"War Communism" as Revolution

Historical Materialism Book Series

VOLUME 391

The titles published in this series are listed at *brill.com/hm*

"War Communism" as Revolution

Lev Kritsman's *The Heroic Period of the Great Russian Revolution* (*an attempt at an analysis of so-called "War Communism"*)

Translated, annotated and introduced by

Frederick C. Corney

BRILL

Originally published as L.N. Kritsman, *Geroicheskiy period velikoy russkoi revolyutsii* [Heroic Period of the Great Russian Revolution]. Moscow–Leningrad: Gosudarstvennoe izdatel'stvo, 1924; reprinted 1926.

ISSN 1570-1522
ISBN 978-90-04-76530-6
ISBN 978-90-04-76531-3 (PDF)
DOI https://doi.org/10.1163/9789004765313

Library of Congress Control Number: 2026945335

Brill and Koninklijke Brill BV are part of De Gruyter Brill.
www.degruyterbrill.com

Questions about General Product Safety Regulation: productsafety@degruyterbrill.com

Contents

Preface

This volume contains the only complete, annotated translation into English of Lev Kritsman's seminal 1924 political and economic analysis of the first tentative years of the Soviet state. His work is ever-present in the footnotes and bibliographies of Russian and foreign studies of this period of Soviet history. Its detailed contents, however, have been inaccessible to those unable to read the Russian original or its German translation.

1 A Note on the Translation and Annotations

I employ the past tense for my translation (unlike much of Kritsman's original), as I think this sounds better to the modern ear. Kritsman's footnotes are sometimes partial, and randomly formatted, and I have chosen not to convert these footnotes into a modern format. Instead, I have compiled from his footnotes a bibliography with as complete source entries as possible. A footnoted source in square brackets indicates that it is not from the original text, but is additional information supplied by me. In my introduction to this volume, I have added a bibliography as a research tool, including as comprehensive a list of Kritsman's published works as I have been able to locate. I have also integrated the errata listed at the end of the book into this translated version. The various terms denoting geographical spaces in the tsarist and Soviet space can be confusing. Tsarist and Soviet Russia were divided into *guberniias*, which were subdivided into *uezds*, which in turn were subdivided into volosts. When the *guberniias* were replaced with oblasts from 1929, oblasts were subdivided into okrugs, which were subdivided into *raions*. I have tried to be consistent throughout by translating *guberniia* as province, *oblast'* as region, *krai* as territory, *uezd* as county, *raion* as district, and *volost'* as rural district.

2 A Note on the Glossary

The glossary at the end of this translation is intended as an essay-in-notes. Each entry focuses upon the broader period pertaining to Kritsman's work on this volume. Reading through the entries, the reader will gain a detailed picture of the state of early Soviet economics and many of its main actors, as well as of its linguistic, political, social, and cultural impact in these years of intense political upheaval, wartime strife, and postwar reconstruction. The perceptive reader of this glossary will note that Kritsman's volume spends little time or space on his main rivals in agrarian economics, many of whom were gathered around his main competitor, Alexander Chaianov. Where Kritsman's volume shows the micro-functioning of the fledgling regime of a self-consciously novel world order, the glossary reveals the sinews of continuity between the old tsarist and the new Soviet polity. These sinews were the *batraki, bedniaki, seredniaki, kulaki*, the *meshchane*, *melkie burzhuazy*, *spetsy*, *nepmen*, and *meshochniki*, they were the *sosloviia* and *klassy*. They were also bearers of significant strain and sites of rupture at key moments. The Bolsheviks (and other radical groups) would have acknowledged them less as sinews connecting the old and the new systems than as bacilli within the new, threatening infection of the Soviet body politic. The spectre of a regime eventually strong enough to purge itself of them was ever-present. The plethora of new entities and the acronyms they spawned in the new Soviet lexicon can bewilder, but these glossary entries reveal a system of institutions and organisations overburdened and often overwhelmed with responsibilities and duties. They often responded ad hoc to the immediate and pressing concerns of existence, and not infrequently encroached upon each others' spheres of activity and power. The glossary also profiles the main protagonists in Kritsman's quite circumscribed academic world of economists, statisticians, and demographers, upon whose research and writing he so copiously drew for his book. Their professional expertise was a product in most cases more of prerevolutionary professional practical experience than ideological belief, at least through the 1920s. The ultimate fates of a disturbingly large number of them in the 1930s were grotesque markers of the changing times in Soviet Russia.

Acknowledgements

My thanks are due my editors at Brill, Sébastien Budgen and Danny Hayward, for proposing what seemed at the outset – and turned out to be – a daunting project. I also thank them for their patience with a project that took me far longer than it should have. It has taken a hundred years for this book finally to appear in English translation, not all of the delay my fault. My thanks go, as always, to my dear friends and colleagues, Sasha and Lena Prokhorov, who helped me with stubborn points of translation. As ever, the excellent staff at the Inter-Library Loan section of Swem Library at William & Mary kept up a steady supply of books and articles. I conducted some source work also at Columbia University's Butler Library, and I thank the staff there also, particularly those in the Microfilm Reading Room. I acknowledge herewith another priceless resource, namely the Summer Lab at the University of Illinois at Urbana-Champaign, which for years now has generously opened up its unparalleled holdings to scholars of Eastern Europe and Russia. Research for this book has been supported by grants from the Department of History at William & Mary, not least the Harrison Ruffin Tyler Fund and the Keith and Sandy Dauer Fund. My final thanks go, as ever, to the constants of my life, Caroline, Sarah, and Rachel, with love.

Introduction: The Political Economy of Lev Kritsman

Frederick C. Corney

> Our own Russia, as young and orphaned as these abandoned children, as visionary and embittered, without a corner of her own, with never a caress, with no one to look after her. (Il'ya Ehrenburg)

> No one dared to admit that it would not work. (Victor Serge on 'War Communism')

> The revolution was not defeated, it retreated. This was the first serious foray by mankind into the foggy terrain of its future. (Lev Kritsman)

Lev Natanovich Kritsman was a chemist by training, an economist by profession, and a Marxist fully committed to the revolutionary project in Soviet Russia. Immediately after the Bolshevik takeover, he turned his considerable professional skills to an analysis of this novel socialist economy as it was developing in utero, so to speak, before it even truly existed as a viable entity. In a steady stream of publications from 1918 onwards, he – and his fellow economists and statisticians in the newly created administrative bodies of the post-October state – kept up a tireless analysis of the early Soviet economy at its most vulnerable during the brutal and devastating years of the Civil War and the precarious first years of the New Economic Policy (NEP). Kritsman was not just documenting, recording and analysing, he was arguing for a particular interpretation of the ideological and political meaning of the economic policies that had been put in place at the time. He was, then, also making a case for how these early policies deployed during the Civil War era might yet feature in Soviet Russia's peacetime economic system and in the socialist project writ large. His research on these early critical years found its most articulate and finished form in his *The Heroic Period of the Great Russian Revolution* (*an attempt at an analysis of so-called 'War Communism'*), written over a period of two years and published in 1924.[1] He previewed various aspects of this work

1 L. Kritsman, *Geroicheskii period Velikoi Russkoi Revoliutsii* (*opyt analiza t.n. 'Voennogo kommunizma'*) (Moscow: Gosudarstvennoe izdatel'stvo, n.d.). It included as an appendix a reprint

 | HTTPS://DOI.ORG/10.1163/9789004765313-002

in a range of earlier articles (see the bibliography at the end of this introduction). In 1928, the prominent Soviet historian Mikhail Pokrovsky praised it as one of three major contributions to a deeper understanding of Russia's revolution published since 1917, and the first a posteriori 'attempt at a theoretically sophisticated economic history of our revolutionary years'.[2] Kritsman's statistics, if not his overall Marxist argument and analysis, have been omnipresent sources in Soviet and Western studies of the Soviet Republic's early economics.[3]

This introduction examines Kritsman's work explicitly within the formative contexts that shaped his research and writing. It covers his consciously Marxist approach to socioeconomics, the evolution of his specific views on the early Soviet economy, and also the respective communities of economic research

---

of a related journal article by him (Lev Kritsman, 'Tri goda Novoi Ekonomicheskoi Politiki proletariata Sovetskogo Soiuza,' *Zvezda*, no. 3, 1924, pp. 108–135). This edition appeared in a print-run of 10,000 copies. A large section of this book was featured in a thick journal in late 1924 (Lev Kritsman, 'Geroicheskii period Velikoi Russkoi Revoliutsii (opyt analiza t. n. 'Voennogo kommunizma'),' *Vestnik kommunisticheskoi akademii*, no. 9, 1924, pp. 1–146). A second edition of the monograph appeared in 1926 in a print-run of 5000 copies, Kritsman noting in his preface that it had 'only the most insignificant changes in comparison with the first edition' (Lev Kritsman, *Geroicheskii period Velikoi Russkoi Revoliutsii (Opyt analiza t. n. 'Voennogo kommunizma')* [Moscow-Leningrad: Gosudarstvennoe izdatel'stvo, 1926], p. 7). Publishers added a second appendix, a reprint of another of his journal articles (L. Kritsman, 'Soiuz proletariata i bol'shinstva krest'ianstva v SSSR posle pobedy revoliutsii,' *Bol'shevik*, no. 2[18], 31 January 1925, pp. 40–55). Part of the first chapter of the volume was included in a collection of his writings in 1929 (L. Kritsman, 'Agrarnaia revoliutsiia i sel'skoe khoziaistvo,' in L. Kritsman, *Proletarskaia revoliutsiia i derevnia* [Moscow-Leningrad, Gosudarstvennoe izdatel'stvo, 1929], pp. 79–116). A third edition was recently published in commemoration of the centenary of the USSR (L.N. Kritsman, *Geroicheskii period Velikoi Russkoi revoliutsii: Opyt analiza tak nazyvaemogo voennogo kommunizma*. no. 286 [Moscow, 2022]). Kritsman's volume was translated into German a few years after its initial publication (L. Kritsman, *Die heroische Periode der Grossen Russischen Revolution. Ein Versuch der Analyse des sogenannten 'Kriegskommunismus'* [Vienna-Berlin: Verlag für Literatur und Politik, 1929]). This edition included in German translation the two appendices from the earlier Russian editions, and added a third (L. Kritsman, "Desiat' let na agrarnom fronte proletarskoi revoliutsii," *Na agrarnom fronte*, no. 11 and 12, 1927, pp. 3–8). This German-language version appeared in a later reprint (L. Kritsman, *Die heroische Periode der Grossen Russischen Revolution. Ein Versuch der Analyse des sogenannten 'Kriegskommunismus'* [Frankfurt: Verl. Neue Kritik, 1971]).

2 Pokrovskii 1928, p. 14. The other two works were Lenin's *State and Revolution* (1917) and Bukharin's *Economics of the Transition Period* (1920), ibid., pp. 12–14.

3 The current volume represents the first complete English translation of the Russian original. Only the introduction and first chapter have appeared in English elsewhere (see Kowalski 1989, v-13). I have retranslated these sections for the sake of consistency in my translation of the entire work, although Kowalski's excellent work served as a valuable guide in this endeavour.

he inhabited and their navigation of increasingly difficult political waters. At one level, his career charted the rewards and risks of economic research in Soviet Russia as the limits of the politically possible changed drastically in its first decade and a half. Unsurprisingly perhaps, economists, statisticians, and demographers placed their faith in the meticulous gathering and weighing of economic data in order to produce an explanatory narrative of the recent past as a guide to the future. Some had accumulated years of practical experience in the zemstvo system of local rural self-administration set up by imperial statute in 1864, which had opened for them a window onto the state of the agrarian economy in late tsarist Russia. While many did not commit themselves to the politics of the Soviet era, they applied their cumulative experience to an analysis of its complex economics. Others, like Kritsman, learned their methodological and analytical skills in foreign universities during years spent in Western European exile, having fled political persecution for their revolutionary activities in Tsarist Russia. They returned to Soviet Russia after the fall of tsarism to hone and apply their skills to the challenges of its early years. While many had been revolutionary activists for decades before 1917, they were by no means all Bolsheviks. Some were affiliated with other leftist parties, and some of those who later joined the Bolshevik Party complicated their revolutionary pedigree with memberships in various dissident factions within the party post-1917. All of them, though, shared a belief in the need to undertake serious and detailed study of this new economy – and of the economic wreck it inherited from the First World War and the Civil War – if there were to be any confidence in how it should be administered during peacetime.

The introduction will offer an analytical narrative of these few short years as far as possible in the contemporaries' own words. This narrow focus resists the temptation to view these early years through the retrospective lens of later events that would inevitably come to frame perception of them (especially the Great Turn, forced collectivisation and rapid industrialisation, and the repressions of the 1930s). While this introduction certainly highlights the role of coercion in early Soviet economic management, for example, it cannot yet conclude that this coercion is a routinised part of future Soviet economic politics writ large. It returns the years 1917–24 to their formative contexts, and views 'war communism' and the 'NEP' as discursive strategies that eventually came to define each other. Moreover, it resituates the changing role of the urban-rural relationship in economic policy within these short years, removing them from the shadow of later political contexts. Of course, 'war communism' and the NEP became foundation-stones of the historiography of the early Soviet Republic both in Soviet Russia and abroad, and relevant exegeses on their treatment in the later historiographies can be found in the footnotes.

Kritsman believed firmly in the power of numbers, although he also cautioned that a 'number, even a statistic, must not be fetishised', and that anyone who made use of a statistic must inform the reader about 'its potential and probable deviation from reality'. His concern stemmed from what he considered to be the 'outrageous state of our statistical materials, whose unreliability and shoddiness, bordering at times on sheer sloppiness, is quite extraordinary'. He believed that the correct juxtaposition of individual data, 'scrupulously' analysed, was the only way to produce a 'concrete analysis of our revolution', and to avoid its 'trivialities'.[4] He was also fully convinced of the unprecedented historical significance of the 'Great Russian Revolution', which he viewed as the 'empirical confirmation of the correctness of the revolutionary worldview of the proletariat, of the correctness of Marxism that predicted many decades ago the inevitability of everything that has come to pass in Russia since 1917'.[5] His methodological and ideological approach all but ensured that his book would be a comprehensive, detailed – and dry – analysis of Soviet Russia's first, halting economic steps. His portrait of the industrial and agricultural landscape was by any measure an extraordinarily detailed and meticulously argued case for a particular understanding of the economic policies of the Civil War years and of the form they took at the time, and also for their potential import for the future of the Soviet economic system.

1 Actually Existing 'War Communism'

Kritsman sought to convey the enormity of the changes in the Russian economy and society during the Civil War years through the sheer weight of his statistics and the power of his analysis. He detailed the 'catastrophic *decline in living standards*' as a result of the virtual collapse of industrial productivity. Workers' wages had fallen by two-and-a-half times by 1920, compared with prewar levels, while agriculture had contracted by one-and-a-half times, transportation by five times, and total national income by at least two-and-a-half times.[6] He acknowledged the awful effects of rationing particularly on the children of workers and peasants who were already near starvation. He wrote of the colossal epidemic of five million people in European Russia suffering from

4 Kritsman, The Heroic Period, pp. 65n2, 65–66.
5 Kritsman, The Heroic Period, p. 68.
6 Kritsman, The Heroic Period, p. 255. (original emphasis).

typhus in 1919 and 1920, a thirty-seven-fold increase over 1914. These numbers were even higher, he observed, when smallpox, scarlet fever, malaria, and cholera were included.[7] But he also acknowledged the inevitable inadequacy of this telling of the suffering: 'These dry figures conceal hunger and cold, disease and death, children starving to death before the eyes of their loved ones'.[8] His statement was especially poignant, given that his own nine-year-old son, Iurii, succumbed to disease in 1920, a death he memorialised with his son's portrait at the front of his book. The conditions of the times also took their toll on Kritsman's own body, and he was forced to spend several months abroad recuperating in 1922.

Nonetheless, Kritsman's work is not the best place to get a sense of the existential and visceral nature of the suffering widely experienced during and after the years of war and civil war.[9] Nor is it therefore the place to get a sense of widespread attitudes to the new regime. Before we delve into the economics and politics of the era as seen through the lens of Kritsman's 1924 volume, an analysis that by definition creates a scholarly distance from their visceral effects, it seems fitting to offer a sense of life caught unawares (*zhizn' vrasplokh*) at the time (as the avant garde film-maker, Dziga Vertov, termed it). This land of extreme scarcity had an abundance of suffering, as did many of the postwar states of Europe. Its witnesses were members of all classes and all political dispositions who experienced the tribulations on their own livelihoods and bodies. Millions of people died of war, hunger, and disease. Millions were forcibly expelled or left the country voluntarily (if that word had any real meaning at that time). For the many millions who survived, these experiences were indelibly etched into the personal and collective memories accompanying them as they lived their lives as willing or unwilling Soviet citizens. Notwithstanding his stated desire to avoid 'trivialities' in his analysis of early Soviet Russia's economic state, Kritsman's rather bloodless, macroscopic view can be fruitfully juxtaposed against some visceral, microscopic vignettes of suffering:

7 Kritsman, The Heroic Period, p. 259.

8 Kritsman, The Heroic Period, p. 258.

9 The post-WW2 turn to social and labour history produced excellent studies of the existential impact of the First World War, Revolution, and Civil War on the lower classes of the former Russian Empire and the USSR (among many, Hessler 2004; Ball 1994; Lih 1990a; Koenker, Suny, and Rosenberg (eds.) 1989–1989). Significant studies have also been undertaken of the prerevolutionary professionals and technical personnel who continued to work into the 1920s in their positions at the sufferance of the new Soviet administration (among many, Chamberlain 2007; Finkel 2007; David-Fox, 1997; Tolz 1997; Byrnes 1991, pp. 297–308). The tsarist elites who suffered during these first years or fled for foreign shores also have their chroniclers (among many, Smith 2012; Alexopoulos 2003; Raeff 1990).

human colour for the grey statistics. After all, these analyses by Kritsman – and those of other economists, some of whom agreed and some of whom disagreed with him – would one way or another help to shape Soviet Russia's future economic, political, and social policy in the turbulent years ahead. The visceral suffering that the new policies of collectivisation and rapid industrialisation ushered in through the 1930s, for example, would surely have already seemed intimately familiar to Soviet citizens who had experienced the first years of the Soviet regime.

Many eloquent observers came to 'watch the Revolution' in Soviet Russia – even testify to it – during these difficult years, not least the now-famous John Reeds, Louise Bryants, and Bertrand Russells from America and England, the 'poetic journalists and journalistic poets', as they were called.[10] Others, it should be said, came to watch the inevitable collapse of the 'coup'. They all bore witness to the things so meticulously documented by Kritsman: the half-empty cities, the idle factories, the burgeoning new bureaucracies and the growth of insider privilege these bureaucracies brought with them, the crumbling urban infrastructure of burst water pipes and crumbling buildings, the non-existent public transport, the scant supplies of raw materials and food trickling into the cities, the rationing, the rampant inflation and ever-present bartering for goods on the ubiquitous (and vital) black market, the disease, the death. But their impressionistic and arresting observations often captured more evocative, if fleeting, truths. Soon after his arrival in Moscow in 1919, the British novelist and correspondent for the *Manchester Guardian*, Arthur Ransome, was confronted by the curious sight of a bedraggled man driving a sled loaded with horsemeat bones while beating back a flock of starving crows pecking away at them. He also watched starving crows forcing their way into his hotel in search of scraps. He knowingly acknowledged the absence of the usually ubiquitous pigeons from the city.[11] It was worse in the villages consigned to hunger by the forced requisitioning of their grain. 'People deranged from hunger are wandering about like packs of wolves', a delegation from Samara reported, 'tearing apart the burrows of rodents, digging up the carcasses of diseased cattle, and grinding their half-decayed bones into flour'.[12] The anarchist firebrand and newfound Bolshevik, Victor Serge, reported that 'children and feeble old folk died in their thousands'. 'People dined on a pittance of oatmeal or half-rotten horsemeat', he continued,

10 von Mohrenschildt 1943–44, p. 65.
11 Ransome 1919, p. 42.
12 Cited in Ball 1994, p. 8.

> a lump of sugar would be divided in tiny fragments among a family, and a single mouthful taken out of turn would start angry scene ... Requisitioning detachments were sent out into the outlying countryside, only to be driven away, as likely as not, or sometimes even massacred by muzhiks wielding pitchforks. Savage peasants would slit open a commissar's belly, pack it with grain, and leave him by the roadside as a lesson for all.[13]

It was well-nigh impossible for observers to miss the seven million (by 1922) orphaned and abandoned children [*besprizornye*] in Soviet Russia, 'whole armies of children – grimy, starving vagrants', raised by war, famine, and neglect, 'ragged flocks of animated scarecrows'.[14] They were, to the eyes of the passersby, hapless victims of fate or dangerous, drug-addled predators, or perhaps both, sleeping rough in train stations or on the docks, and permanent fixtures in the many bazaars that popped up throughout the cities. Family suicides were not unheard of.

A British engineer, recently returned from work in Russia, nostalgically rued the disappearance of the 'brilliantly uniformed officers', the 'smart carriages' and 'luxurious motor-cars', and the 'well-dressed men and women' of the old days, now replaced in Petrograd by 'slovenly-looking Red Guards', 'broken-down cabs with half-starved horses', and 'drab, anxious-looking crowds'. He saw emaciated horses lying dead in the streets, being ripped apart by hungry dogs. Petty crime and graft were the order of the day on the streets, as he saw it.[15] Paul Dukes, a British secret agent in both Tsarist and Bolshevik Russia, painted a vivid image of the impromptu street markets, where not only the 'educated class' but also 'peasants, servant-girls, and street-urchins' sold off whatever they had for food and fuel: 'Old clothing, crockery, toys, knick-knacks, clocks, books, pencils, pens, pictures, pots, pans, pails, and postcards'. A few streets away from the markets stood even sadder individual figures, 'speculators' offering 'half-a-dozen lumps of sugar for sale', 'unappetizing viands', 'bread patties of a greenish-brown colour', even 'salt-herrings', all at impossibly high prices, the sellers always at risk of arrest by Red Guards or sailors.[16] Serge painted an eerie picture of a Petrograd emptied of people and automobiles. Petrograd and

13 Serge 2012, pp. 136, 137.

14 Cited in Ball 1994, pp. 1, 9, xi.

15 'Life in Petrograd Under the Bolsheviks'. *Manchester Guardian*, 16 December, 1918, p. 4.

16 Paul Dukes, 'Under Bolshevist Rule: II. Food and Fuel,' *Illustrated London News*, 13 December 1919, p. 978; see also idem., 'Under Bolshevist Rule: I. Family Life,' *Illustrated London News*, 6 December 1919, p. 926; idem., 'Under Bolshevist Rule: III. Suppressing Revolt,' *Illustrated London News*, 20 December 1919, p. 1030.

Moscow lost two-thirds and half of their populations respectively between 1917 and 1920.[17] He discerned 'gentle ghostlike hints of life' as he approached the city centre. Starving horses pulled open sleds slowly through the snow, occasional passersby 'eaten by cold and hunger, had faces of ghastly white', 'half-ragged soldiers, their rifles often hanging from their shoulders by a rope, tramped around'. Typhus corpses lay unburied, but 'luckily' frozen. He conjured surreal images of peasants taking anything they could carry back to their villages, including 'gilded chairs, candelabras, and even pianos', and even 'streetlights'. Serge called Petrograd 'the metropolis, of Cold, of Hunger, of Hatred, and of Endurance'.[18]

Letters from citizens to Bolshevik leaders in these hard times, sequestered in the Soviet archives and published only decades later under *glasnost'*, attested to the sense of a world out of control and out of time. One spoke of the 'abyss of grief, despair, human malice and tears', in which 'unhappy Russia' found itself. Another decried the unprecedented 'arbitrariness, oppression, and lawlessness' of the times. One young man wrote to Vladimir Lenin that, in this new regime, power is 'in the hands of people without consciousness [*bessoznatel'nyi*]' and weapons are 'in the hands of madmen'.[19] Sympathetic observers did not see the socialism they had been hoping to see in their aspirational visits to the Land of the Soviets. The French communist Alfred Rosmer, who spent significant periods of time in Russia between 1920 and 1924, saw precious little 'communism' in 'war communism', for communism 'supposes abundance and this was scarcity'. The regime of that name 'had been born with the war and should have died with it'. He attributed the persistence of the wartime economic policies to hesitation and inertia, to people 'groping, searching and failing to make decisions'.[20] Serge too focused on the failings, contrasting the 'famished populace in the streets' with the 'elegant gentlemen, pretty and irreproachably powdered typists' in the commissariats, with their 'chic uniforms' and their access to the 'racket' of privilege and favour.[21] Ransome's testament to the 'extraordinary vitality' he saw in Moscow 'even in those dark days of discomfort, disillusion, pestilence, starvation and unwanted war' might well have involved some wish-fulfillment on his part.[22]

---

17 Ball 1990, p. 8.

18 Serge 2012, pp. 82, 85.

19 *Golos naroda. Pis'ma i otkliki riadovykh sovetskikh grazhdan o sobytiiakh 1918–1932 gg.* (Moscow: ROSSPEN, 1998), pp. 45–46. See also Iarov, *Gorozhanin kak politik*; idem., *Krest'ianin kak politik*.

20 Rosmer 1971, pp. 133–134.

21 Serge 2012, 87.

22 Ransome 1919, p. x.

Some foreign visitors indeed chose to accentuate the positive, the British artist, Arthur Bridge, sketching lively celebrations of the revolution, and cosy scenes of communal soup kitchens full of well-fed, bantering men, women, and children, where 'every class of the community mingled together'.[23] If the great anarchist, 'Red' Emma Goldman, nurtured any such comforting expectations when she first arrived in Russia after being deported from America in 1919, they were quickly dispelled by the reality she witnessed. She spoke in 1919 of waking slowly as if from a 'ghastly dream'. She was less concerned about the 'incompetent and inefficient' bureaucratic state than with the persistence of human brutality: political activists arrested by the Cheka, workers conscripted like 'chattel-slaves' for their labour, and peasants 'helpless prey' to forced food collections.[24] The famous British novelist H.G. Wells, who met with Lenin and other Bolshevik leaders in Russia in 1920 and was by no means ideologically ill-disposed to the Bolshevik project, documented the predations of the Red Terror and his own disillusion with the conditions he saw on the ground.[25] In the same year, the British philosopher Bertrand Russell spent a month in Moscow and Petrograd with a British Labour Delegation. He 'went to Russia a Communist', he wrote, but left it with doubts about those who held 'a creed so firmly that for its sake men are willing to inflict widespread misery'.[26] For many committed socialists, this regime looked less Time Forwards than Time Backwards. Ransome shared a joke he had been told about Soviet Russia's apparent direction: 'In ten years we shall be running about on all fours. And in twenty we shall begin sprouting tails'.[27]

Kritsman, his sights set firmly on the socialist progress to come, would have no doubt been appalled at such gallows humour. It seems fair to assume that while these vignettes of suffering might have moved him emotionally, they would not have caused him to doubt his ideological core. While the situation on the ground was indeed improving as he was putting his monograph together, it was not this relative improvement or the brief passage of time that lent his 1924 analysis such sang-froid, even callousness. His Marxist outlook shaped profoundly how he understood these catastrophic effects on the population, providing a historical justification for the regrettable but necessary sac-

23 'Among the Bolshevists: A British Artist's Experiences,' *Illustrated London News*, 27 September 1919, p. 474.

24 Emma Goldman, 'What I Saw in Russia,' *Illustrated London News*, 22 November 1924, 988. Serge too very explicitly condemned the practices of the Cheka as akin to those of the Inquisition (Serge 2012, p. 94).

25 Wells 1921.

26 Russell 1920, p. 42.

27 Ransome 1919, p. 86.

rifices. They were the 'costs', as Kritsman frequently termed them, of ensuring the victory of the Russian Revolution against foreign aggressors and recidivist capitalism. The dry figures, he wrote, 'show more clearly than anything else the extraordinary heroism of the workers' revolution'.[28] This ideological cant augured a quite dispassionate set of conclusions from the devastating sets of statistics he marshalled from his own and his comrades' research. Fully committed to the dictatorship of the proletariat, Kritsman discerned a class hierarchy of 'legitimate' suffering reflected in it. He saw in his statistics prima facie evidence of the correctness of his Marxist worldview. The 'bony hand of hunger' that lay heavily upon the population was an indictment of 'world capital' whose hand it in fact was. The starving children of the workers and peasants exposed the reluctance of the 'sybaritic bourgeoisie' to give up any of their own rations to them, even as starving Leningrad workers 'gave up part of their hunger rations every day even for the children of the bourgeoisie'.[29] His book's dedication emptily honoured 'the memory of the many children who fell victim to the intervention by world capital'.[30] While he acknowledged the suffering of the peasants, and praised their support for 'Red Russia against the Whites', he added that his work would show that 'it was not the petty bourgeois village but the heroic proletarian city that bore the heaviest sacrifices during the Civil War'.[31] Indeed, his political commitment to a state anchored in a determined and conscious working class rather than a vacillating and unreliable peasant class was a key factor in his decision to divide, say, grain consumption statistics into urban and rural categories. Soviet Russia's very existence and survival was invested in the working class, and, he implied, grain shortages were therefore *by definition* worse for urban workers and therefore the state.

Especially revealing of Kritsman's mindset was a laconic aside on the changes in occupation density of urban apartments that had given workers more living space by 1923 than ever before. While by no means ignoring the massive population shifts of the Civil War years, Kritsman chose to focus on the rapid repopulation of urban areas in the early years of the 1920s.[32] He acknowledged that this had been made possible by the 'expropriation of domiciles, furniture, utensils, bedding…, linen, etc through evictions, confiscations, and one-time seizures (in-kind taxation)'. He explicitly removed the human dimension from this intensely inhumane process, casting this expropriation as having

28 Kritsman, *The Heroic Period*, p. 258.
29 Kritsman, *The Heroic Period*, pp. 256, 257.
30 Kritsman, *The Heroic Period*, p. 60.
31 Kritsman, *The Heroic Period*, p. 251.
32 Kritsman, 'Three Years of the New Economic Policy,' in Kritsman, *The Heroic Period*, pp. 322–3.

'a mass, class aspect to it, but not a personal aspect, just as, whenever capitalist society threw proletarians out into the street during a crisis or physically destroyed proletarians during the imperialist war, it is not personal but class in nature: capital does not ask about the individual proletarian's personal guilt'.[33] Perhaps he had not witnessed what Serge had witnessed in the winter of 1920–21 while the latter was searching for staff accommodations in downtown Petrograd: 'whole rooms plastered with frozen excrement. The WCs would not flush ... Many houses were in a similar condition; when spring came and the excrement began to run all over the floors, anything might happen to the city. Compulsory clearance squads were organized hastily'.[34] Kritsman, rather, grouped some of the Soviet polity's most inhumane and harsh policies under what he euphemistically termed 'consumer communism', namely

> a revolution in everyday life. Immediately and in practice it destroyed the outrageous luxury, crushed the smug security, broke the ruling customs of the former ruling classes, toppled – a method which the most backward, undeveloped proletarian could appreciate – the members of the former ruling classes from their social pedestal, and created in the proletariat and its affiliated social groups the feeling of true liberation, the sensation of true upheaval, and powerful, revolutionary enthusiasm. This destruction of class inequality is best illustrated by data on the change in the distribution of domiciles.[35]

Serge had earlier already seen these Marxist blinkers worn by the Soviet economic administrators with whom he had had the opportunity to speak. When he asked Aleksandr Tsiurupa, sometime People's Commissar of Food and organiser of the food detachments in 1918, about the Soviet system of rationing and supply, Tsiurupa showed him 'beautifully drawn diagrams from which the ghastly famine and the immense black market had vanished without trace'. The danger here, Serge noted, was that Tsiurupa was a 'captive of his system' and was being 'primed with lies' by his comrades in the administration.[36]

Nonetheless, Western observers generally cast a forgiving – or perhaps hopeful – eye on the economic realm in Soviet Russia. A *Times Literary Supplement* review in 1924 of a recent Soviet work on the state of the economy pointed out that it was suspect because it drew upon officially published statements and statistics by the Soviet government. But it should be taken seriously, it

33 Kritsman, The Heroic Period, p. 261.

34 Serge 2012, p. 138.

35 Kritsman, The Heroic Period, p. 261.

36 Serge 2012, p. 132.

continued, because many of the statistics were compiled by 'honest economists pressed into the Government service', and because in-fighting amongst the Bolsheviks over policy meant that different groups used the 'best figures available' to expose their opponents' methodological failings.[37] Other commentators looked for any signs of development of a more robust (i.e. 'free') Soviet economic marketplace, particularly within the burgeoning cooperative movement and the NEP. Some foreign observers even began looking at the emergent, post-Civil War Soviet economic order for potential pointers for their own postwar state-capitalist economies.[38] This was certainly a less jaundiced eye than the one they cast on the shrinking realm of the politically possible in early Soviet Russia. The banning of the oppositional press, the wartime military tribunals, the activities of the Cheka and institutionalised political repression, the rising voices against Lev Trotsky and other Bolshevik 'oppositionists', not to mention the peasant and urban unrest and the mutiny of the Kronstadt sailors in early 1921, were watched closely, not least by the engaged exiles from Soviet Russia who were streaming into the burgeoning *émigré* centres of Europe. As the mock performative agitation 'trials' in the early 1920s of the 'heroes' of the revolution (the Communist Party, the October Revolution, the Red Army, and Lenin) were giving way to judicial trials of 'political saboteurs' with graver consequences (e.g. the trial of twelve Socialist Revolutionaries in 1922), even the casual observer could see a rising inquisitorial animus in Soviet Russia bent on rooting out heresies committed, yet to be committed, or yet to be imagined.[39]

2 Economic Transition and Ideological Uncertainties

Every political economy is a function of certain theoretical postulates, political frameworks, and domestic and international conditions. This is as true of capitalist regimes as it is of socialist regimes. This post-WWI Soviet economy was often dismissed as unrealistic and impractical, even utopian and unnatural. This dismissal had much to do with the normative assumptions of capitalist

37 'Bolshevist Economics' (review of *The Economic Condition of Soviet Russia* by S.N. Prokopovich), *The Times Literary Supplement*, 10 July 1924, p. 426.

38 A.M. Asancheyev, 'Renewing Commerce with Russia: Her Co-Operative System,' *Illustrated London News*, 24 January 1920, p. 116; see 'The Socialization of Industry,' a review of *La Marche Au Socialisme* by Edgard Milhaud, in *The Times Literary Supplement*, 18 March 1920, p. 179; 'Bolshevist Russia. Review of *Bolshevist Russia* by Etienne Antonelli,' *The Times Literary Supplement*, 29 April 1920, p. 264; Marcel Mauss, 'Socialisme et Bolchévisme,' *Le Monde Slave* (2), no. 2, 1925, pp. 201–222.

39 Wood 2005; Shub 1964, pp. 362–69; Cassiday 2000.

economies that had had plenty of time to embed themselves as the dominant discourse of economics. The Bolsheviks were confronted by a complex task: how to explain their early economic measures in ways that were not defined and confined by the dominant economic discourse of capitalism as the most 'expedient' or 'natural' economic system, even as they invoked their Marxist and Leninist guides. Kritsman referred repeatedly in his work to the need for socialist economic policy to go beyond 'bourgeois-capitalist, and petty bourgeois thinking', namely that the revolution was not to be limited by considerations of economic expediency. Or as he succinctly put it, 'Economic inexpediency becomes revolutionary necessity'. The revolution's true challenge, then, was the creation of a fundamentally novel economic system that so contradicted historically accepted notions of what constituted a 'proper' economy that it would inevitably trigger 'resistance from opposing forces'.[40]

When the New Economic Policy was introduced at the Tenth Party Congress in March 1921, the economic measures that had been deployed by the young Soviet government between 1918 and 1921 were abolished or at least significantly modified, leading to disagreement over their precise significance for the future of Soviet Russia. Serge conveyed succinctly the unprecedented nature of these changes: nationalisation of all industries; centralisation and hierarchisation of industrial management; state control of foreign trade; strict labour discipline; obligatory labour duty for all classes; forced requisitioning of agricultural surplus from the peasants for distribution to the rest of the population, especially those in urban areas; rationing of vital foodstuffs and other goods; banning of private enterprise and the market; state control of the railways and waterways. Accompanying these measures, he pointed out, had been a 'monopoly of power tending towards the single Party and the suppression of all dissent, ... a state of siege, and the Cheka'.[41]

Of course, these individual policies had not always been fully realised in practice. The supply of grain and other products to the cities remained inadequate, peasant resistance to force abounded, and a vibrant underground market persisted, indeed thrived. Nonetheless, individuals in city and village experienced these policies to varying degrees first hand, and the softer measures announced with the NEP would surely have looked vastly different to them: non-state enterprises were permitted; profit incentives were introduced into nationalised industries; forced grain requisitioning was ended, as was the ban on private trade, to be replaced by a tax-in-kind [*prodovol'stvennyi nalog*, or

40 Kritsman, The Heroic Period, pp. 67, 118, 305.

41 Serge 2012, p. 138.

prodnalog] and limited retail trade; individual non-state enterprises and foreign companies were granted concessions. Here again, though, intent outstripped practice: foreign concessions were granted at the pleasure of the state, concessions to non-state enterprises could be withdrawn at will, taxation reintroduced, or the enterprises closed. Nor was peasant control of farming and selling by any means guaranteed, and the toleration of profit as an economic tool could be reversed. Even with all of these caveats, potential or otherwise, it might be argued that the Soviet economic system was no longer defined by the formerly dominant capitalist terms of debate. 'For all the fluctuations in Soviet policy that raise questions about the nature of Soviet socialism', argues historian Yanni Kotsonis, '–state capitalism in 1918, War Communism in 1919, New Economic Policy in 1921, the Great Turn of 1929–the system's underlying stability and safeguard was state ownership and party control'.[42]

Like all the major political clashes within the party in these early years (the quarrels over the Brest Peace in 1918 and over the role of trade unions in 1920, to name but two),[43] the NEP was accompanied by a veritable publicity campaign for the new policies, spearheaded by Lenin himself. Throughout 1921 and into 1922, the Bolsheviks took their message directly to a wide array of party and non-party congresses, conferences, and meetings, onto the pages of economic journals, and into the party and government press, namely *Pravda* and *Izvestiia*. This messaging included the invention of a term that would be used to neatly define those earlier policies, to draw a sharp line between the economic policies that 'the war and the ruin' had forced upon the Soviet state and the economic policies of the NEP that the state now tailored to current exigencies. That term was 'War Communism'. 'It was not, and could not', Lenin added, 'be a policy that corresponded to the economic tasks of the proletariat. It was a makeshift'.[44] Unlike the NEP, which was publicised as a measured, considered, and holistic response to the current economic and political crisis, the term 'war communism' was intended to convey ad hoc contingency rather than planned

42 Kotsonis 2014, pp. 298–299.

43 On the former, see the criticism of Left Communists in V.I. Lenin, '"Left-Wing" Childishness and the Petty-Bourgeois Mentality,' in Lenin, *Collected Works*, v. 27 (Moscow: Progress Publishers, 1965), pp. 323–354; on the latter, see the specific criticisms of Trotsky and Bukharin in V.I. Lenin, 'The Trade Unions, the Present Situation and Trotsky's Mistakes. Speech Delivered at a Joint Meeting of Communist Delegates to The Eighth Congress of Soviets, Communist Members of the All-Russia Central Council of Trade Unions and Communist Members of the Moscow City Council of Trade Unions, December 30, 1920,' idem., *Collected Works*, v. 32, pp. 19–42.

44 'The Tax in Kind (The Significance of the New Policy and Its Conditions),' *Collected Works*, v. 32, p. 343.

coherence. Lenin used the term dismissively and always in quotation marks.[45] The measures undertaken during the Civil War years were not, he wrote baldly, 'an economic system or an economic plan for a policy, adopted from a number of policy choices'.[46] Referring to the forced requisitioning measures introduced at the time, and the belief that they would generate the requisite supplies to the workers and army for the war effort, he said: 'I cannot say that we pictured this plan as definitely and as clearly as that; but we acted approximately on those lines. That, unfortunately, is a fact'.[47] In being denied the coherence of a policy and the currency of legitimised usage, 'war communism' was not permitted to figure in the current economic debate on the same terms as the NEP.[48]

---

45 The English translation of Lenin's collected works for the most part dropped the quotation marks, despite their presence in the original Russian texts (cf. V.I. Lenin, *Polnoe sobranie sochinenii*, v. 43, pp. 219–220, 230, 243, 379, 381). The term had been used before in a different context in 1917 by Alexander Bogdanov, non-party socialist, philosopher, and long-time ideological thorn in Lenin's side, which would not have made the term any more palatable to Lenin. Bogdanov had regarded the October Revolution as bourgeois rather than socialist, due to the preponderance of the peasantry (i.e. the army) rather than the quasi-peasant proletariat. He called the 'workers-soldiers party' in reality 'simply a soldiers party'. He saw the causes of what he termed 'war communism' in the collapse of the world economy in the First World War and the militarisation of society in various wartime states, Germany included. It had been needed to deal with existential crises in food consumption, productivity, and distribution. This had involved incremental measures, including the regulation of production, obligatory labour service, price regulation, and finally monopolies of individual products. In the case of Russia, Bogdanov used the term consumer communism [*potrebitel'skii kommunizm*], because true socialism meant production collectivism. He doubted that the old coercive measures of war communism would easily disappear once the war was over. Lenin's analysis in 1921 was, in fact, not a million miles away from Bogdanov's (see Pliutto 1992, pp. 46–52).

46 'Report on the Tax in Kind Delivered at a Meeting of Secretaries and Responsible Representatives of R.C.P.(B.) Cells of Moscow and Moscow Gubernia. April 9, 1921,' *Collected Works*, v. 32, pp. 290.

47 'The New Economic Policy and the Tasks of the Political Education Departments. Report to the Second All-Russia Congress of Political Education Political Education Departments,' October 17, 1921, *Collected Works*, v. 33, p. 62.

48 Unsurprisingly, Lenin's representation of 'war communism' came to dominate much Soviet, post-Soviet, and Western historiography of the early Soviet Republic. Rare was the work that eschewed the term completely in analyses of these early policies or acknowledged it only briefly as an ex post facto framing device (see Döring 1970); Weiss 1937. More often, the term has been used as an all too convenient shorthand, sometimes with, sometimes without, the early ubiquitous quotation marks. All scholars who study these early policies acknowledge the critical significance of the wartime context, focusing on the Bolshevik regime's most extreme state policies adopted between mid-1918 and early 1921 which sought to marshal all necessary resources to win this exhausting and existential civil war (the central procurement and distribution of resources, including labour, mon-

The Tenth Party Conference in late May 1921 was convened primarily for the purpose of relaying – and explicating – the NEP to the Party and Soviet workers in the localities.[49] In a series of *Pravda* articles in April 1921, Lenin laid

etary control, and an end to the private market). Some place these policies on a broader historical continuum, for example, the prerevolutionary, antidemocratic tradition of tsarist Russia's semi-feudal and semi-industrial system with its significant levels of industrial and financial concentration and monopoly (the First World War merely exacerbated this both in Russia and the other warring states) in a sense rendering the early Soviet economic policies less novel (see A.F. Dowlah, 'Soviet Socialism: The Era of War Communism,' *International Journal of Social Economics* 20, no. 5, 1993, pp. 57–83). Others place it quite productively into a continuum of 'crisis socialism' throughout the Soviet era, a way of avoiding the ideological pitfalls of the term itself (see Hessler, *A Social History of Soviet Trade*). Studies of 'war communism' particularly in the 1920s sought to identify an underlying ideological rationale, a perceived opportunity in the eyes of many Bolsheviks to introduce a militantly socialist system of production, an uncompromising push for immediate socialism. This view points to early intent as ideological evidence, namely the introduction already by mid-December 1917 of socialist measures, including the land decree, workers' control, nationalisation of the banks, and the establishment of the Supreme Council of the National Economy (VSNKh) with its brief for central planning and for the right to requisition and confiscate. These views sometimes offer the caveat that policy was not always practice, and point to the sheer chaos of these years, the autonomy of local actors, and the difficulty of instituting top-down policies in the midst of brutal want and privation. They also note that not all Bolsheviks at that time were singing from the same ideological hymnal, or at least not singing quite as loudly as others. Some Bolsheviks believed that this was indeed what Kritsman termed 'the heroic period of the Great Russian Revolution,' namely that Soviet Russia was already on the path to socialism, perhaps even to full communism. Others felt that that claim, though ideologically desirable, was still premature. Still others saw only the excesses of the policies, and sought a different path to eventual communism. The respective attitudes of these individuals to the announcement of the NEP followed accordingly (see Nove 1972, pp. 46–52; 78–82; Lewin 1974, pp. 73–96). These approaches were eclipsed somewhat by a later view of war communist policies as ad hoc measures driven by civil war, namely temporary, emergency improvisations to combat the crippling economic scarcity and inflation and to meet urgent military needs (for excellent historiographic surveys of this trend, see Malle 2002, pp. 1–28; Roberts 1970, pp. 238–61; on the perestroika-era 'rediscovery' of the ideological argument, see the collection of translated late-Soviet articles, and their introduction by Bradley 1994). One scholar has argued that this historiographic shift derived from over-reliance on the research of three deans of Soviet economic and political history – Maurice Dobb, E.H. Carr, and Alec Nove – and that this in fact held back serious treatment of the role of ideology in assessments of 'war communism' (Boettke 1988, pp. 152, 149). Finally, the approaches discussed above are often fruitfully complicated by studies that focus on a specific aspect of economics over the longue durée, such as Russia's food crisis, the cooperative movement, or national income (Lih 1990a; Kotsonis 1999; Veselov 1994, pp. 52–71; Markevich and Harrison 2011, pp. 672–703).

49 'Speech in Closing the Conference May 28,' *Collected Works*, v. 32, pp. 436; see also 'Draft Resolution on Questions of the New Economic Policy,' *Collected Works*, v. 32, pp. 433–435;

out his rationale for the course change, a model of *realekonomik* in the service of *realpolitik*. Forcible appropriation of peasant surpluses, essentially without remuneration, had been the only way to secure enough grain to feed a starving, malnourished working class, in order that it could maintain the army and what was left of industry. 'We had', he wrote, 'no other way out'.[50] By the end of the year, his message was even more direct: 'we have had to retreat to state capitalism, retreat to concessions, retreat to trade'. With the NEP, he prioritised the restoration of 'proper [*pravil'nye*] relations with the peasants' after the devastation of war and the threat of Kronstadt as the only path to rebuild a weakened large-scale industry. If not, the widening gulf between the proletarian vanguard and the peasantry would become unbridgeable. This was why the NEP policy had to be 'in earnest and for a long time, but, of course, ... not for ever'.[51]

Many of his comrades, he noted, had underestimated the crucial role to be played by the peasantry in Soviet Russia's survival and reconstruction. 'Ours is not actually a workers' state', Lenin explained to them, 'but a workers' and peasants' state'.[52] For this reason, he spent more time explaining the tax-in-kind than any other single element of the new policy, and he did not mince his words:

> The correct policy of the proletariat exercising its dictatorship in a small-peasant country is to obtain grain in exchange for the manufactured goods the peasant needs. That is the only kind of food policy that corresponds to the tasks of the proletariat, and can strengthen the foundations of socialism and lead to its complete victory. The tax in kind is a transition to this policy. We are still so ruined and crushed by the burden of war (which was on but yesterday and could break out anew tomorrow, owing to the rapacity and malice of the capitalists) that we cannot give the peasant manufactured goods in return for all the grain we need. Being aware of this, we are introducing the tax in kind, that is, we shall take the minimum of grain we require (for the army and the workers) in the form of a tax and obtain the rest in exchange for manufactured goods. There is something else we must not forget. Our poverty and ruin are so great that we cannot restore large-scale socialist state industry at one stroke.[53]

'Speech Delivered at the Third All-Russia Food Conference, June 16, 1921,' *Collected Works*, v. 32, pp. 444.

50 'Report on the Tax in Kind Delivered at a Meeting of Secretaries and Responsible Representatives of R.C.P.(B.) Cells of Moscow and Moscow Gubernia. April 9, 1921,' *Collected Works*, v. 32, pp. 290.

51 'The Home and Foreign Policy of the Republic,' *Collected Works*, v. 33, p. 160.

52 'Party in Crisis,' Lenin, *Collected Works*, v. 32, p. 48.

53 'The Tax in Kind (The Significance of the New Policy and Its Conditions),' *Collected Works*, v. 32, p. 343.

'Economics in the spring of 1921', he stated bluntly, 'transformed into politics: "Kronstadt"'. He assured detractors that this new policy would be achieved not by a wager on the kulak, who would remain 'in the cold', or on the poor peasant, but on a better relationship with the middle peasant, the 'industrious peasant'. This relationship would be built in small collective farms, cooperatives, through electrification, and by reducing the 'evil of bureaucracy (its economic roots)'. In this way, the tax-in-kind would bring a transition 'from surplus-grain appropriation to commodity exchange' and thus 'from 'War' Communism to a proper [*pravil'nyi*] socialist foundation'.[54] 'Why the peasants and not the workers?' he asked rhetorically. The workers' condition could not improve without grain and fuel, he said, and grain could be produced and fuel delivered only if the peasants' condition could be improved enough to raise their productivity. 'We must start with the peasantry'.[55] He spelled out for his comrades the scale of the disaster in peasant farming in the spring of 1921: 'an extremely severe crisis caused by the war-time ruin and aggravated by a disastrous crop failure and the resultant fodder shortage ... and loss of cattle; ... peasant farming ... in many places was doomed to utter ruin'.[56] Lenin had moved the peasantry centre-stage in the dictatorship of the proletariat. This was no infringement on the prerogatives of the dictatorship of the proletariat, for, he assured them somewhat tautologically, the dictatorship decided the 'direction of policy', and this was the direction it had decided. 'State supervision, accounting, and control'[57] would keep in check the inevitable private capitalism that would emerge under the NEP. He hinted though that for this to be assured a measure of internal housekeeping might be needed. The existing problems of bureaucratic inertia, red tape, bribe-taking, 'communist conceit' in the Soviet state might well require the party to expel 'a hundred thousand to two hundred thousand Communists' who were unable or unwilling to fulfill their communist duties.[58]

Lenin, then, openly admitted that the NEP was a strategic retreat. The changes in policy, including concessions to foreign capitalists, leased enter-

54 'Plan of the Pamphlet 'The Tax in Kind',' *Collected Works*, v. 32, pp. 327, 320–321.

55 'The Tax in Kind (The Significance of the New Policy and Its Conditions),' *Collected Works*, v. 32, pp. 341.

56 'Report on the Tax in Kind Delivered at a Meeting of Secretaries and Responsible Representatives of R.C.P.(B.) Cells of Moscow and Moscow Gubernia. April 9, 1921,' *Collected Works*, v. 32, p. 287.

57 'The Tax in Kind (The Significance of the New Policy and Its Conditions),' *Collected Works*, v. 32, pp. 364.

58 'The New Economic Policy and the Tasks of the Political Education Departments. Report to the Second All-Russia Congress of Political Education Political Education Departments,' October 17, 1921, *Collected Works*, v. 33, pp. 77, 75.

prises to private capitalists, and free trading by peasants of their surpluses meant 'reverting to capitalism to a considerable extent'.[59] He still argued, however, for a fundamental continuity of communist principles underpinning both the measures deployed under what he termed 'war communism' and those now being deployed under the NEP. In another speech also delivered in late 1921, he said that the government and party called the NEP new, but that 'this new policy contains more elements of the old than our previous economic policy did'.[60] He quoted from his own writings from 1918 to display his consistency of thought and, by immodest analogy, the essential continuity of Soviet economic policy. As a 'transitional' system from capitalism to socialism, the Soviet economic system incorporated 'elements, particles, fragments' from patriarchal peasant agriculture, small commodity production, mostly by peasants, private capitalism, state capitalism, and socialism. In those earlier writings, he had already pointed out that his call for a transition to 'state capitalism' might be seen by some as a 'betrayal of socialism', but added that 'it is not state capitalism that is at war with socialism, but the petty bourgeoisie plus private capitalism fighting together against state capitalism and socialism'. He emphasised the difference between the state capitalism of, say, bourgeois imperialist Germany that was economically grounded in the private ownership of large-scale industry, and the state capitalism of socialist Soviet Russia that was economically grounded in the proletarian ownership of large-scale industry. While some fragments of private capitalism might briefly flourish in NEP Russia, they would be held in check by a novel state capitalism of nationalised commanding heights in the hands of the dictatorship of the proletariat.[61]

The system, then, was retreating not to capitalism but to state capitalism. In a report on the NEP to the Seventh Moscow Regional Conference of the party at the end of October 1921, Lenin pointed out some lessons learned from the Soviet state's earlier economic policies. After the Brest Peace in March 1918, and before the Civil War had heated up with the Czechoslovak mutiny in the summer, 'the question was raised of transferring our activities from the task of expropriating, of smashing the power of the exploiters and expropriators,

59 'The New Economic Policy and the Tasks of the Political Education Departments. Report to the Second All-Russia Congress of Political Education Political Education Departments,' October 17, 1921, *Collected Works*, v. 33, p. 64.

60 'The New Economic Policy and the Tasks of the Political Education Departments. Report to the Second All-Russia Congress of Political Education Political Education Departments,' *Collected Works*, v. 33, p. 61.

61 'The Tax in Kind (The Significance of the New Policy and Its Conditions),' *Collected Works*, v. 32, pp. 330–334. The work he referenced from 1918 was Lenin, ''Left-Wing' Childishness,' p. 335 ff.

to that of organising accounting and control, to the, so to speak, prosaic tasks of actual economic development'. This had involved certain compromises, he noted, with bourgeois specialists, for example, being paid at higher 'bourgeois' rates than initially permitted. The Bolsheviks had been guilty at the time of a too narrow view of their economic remit: 'We assumed that we could proceed straight to socialism without a preliminary period in which the old economy would be adapted to socialist economy. We assumed that by introducing state production and state distribution we had established an economic system of production and distribution that differed from the previous one'. He implied that the party needed to take a more capacious view now. It had become clear by spring 1921, he told them, that the attempt to introduce 'socialist principles of production and distribution by "direct assault"' had failed.[62]

This acknowledged need for extended explication rather than summary proclamation of the NEP attested to the precarious position in which the Bolsheviks found themselves in the midst of their 'Kronstadt moment'. It was the antithesis of the summary introduction of the economic measures during the Civil War. The chaotic, brutal, and devastating years from 1918 to 1921 had undoubtedly won over many to the Soviet cause… and also alienated many. Soviet Russia's first years had spawned a range of emotions in the population: joy, anger, grief, relief, disappointment, disillusionment, and animosity. The announcement of the NEP created new wellsprings of relief and disappointment, although presumably not in equal measure. In his speeches and writings, Lenin explicitly addressed the more harmful of these emotions, at least as he saw them. He referred to 'wavering and uncertainty', to 'despondent, almost panic-stricken' comrades, and as late as October 1921 brought up the 'complaints, lamentations, despondency and indignation' that the transition might yet still elicit.[63] His own lieutenants and theoreticians of the party, Nikolai Bukharin and Evgenii Preobrazhenskii, were among the disillusioned. In 1919, they had praised the coercive, militarised, and mobilisational measures of the Civil War as prima facie evidence of the intrinsic value of the socialist state and of the inevitability of Communism's victory. This was a new form of civil war, they wrote, namely an 'extremely intensified class war', the very 'manifestation

62 'Seventh Moscow Gubernia Conference of the Russian Communist Party,' *Collected Works*, v. 33, pp. 88, 93.

63 Respectively, 'Speech Delivered at the Third All-Russia Food Conference, June 16, 1921,' *Collected Works*, v. 32, pp. 444; 'The New Economic Policy and the Tasks of the Political Education Departments. Report to the Second All-Russia Congress of Political Education Political Education Departments,' October 17, 1921, *Collected Works*, v. 33, pp. 63; 'Seventh Moscow Gubernia Conference of the Russian Communist Party,' October 29–31, 1921, *Collected Works*, v. 33, pp. 93.

of the revolution', and it thus *demanded* 'the sacrifice of persons and the sacrifice of material values'. These very costs meant that 'we must not ... set our faces against revolution'.[64] In their view, the class war should be continued rather than abandoned, even temporarily. Along with Iurii Larin, a major force in shaping early Soviet economic policy, they embraced the increasingly moneyless Soviet economy and the inflationary printing press as valuable rearguard attacks on the bourgeois monetary system.[65] Bukharin's eager commitment to immediate socialism by way of the hard-left policies already deployed during the years of civil war, particularly the state nationalisations of industry and the grain requisitioning policies from May 1918 onwards, was most in evidence in his 1920 publication *The Economics of the Transition Period*. He insisted on the need under socialism for conscious planning and guidance of the production process with set goals – the opposite of world capitalist 'anarchic' practices, Still, his insistence did not blind him to the reality on the ground at the time, namely that military needs were stripping the economy of the very means of its reproduction in terms of industrial products, consumer goods, finance, and labour.[66]

Bukharin's views were by no means exceptional among Bolsheviks at the time, Lenin and Trotsky included. In an extended speech at the Ninth Party Congress in March–April 1920, Trotsky made his most forthright case for the retention of some of these early policies. With the Civil War won, he sought to apply his organisational skills and experience to longer-term economic reconstruction, but most immediately to the devastating food crisis of the moment. He planned to form labour armies by mobilising peasants essentially as 'military units', replete with a command structure, and supervised by communist cells. The 'inevitability and progressiveness of military compulsion', he said, were essential for this 'revival of the economy'.[67] Trotsky's proposal for forced labour mobilisation would not have shocked the delegates.[68] After all, it was

64 Bukharin and Preobrazhensky 1969, pp. 173, 174, 182, 183.

65 Dobb 1967, p. 122.

66 See the editor's introduction in Bukharin 1979, pp. 1–25.

67 *Deviatyi s'ezd RKP(b). Mart-aprel' 1920 g.* (Moscow: Partiinoe izdatel'stvo, 1934), p. 99; also Leon Trotsky, 'On Mobilising the Industrial Proletariat, on Labour Service, on Militarising the Economy, and on the Utilisation of Army Units for Economic Needs,' in Trotsky 1981, pp. 69, 70.

68 Although best known for its labour militarisation proposal, Trotsky's speech also advocated other measures that found some favour within the party's Central Committee. He accused the Bolsheviks of undervaluing the peasantry, and he called for improved mutual understanding between industry and agriculture. He railed against stagnation in the new Soviet economic bureaucracy and called for a more decentralised system of regional eco-

something of a continuation of a raft of such coercive measures that had been adopted since September 1918 in response to the perennial food shortages and low productivity rates in the besieged Soviet economy. Even Lenin's would-be pretender, Iosif Stalin, as late as the Twelfth Party Congress in April 1923, criticised the 'corrupting influence' of elements of the NEP, by which he meant a corruption of the promise of the policies of immediate socialist construction he had supported so readily up to 1921.[69]

Kritsman would have found much to like in the utterances of these party leaders at the time. Since 1918, he had been following closely and writing regularly about the economic policy shifts of the day. Bolshevik policies until mid-1918 had permitted the relatively relaxed coexistence of socialist initiatives with concessions to prerevolutionary economic elements in the interest of continuity of production. While coercion still played an integral role in these early months, only from mid-1918 were the full-on coercive nationalisations and requisitions introduced that came to stamp this period. In May 1918 in the journal *Kommunist*, Kritsman endorsed this shift, arguing that the proletariat's assumption of political power would be meaningless without an 'economic takeover [*perevorot*]', namely all 'necessary decisive measures' to establish 'economic domination over the class enemy'. He left no doubt about his support for the aggressive intent behind these more assertive policies, noting that seizure of the banks was the 'first word' of the economic revolution, although he added that the 'concrete organisational forms' this revolution might take were still 'as if in a predawn fog'. He was certain, though, that these transitional measures would serve as a 'bridge to the complete realisation of socialism'. Despite this lack of clarity as to how to proceed, Kritsman called on the proletariat 'to begin to take control of economic life, as to refuse to do so would mean to renounce the revolution'. He rejected as incoherent the idea that workers' control would limit the actions of capitalists, that the bourgeoisie would willingly bequeath their administrative, technical, or commercial expertise to the workers, and he argued that efforts at worker management of enterprises had been nothing but a failure. Instead, he saw a useable model in the syndicates and trusts that had been set up by the state in heavy industry in order to mobilise industry for

---

nomic centers. He explicitly supported the establishment of a unitary system of state planning. He may even have implied in some of his speeches that forced requisitioning should be abandoned in favour of a legal free market in agricultural goods (Remington 1977, pp. 44–60). The seriousness of this latter measure, and whether Trotsky was justified in representing himself in retrospective writings as 'a NEPist before NEP' (ibid., p. 54), has been disputed (see Richard B. Day's comment and Remington's riposte (ibid., pp. 60–68); Day 1973).

69 Quoted in Himmer 1994, p. 516.

the needs of war. These he saw as the model for proletarian organisation in economic branches, but only after the old enterprises had been driven out or their managements' power diminished.[70] Kritsman's first foray into the politics of economics, then, implied a militarised, classist, exclusionary approach to economic policy that eschewed tsarist expertise in the transition to socialism, relying instead on a literal interpretation of the dictatorship of the proletariat in this overwhelmingly peasant state. The coerced mobilisation of all sectors of society was implicit here.

Two months later, his language was similarly uncompromising, almost visionary. The 'fortress of Russian capitalism' had been taken 'by storm', and from its wreckage ('there is no other material'), a 'new fortress' would be built. This task could only be in the hands of the proletariat, as the petty bourgeoisie was 'organically incapable'. The many projects being planned for the new Soviet state, he wrote, such as the cultivation of new sources of land, the exploitation of new sources of energy (electrification, etc), and the establishment of new means of communication, were all fine and good, but they could not solve the immediate crisis in Soviet Russia and they lacked any 'long-term prospects' of success. The 'ideological revolution' had successfully taken control of political power, but now the economic revolution was needed. Ultimately, it would be necessary to '*change the relationship of the social individual with nature* (in the sense of increasing the individual's mastery over it), in short, *a revolution [perevorot] in technology*'. Before this could happen, though, *the relationship among individuals in the production process* had to be changed, wherein the capitalist anarchic mode of production had to be replaced by a socialist planned mode, and the commodity-monetary economy had to be replaced by the planned supply and distribution of goods. This was the '*immediate task*' of the revolution, a 'grandiose' one, he conceded, given that the civil war was heating up. Capitalism had created a world economy, and now it was socialism's task to bring about nothing less than the 'actual and complete economic unification of all states into a single whole'. This was predicated on the 'strictest centralisation of economic life', under the newly created highest organ of economic life in this new state, the Supreme Council of the National Economy (VSNKh).

His proposed solutions were the same ones he had proposed in his earlier article, but his vision of unitary planned control was almost Zamiatinian in its reach. Given the rapidly deteriorating situation inside Soviet Russia at the time, it might well have struck some of his comrades as a not especially timely

70 Lev Kritsman, 'Ob organizatsionnykh putiakh sotsialisticheskago stroitel'stva khoziaistvennoi zhizni,' *Kommunist*, no. 3, 16 May 1918, pp. 153, 154, 158.

or realistic exhortation.[71] Indeed, some of the specialists pressed into Soviet economic service during these years found the project more mystical than visionary. One such specialist, a textile engineer, recounted how his Communist boss had told him that the old 'accounting in banknotes [*uchet v denezhnykh znakakh*]' under capitalism had to be replaced by 'direct labour accounting [*neposredstvenno-trudovyi uchet*]' under 'war communism', although neither had any idea what that actually meant. It was not possible, he added, to work 'productively' under such conditions. Even Communists like I.A. Kalinnikov, a Russian academic and engineer who worked in the industrial section of Gosplan, described the experience of working under 'war communism' in less than glowing terms: 'It was constantly necessary to hypnotise oneself with the thought that this irrational system is an ideal system, and, as such, is being established for eternity'. He likened this to the fictional fabulist and terminally self-delusional Baron Munchausen trying to pull himself out of a swamp by his own hair. The introduction of the NEP, he added, had raised the spirits of many of his colleagues, and made them feel as if they were jumping 'from the moon [back] to the earth'.[72]

Kritsman's somewhat wide-eyed enthusiasm apparently remained undampened by what he had witnessed during the years of civil war. Writing in August 1920, he boasted of the 'complete victory on all fronts' in the Civil War, and offered an early defense – and a preview of the argument he would offer in his 1924 volume – of the ideological inspiration behind the economic policies that had brought that very victory. He laid out his argument in a step-by-step riposte to actual – and anticipated – criticisms of those policies. The 'tempestuous activity of revolutionary proletarian (and peasant) spontaneity' after the October Revolution, he wrote, was the driving force in this economic realm. This spontaneity, he added, had not come out of nowhere. It had been primed ideologically long before 1917 by the effects of bourgeois lockouts and shutdowns that had ultimately led to the rise of factory-plant committees and to the very idea of workers' control over economic enterprises. The proletariat was ideologically ready 'to seize command power in production'. From the outset, this revolutionary spontaneity had been harnessed (if incompletely) in the economic sphere by the introduction of 'planned organisation [*planomernaia organizovannost'*]'. Local economic organs of Soviet power had arisen not by fiat from the centre but in response to the local 'economic chaos' generated

71 'Ob ocherednoi zadache proletarskoi revoliutsii v Rossii,' *Narodnoe khoziaistvo*, no. 5, 15 July 1918, pp. 1–3.

72 Valentinov 1991, pp. 60–61.

by 'revolutionary spontaneity and economic destruction' and had tended naturally – if not always smoothly – towards unification. This had been the very first steps in the 'replacement of the dictatorship of capital by the dictatorship of the proletariat', at a time when the preexisting central apparatus was hostile to it, and a central socialist apparatus had yet to be established. As the old economic forms disintegrated, he continued, this absence was corrected over the next three years by the dictatorship of the proletariat, as it set about building brick by brick the central apparatus of a socialist economic system, 'guided by the idea of a unitary economic plan, of the introduction of planning into all economic activity'. He implied that these economic measures might have seemed at the time like ad hoc responses to the pell-mell of the chaos of war, that this all bore 'the inevitable stamp of theoreticality and artificiality [*teoretichnost' i nadumannost'*]'. But as the center and the localities felt each other out and learned how to work together 'in the common task of destroying the old and building the new', albeit with 'endless frictions and partial failures', the economic activity at the local level lost its limited aspect [*ogranichennost'*], becoming part of a greater whole. Moreover, the activity at the centre lost its theoreticality, 'becoming practical and therefore true leadership'. This 'new mechanism of the national economy' was beginning to work. He conceded that 'no actual unitary center of organisation of the national economy' yet existed. Still, he added, the recent discussions about not demobilising the Red Army but rather utilising the soldiers as a labour army for peacetime construction, and the current work being undertaken to work out the contours of a 'general economic plan' (e.g. the GOELRO electrification project), seemed to him to be powerful arguments for staying the course. Moreover, these past three years of a centralised and rationalised national economy had taken the proletariat from 'organisational (socio-economic) activity' to 'production (economic-technical) activity' and had eliminated the commodity economy through the 'state-organised collaboration of town and countryside'. This put Soviet Russia, he ended, in a better position than the hostile Western powers to take on peacetime construction in the face of similar economic challenges.[73]

It is hard to imagine a more full-throated endorsement of the spirit of the policies deployed during the first three years of the Soviet Republic. Kritsman quickly pressed his case for centralised state planning in a series of articles published in *Ekonomicheskaia zhizn'* between December 1920 and February 1921,

---

73 L. Kritsman, 'Organizatsiia narodnogo khoziaistva v Sovetskoi Rossii (1917–1920),' in *Ocherk khoziaistvennoi zhizni i organizatsiia narodnogo khoziaistva Sovetskoi Rossii, 1 noiabria 1917–1 iuliia 1920 g.*, ed. Iu Larin and L. Kritsman (Moscow: Gos. Izd-vo, 1920), pp. 125, 112–113, 114, 112, 113, 125, 137, 136, 141.

acknowledging their 'crudest general outlines', but claiming that nothing was more urgent in early 1921 than the 'economic plan'.[74] He rather cheekily invoked Lenin's earlier declaration that 'socialism is accounting [*sotsializm eto uchet*]' to make the case for the indispensability going forward of the Commission for the Utilisation of Material Resources, the organisation he now headed.[75] This body, he argued, should offer the coordinated, systematic, centralised planning that Soviet Russia needed for the peacetime era, if it was to move on once-and-for-all from capitalism and repair the destruction wrought by capital on the Soviet Republic. The 'anarchy' of capitalism's supply and distribution system, indeed of economic life in general, had been tempered somewhat by a degree of planning imposed by the needs of war. Capitalist production was still, he wrote, 'better than ours'. This was in spite of the fact that Soviet Russia had set up a plethora of organisations under VSNKh to carry out organised individual plans for the accounting, acquisition, and distribution of all manner of goods, labour power included, and had drawn upon the expertise of the earlier system (those bourgeois specialists, for example, that Lenin would soon defend). Nonetheless, three years after the establishment of proletarian power, he noted, these efforts had remained terminally uncoordinated, and there existed no single economic plan, nor any single organ that could devise one. 'Capitalist anarchy had been replaced by proletarian anarchy', he wrote, although he conceded that this had had much to do with the exhausting fight for survival during the war that had left no energy, resources, or forces for economic work. His commission, he implied, if given the needed authority and resources, would bring organisation and planning – however inadequately at first – to this anarchy. His promise was simple in its intent, and extraordinarily ambitious in its scope:

> The basic task of the Utilisation Commission is the compilation of utilisation plans ... The utilisation plan for each product must determine how much of it goes for industrial consumption, how much of it is for the satisfaction of the population's personal consumption, how much of it is destined for export abroad, and how much of it is held back in reserve (for the satisfaction of unforeseen needs).

---

74 L. Kritsman, 'O khoziaistvennom plane,' *Ekonomicheskaia zhizn'*, no. 38, 20 February 1921, p. 1.

75 L. Kritsman, 'Edinyi khoziaistvennyi plan i Komissiia ispol'zovaniia,' in *Ob edinom khoziaistvennom plane* (*raboty 1920–1921 godov*) (Moscow: 'Ekonomika,' 1989), p. 135; he is referring to Lenin, 'Can the Bolsheviks Retain State Power?' *Collected Works*, v. 26, p. 105. Alongside other writings on planning by leading Bolsheviks, this 1989 volume also included several of the major decrees on planning enacted at the time.

Kritsman uncompromisingly called for the revolution's fourth year to be devoted to 'carrying out the second half of the communist economy: without exploiters, but on the basis of a rigorously devised plan'.[76]

In 1920 at least, Bukharin had praised Kritsman's 'sharp-witted [*ostroumnye*]' writings, but he also saw naïveté in them.[77] He implied that Kritsman had an unrealistic grasp of the current state of affairs and tended to oversimplify the task of dismantling the capitalist organisation of the economy, which Kritsman had dismissively likened to being 'shucked off like a husk'.[78] 'The new society', as Bukharin put it, 'cannot suddenly appear like a *deus ex machina*'.[79] By early 1921, reminders of capitalism's anarchic features would not have sat well with those now touting the New Economic Policy and the apparent return of state capitalistic measures to peacetime economic reconstruction. Indeed, Kritsman soon found himself the target of Lenin's sharp tongue. Lenin dismissed his writings as full of 'empty talk and word-spinning', and for refusing to see what had already been achieved in this realm. He called out other comrades by name, including the prominent economists V.P. Miliutin and Larin, who 'all have the same basic defects as Kritsman's articles'. They exhibited the 'dullest sort of scholasticism' rather than a practical focus on the past experience that the transitioning economy so desperately needed. Lenin pilloried the 'intellectualist conceit of the Communist literati', with their constant calls for more and more theoretical discussions and plans and approval procedures, and their willingness to ignore the practical experience being accumulated in the centre and at the local level often by those with seemingly less unimpeachable revolutionary credentials. The Communists, he wrote, should be learning all they could from the 'bourgeois specialists and scientists, and cutting out the administrative game'. He would gladly swap 'dozens' of the former for 'one conscientious qualified bourgeois specialist', notwithstanding the inevitable 'strong bourgeois habits' of the latter. It was true, he allowed, that for a long time Communists had been learning how to 'mistrust' and 'expose' the bourgeois specialists. Now, though, 'we must learn to run the country'.[80] He did not

76 Kritsman, 'Edinyi khoziaistvennyi plan i Komissiia ispol'zovaniia,' pp. 134, 136, 142, 153.

77 Bukharin acknowledged a debt to Kritsman's schema of revolutionary phases – from ideological to political to economic to technical revolution – outlined in the above article (Bukharin 2003, pp. 100, 218n14).

78 Bukharin is quoting from L. Kritsman, 'Osnovnye tendentsii sotsial'noi revoliutsii proletariata,' *Narodnoe khoziaistvo*, no. 3, 1919 (see Bukharin 2003, p. 215n1).

79 Bukharin 2003, p. 94.

80 'Integrated Economic Plan,' *Collected Works*, v. 32, pp. 137, 138, 143, 144, 145. Lenin argued here that the work that had already been carried out on his pet project, the GOELRO (State Commission for the Electrification of Russia) plan, was not fully appreciated, although

restrict his ire to just one speech. At other venues, he blasted the 'feverish upper ranks' of the party who used 'empty, highbrow chatter' to advocate for labour policies that were a continuation of a militarised economy.[81] They were still in the thrall of revolution, he implied, and their unrealistic designs were a misunderstanding of what was required in Soviet Russia at this particular moment in time. He later reminded his comrades that he had cautioned them in 1918 not to be unrealistic in their communist aspirations and not to get carried away by the ''dazzling' revolutionary spirit'.[82] Lenin's defense of bourgeois specialists and of rolling back the militarisation in the economy were but two of the starkest illustrations of the clash in 1921 between the economic pragmatism that Lenin saw at the heart of the NEP era and the ideological aspirations that Kritsman and others saw at the heart of the economic policies of the Civil War era.

On the occasion of the Fourth Anniversary of the October Revolution, Lenin continued to attribute the discomfit within the party ranks with these changes in economic policy to the fact that during the Civil War comrades had been 'borne along on the crest of the wave of enthusiasm, rousing first the political enthusiasm and then the military enthusiasm of the people'. The rank-and-file had thus expected a similar surge of enthusiasm to make a success of the economic measures introduced at that time.[83] Their enthusiasm, he implied, was understandable, even laudable, but premature. In response to the overwhelming problems of the war, among other issues, the Bolsheviks had made the mistake of going 'directly to communist production and distribution', Lenin wrote, i.e. to the forced requisitioning system that would extract the resources they needed from the peasants.[84] The implication was clear. The goal was sound, but the timing was wrong. He directly addressed those who felt that the party had lost its ideological bearings with the NEP:

> Some people think it is very queer and even very terrible. They say: If Communists have gone to the length of saying that the immediate task is to engage in trade, in

---

Kritsman had in fact singled this project out as an example of how fruitfully to move forward with planning.

81 'Party in Crisis,' Lenin, *Collected Works*, v. 32, p. 43.

82 'The Tax in Kind (The Significance of the New Policy and Its Conditions),' *Collected Works*, v. 32, p. 340.

83 'Fourth Anniversary of the October Revolution,' *Collected Works*, v. 33, p. 58.

84 'The New Economic Policy and the Tasks of the Political Education Departments. Report to the Second All-Russia Congress of Political Education Political Education Departments,' October 17, 1921, *Collected Works*, v. 33, p. 62.

> ordinary, common, vulgar, paltry trade, what can remain of communism? Is this not enough to make anyone throw up his hands in despair and say, 'All is lost'?[85]

Lenin had importuned such doubters to stay their short-term pessimism in favour of a longer-term view of the new Soviet state: 'The policy is…being adopted in earnest….[O]wing to the gossip habit, rumours are being spread that we are indulging in a policy of expedients, that is to say, political trickery, and that what is being done is only for the present day'.[86] At the Tenth Party Congress in March 1921, while acknowledging that a socialist revolution had to be started by 'dreamers', Lenin chided those very communist dreamers 'who thought the economic basis, the economic roots, of small farming could be reshaped in three years'.[87] Clinging to earlier dreams, he warned at the Eleventh Party Con-

---

85 'Seventh Moscow Gubernia Conference of the Russian Communist Party,' October 29–31, 1921, *Collected Works*, v. 33, p. 97.

86 'Summing-up Speech on the Tax-in-Kind. May 27,' *Collected Works*, v. 32, p. 429.

87 'Tenth Congress of the R.C.P.(B.). March 8–16, 1921,' *Collected Works*, v. 32, pp. 216–217. Lenin's cautions to the 'Communist dreamers' seduced by the promise of an illusory short-cut to socialism through 'war communism' were eagerly embraced by those scholars who argued that Marxism was fundamentally inapplicable to backward Russia (for example, Patenaude 1995, pp. 552–70; Lewin 1968, ch. 2). Some scholars attributed the failure of this Soviet socialist experiment to precisely such 'flights of leftist fancy' (Dobb 1967, p. 122). Others saw this early failure as an indictment *tout court* of the delusional nature of the entire Communist project. As historian Martin Malia famously observed, scholars' attitudes to the events of October 1917 had much to do with whether they believed Soviet Russia to be a legitimate or an illegitimate state and vice versa (Malia 1992, p. 9; also Malia 1994]). So it was with 'war communism'. Was it 'true socialism … or an aberration'? (Bradley 1994, p. 3). Often, the NEP was viewed as the cold compress on the revolutionary's brow after the fever-dream of 'war communism' finally broke. Scholars have argued that this assumption has produced a distorted evaluation of individual policies of 'war communism,' for example the establishment of sowing committees (*posevkomy*) intended to tackle the agricultural crisis in late 1920 (Lih 1990b). With similar astuteness, Boettke points out that historiographic discussions about the meaning of 'war communism,' rather than about the specific economic policies it actually introduced, had less to do with economics than with 'intellectual history and political economy'. Scholars have had it both ways in a sense, he implied, as those who indeed saw these policies as animated by ideology could interpret their often disastrous effects as a failure of 'Marxian socialism,' which had underperformed capitalism. Those who saw them as ad hoc responses to war emergencies and military necessity argued that they were in fact not a testing ground for socialist economics at all. For Boettke, this dismissiveness is only possible because scholars have failed to take serious account of the broader ideological and historical context, namely the 'policy prescriptions of early twentieth-century European and Russian Marxism' as the best way to understand them (see Boettke 1988, 149–159). Moreover, Lenin's perhaps expedient but very public disavowal of Communist dreams and utopian illusions in the launch of the NEP also cleared a historiographic path for the cynics' view that Soviet Russia was now in

gress a year later, was a dangerous luxury that Soviet Russia could ill afford at this moment in its history. Such sentiments, he continued, could only serve to feed the widespread belief among Soviet Russia's enemies, many now in forced emigration, that socialism under NEP was becoming an empty signifier, and that its use of specialists from the former regime, for example, would ensure that it would evolve over time into an 'ordinary bourgeois state'. These were not just isolated *émigrés*, he warned, but individuals who 'express the sentiments of thousands and tens of thousands of bourgeois, or of Soviet employees whose function it is to operate our New Economic Policy. This is the real and main danger'.[88]

It might seem paradoxical that this retreat from militarised practices in the economic sphere was accompanied by precisely the opposite in the political sphere. In March 1921, the Tenth Party Congress adopted a ban on intraparty factions, another ripple from the Kronstadt events.[89] This latter development undoubtedly had a chastening effect on the political viability of economic policy debates moving forward. Lenin's analysis and statements in this seminal year set the contours of future debates and discussions in all realms of this postwar Soviet Republic. His pronouncements – both his analysis of the transition and the language he employed – were not draft policies seeking approval, but adopted policies requiring approbation. It was the blueprint

the hands of those 'only interested in power' (Kotsonis 2014, esp. pp. 296–298). In short, the historiographic view scholars took of the 'war communism' period (and the preservation of quotation marks around the term was often a tell) helped shape their treatment of a number of key themes now etched into Soviet historiography: the relationship between Leninism and Stalinism; the relationship between the requisitioning and centralisation policies of 'war communism' and the collectivisation and industrialisation policies of later Stalinism; indeed, the role of coercion in political and economic policy throughout the Soviet era. For the Polish philosopher, Leszek Kolakowski, for example, 'war communism' was undeniably an ideological project of the Bolsheviks from the outset and was thus one of the 'main stages of Stalinist totalitarianism' (Kolakowski 1999, p. 160).

88 'Eleventh Congress of the R.C.P.(B.), March 27–April 7, 1922,' *Collected Works*, v. 33, pp. 286–287. He was referring specifically to a disparate group of *émigrés* in Europe, who were buoyed by what they saw as a revival of basic elements of capitalism under the NEP. They coalesced around a 1921 publication, *Smena vekh* [*Change of Signposts*], and a journal of the same name that was published in Paris for several months after October 1921. *Émigrés* later drew a direct line in their critiques of the coercive policies of collectivisation and planning back to the early socialist experimentation with 'war communism,' sometimes marshalling Kritsman's work in support of their condemnation (see, for example, Prokopovich 1934, pp. 37, 54).

89 'Preliminary Draft Resolution of the Tenth Congress of the R.C.P. on Party Unity,' *Collected Works*, v. 32, pp. 241–244. The most exhaustive documentary record of this factionalism can be found in Allen (ed.) 2021. For more on this development, see Daniels 1960.

for Soviet Russia's economic and political future. At the end of December, the Politbureau of the party called on 'all economic bodies' to stop talking and instead to act, as the 'New Economic Policy has been quite firmly and clearly established', and needed to be tested on the ground as widely as possible:

> All general arguments, theoretical arguments and debates on the subject of the New Economic Policy must be relegated to debating clubs, partly to the press. They must be rooted out relentlessly from the Council of People's Commissars, the Council of Labour and Defence and all economic bodies … The Higher Economic Commission should be turned into a body engaged solely in classifying and pooling the economic acts promulgated by the state.[90]

Advocates of the earlier policies, including Stalin and Bukharin, had begun abandoning their positions and embracing the NEP from early 1921, although the sincerity of their epiphanies was not always clear.[91] Kritsman did not follow their lead. Economists and statisticians like him were surely mindful of these official admonitions and public mea culpas, as they set about their research on the early economic state of the Soviet Republic, but their economic field of play was not yet the increasingly polemical minefield of the political realm. As observed at the time, the first half of the 1920s saw a deluge of monthly economic journals, regular published yearbooks of industrial and financial statistics, and monographic examinations of the new Soviet economy.[92] Even in the political journals, Kritsman found some room to breathe. In the pages of the journal of the Socialist Academy between 1922 and 1924, he debated the earlier economic policies quite forthrightly with Preobrazhenskii, Miliutin, Larin, and ex-Menshevik B. Gorev, among others. They discussed whether the policies had indeed been 'transitional to socialism', whether key parts of the Bolshevik agenda, such as all-out nationalisation, ending petty trade, and so on, had merely been forced upon them by the Civil War, and whether 'catastrophe' or 'communism' had in fact driven the policies.[93]

In early 1924, Kritsman offered a report-card in the journal *Zvezda* on the first three full years of the NEP. He threw Lenin's own words back at him:

90 'Draft Directive of the Political Bureau on the New Economic Policy,' *Collected Works*, v. 33, p. 197.

91 On doubts about Stalin's supposed NEP-iphany, see Himmer 1994, pp. 515–29.

92 Méquet 1929, pp. 399–410.

93 Nove 1972., pp. 79–80.

> Since the announcement of the New Economic Policy – in earnest and for a long time, but not for ever – three years have passed.…Is the newly created proletarian society developing, strengthening politically, and most importantly, economically under these conditions of retreat of the proletarian revolution? Or is the petty bourgeois, and this means bourgeois, flood washing away the solidified lava of the proletarian revolution?

While no longer explicitly defending the earlier policies, he did so implicitly by criticising the NEP at its ideological core. He praised the successes of the NEP (particularly in light of the economic and human misery and devastation that had precipitated its introduction three years before), chronicling these successes between 1921 and 1924 with a litany of impressive economic statistics in both industry and agriculture. In his view, though, the very outward economic successes of the NEP were evidence of its inherent ideological failure. The market was 'capital's source of life, the source of its power, and thus of its counter-revolutionary power', and its earlier suppression, he argued, had been central to crushing the counter-revolution, even though the peasantry had only ever grudgingly supported that suppression. The revival of market relations under the NEP, then, had removed central prerequisites for the 'victory of the peasant revolution'. For this reason alone, it qualified as a 'retreat from the proletarian revolution'. The NEP had so held back both the peasant and proletarian revolutions, he argued, that the Soviet system was still not yet a socialist system, but in a transitional stage to it. The 'class of capitalists', much diminished in power to be sure, still existed, and so 'class exploitation' still existed, albeit restricted in scope. Notwithstanding the improved economic indices, factors like poverty, hunger, unemployment, prostitution, homelessness, and the 'well-fed Nepman', persisted for some, while 'shameless luxury' persisted for others. The NEP, he offered, had indeed done some things correctly. It had made sure to retain political power over the basic means of 'social production and exchange' in the proletarian class, but the peasant and household economy continued to exist, as did all the 'narrowness and limitedness of peasants and women' that went along with it. He still saw planning of all aspects of the economy as the antidote to the 'commodity anarchy of economic life'.

Kritsman drew some hope for the future from the scissors' crisis of 1923. The growing gap between industrial prices and agricultural prices seemed to him blunt evidence of the ever-present threat from the anarchy of the market under the NEP, and ran the risk of a peasant withdrawal from the economy. He welcomed the state regulation of trade and monetary reform that had emerged in response to it, which seemed to be 'not only a turn away from retreat before the elemental forces of the market and a move towards attempts to regulate it, but also a turn away from any collaboration with trade capital to fight against it'. Still, the 'elemental' market persisted, as did collaboration with the bourgeoisie. He conceded that it had earlier been necessary to put energy into the alliance [*smychka*] of the proletariat and peasantry in order to restore economic relations and production after the Civil War, but, in the absence of adequate proletarian economic organisations, capital turned out to have a 'virtual monopoly on the restoration of the missing (destroyed) economic connections'. Capital's pledged recognition of the Soviet system could not be trusted, and indeed capital had exploited state economic organs as well as the urban/rural economic connections often through bribes, as it sought to turn the former 'into an (illegal) tool of capitalist exploitation', with some success, Kritsman noted. The proletariat's acceptance of this 'collaboration with trade capital' was, then, the 'sharpest expression of the proletariat's retreat'. At least, he wrote, state (and cooperative) trade and capitalist trade were no longer treated as equals after the 1923 crisis. 'Trade capital became the enemy' and was no longer a target of state collaboration. It ushered in a welcome second phase of the NEP, a 'shift *from retreat* to careful and methodical *attack*'.[94]

3 The 'Heroic Period' of the Great Russian Revolution

While Lenin was busy explaining the finer points of the NEP and while key planks of the economic policy were being put into place, Kritsman was diligently working from 1922 onwards on his opus, a statistically girded endorsement of the ideological rationale for the Soviet economic policies that had been deployed prior to the NEP.[95] Beginning in 1923, he shifted from his earlier

94 L. Kritsman, 'Tri gody Novoi Ekonomicheskoi Politiki proletariata Sovetskogo Soiuza'. *Zvezda*, no. 3, 1924, pp. 108–134 (all quotations are from the translated appendix in Kritsman, The Heroic Period, pp. 330–32 [emphases in original]). A year earlier, he had published a similar appraisal after two full years of the NEP (L. Kritsman, *Dva goda Novoi Ekonomicheskoi Politiki proletariata SSSR* [Moscow: 1923). I have been unable to locate a copy of this article.

95 In Soviet historiography, Kritsman's volume ensured that he would become something of an exemplar of 'mistaken' evaluations of these early economic policies, particularly his view of them as a 'direct transition to the Communist society'. Charges that they contradicted the 'Leninist conception of the history of the Great October Socialist Revolution and the Civil War' did not, however, dissuade Soviet historians from drawing upon the voluminous economic statistics he marshalled in this volume (Gimpel'son 1973, pp. 248–259). Western historians have praised the volume both for its 'fecundity of Marxist thought' in the early years of Soviet Russia, which contrasted with the 'sterile dogmatism' embraced in the Stalinist years, and for its efforts to avoid the 'crude economic determin-

administrative positions to the life of an academic on the Presidium of the Communist Academy, a move that undoubtedly afforded him more time for his own research and writing. It also gave him, perhaps, the illusion of a safe economic port in a rising political storm. He joined a special commission set up under the Communist Academy for a project to study the history of the agrarian revolution in Russia, with the intention of publishing a series of volumes on key economic topics.[96] In the latter half of the 1920s, he joined the editorial boards of *Pravda*, *Problemy ekonomiki*, and *Na agrarnom fronte*, as well as encyclopedia projects. Unsurprisingly, his earlier articles were in many ways previews of his later more comprehensive study of the pre-NEP economic policies.

Kritsman's monograph was an attempt (his term) at a coherent and reasoned evaluation of the effectiveness of these policies. He explicitly rejected the notion that 'so-called 'war communism'' had been 'a delusion [*zabluzhdenie*] of individuals or of a class'. It had in reality been 'an anticipation of the future – although not in a pure sense but with certain distortions, an intrusion by this future into the present (now already the past)'. He used the term 'war communism' only five times in the entire manuscript, only ever in quotation marks, and generally to dismiss it – 'so-called 'war communism',' as he put it in the very title of his opus. He believed the term was unhelpful, and that it distracted from real analysis. He referred dismissively to 'very quick-witted individuals' whose application of the term to the economic system from 1918 to 1920 was 'unjustified and extremely superficial' (was he including Lenin among these individuals?). He accused them of portraying the policies as merely 'simulating the transition to socialism', and of believing that the policies were in fact merely 'organising the 'rear',' i.e. that they were not in fact a response to long-term socialist aspirations but to short-term wartime conditions. He implied that this was just a sloppy adaptation of 'so-called 'war socialism',' an earlier term coined to describe (wrongly, he opined) the economic regime of wartime capitalist states as a 'purely consumer economy' involving the rationing of consumer needs under temporary siege conditions. The term 'war communism', he added, was misleading because it did not convey the true rationale of the economic policies deployed in Soviet Russia at that time. The organisation by the proletariat of production and reproduction was not something imposed upon

ism' with which Marxism had long flirted (Kowalski, 'Geroicheskii period Russkoi Revolutsii. Translator's Introduction,' p. vi). Others, while praising the data and information it deployed, described it as an 'apologia on behalf of those who had given their devotion to the revolutionary drive' and as embodying 'the bias of any heroic chronicle' (Malle, *The Economic Organization of War Communism*, p. 9).

96 Cox and Littlejohn (eds.) 1984, p. 9n1.

the Soviet state from outside by the war. On the contrary, it took place in conditions of '*civil war*', which was 'nothing less than the climax of the revolution', and in the economic realm this signified '*an attempt to take the first steps of the transition to socialism*'. As defining terms, both 'war socialism' and 'war communism' were 'equally useless and no better than their originators' (original italics).

In *The Heroic Period of the Great Russian Revolution*, Kritsman moved from the general to the specific. He extolled the 'unique' nature, 'profundity' and 'reach' of the Great Russian Revolution, his analysis then giving way over thirteen chapters to ever more sobre and detailed analyses of the economic specificities of the period as they had played out in reality. The true impact of these events in Russia in 1917 and afterwards, he argued, was epistemological in nature, a deep psychological blow to a capitalist world which was conceptually incapable of understanding the Russian Revolution because it lacked the requisite terms of reference to do so. Capital's abiding arrogance was to conceive of itself not just as a dominant form of societal organisation but as a 'natural' one. Even if the revolution had lasted only a few weeks, he noted, it had already shattered received notions of how the world operated, just as a volcanic eruption shook one's faith in the solidity of the earth, revealing for the first time the ever-present 'fiery matter beneath'.[97]

Kritsman's true intended audience though was not the world of capital but the world of Soviet Marxism. With albeit brief nods to the works of founding fathers like Marx and Lenin, he had outlined his own model of sequential and interconnected revolutionary development first in 1918.[98] He elaborated on it in his 1924 work, charting the course of proletarian revolution across five phases. The first *ideological* phase of revolution wins over people's minds, allowing them to conceive of agitating for a political overthrow, and ushering in the second phase, namely a *political* revolution that destroys the old political system and replaces it with radically restructured political relations. The revolutionary masses that emerge in the first phase are essential to the success of the second phase, and this allows for the *economic* third phase of the revolution, namely the final destruction of the old antagonistic and exploitative productive forces of society. A fourth phase (no longer, in Kritsman's view, a truly revolutionary phase) creates fundamentally new productive forces of economic development. This process, as laid out by Kritsman, signifies a novel development – a move away from the wasteful 'anarchy' of market forces and

97 Kritsman, *Heroic Period*, 68.

98 L. Kritsman, 'Ob ocherednoi zadache proletarskoi revoliutsii v Rossii,' *Narodnoe khoziaistvo*, no. 5, 15 July 1918, pp. 1–5.

towards a 'rational' and 'planned' mode of production in the new workers' state. Only when this has been achieved, could a final, fifth, phase occur (the revolution itself has started to 'fade away' by now), when the most fundamental technological relationships of society – still redolent with the 'former antagonistic economic structure' – could be remade for the new socialist economy. For its part, agrarian revolution passes through similar phases of development. However, its own scattered and atomised nature – a product of petty-peasant economy – holds it back from moving beyond the inchoate revolts so common in history (and especially in Russian history) and onto the second phase of revolution (political revolution). For this to occur, Kritsman argued, it would require the guidance of a truly revolutionary class, the proletariat, which in turn would draw on the support of the masses of the peasantry for its own progress through the five phases of revolution. This would take the peasantry from the ideological and political phases to the destruction of feudal landholding, through revolutionary land reorganisation, and finally to the destruction of those features of peasant agriculture (distant fields, strip-farming, etc) that had so held it back in Tsarist Russia.

Kritsman argued, however, that Russia's actual revolution was far more complex than his theoretical model. It was not a 'purely proletarian (anti-capitalist) revolution or a purely peasant (anti-feudal) revolution', because it still had 'vestiges of pre-capitalist economic formations'. These vestiges had helped delay the onset of a full bourgeois revolution, the much-discussed and long-anticipated prerequisite of Russia's proletarian revolution. This was a blessing, he added, because the new Soviet government was not weighed down by a full bourgeois stage of the revolution. Even more important than this, though, were the predations of the First World War, Civil War, and foreign intervention, which had seen a crippling and protracted economic crisis, an end to the arms monopoly of the ruling classes, and an arming of both the workers and the peasants. The peasant masses had always been historically slower than the working masses to realise the state of their oppression by capitalism, a result of their historically dispersed nature. War and intervention overcame their dispersal, their 'atomization', as he put it, and their defenselessness. Under these conditions, and forced to take unprecedented measures for survival, the new Soviet government expropriated capital, confiscated the property of the ruling classes, suppressed the market, and restructured the national economy along proletarian principles that eliminated exploitation. Socialism was to be neither deferred nor delayed, and this 'first major attempt at a proletarian natural economy' that took shape between 1918 and 1920 was prima facie evidence for Kritsman of the rightness of these early policies. This moment had presented a golden opportunity, which those who had put in place the economic policies during these years had seized with both hands. This was not simply a few years of improvised survival, in his view, but an era of heroism, for both the proletariat and the peasantry had finally been able to conceive of their respective roles as vanguards of world proletarian and world peasant revolution. Both could now see themselves as the liberators of oppressed nations from both capitalism and colonialism. Given the continuing dominance of finance capital on the world stage, this was a crucial asset for the socialist project.

Writing at a time when Lenin and his comrades were turning away from these earlier economic and administrative policies towards the NEP, Kritsman, not accidentally, devoted the major part of his book to understanding the now squandered opportunity that he believed these earlier policies had in fact represented at the time. He saw the turn to the NEP as a fundamental error by the Soviet government. Treating the first wartime years of the proletarian state as a period of transition rather than as an era of immediate socialist transformation, Kritsman argued, had revealed 'half-heartedness' on the part of the new Soviet government. It was not just 'utopian' to think that the proletarian state could initially coexist with a hostile capitalist sector in the hope of learning 'from the class enemy the art of managing all aspects of an enterprise – technical, administrative, commercial'. It had been an illusion because hostile entrepreneurs would never collaborate in their own demise. Worse yet, even a transient desire 'to accommodate capital' deeply undermined the effectiveness of the perfectly good (if incomplete) socialist initiatives that had already been launched, not least workers' control, nationalisation of banks and transport, loan cancellation, and joint shareholding companies. Furthermore, the proletariat's concession to the peasant majority to enact a 'peasant agrarian programme' (the nationalisation of the land that had been a long-standing plank of the Party of Socialist Revolutionaries (PSR), as Kritsman helpfully reminded everyone), had been a significant coup for the Bolsheviks, even it was not an explicitly 'proletarian agrarian programme'. It had brought about the '*merger of the two revolutions*', securing the peasantry's support for the transfer of power to the proletariat, even though it had also led to the ideologically hazardous emergence of a 'small-peasant economy, more like a consumer economy'.

This missed golden opportunity that Kritsman saw in the economic and administrative policies of the Civil War era in no way blinded him to the realities of those policies as practiced. He neither glossed over the statistics he so meticulously featured in his book, nor downplayed or sugar-coated the enormity of the destruction wrought during the Civil War years. Indeed, he mercilessly called out by name those fellow economists who interpreted their statistics in ways that offered a too rosy picture of, for example, labour productivity. For his part, he described the parlous economic situation as 'completely unstable', productive forces as in 'appalling decline', working and living conditions as 'horrendous', and industrial plants as 'exhausted'. The very fabric of a modernising economy, he argued, was coming apart at the seams, precisely the intent of the protracted siege by the 'imperialist and capitalist powers'. Cities had been depopulated both by war needs and by a shortage of goods. Construction projects large and small had ground to a halt. Logging was severely curtailed. Factories and railways were on life support, absenteeism was rife, and labour productivity was in steep decline. The peasants were withholding their grain, and grain surpluses were disappearing, a process mitigated not by persuasion but by often violent requisitioning. The bourgeois specialists were either indifferent or openly hostile to their work. The standard of living (or 'standard of dying' as Kritsman artfully put it) was execrable. Starvation and epidemic disease were the daily companions of the population.

But the very severity of this system in extremis, he argued, was the price to be paid for ending capitalism. It had compelled the proletariat and the peasantry to look beyond the 'fetishistic approach to the economy' of capitalism and to be guided instead by the 'rationality' of the new Soviet approach. Kritsman invoked the French Revolution: 'A mad God ruled the world, from now on Reason rules everything'. Russia's workers and peasants were forced to look for their survival no longer to the old economic order but to the 'new social order'. The unprecedented suffering had demanded their commitment to the 'Soviet platform' with its 'integrated economic terrain'. In so doing, it caused the workers and peasants to begin to conceive of their lives and their labour in fundamentally novel ways, something that would have been impossible while capitalist elements persisted in the new Soviet economic system. This was, in fact, what had made the years between 1918 and 1921 truly 'heroic' years. The 'proletarian natural economy' he so praised in his book had certainly encountered major problems. He had argued years earlier that the anarchic practices of the capitalist economy had been replaced by the anarchic practices of the proletarian economy during these years. But the theory of the proletarian natural economy was sound, he implied, only its practice had been flawed. With private trade banned and the free market eradicated (*'for the first time in the history of mankind'*), and with traditional individualistic actions being replaced by collectivism, collegiality, and communalism, the emerging economy had set about bringing order to the anarchy through a consistent strategy of centralisation and planning. Of course, he conceded, there had been too many 'mutually independent economic plans' and too much 'bureaucratism' getting in the way. Indeed, the major flaw had been the absence throughout of an 'actual, unitary centre of organization of the national economy' and of a 'single national economic plan', a flaw which had prevented the proletarian natural economy from being a *socialist* economy. Notwithstanding these flaws, Kritsman was careful to point out some 'famous successes' of the proletarian natural economy during the war, particularly in the arms industry and in supplying the Red Army. He even footnoted (perhaps unwisely given the volatile political situation) a 1919 speech by Trotsky in this regard. At the end of his book, he recast the meaning of the Civil War from a war of naked survival and internal and external aggression to a crucible of the goals of revolution: to destroy capital, to create a proletarian economic system, and to reengage that new system with the world economy. If the next steps towards socialism were to be taken now, then more planning was needed, not less. The NEP, he implied, was marching in precisely the wrong direction, away from socialism, and had eschewed this golden opportunity offered by the 'heroic' policies boldly deployed in the years of the Civil War.

4 Life after 'War Communism'

By 1924–25, the scope of the politically possible – and of the politically wise – was changing even for economists, and Kritsman's book landed at something of an unfortuitous moment for many individuals in Soviet politics.[99] Bukharin, former heavyweight in the defense of these policies and Kritsman's sometime admirer, had early in 1924 taken up the cudgel of the recently deceased Lenin against those who had represented the transition to the NEP as the 'collapse of the illusions of the proletarian revolution', by which he meant the collapse of the 'ideology of war communism, i.e. those illusions that had been present in our party'. Channeling Lenin quite literally, he pilloried the 'enemies of communism', the 'empty Menshevik and SR windbags' and the 'vile oracles of the liberal bourgeoisie' who 'evaluated and continue to evaluate the transition to the New Economic Policy as the collapse of communism'. While he conceded that the foreign and domestic blockade had forced these policies of 'war communism' upon Soviet Russia, this did not mean that they had 'in its essence' been wrong for the time, although the Bolsheviks had not 'appreciated the full conditional nature [*otnositel'nost'*] of the war communist policy'. He conceded further that he, among others, had believed that post-Civil War economic policy would be a 'continuation of the centralised planned economy of this era', as enough had already been 'centralised' to suggest that the 'socialist planned economy' was already on its way. 'We conceived of war communism',

99 On the rise of the polemical in the political sphere, see Frederick C. Corney, 'Anatomy of a Polemic,' in Corney 2015, pp. 1–85.

he wrote, 'not as a response to 'war', i.e. suitable only for a particular stage in the development of the Civil War, but as a universal, general, and so to speak, 'normal' form of economic politics of the victorious proletariat'.[100] Furthermore, the party's multipronged polemic against Trotsky was heating up at this time. One protagonist in this polemic, Lev Kamenev, singled out Trotsky's call at the time to 'tighten the screws of war communism', rather than follow Lenin to the NEP. This exhibited, he said, a 'repeated underestimation of the peasantry, the tendency to get carried away by external forms, methods of 'pressure' and 'administration from above''.[101] While Kritsman was not implicated directly in either Bukharin's or Kamenev's criticisms, his views were similar enough that it was not beyond the realm of possibility that he could be.

Kritsman had made no attempt to thread any ideological or political needle for so-called 'war communism' with his book, and he stayed above the fray as much as possible. He perhaps thought that now, as charges of anti-Trotskyism reverberated throughout the Soviet body politic, discretion was the better part of valour. Or perhaps he felt he had said all he could say of substance in his ultimately futile championing of the early economic policies of the Soviet Republic before the transition to the NEP. His earlier work was underpinned by the deeper issue of the putative relationship between the proletariat and the peasantry, and by the nature of the development of peasant social structure under changing socioeconomic and political conditions. It was a topic that had animated Marxist thinking since, well, Marx, and it was to this that he devoted himself wholeheartedly from now on. In a January 1924 article, he called the *smychka* (merger) between the proletariat and the peasantry, 'the *central* problem of the day', adding later that this term, though ubiquitous, was imprecise.[102] In another article a year later, he eschewed this word in favour of *soiuz* (alliance or union), while still arguing that this too was imprecise. The socio-economic stratification of the agrarian population meant that the peasantry as such should no longer be treated as a single entity [*kak tseloe*], and yet this concept took neither positive nor negative account of the 'differentiation of the peasantry...into the classes of capitalist society – the bourgeoisie and the proletariat'. Soviet Russia's earlier battle with the remnants of feudal-

100 N.I. Bukharin, 'O likvidatorstve nashikh dnei,' *Bol'shevik*, no. 2, 1924, pp. 3, 4. Lih argues that too much historiographic weight is given to Bukharin's oft-quoted article, and that in fact his positions on 'war communism' and the NEP were marked more by continuity than by the discontinuity in his views that this statement has conveniently been taken to suggest (Lih 2000, pp. 417–60; also Lih 1996, pp. 494–96).

101 See Corney 2015, doc. 8, pp. 247–248; also doc. 30, p. 687.

102 Reprinted in Kritsman, *Heroic Period*, Appendix, p. 330 [italics in original].

ism in the countryside, he argued, was now a battle with the capitalist elements emerging within a steadily stratifying peasantry, elements that would impede the proletariat's efforts to enact policies to advance socialism. A 'socialist line of development of the small-scale economy' was necessary, he wrote, and this would entail the 'extra-economic coercion' that had been deployed to eradicate capitalism during the Civil War years. Kritsman concluded his piece with a set of recommendations as to what a more defined alliance of the proletariat and a majority of the peasantry would require: unfettered development of the small-scale economy; organisational and material (credit) support for the 'comradely association of small households into collectives' and for 'state large-scale agriculture (*sovkhozy*)'; organisation and defense of the 'interests of the agricultural proletarian-labourers [*proletarii-batraki*]' and of all peasants who sold their own labor power; and economic struggle against 'agricultural capitalists of state and comradely (collective) large-scale agriculture'.[103]

The economic policies of the civil war period had by no means animated – let alone consumed – the entire field of Soviet economic research, far from it. One of the most prominent economists of this era, Alexander Chaianov, a non-Marxist economist tolerated by the regime, was not mentioned at all in Kritsman's volume, nor were his influential works cited. As Director of the renowned Institute of Agricultural Economics of the K.A. Timiriazev Agricultural Academy [*Institut Sel'skokhoziaistvennoi Ekonomiki pri Sel'skokhoziaistvennoi Akademii im. K.A. Timiriazeva*] in Moscow, Chaianov attracted a formidable band of professionals, many of whom had been agronomists in the prerevolutionary zemstvo system of rural administration. This group of agrarian economists, the Organisation-Production School [*Organizatskionno-proizvodstvennaia shkola*], had been active since 1915, and had managed to navigate the 1917 ideological divide, for now at least. Kritsman's own institutional power-base derived from his position as Director of the Agrarian Section of the Communist Academy [*Agrarnaia sektsiia Komakademii*] set up in mid-1925 (and elevated to an institute in 1928) to help develop an explicitly Marxist approach to the study of the peasantry and the agrarian economy. It drew in younger scholars, some of whom had in fact earned their laurels as recent graduates of the Timiriazev Academy and as former students of Chaianov. This group became known as the Agrarian Marxists [*argrarniki-marksisti*].[104]

---

103 L. Kritsman, 'Soiuz proletariata i bol'shinstva krest'ianstva v SSSR posle pobedy revoliutsii,' *Bol'shevik*, no. 2(18), 31 January 1925, pp. 40, 43–55.

104 An upsurge of academic interest in agrarian history was concentrated around *The Journal of Peasant Studies* founded in 1973. It was particularly interested in the question of differentiation – class or otherwise – within the peasantry in developing countries, and it fueled

Chaianov argued for the inherent viability of peasant agriculture, which would allow it to transcend difficult challenges, such as resisting encroachments from any large capitalist farms that were developing. He saw neither a capitalist nor a socialist path forward for peasant farming but rather a specifically peasant future grounded in family small-holdings. The peasantry, he believed, was not becoming more differentiated by class, although he conceded that some non-exploitative differentiations were developing.[105] Not surprisingly, Kritsman's shift in the focus of his research to class differentiation within the peasantry, and his diametrically opposed view of the future development of the agrarian economy in Soviet Russia, soon brought him into direct conflict with Chaianov and his group. Kritsman expressed his early disagreements with Chaianov's work in disarmingly direct fashion in a highly critical introduction he wrote for a 1924 volume by Chaianov. Offering faint praise for Chaianov's use of empirical statistics, especially budgetary statistics, Kritsman accused him of failing to appreciate the capitalist content or inherent instability of the peasant household economy. Worse, he added, Chaianov had laid out nothing less than an internally contradictory 'system of non-Marxist views, i.e. non-proletarian views…expressing the ideology of the pre-capitalist (and thus in the age of capitalism anti-capitalist) petty bourgeois'. These were by no means petty academic jibes within the context of the time. Chaianov was no 'theoretician', implied Kritsman, and his 'theory of the so-called labour peasant economy [*trudovoe krest'ianskoe khoziaistvo*]' took account only of the 'physiology and psychology of the peasant', while ignoring all 'material production forces and their changes', most egregiously the effects of technology on the growth of productive forces in the countryside. In short, Kritsman wrote, Chaianov ascribed the rise or fall of the peasant household only to natural [*estestvennye*] rather than social factors. He derided the naïveté and narrowness of Chaianov's views of the peasant, and for drawing conclusions from these views about the entire social economy of the peasantry, a theory, he added, 'clearly at odds with reality'. He bluntly likened Chaianov to an astronomer trying 'to come up with

a surge of Western and Soviet studies of the peasantry in Tsarist and Soviet Russia (see Hobsbawm 1973, pp. 3–22; Shanin 1972; Shanin 1980, pp. 83–104). For a more recent and thought-provoking treatment of the nature of the peasantry in the tsarist period, see Kotsonis 1999. Chaianov's Organisation-Production School drew the most Western attention initially (Harrison 1975, pp. 389–417; more recently, Bernstein 2020, pp. 32–38). Kritsman's Agrarian Marxists were often viewed as poorer cousins, as economists devoted to more empirical, less theorised methods, and ideologically over-preoccupied with the issue of class stratification within the peasantry (Solomon 1977, pp. 32–33). For continued interest in these debates, see Dobronozhenko 2020, pp. 55–62.

105 Chaianov 1924.

a theory of the motion of celestial bodies while ignoring the effects of gravitational forces'. Chaianov's reduction of all factors of the social economy to physiological factors meant that he had gone 'further than Malthus' and the latter's pessimistic examination of projected food production and population increase.[106]

Having set out his theoretical and political stall vis-à-vis the Chaianov group, Kritsman developed his ideas on peasant differentiation in a series of short articles in 1925 in the journal edited by his section at the Communist Academy, *Na agrarnom fronte*, as well as in a speech to the Communist Academy in November of that year.[107] While proclaiming the inherent 'inevitability of the subsequent class stratification of the peasantry', particularly since the advent of the NEP, he conceded the 'objective difficulty' of actually elucidating it, in part because various strata of the peasantry sought to conceal the 'actual state of affairs', just as they had done during the Civil War years. Broad generalisations from USSR-wide aggregate data, he added, would not be able to illuminate the process of differentiation, and so he and his group undertook more detailed analyses of partial data from individual small regions.[108] This task of eliciting, compiling, and analysing local data was an ambitious one. He published his early findings and more in a single volume in 1926, reiterating his long-standing frustration with the poor state of reliable and useable Soviet statistics on the agrarian economy. Available resources on this issue, he complained, were 'indirect' and 'incomplete', and he and his group could thus draw only tentative conclusions about class differentiation, 'hidden capitalist forms' (and thus hidden forms of exploitation), and the rise of a middle peasantry in the countryside.[109] He supplemented his findings with a new series of articles a year later. He took issue with members of the Chaianov group, including V.S. Nemchinov and S.I. Raevich, not least over the indices might best be used

---

106 Kritsman's foreword to Chaianov, *Ocherki po ekonomike trudovogo sel'skogo khoziaistva*, pp. 3, 4, 6, 16.

107 L.N. Kritsman, 'K voprosu o klassovom rassloenii sovremennoi derevni,' *Na agrarnom fronte*, no. 2, no. 7–8, no. 9, no. 10, 1925; L.N. Kritsman, 'Klassovaia differentsiatsiia krest'ianstva v sovremennoi sovetskoi derevne,' *Vestnik kommunisticheskoi akademii*, no. 14, 1926 [reproduced in Kritsman, *Proletarskaia revoliutsiia i derevniia*, pp. 268–301].

108 Kritsman, 'K voprosu o klassovom rassloenii sovremennoi derevni,' no. 2, 1925, pp. 49, 51, 55.

109 L. Kritsman, *Klassovoe rassloenie v sovetskoi derevne: po dannym volostnykh obsledovanii* [Moscow: Izdatel'stvo kommunisticheskoi akademii, 1926 (references to this volume are to the reprint in Kritsman, *Proletarskaia revoliutsiia i derevniia*, pp. 302, 293). It was published in a condensed and edited English translation in *Kritsman and the Agrarian Marxists*, 1984, pp. 85–143.

to measure any class differentiation (e.g. land sown, cattle or horses owned or equipment used in a household, use of wage labour, or entrepreneurial component, and so on).[110]

Kritsman would surely have seen little cause for optimism either in the developing Soviet information state or in the possibilities of serious debate in the increasingly polemical atmosphere – now also in the economic realm – in the course of the 1920s. His own methods came under the kind of political scrutiny he had earlier levelled at Chaianov. Kritsman's conclusions on differentiation within the peasantry were criticised in 1925 for their 'general' and 'abstract' nature and for lacking 'a concrete context', a critique that was often broadened out to include parts of his earlier work on so-called 'war communism'. His approach was accused of 'deviation from Leninism' and of being dismissive of the dictatorship of the proletariat and the socialist management of industry. He had overestimated 'war communism', and underestimated the NEP, viewing it as a 'utopian attempt' to eliminate capitalism from agriculture.[111] The 'nebulosity [*tumannost'*] of his conclusions was challenged, as was the 'tone-deafness [*oglushenie*]' of his methods.[112] Serious academic economic debate was no bulwark against political animus, indeed it foundered upon it.

Chastened perhaps by the extraordinary challenges of the Civil War years, Soviet leaders all understood the vital role of economics in the very viability of the Soviet state. Their various disagreements over the relative balance at any given time between extreme state control of the means of production and a measure of market freedom, between industrial production (the worker) and agricultural production (the labouring peasant), between the individual peasant farm and the collective, and between economic autarky and global interdependence, were all suffused with ideological and political considerations. They drew at various times on the opposing arguments of the Kritsman and Chaianov groups, and on other economists and statisticians besides, and fortunes within these groups rose and fell as a result. Theirs had been

110 L. Kritsman, 'O statisticheskom izuchenii klassovoi struktury sovetskoi derevni,' *Na agrarnom fronte*, no. 2, 1926; no. 8–9, 1927; no. 10, 1927 [reproduced in Kritsman, *Proletarskaia revoliutsiia i derevniia*, pp. 433–503]. This aspect of Kritsman's research has received careful and serious study, although not until the 1980s when scholars sought to bring Kritsman out of Chaianov's historiographic shadow, and to examine his empirical data and tentative conclusions on class differentiation in their own right (see Cox and Littlejohn (eds.) 1984; Cox 1986). Their work pushed back against earlier conclusions about the Kritsman group in Solomon, *The Soviet Agrarian Debate*.

111 Batyrev, 'Po povodu stat'i tov. Kritsmana,' *Bol'shevik*, nos. 5–6 (21–22), March 1925, pp. 90, 100, 97.

112 Gol'tsman 1925, pp. 76, 75.

no dispassionate academic debate among economic professionals about the specific contours of a state's economic development. Nor had it been about the development of ideas that would be tried, tested, and finessed in the real world, so to speak. Politics and ideology were ever in the fray. Still, if relatively pallid in its early years, Soviet economic debate took on a new complexion from early 1927. This became evident in meetings held at this time in the Timiriazev Academy involving both the Kritsman and the Chaianov groups over the issue of class stratification within the peasantry. They disagreed forcefully over whether the Soviet rural sector was indeed becoming more capitalist or whether it was still anchored in the family farm. This ever-sharpening dispute between these groups was rendered moot by the Communist Party's decision at the Fifteenth Party Congress in December 1927 to collectivise and mechanise individual peasant holdings. At a stroke, the past research of both the Organisation-Production School and the Agrarian Marxists was rendered irrelevant – and now became potentially dangerous. As the 'pre-socialist' economic approach now became 'bourgeois science' in the rhetoric of 1928 and 1929 and had to give way to an explicitly Marxist approach to the study of economics, Chaianov switched to studying state and collective farms. But no amount of mea culpas, renunciations of earlier allegiances, or embraces of the new policy could save him and his group. As for Kritsman, drafts of the First Five-Year Plan prepared in 1928 might have given him real hope that his own early embrace of state planning and the strong Marxist credentials of his group would put him in a stronger position. Indeed, he might even have felt encouraged to see members of the Frankfurt School taking an interest in his earlier work on economic planning during a fact-finding trip to Moscow, some of whom even attended the Tenth Anniversary celebrations of the October Revolution.[113]

Yet Kritsman's persistence in researching and publishing on class stratification within the peasantry and arguing for the increasingly capitalistic nature of the agrarian economy opened him and his group to criticisms that he had taken insufficient stock of the developing communism within the cooperative movement and threw his Marxist credentials into doubt, at least as a political pretext.[114] Stalin's rather sudden wager on the forced collectivisation of agricul-

113 One of them, Friedrich Pollock, a German Marxist economist with a by no means unskeptical attitude towards the Soviet revolutionary experiment, drew upon Kritsman's early research for his doctoral thesis on Soviet Russia's experiences with economic planning (see Pollock 1929, esp. ch. 2]). For more on Pollock's views at the time, see Lenhard 2024, pp. 63–68. My thanks to Véronique Mickisch for bringing this to my attention.

114 Solomon 1975, pp. 571–580.

ture and planned heavy industrialisation left no room for the protracted and careful rural research of either a Chaianov or a Kritsman.

5 A Matter of Life and Death

In fact, it left no room for them personally either. The Shakhty Affair [*Shakhtinskoe delo*] in 1928, which inculpated engineers and specialists for alleged sabotage of the economy, was a ghastly sign of the changing times. In 1930, the OGPU 'uncovered' – with sadly predictable consequences – a Toiling Peasant Party [*Trudovaia Krest'ianskaia Partiia*], a 'massive' counter-revolutionary conspiracy of members allegedly bent on 'wrecking' the Soviet economy. They had allegedly infiltrated everything from agricultural cooperatives and credit unions to the Commissariats of Agriculture and of Finance, as well as research institutes of agricultural economics, notably the Timiriazev Academy.[115] More economic wrecking activities among the *spetsy* would be 'exposed' later that same year at the Industrial Party Trial [*Protsess Prompartii*] and again at the March 1931 trial of the Union Bureau of the Central Committee [*Soiuznoe Biuro Tsentral'nogo Komiteta*] of the Menshevik Party. The OGPU had fabricated a broad web in which to ensnare a shocking number of the economists and statisticians of the 1920s.

The very same prerevolutionary credentials that had rendered Chaianov and his colleagues of use to the Soviet government in the early years were now the stains of their intractable and incorrigible views. Within Chaianov's immediate circle, N.P. Makarov survived a period of imprisonment in the first half of the 1930s but was able to resume his work as an agronomist until 1947, dying in 1980; A.N. Chelintsev spent three years in internal exile working as an agronomist in Voronezh, eventually dying in 1962; A.L. Vainshtein endured multiple periods of exile up to 1949, although upon release was able to return to professional work until his death in 1970. Others were not so fortunate (if these fates can be deemed fortunate). A.A. Rybnikov, N.D. Kondrat'ev, and Chaianov himself were arrested in the Toiling Peasant Party Affair. They were shot in 1937 or 1938. More distant colleagues were swept up in either the Industrial Party Trial or the Kondrat'ev affair: S.A. Fal'kner was shot in 1938 and L.N. Litoshenko died in a gulag camp in 1943. Solid Marxist credentials offered little protection as the Kritsman group soon discovered. A. Gaister, M.I. Kubanin, and I.D. Vermenichev were shot in 1937 or 1938, while M.V. Sulkovskii died of unknown

115 See Bailes 1978, ch. 3; Medvedev 1973, pp. 113–117.

causes in 1937. Whether Kritsman himself suffered their tragic fates is not certain, although he was sidelined from his official positions in the course of the 1930s until his death in 1937.[116] His earlier criticism of Chaianov for his lack of Marxist credentials and of some of his fellow economists and statisticians for their perceived methodological and statistical sloppiness might have seemed relatively benign in 1924. In the vicious climate of repression of the early 1930s, however, they became potential fuel for the Soviet authorities to fan the flames, and Kritsman by one account was directly culpable in the denunciations.[117] Being outside of the immediate orbits of Chaianov and Kritsman was no guarantee of safety. The prominent economists I.A. Teodorovich, N.M. Vishnevskii, and N. Osinskii were all shot in 1937 or 1938. Others, such as S.M. Dubrovskii, L.B. Kafengauz, and N.P. Oganovskii, spent significant periods in exile or in the gulag in the 1930s and beyond. Ultimate rehabilitation in the waves of political relaxation in Soviet Russia in the 1960s, the 1980s, and the 2000s was surely cold comfort for those who still remembered these individuals. No history of early Soviet economics should be written without this ghastly coda.

Bibliography

Author's Works (by Date of Publication)[118]

Kritsman, L. 1918. 'Ob organizatsionnykh putiakh sotsialisticheskago stroitel'stva khoziaistvennoi zhizni'. *Kommunist*, no. 3, 16 May.

Kritsman, L. 1918. 'Ob ocherednoi zadache proletarskoi revoliutsii v Rossii'. *Narodnoe khoziaistvo*, no. 5, 15 July, pp. 1–5.

Kritsman, L. 1919. 'Osnovnye tendentsii sotsial'noi revoliutsii proletariata', *Narodnoe khoziaistvo*, no. 3.

116 Solzhenitsyn lists Kritsman among those shot in 1937 (Solzhenitsyn 2002, p. 300). A source that draws on Kritsman's personal papers in the Archive of the Academy of Sciences (*Arkhiv Akademii nauk*) disputes this, ascribing his death in mid-1938 [*sic*] to a protracted illness ('Igor' Anatol'evich Kuznetsov o L've Natanoviche Kritsmane (1890–1938),' https://vas-s-al.livejournal.com/895312.html).

117 Kritsman, The Heroic Period, pp. 43n106, 43–44. Solzhenitsyn accused Kritsman of playing a key role in the persecution of Kondrat'ev and Chaianov (Solzhenitsyn, *Dvesti let vmeste*, p. 272). Some of the persecuted indeed participated in the denunciations of their colleagues (Solzhenitsyn 1989, book 1, pp. 238–239).

118 I build here upon the excellent bibliography of Kritsman works compiled in Cox 1986, pp. 258–260.

Kritsman, L. 1920, 'Organizatsiia narodnogo khoziaistva v Sovetskoi Rossii', in Larin, L., and L. Kritsman, *Ocherk khoziaistvennoi zhizni i organizatsiia narodnogo khoziaistva sovetskoi Rossii, 1 noiabria 1917–1 iuliia 1920 g*. Moscow: Gosudarstvennoe izdatel'stvo, pp. 105–141.

Kritsman, L. 1920. 'Tezisy po voprosu o reorganizatsii Komproda'. *Ekonomicheskaia zhizn'*, 27 March.

Kritsman, L. 1921. 'O khoziaistvennom plane'. *Ekonomicheskaia zhizn'*, no. 281, 14 December 1920, p. 1; no. 289, 23 December 1920, p. 1; no. 28, 9 February 1921, p. 2; no. 34, 16 February 1921, pp. 1–2; no. 38, 20 February, p. 1.

Kritsman, L. 1989. *Edinyi khoziaistvennyi plan i Komissiia ispol'zovaniia*. Moscow: Gosizdat, 1921 [reprinted in *Ob edinom khoziaistvennom plane* (*raboty 1920–1921 godov*). Moscow: 'Ekonomika', 1989, pp. 132–153].

Kritsman, L. 1921. *Sel'skokhoziaistvennaia promyshlennost'*. Moscow: Gosizdat.

Kritsman, L. 1921. *Kapitalisticheskoe rabstvo, velikaia rabochaia revoliutsiia, osvobozhdenie rabochego klassa*. Moscow: Gos. Izd-vo.

Kritsman, L. 1921, and Larin, Iu., *Wirtschaftsleben und wirtschaftlicher Aufbau in Sowjet-Russland, 1917–1920*. Hamburg: C. Hoym Nachf.

Kritsman, L. 1921. *Obshchestvennyi trud rabochego i edinolichnyi semeinyi trud krest'ianina*. Moscow.

Kritsman, L. 1922. *Novaia ekonomicheskaia politika i planovoe raspredelenie*. Moscow: Gosizdat.

Kritsman, L. 1925. *Sel'skoe khoziaistvo na putiakh vosstanovleniia*. Moscow.

Kritsman, L. 1922. 'O Russkoi Revoliutsii'. *Vestnik sotsialisticheskoi akademii*, no. 1: 55–66.

Kritsman, L. 1923. *Dva goda Novoi Ekonomicheskoi Politiki proletariata SSSR*. Moscow.

Kritsman, L. 1923. 'Krupnoe i melkoe khoziaistvo v zemledelii'. *Vestnik sotsialisticheskoi akademii*, no. 3, [reproduced in Kritsman, *Proletarskaia revoliutsiia i derevniia*, pp. 533–539].

Kritsman, L. 1923. 'O nakoplenii kapitala i 'tretikh' litsakh'. *Vestnik sotsialisticheskoi akademii*, no. 5: 51–73.

Kritsman, L. 1923. 'Ot tiagi k zemle k tiage k rynku'. *Sotsialisticheskoe khoziaistvo*, nos. 4–5, [reproduced in Kritsman, *Proletarskaia revoliutsiia i derevniia*, pp. 539–548].

Kritsman, L. 1924. *Geroicheskii period Velikoi Russkoi Revoliutsii*. Moscow: Gosudarstvennoe izdatel'stvo.

Kritsman, L. 1924. 'Geroicheskii period velikoi russkoi revoliutsii (Opyt analiza t. n. 'Voennogo Kommunizma')'. *Vestnik kommunisticheskoi akademii*, no. 9: 1–146.

Kritsman, L. 1924. 'Tri goda Novoi Ekonomicheskoi Politiki proletariata Sovetskogo Soiuza'. *Zvezda*, no. 3, pp. 108–134.

Kritsman, L. 1924. 'Sel'skoe khoziaistvo v sisteme narodnogo khoziaistva v pervye tri goda Novoi Ekonomicheskoi Politiki'. In *Tri goda Novoi Ekonomicheskoi Politiki*. Moscow.

Kritsman, L. 1924. 'Sovremennaia melko-burzhuaznaia politicheskaia ekonomiia'. *Vestnik Kommunisticheskoi Akademii*, no. 7, [reproduced in Kritsman, *Proletarskaia revoliutsiia i derevniia*, pp. 548–567].

Kritsman, L. 1925. 'Kolkhoznoe dvizhenie (o ego literaturnom otrazhenii)'.

Kritsman, L. 1925. *Sel'skoe khoziaistvo na putiakh vosstanovleniia*. Moscow, 1925.

Kritsman, L. 1925. 'Soiuz proletariata i bol'shinstva krest'ianstva v SSSR posle pobedy revoliutsii'. *Bol'shevik*, no. 2(18), 31 January, pp. 40–55. [reproduced in Kritsman, *Proletarskaia revoliutsiia i derevniia*, pp. 26–46].

Kritsman, L. 1925. 'Perezhitki ideologii krepostnichestva v nashei statistike'. *Na agrarnom fronte*, no. 1, 1925. [reproduced in Kritsman, *Proletarskaia revoliutsiia i derevniia*, pp. 530–533].

Kritsman, L. 1925. 'Arifmetika i znanie dela (o trudakh zemplana i o professorakh Kondratieve i Oganovskom)'. *Na agrarnom fronte*, no. 1.

Kritsman, L. 1925. 'Stikhiia oproberzheniia i ee zherta (po povodu pisma prof. Oganovskogo)'. *Na agrarnom fronte*, no. 2.

Kritsman, L. 1925. 'K voprosu o klassovom rassloenii sovremennoi derevni'. *Na agrarnom fronte*, no. 2, 1925; no. 7–8, 1925; no. 9, 1925; no. 10.

Kritsman, L. 1925. 'Lenin i put k sotsializmu'. *Na agrarnom fronte*, no. 3, 1925 [reproduced in Kritsman, *Proletarskaia revoliutsiia i derevniia*, pp. 13–25].

Kritsman, L. 1925. 'Ob osnovakh perspektivnogo plana razvitiia sel'skogo i lesnogo khoziaistva'. *Na agrarnom fronte*, nos. 7–8.

Kritsman, L. 1925. 'Novyi etap (K proektam 'Obshchikh nachal zemlepol'zovanii i zemleustroistva')', in Kritsman, *Proletarskaia revoliutsiia i derevniia*, pp. 46–67.

Kritsman, L. 1925. 'Plan sel'skogo khoziaistva i industrializatsiia'. [reproduced in Kritsman, *Proletarskaia revoliutsiia i derevniia*, pp. 67–78].

Kritsman, L. 1926. *Geroicheskii period Velikoi Russkoi Revoliutsii (opyt analiza t. n. 'Voennogo kommunizma')*. Moscow: Gosudarstvennoe izdatel'stvo.

Kritsman, L. 1926. 'Klassovaia differentsiatsiia krest'ianstva v sovremennoi sovetskoi derevne'. *Vestnik kommunisticheskoi akademii*, no. 14, 1926 [reproduced in Kritsman, *Proletarskaia revoliutsiia i derevniia*, pp. 268–301].

Kritsman, L. 1926. 'Razvitie kapitalizma i progress tekhniki'. *Vestnik kommunisticheskoi akademii*, no. 16.

Kritsman, L. 1926. *Klassovoe rassloenie v sovetskoi derevne: po dannym volostnykh obsledovanii*. Moscow: Izdatel'stvo kommunisticheskoi akademii [reproduced in Kritsman, *Proletarskaia revoliutsiia i derevniia*, pp. 117–268; and in English in *Kritsman and the Agrarian Marxists*, 1984, pp. 85–143].

Kritsman, L. 1927. 'O statisticheskom izuchenii klassovoi struktury sovetskoi derevni', *Na agrarnom fronte*, no. 2, 1926; no. 8–9, 1927; no. 10, 1927 [reproduced in Kritsman, *Proletarskaia revoliutsiia i derevniia*, pp. 433–503].

Kritsman, L. 1927. 'Desiat' let na agrarnom fronte proletarskoi revoliutsii'. *Na agrarnom fronte*, no. 11–12, pp. 3–8 [reproduced in Kritsman, *Proletarskaia revoliutsiia i derevniia*, pp. 5–13].

Kritsman, L. 1927. 'Novyi etap. (k proektam 'obshchikh nachal zemlepol'zovaniia i zemleustroistva,)'.

Kritsman, L. 1928. 'Klassovye gruppirovki krest'ianskikh khoziaistv'. *Na agrarnom fronte*, no. 4, [reproduced in Kritsman, *Proletarskaia revoliutsiia i derevniia*, pp. 386–433].

Kritsman, L. 1928. 'Ob analize klassovoi struktury krest'ianstva'. In *Rassloenie sovetskoi derevni*, ed. A.I. Gaister. Moscow [reproduced in Kritsman, *Proletarskaia revoliutsiia i derevniia*, 301–342].

Kritsman, L. 1928. 'O Samarskom obsledovanii'. In *710 khoziaistv samarskoi derevni*, ed. I. Vermenichev, Gaister. Moscow [reproduced in Kritsman, *Proletarskaia revoliutsiia i derevniia*, pp. 342–386].

Kritsman, L. 1928. *Osnovnye elementy i produktsiia sel'skogo khoziaistva SSSR za 1925/26–1928/29 gg: s prilozheniem predpolozhitel'nogo khlebo-furazhnogo balansa na 1928/29 g*. Moscow: Izd. TsSU SSSR.

Kritsman, L. 1928. *Materialy po istorii agrarnoi revoliutsii v Rossii*. Two volumes. Moscow: Kommunisticheskaia akademiia.

Kritsman, L., and A. Gaister 1928, *Rassloenie sovetskoi derevni*. Moscow: Izdatel'stvo kommunisticheskoi akademii [Kritsman's introduction reproduced in Kritsman, *Proletarskaia revoliutsiia i derevniia*, pp. 301–342].

Kritsman, L. 1929. *Proletarskaia revoliutsiia i derevniia*. Moscow and Leningrad: Gosudarstvennoe izdatel'stvo.

Kritsman, L. 1929. 'Ob osnovnykh metodakh razrabotki massovykh statisticheskikh materialov nashei agrarnoi revoliutsii'.

Kritsman, L. 1929. 'O vnutrennikh protivorechiiakh krest'ianskogo dvora'. In M. Kubanin, *Klassovaia sushchnost' protsessa drobleniia krest'ianskikh khoziaistv*. Moscow, Izd-vo Kommunisticheskoi akademii [reproduced in Kritsman, *Proletarskaia revoliutsiia i derevniia*, pp. 504–529].

Kritsman, L. 1929. *Die Heroische Periode der Grossen Russischen Revolution. Ein Versuch der Analyse des sogenannten 'Kriegskommunismus'*. Vienna and Berlin: Verlag für Literatur und Politik.

Kritsman, L. 1930. 'O kharaktere nashei revoliutsii'. *Na agrarnom fronte*, no. 4.

Kritsman, L. 1930. 'The Process of Socialisation of Agriculture in the USSR'. *Proceedings of the Conference of Agricultural Economists, New York*.

Kritsman, L. 2022. *Geroicheskii period velikoi russkoi revoliutsii: opyt analiza tak nazyvaemogo voennogo kommunizma*. Moscow.

Works Consulted

1974, *A Selection of Official Documents on Internal Policies*. Edited by Mervyn Matthews. New York: Taplinger Publishing Co., Inc.

Alexopoulos, Golfo 2012. *Stalin's Outcasts: Aliens, Citizens, and the Soviet State, 1926–1936*. Ithaca, New York: Cornell University Press.

Bailes, Kendall E. 1978, *Technology and Society under Lenin and Stalin. Origins of the Soviet Technical Intelligentsia*. Princeton, NJ: Princeton University Press.

Ball, Alan M. 1990, *Russia's Last Capitalists: The Nepmen, 1921–1929*. Berkeley, CA: University of California Press.

Ball, Alan M. 1994. *And Now My Soul is Hardened: Abandoned Children in Soviet Russia, 1918–1930*. Berkeley: University of California Press.

Batyrev 1925. 'Po povodu stat'i tov. Kritsmana'. *Bol'shevik*, nos. 5–6 (21–22), March, pp. 90–100.

Bernstein, H. 2020, 'Shanin, Chayanov and Peasant Studies of Russia and Beyond'. *Krest'ianovedenie* 5, no. 4: 32–38.

Boettke, Peter J. 1988, 'The Soviet Experiment with Pure Communism'. *Critical Review* 2, no. 4, pp. 149–82.

Bradley, Joseph 1994. 'Editor's Introduction' [for a special edition on 'War Communism']. *Russian Studies in History* 33, no. 1, pp. 3–7.

Bukharin, N.I. 1924, 'O likvidatorstve nashikh dnei'. *Bol'shevik*, no. 2, pp. 3–9.

Bukharin, N.I. and E. Preobrazhensky 1969. *The ABC of Communism*. Edited by E.H. Carr. Harmondsworth, England: Penguin.

Bukharin, N.I. 1979. *The Politics and Economics of the Transition Period*. London and New York: Routledge.

Bunyan, James and H.H. Fisher 1961, *The Bolshevik Revolution 1917–1918. Documents and Materials*. Stanford, California: Stanford University Press.

Byrnes, Robert F. 1991, 'Creating the Soviet Historical Profession, 1917–1934'. *Slavic Review* 50, no. 2, pp. 297–308.

Cassiday, Julie A. 2000. *The Enemy on Trial: Early Soviet Courts on Stage and Screen*. DeKalb, Illinois: Northern Illinois University Press.

Chaianov, A.V. 1924. *Ocherki po ekonomike trudovogo sel'skogo khoziaistva*. Moscow: Izdatel'stvo Narkomzema.

Chamberlain, Lesley 2007. *Lenin's Private War: The Voyage of the Philosophy Steamer and the Exile of the Intelligentsia*. New York, NY: St. Martin's Press.

Corney, Frederick C. 2015. *Trotsky's Challenge. The 'Literary Discussion' of 1924 and the Fight for the Bolshevik Revolution*. Leiden and Boston: Brill Academic Publishers.

Cox, Terry 1986. *Peasants, Class, and Capitalism: The Rural Research of L.N. Kritsman and His School*. New York: Oxford University Press.

Daniels, Robert V. 1960. *The Conscience of the Revolution. Communist Opposition in Soviet Russia.* Cambridge, Mass.: Cambridge University Press.

David-Fox, Michael 1997. *Revolution of the Mind. Higher Learning Among the Bolsheviks, 1918–1929.* Ithaca: Cornell University Press.

Day, Richard B. 1973. *Leon Trotsky and the Politics of Economic Isolation.* Cambridge: Cambridge University Press.

1989. *Deiateli SSSR i revoliutsionnogo dvizheniia Rossii. Entsiklopedicheskii slovar' Granat.* Moscow: Sovetskaia entsiklopedicheskii slovar' Granat.

1985. *Demograficheskii entsiklopedicheskii slovar'.* Moscow: Sovetskaia entsiklopediia.

1934. *Deviatyi s'ezd RKP(b). Mart-aprel' 1920 g.* Moscow: Partiinoe izdatel'stvo.

1970. *Dictionary of Russian Historical Terms from the Eleventh Century to 1917.* Edited by and edited by George Vernadsky and Ralph T. Fisher compiled by Sergei G. Pushkarev. New Haven: Yale University Press.

Dobb, Maurice. 1967. *Soviet Economic Development Since 1917.* New York: International Publishers.

Dobronozhenko, G.F. 2020. 'Diskussii v ekonomicheskoi literature 1920-kh godov: O differentsiatsii krest'ianstva v NEPovskii period', *Vestnik Syktyvkarskogo Universiteta. Seriia gumanitarnykh nauk*, no. 2; pp. 55–62.

Döring, Falk 1970. *Organisationsprobleme der Russischen Wirtschaft in Revolution und Bürgerkrieg (1918–1920). Dargestellt am Volkswirtschaft für den Nordrayon (SNChSR).* Hanover: Verlag für Literatur und Zeitgeschehen GmbH.

1923. *Dvenadtsatyi s'ezd RKP (bol'shevikov). 17–25 aprelia 1923 g.* Moscow: Izdanie RIO VtsIK.

Finkel, Stuart 2007. *On the Ideological Front: The Russian Intelligentsia and the Making of the Soviet Public Sphere.* New Haven: Yale University Press.

1970. *First Decrees of Soviet Power.* Edited by Yuri Akhapkin. Lawrence & Wishart.

1973. Gimpel'son, E.G. *Voennyi kommunizm: Politika, praktika, ideologiia.* Moscow: Mysl'.

Goldman, Emma 1924. 'What I Saw in Russia'. *Illustrated London News*, 22 November, 988.

1988. *Golos naroda. Pis'ma i otkliki riadovykh sovetskikh grazhdan o sobytiiakh 1918–1932 gg.* Moscow: ROSSPEN.

Gol'tsman, A. 1925. 'Nashi zadachi v derevne (po povodu st. tov. Kritsmana 'Souiz proletariata i bol'shinstva krest'ianstva')'. *Bol'shevik*, nos. 5–6 (21–22), March, pp. 73–89.

Harrison, Mark 1975. 'Chayanov and the Economics of the Russian Peasantry'. *The Journal of Peasant Studies* 2, no. 4, pp. 389–417.

Hegel, G.W.F. 1894. *Lectures on the Philosophy of History.* London: George Bell & Sons.

Hessler, Julie 2004. *A Social History of Soviet Trade. Trade Policy, Retail Practices, and Consumption, 1917–1953.* Princeton, NJ: Princeton University Press.

Himmer, Robert 1994. 'The Transition from War Communism to the New Economic Policy: An Analysis of Stalin's Views'. *Russian Review* 53, no. 4, October, pp. 515–29.

Hobsbawm, E.J. 1973. 'Peasants and Politics'. *The Journal of Peasant Studies* 1, no. 1, pp. 3–22.

Iarov, S.V. 1999. *Gorozhanin kak politik. Revoliutsiia, voennyi kommunizm i NEP glazami Petrogradtsev*. St. Petersburg: 'Dmitrii Bulanin'.

Iarov, S.V. 1999. *Krest'ianin kak politik. Krest'ianstvo Severo-Zapada Rossii v 1918–1919 gg.: Politicheskoe myshlenie i massovyi protest*. St. Petersburg: 'Dmitrii Bulanin'.

Iarov, S.V. 1999. *Proletarii kak politik. Politicheskaia psikhologiia rabochikh Petrograda v 1917–1923 gg*. St. Petersburg: 'Dmitrii Bulanin'.

1936. *Intervention, Civil War, and Communism in Russia, April–December 1918*. Edited by James Bunyan. Baltimore: The Johns Hopkins Press.

2007. *Istoriia ekonomicheskoi mysli Rossii v litsakh. Slovar'-spravochnik*. Edited by N.N. Dumna, and O.V. Karamova. Moscow: KNORUS.

Kojima, Shuichi 2014. 'Russian Liberal Visions of Agricultural Development at the Beginning of the Twentieth Century – Litoshenko and Brutzkus'. *Œconomia – History / Methodology / Philosophy* 4, no. 1, 2014: 55–76.

Kol'man, E. 1931. 'Vreditel'stvo v nauke', *Bol'shevik*, no. 2, pp. 73–81.

Kotsonis, Yanni 1999. *Making Peasants Backward. Agricultural Cooperatives and the Agrarian Question in Russia, 1861–1914*. Palgrave Macmillan.

Kotsonis, Yanni 2014. *States of Obligation. Taxes and Citizenship in the Russian Empire and Early Soviet Republic*. Toronto: University of Toronto Press.

Kowalski, Ronald 1989. 'Geroicheskii period Russkoi Revoliutsii. Translator's Introduction'. *Revolutionary Russia* (2), no. 2, pp. v-13.

1984, *Kritsman and the Agrarian Marxists*. Edited by Terry Cox and Gary Littlejohn. London: Cass.

Lenhard, Philipp 2024. *Friedrich Pollock, The Éminence Grise of the Frankfurt School*. Leiden: Brill.

Lenin, V.I. 1960–70. *Collected Works*. 45 volumes. Moscow: Gosudarstvennoe izdatel'stvo politicheskoi literatury.

Lewin, Moshe 1968. *Lenin's Last Struggle*. New York: Monthly Review Press.

Lewin, Moshe 1974. *Political Undercurrents in Soviet Economic Debates. From Bukharin to the Modern Reformers*. Princeton, NJ: Princeton University Press.

Lih, Lars T. 1990a. *Bread and Authority in Russia, 1914–1921*. Berkeley, CA: University of California Press.

Lih, Lars T. 1990b. 'The Bolshevik Sowing Committees of 1920: Apotheosis of War Communism?' *The Carl Beck Papers in Russian and East European Studies*, no. 803.

Lih, Lars T. 1996. 'Bertrand Patenaude's 'Peasants Into Russians'.' *Russian Review* 55, no. 3, pp. 494–96.

Lih, Lars T. 2000. 'Bukharin's 'Illusion': War Communism and the Meaning of NEP'. *Russian History/Histoire Russe* 27, no. 4, Winter, pp. 417–60.

Malia, Martin 1992. 'Why Amalrik Was Right'. *Times Literary Supplement*, no. 4675, 6 November, p. 9.

Malia, Martin 1994. *The Soviet Tragedy. A History of Socialism in Russia, 1917–1991*. New York: The Free Press.

Malia, Martin 2004. 'The Archives of Evil'. *The New Republic*, 29 November, p. 34.

Malle, Silvana 2002. *The Economic Organization of War Communism 1918–1921*. Cambridge, Mass.: Cambridge University Press.

Markevich, Andrei, and Mark Harrison 2011. 'Great War, Civil War, and Recovery: Russia's National Income, 1913 to 1928'. *Journal of Economic History* 71, no. 3, pp. 672–703.

Mauss, Marcel 1925. 'Socialisme et Bolchévisme', *Le Monde Slave* 2, no. 2, pp. 201–222.

Medvedev, Roy A. 1973. *Let History Judge. The Origins and Consequences of Stalinism*. New York: Vintage Books.

Méquet, G. 1929. 'La vie économique dans la Russie Révolutionnaire. Sources et instruments de travail'. *Annales d'histoire économique et sociale*, no. 3, pp. 399–410.

Minskii, Nikolai 1989. *Russkie pesni i romantsy. Klassiki i sovremenniki*. Moscow: 'Khudozhestvennaia literature'.

Nove, Alec 1972. *An Economic History of the U.S.S.R.* London: Pelican Books.

Otkrytyi spisok [website listing of politically repressed: https://ru.openlist.wiki/]

Koenker, Diane P., Ronald Grigor Suny, and William G. Rosenberg (eds.) 1989. *Party, State. and Society in the Russian Civil War. Explorations in Social History*. Bloomington and Indianapolis: Indiana University Press.

Patenaude, Bertrand M. 1955. 'Peasants into Russians: The Utopian Essence of War Communism'. *Russian Review* 54, no. 4, October, pp. 552–70.

1980. *Peasants in History. Essays in Honour of Daniel Thorner*. Edited by E.J. Hobsbawm, K.N. Raj, Ashok Mitra, Witold Kula. Calcutta, India: Oxford University Press.

Pliutto, Petr Alexandrovich 1992. 'Aleksandr Bogdanov on the Period of 'War Communism'.' *Revolutionary Russia* 5, no. 1, pp. 46–52.

Pokrovskii, M.N. 1928. 'Obshchestvennye nauki v SSSR za 10 let'. *Vestnik kommunisticheskoi akademii* 26, pp. 3–30.

Pollock, Friedrich 1929. *Die Planwirtschaftlichen Versuche in der Sowjetunion 1917–1927*. Leipzig: Verlag von C.L. Hirschfeld.

Prokopovich, S.N. 1934, *Ideia planirovaniia i itogi piatiletki*. Paris: Respublikansko-demokraticheskoe Ob'edinenie.

Raeff, Marc 1990. *Russia Abroad. A Cultural History of the Russian Emigration 1919–1939*. Oxford: Oxford University Press.

Ransome, Arthur 1919. *Russia in 1919*. New York: B.W. Huebsch.

Remington, Thomas 1977. 'Trotsky, War Communism, and the Origin of the NEP'. *Studies in Comparative Communism* 10, no. 1–2, Spring-Summer, pp. 44–60.

Roberts, Paul Craig 1970. ''War Communism': A Re-Examination'. *Slavic Review* 29, no. 2: 238–61.

Rosmer, Alfred 1971. *Lenin's Moscow*. Translated by Ian Birchall. London, Chicago, and Melbourne: Bookmarks.

Russell, Bertrand 1920. *The Practice and Theory of Bolshevism*. London: George Allen & Unwin Ltd., p. 42.

1982. *Selected Writings on the State and the Transition to Socialism*. Ed. by Richard B. Day. Armonk, NY: M.E. Sharpe.

Serge, Victor 2012. *Memoirs of a Revolutionary 1901–1941*. New York: New York Review of Books.

Shanin, Teodor 1972. *The Awkward Class. Political Sociology of Peasantry in a Developing Society, Russia 1910–1925*. Oxford, Great Britain: Clarendon Press.

Shanin, Teodor 1980. 'Measuring Peasant Capitalism. The Operationalization of Concepts of Political Economy: Russia's 1920s-India's 1970s'. In *Peasants in History. Essays in Honour of Daniel Thorner*, ed. E.J. Hobsbawm and Ashok Mitra Witold Kula, K.N. Raj, 83–104. Calcutta, India: Oxford University Press.

Shub, David 1964. 'The Trial of the SRs'. *Russian Review* 23, no. 4.

Smith, Douglas 2012. *Former People: The Final Days of the Russian Aristocracy*. Farrar, Straus and Giroux.

Solomon, S.G. 1975. 'Controversy in Social Science: Soviet Rural Studies in the 1920s'. *Minerva* 13, no. 4, pp. 554–82.

Solomon, S.G. 1977. *The Soviet Agrarian Debate: A Controversy in Social Science 1923–1929*. Boulder, Colorado.

Solzhenitsyn, A.I. 2002. *Dvesti let vmeste*, part II. Moscow: Russkii put'.

2021. *Sovetskaia istoricheskaia entsiklopediia*. Moscow: Izdatel'stvo 'Sovetskaia Entsiklopediia', 16 vols.

The Workers' Opposition in the Russian Communist Party. Documents 1919–1930. Edited by Barbara C. Allen. Leiden & Boston, MA: Brill.

Tolz, Vera. *Russian Academicians and the Revolution. Combining Professionalism and Politics*. Basingstoke, England: Macmillan Press Ltd, 1997.

Trotsky, Leon. *How the Revolution Armed: The Military Writings and Speeches of Leon Trotsky*, 5 vols. London: New Park Publications, 1981.

Trotsky, Leon. *The Stalin School of Falsification*. New York: Pioneer Publishers, 1937.

Tucker, Robert C. *Stalinism. Essays in Historical Interpretation*. London: Routledge, 1999.

Valentinov, N. (N. Vol'skii). *Novaia Ekonomicheskaia Politika i krizis partii posle smerti Lenina. Gody raboty v VSNKh vo vremia NEP. Vospominaniia*. Moscow: 'Sovremennik', 1991.

Velikaia Oktiabr'skaia sotsialisticheskaia revoliutsiia. Moscow: 'Sovetskaia Entsiklopediia', 1987.

Veselov, S.V. 1994. 'The Cooperative Movement and Soviet Rule. The Period of 'War Communism''. *Russian Studies in History* 33, no. 1, pp. 52–71.

Von Mohrenschildt, Dimitri 1943–44. 'The Early American Observers of the Russian Revolution 1917–1921'. *Russian Review*, no. 1.

1989. *Vozvrashchenye imena. Sbornik publitsisticheskikh statei v dvukh knigakh*. Moscow: Izd. Agentstvoa pechati Novosti.

Weiss, Helmut 1937. *Das erste kommunistische Experiment Sowjetrusslands in den Jahren 1919 bis 1921 während des sog. 'Kriegskommunismus'*. Würzburg: Verlag wissenschaftl. Werke Konrad Triltsch.

Wells, H.G. 1921. *Russia in the Shadows*. New York: George H. Doran Company.

Wood, Elizabeth A. 2005. *Performing Justice: Agitation Trials in Early Soviet Russia*. Ithaca, N.Y.: Cornell University Press.

Zhertvy politicheskogo terrora v SSSR [website listing of politically repressed: https://base.memo.ru/]

1911–1920

L. Kritsman

the Heroic Period of the Great Russian Revolution

(an Attempt at an Analysis of So-Called 'War Communism')

Gosudarstvennoe Izdatel'stvo

Moscow

This book is dedicated
To the memory of young Yuri,
To the memory of my only child,
To the memory of the many children
Who fell victim to the intervention
By world capital,
And to those who did not perish,
And were able to become now
The bold pioneers of this wonderful country
Of happy children of the future.

Contents

Foreword

This book is part of a study of our revolution which I am preparing for publication. As its author, I did not want to submit this book for publication yet. Firstly, its analysis of our revolution in the final stage of the Civil War is *incomplete* because it does not adequately deal either with the context of the revolution – something I have done, as much as I have been able to, in my earlier work – or with its transition to the next stage (something I must do in future parts of this work). An event can be understood only within the context of its development, i.e. including its emergence and its demise. Secondly, a revolution, and *this* revolution in particular, is a subject without end, and so vital that there is always a natural desire to revise and supplement it constantly.

Nonetheless, the need to provide, even to a small degree, an inexhaustive but overarching analysis of the revolution is so great (my interactions with our committed proletarian youth have convinced me of this) that I can no longer permit myself to delay publishing the portion that is ready for print.

This work aims to provide a *concrete* analysis of our revolution. This does not mean an analysis of the details, the trivialities, but of the historical particularities of our revolution, the features peculiar to it. It does not mean, however, an analysis of the transition of abstract capitalism to abstract socialism, although of course an analysis of our revolution is *impossible* without this (and comrade Bukharin has already done this analysis, still unsurpassed, in his *Economics of the Transition Period*, fittingly subtitled 'The General Theory of the Transformation Process').[1] It means an analysis of the concrete nature of *our* revolution.

This analysis is extremely difficult not only because the theoretical questions associated with it are still inadequately explained or because the abundance of materials can only be worked through collectively (I hope that comrades from our Institute of Red Professors can be found to take part in this). It is difficult because of the outrageous state of our statistical materials, whose unreliability and shoddiness, bordering at times on sheer sloppiness, is quite extraordinary. Readers can find examples below.[2]

1 [Nikolai Bukharin, *The Politics and Economics of the Transition Period* (London: Routledge, 2003)].

2 Of course, statistics must never be used to present falsified figures instead of the actual figures received. But a number, even a statistic, must not be fetishised. A statistician, or anyone for that matter, who first puts a number into general circulation, is duty bound (if he does not want to mislead the readers and if he is not completely deaf to the significance of his work) to inform the reader about the number's accuracy, i.e. about its potential and probable deviation from reality.

The author, then, must inform the readers that, at the present moment when all of the evidence has not yet been meticulously and scrupulously analysed (beyond the powers of any single author of course), and wherever this work utilises statistical evidence, the emphasis must be not on the individual data, whose reliability is highly dubious (or rather, whose degree of reliability has not yet been ascertained), but in their *juxtaposition*. The author hopes that his general understanding of this period will allow him in most instances to evaluate correctly the utility of these materials. That all these materials can be accommodated within a general system, without being shoe-horned into it, can serve as something of an assurance that this hope is not unjustified.

Moscow, July 1924 *L.K.*

Introduction

The events that have unfolded in Russia over the past five years are so unique, so unlike anything that mankind has ever experienced, that they are changing the very foundations of everyday life.[1] They are, in short, so deeply *revolutionary* that conservative, bourgeois-capitalist, and petty bourgeois thinking, in all its variations including contemporary Social Democratic thought, is completely unable to acknowledge the profound *reality* of these events, or the fact that they have been shaped historically by all preceding world development, or that their *essential* character flows from the course of events. On the contrary, this kind of thinking sees these events both as a historical accident and as a product of the evil will of a band of fanatics, – in short, as something imposed on history from outside and thus illusory.

In bourgeois capitalist thinking, capitalist societal order is natural and immanent, and is therefore the only realistic societal order. *Non*-capitalistic societal manifestations, the expression of a newly developing non-capitalistic societal order, cannot therefore be understood as real *societal* phenomena; on the contrary, they strike that mindset as unreal and non-societal, illusory and artificial.

Furthermore, modern Social Democratic thought (when it is not simply hypocrisy) has been completely unable to grasp the *class* nature of the Great Russian Revolution, precisely because it has been incapable of understanding the societal nature of the revolutionary events. Trite discussions in the press and the 'scientific' works of the Second and the Two-and-a-Half Internationals portray the events of 1917–1920 and the subsequent years as a 'dictatorship of the party' or a 'dictatorship of the Kremlin', even a 'dictatorship of Lenin', denying the reality of the class dictatorship of the proletariat in Russia and depicting the Russian proletariat as an oppressed class.[2] These discussions do not only

1 This introduction is the introduction for the entire book.

2 We will limit ourselves to a single quotation from F-D [Translator: Fedor Dan] which places the Bolsheviks in direct classical contrast with all classes of Russian society: 'The Bolsheviks launched their state career with the proclamation of the *dictatorship of the proletariat*. But since this slogan turned out to be purely utopian within the social conditions of Russia, they were forced very quickly to *put into practice a party dictatorship over the proletariat*, and over all other classes' (F-D, 'Krizis bol'shevizma,' 'Sotsialisticheskii vestnik' no. 6 (28)). All italics are the author's, who, seemingly, divides society into the Bolsheviks on one side and all other classes on the other. A dictatorship over the proletariat and over all other classes which, as is well known, emerged victorious from the struggle with the entire capitalist world! It must be said that the Bolsheviks are damnably strong, although one thing is unclear: where did they

 | HTTPS://DOI.ORG/10.1163/9789004765313-004

show a stubborn desire to repeat what has already been said, they also reveal an anti-Marxist, extra-class conception of the greatest historical events. If the greatest historical events have nothing to do with classes but only with parties, groups or even individual people, then such a conception of history reveals the class nature of contemporary Social Democracy no less sharply than does its 'extra-class', counter-revolutionary coalition practice.

The bourgeois mindset cannot conceive of a proletariat that is *not* a function of capital, of a proletariat *outside of* its relationship to capital, of a proletariat that works *without* capitalist exploitation.

The Russian revolution has turned the inconceivable into a *reality*.

The *collapse* of the capitalist economy and society, the *expropriation* of capitalist ownership, and the *destruction* of the capitalist state are above all *facts*, facts of universal historical significance, and moreover contemporary facts. For this all happened not in dreams about the future, but in 1917–1920, not on the island of Utopia, but in actual reality, in a country covering one eighth of the earth's surface and inhabited by a twelfth of humanity. Even if it had lasted but a few weeks, the Great Russian Revolution would forevermore have destroyed the faith in the inviolability of the capitalist system and rejected its supposedly natural character, just as a volcanic eruption of only a few hours destroys forever the certainty that the earth's surface is indestructible, once the fiery matter beneath is revealed. But measuring these events in weeks[3] does not convey the enormous world-historical event that is the Great Russian Revolution, but rather the limited thinking of its enemies who have vainly tried to alter its course, and to reward themselves (with success) for this real failure in their world of fantasy. After all, this world, in contrast to the stubborn world of reality, is completely controlled by free, though futile, will.

The Great Russian Revolution is both a (still incomplete) practical and a complete theoretical defeat of capital and its conscious and unconscious apologists. It is the empirical confirmation of the correctness of the revolutionary worldview of the proletariat, of the correctness of Marxism that predicted many decades ago the inevitability of everything that has come to pass in Russia since 1917. It predicted the failure of capitalism, the proletarian revolution, the destruction of the capitalist state, the expropriation of capitalist ownership, and the era of the dictatorship of the proletariat (the era of the proletarian

get this boundless strength from? Marx was evidently correct: a revolutionary era must not be judged by its level of consciousness.

3 It was well-known that for many years the fall of Soviet power was anticipated 'in a few weeks'.

state). The abundance of truly titanic tasks facing the proletarian revolution, the complex nature of the historical situation, the contradictions of the competing forces mean that future developments will not be linear, but will tread a highly complex path with pauses and setbacks. And if the development of the Russian Revolution and its international context sometimes create completely unforeseen situations, if revolutionary practice at times finds its way only tentatively and often runs ahead of ideology, then this shows that Marxist prediction has still much to do. This is no way negates or undermines the fact that the Russian proletarian revolution is simultaneously a theoretical triumph for the proletariat, a triumph of the revolutionary theory of Marxism, and a pledge of its complete practical triumph.

The Great Russian Revolution is a truly national revolution. This is true above all in the sense that, like no other event in Russian history, it captivated the entire population of Russia to its very depths, to its remotest corners, because it was the work of numberless masses of the people, a popular revolution no less, perhaps more so, than the Great French Revolution. The Great Russian Revolution irrefutably demonstrated its inexhaustible social power on the battlefields of a more than three-year armed struggle against the overthrown ruling classes of Russia and against the *entire* capitalist world. The young, still immature system survived the crucial test of fire, iron and blood. And it did so of course not because – at the very moment of its emergence! – it had at its disposal a superior technical organisation, or – in backward and ruined Russia! – a superior technology to that of its enemies. Only the support of the popular masses of Russia and the enthusiasm with which their vanguard defended the new system, alongside the unshakable sympathy of the proletarian masses of the whole world towards this system, can explain an initially inconceivable fact – the fact of Soviet Russia's victory over those powers that had defeated the colossus of German imperialism. Before it won anything, the revolution won over *people*: that is the secret of its victory.

But the Great Russian Revolution is a truly national revolution also because it is completely unique, unparalleled, the *only* such event in the history of mankind, because above all else *it* marks out the history of Russia from the history of all other countries of the world. The Paris Commune, the Bavarian Soviet Republic, even the Hungarian Soviet Republic, when compared with what has unfolded between 1917 and now in Russia, are but moments in the history of those respective countries. By contrast, the Great Russian Revolution is objectively – irrespective of any sympathy or lack of sympathy for it – the *signature* event of Russian history, filling some with pride, and others with rage, and is unsurpassed by no other event in terms of scope or intensity. It is the most profound, the most tragic, and the most significant event.

The Great Russian Revolution distinguishes itself from all preceding revolutions above all by its *profundity*, not because it is a Russian revolution, but because it is a proletarian revolution. By contrast, all preceding revolutions are marked by their superficiality, because they did not penetrate into society's very foundations.

Every revolution means both the political and economic collapse of the class that ruled the society before the revolution. 'Every revolution', says Marx, 'dissolves the old order of society; to that extent it is social. Every revolution brings down the old ruling power; to that extent it is political'.[4]

The great bourgeois revolutions brought about the political and economic collapse of feudal serfdom. Society made a fundamental shift from a feudal serf to a capitalist system. But inasmuch as the revolution was a bourgeois capitalist revolution, it remained a purely *political* one in the strict sense of the word. For only in the realm of politics did a *reconfiguration* of societal relationships occur: the former political ruling class – the feudal lords – lost their ruling position, the former politically oppressed class, the capitalists, took power.

Until the bourgeois revolution, political power was in the hands of the feudal lords and the capitalists had no political power; after the revolution, the political power of capital appeared and the political power of the feudal lords disappeared.[5] In the political sphere, then, a *qualitative* change occurred, capital replaced its own political suppression with political rule.

In the economic sphere, by contrast, no such reconfiguration of societal relationships occurred, but rather a *change in the quantitative interrelationship* between the feudal and capitalist elements that existed alongside each other before the revolution; this change proceeded in the same direction as earlier but at a different, faster pace. *As a result of the revolution*, the former decreased in number, while the latter increased in number. Even before its revolution, the capitalist bourgeoisie was not economically oppressed, but was itself a ruling class, albeit in a restricted sphere. For it, then, revolution did not signify a transition from economic oppression to economic rule, but merely *an expansion of the spheres of this rule*. For precisely this reason, the bourgeois-capitalist revolution, *qua* revolution, restricts itself to the political sphere, while in the economic sphere it is but a jolt that accelerates its bourgeois-capitalist *evolution*. In the economic sphere therefore (in so far as this concerns the mutual rela-

4 [Karl Marx, 'Critical Notes on the Article: 'The King of Prussia and Social Reform. By a Prussian,'' Vorwärts!, no. 64, 10 August, 1844].

5 Political power is by no means merely influence, it is above all the reification of that influence – the apparatus of power, the machinery of state force.

tionship between the feudal lords and the capitalists), no qualitative change occurred, only a *quantitative* one.[6] The influence of the bourgeois-capitalist revolution (like any revolution) was not restricted to the political sphere, it also extended into the economic and technological spheres, but, as a revolution, the bourgeois-capitalist revolution remained a political revolution.

The great bourgeois revolutions (which went beyond their bourgeois-capitalist framework) were, however, also economic revolutions. During these revolutions a *mutation* [*pererozhdenie*] occurred, namely a qualitative change in economic relations as well: *feudal-serf exploitation was destroyed.* It was precisely this that made them great revolutions. The enserfed peasant broke the chains of feudal exploitation and became a laboring proprietor, a free producer of commodities: from the rubble of feudalism, which like its heir, capitalism, was also a system of exploitation, a simple commodity society, free of exploitation, emerged spontaneously. This was the *source of the pathos* of the great bourgeois revolutions (the ideas of equality, freedom of the individual, right to work and so on), this was the source of revolutionary enthusiasm.

But the simple commodity society appears too late to become the dominant form of society: its midwife turns out to be capital, which permits and exploits the emergence of labouring proprietors in the countryside, while at the same time resolutely impeding any efforts by labouring owners at the guild level [*tsekhovoi*] in the cities to set up their own organisations of self-protection.[7]

A truly fundamental bourgeois revolution that also extends into the economy is thus, on the one hand, an *incomplete*, merely *agrarian* revolution, because it does not encompass the entire economy but only its most backward part, namely agriculture. On the other hand, as a revolution it remains incomplete because political power (and thus control of society) shifts not into the hands of the free commodity-producing peasant labourers but into the hands of capital. Destruction of the feudal means of exploitation does not lead to the emergence of a completed society of basic commodity producers, but only individual, although numerous, labouring commodity producers within the developing capitalist society.

---

6 As far as the revolutionary mutation of the economy is concerned, the feudal-serf economy can in no way transform directly into a capitalist one on a mass scale. Between the one and the other stands the simple production society. The bourgeois economic revolution, then, does not create capitalism, just the conditions for its spread.

7 While capital protects with the one hand the emergence of basic commodity production (in the countryside), it strangles it with the other (in the city). Both are historical necessities, because basic commodity production, which develops the productive forces of society in the countryside, hinders their development in the city (guilds).

In contrast, a complete bourgeois-capitalist revolution remains *superficial*, a purely political revolution which does not immediately destroy the feudal economic system but only the obstacles to its destruction.

An economic – and thus partial – revolution is produced, then, by a class that *will not become* a ruling class. By contrast, a class that becomes a ruling class *will not carry out* an economic revolution. For this reason, the great bourgeois revolutions turned out to be shallower, more superficial than proletarian revolutions. As Marx said, the true cause of bourgeois revolution is alienation from political statehood [*politicheskaia gosudarstvennost'*], while the true cause of proletarian revolution is alienation from man's very essence [*chelovecheskaia sushchnost'*].[8] This fundamental difference is why the replacement of the feudal with a capitalist system is but an *exchange of systems of exploitation*, while the replacement of capitalism with the dictatorship of the proletariat is the *elimination of exploitation itself*.

Unlike the great bourgeois revolutions, the Russian proletarian revolution brought to power a class that until then had been oppressed both economically and politically. For that reason, it is not only a whole and complete revolution, but also a profound revolution. It is a social revolution in the fullest sense of the word, for it encompasses both political and economic revolution. The class that has won power, but does not limit itself to that, also carries out, as a class, the economic revolution; the economic revolution is carried out by the class that has become the ruling class. Today's revolution is not a simple exchange of state power, i.e. a purely political revolution that just unleashes a previous economic evolution, just opens the way for the blind or, if one wishes, the 'free' play of economic forces, as the bourgeois revolutions did for capital. No, our revolution upends not indirectly, but directly and immediately, the very foundations of society, its relations of production, and it does so not in the stagnant spheres of the economy, but in the foundational, developing, and critical sphere of the economy – heavy industry. The complete change in the means of production is by no means a simple outcome of the revolution, as was the case for capital in the bourgeois revolutions, but the direct work of the social revolution of the proletariat. In keeping with the distinction between the bourgeoisie and the proletariat, the bourgeoisie, in the course of its revolution, created a new power in place of the toppled old political power, but it destroyed only the old feudal relations of production or allowed for their destruction. It left the final change in the entire means of production, however, and the creation (expansion) of

8 [Marx expanded on his theory of the alienation of individuals from their human nature in, among other writings, Karl Marx, *Economic and Philosophic Manuscripts of 1844* (Moscow: Progress Publishers, 1959)].

new capitalist relations of production, to the future endeavours of individual capitalists. *The proletariat, however, organised a new mode of production*. For this reason, the Great Russian Revolution cannot be compared with any other revolution in world history.

The Great Russian Revolution, however, is distinguished from all earlier great revolutions not only by its profundity, but also by its (territorial) *reach*, although, it is true, this is still taking place below the surface and not out in the open. Unlike the English and the Great French Revolutions and even the 1848 Revolution, the Great Russian Revolution is taking place not in the age of the national economy, like its predecessors, but in *the age of the world economy*. This distinction is apparent in many features of the Great Russian Revolution. In particular, this explains precisely the initially inconceivable reason why, while the bourgeois revolutions first took hold in individual economically more developed countries, the proletarian revolution began and triumphed first in an *economically backward* country. This has all to do with the fact that the economic maturity (for the bourgeois revolution) of England in the mid-17th century or France towards the end of the 18th century should not be compared with the economic maturity (for the proletarian revolution) of Russia at the start of the 20th century, but rather with the maturity of the entire capitalist world. The capitalist world became ripe for proletarian revolution, and *this* made the Russian proletarian revolution a possibility. Within a society that is ripe for revolution, revolution breaks out not where this society is most economically developed, but where *social contradictions have become most prominent*, something that is conditioned not by the level of the economy of the affected sector of society, but by the level of the economy of this society as a whole.

The international reach of the Great Russian Revolution, which is only *Russian* because the flame of world conflagration was ignited *in Russia*, also explains the supranational, world-encompassing, internationalist pathos of the Russian Revolution, a pathos as strong and passionate as the national patriotic pathos of the great bourgeois revolutions.

The Great Russian Revolution is therefore a completely unique revolution. But this uniqueness is only the uniqueness of being the *first* proletarian revolution in history.

The internal forces of the Russian Revolution and the substance of their struggle, which infused the Russian Revolution, do not in themselves constitute *anything specifically Russian* – they are but representations and manifestations of international forces. The true unique feature of the Great Russian Revolution, i.e. that which makes it a Russian Revolution and not just a generic proletarian revolution, is above all a result of its unique international situation, of the effect of this situation on the preparation and development of the revolutionary process being driven by the internal forces of revolution.

The intrinsic, internally conditioned content of the Russian Revolution is not specific; its specific content is shaped not by internal factors but by external influences.

In its *basic* content, the Russian Revolution is the *national* – and for certain historical reasons, Russian – manifestation of an *international* revolutionary crisis, the crisis of world capitalism. Russia is the part of the capitalist world where the hidden became visible, where international, underground forces overcame resistance and rose to the surface, where the international contradictions were exposed. It is where two international foes – capital and the proletariat – and two international principles – capitalism and communism – clashed in a life and death struggle for mastery not of Russia, but of the world. This pitched battle is still going on (and this battle – whether it be a strike, an uprising, a war, or the revolutionary construction of a new social order in the midst of world Reaction – is not exactly a time of economic prosperity), but both sides know very well that when songs of plenty ring out in the land of the Soviets, there will be funeral dirges for world capitalism, and it will find these more terrifying than the language of Red Army cannons and machine-guns.

The essence of the Great Russian Revolution – the revolutionary conflict in the class-struggle between the proletariat and capital – is in no way unique; the class struggle between the proletariat and capital is playing out in all capitalist countries, all across the capitalist world. It is everywhere, and in many countries it has already led to revolutionary conflicts (the Paris Commune, Soviet Republics in Bavaria, Finland, and Hungary; the revolutionary movements of 1919–1920 in Germany and Italy). The paths of all capitalist countries, the course of their social life, do not change direction; Russia has just greatly outstripped the others. In its essence, the Great Russian Revolution is not a national but a world historic event, the culminating phase (for a certain period) in the class struggle between the two primary classes of an international social formation, of capitalism, but within the borders of a national territory and in the form of a national event.

This contradiction between the form of the national event and its international content is a characteristic feature of the Great Russian Revolution, distinguishing it from the great bourgeois revolutions in which the form of the national event corresponded directly with the intrinsic forces and the content of their struggle. This contradiction comes from the fact that the Russian Revolution is taking place in an era not of national economies but of a world economy.

The essence of the Great Russian Revolution – elimination of the capitalist exploitation of the proletariat – is complicated by the elimination of the feudal mode of exploitation of the numerically overwhelming (petty bourgeois) mass of Russia's population, the peasantry. Proletarian revolution is intertwined with agrarian revolution, which is the economic foundation of the great bourgeois revolutions, ensuring that these revolutions did not merely signify an exchange of ruling classes, but that they became truly great and truly popular revolutions, even though the bourgeoisie marched at their head and exploited for their own ends the powerful movement of the popular masses. But precisely because now the proletariat was marching at the head of the revolution, the Great Russian Revolution was at the same time the most complete bourgeois revolution, radically eliminating all the vestiges of feudalism and realising the most extreme dreams of the bourgeois reformers – nationalisation of the land.

That the proletarian revolution is intertwined with agrarian revolution, supporting it and being supported by it up to a certain point, is without doubt a specific feature of the Russian Revolution that, as we shall see later, is a function of the international situation of the prerevolutionary period.

The agrarian revolution is in its core a bourgeois revolution, and its occurrence simultaneously with a proletarian revolution is a consequence of the capitalist backwardness of Russia, i.e. backward vis-à-vis the more advanced capitalist development of other countries; under the influence of this backwardness, the bourgeois revolution in Russia could only triumph as a revolution of the working class. A consequence of this same backwardness is also Russia's semicolonial character, which lent the Russian Revolution certain features of colonial revolution, complicating its basic substance.

The elimination of capitalist and feudal exploitation has also put an end to national oppression within Russia, which had an absolute (feudal) character. The liberation of oppressed nations is a further element of the Russian Revolution that complicates its substance.

Of course, an event of such a scale as the Great Russian Revolution is by definition an event of world historical significance, because it took place in the era of the world economy and encompassed a twelfth of humanity, above all in Europe, where the network of international connections was the densest.

But apart from its scale and apart from the fact that in its essence the Russian Revolution can only be conceived as a world historical event, the concrete historical course of its development can only be understood if it is seen as an international phenomenon, i.e. within its international context. Both the period of its maturation, and the specific features of the two main periods of its development – the Civil War from 1917 to 1920 and the so-called New Economic Policy that began in 1921–are a result of the overwhelming influence of the international context, which *prolonged* each of these periods and sharpened their basic features, in a sense solidifying them.

In the course of this work, we will examine the emergence and development of the revolutionary process: *the prewar period*, the period of preparation and latent development of the revolution together with the revolutionary prologue of 1905; *the period of imperialist war* that directly paved the way for revolution; its culminating period of civil war and *the period of the so-called New Economic Policy*, which is still going on today.

CHAPTER 1

The Mechanism of Revolution

1. The essence of the Russian Revolution. 2. The mechanism of proletarian revolution. 3. The mechanism of agrarian revolution. 4. The complex nature of the Russian Revolution.

The Great Russian Revolution is an exceptionally complex social phenomenon. In all its contradictory complexity, it is a reflection of Russia's aforementioned economic and social contradictions. Nonetheless, the essence of the Russian Revolution, which is becoming strongly evident and which cannot be obscured by superficial factors, is that it is *a social revolution of the proletariat*. Its essence has been thrown into unusually sharp relief by the response to it from both poles of the capitalist world – from world capital and from the world proletariat. It is difficult to point to another national event, another domestic event in the life of a single country, that would have attracted such active attention from all of world capital and from the entire world proletariat as has the Great Russian Revolution.

The preconditions for social revolution by the proletariat – the dominance of capital in the Russian economy, the concentration of industry, transportation, and credit, the development of the internal class contradictions of capitalism, the revolutionary class organisation of the proletariat (its vanguard) and its revolutionary class consciousness – were evident already in prewar Russia. Alone, though, they signified just the *possibility* of proletarian revolution, but by no means its necessity.[1] At that time, capitalism was not yet an obstacle to the development of Russia's productive forces. Their development was impeded not by the capitalist organisation of the economy, but by capital's incomplete control of Russia's economy, first and foremost of its agriculture.

This possibility of proletarian revolution was realized and transformed into a *necessity* by the imperialist world war. The imperialist world war was a crisis of world capitalism, marking a shift from the era of growth of the productive forces of world capitalism to the era of their decline. It marked capitalism's impotence to tackle the tasks of growth or even merely to maintain the pro-

1 Thus, already in 1907 comrade Lenin wrote (in the preface to 'The Development of Capitalism in Russia'): '…the revolution in Russia is, of course, inevitably a bourgeois revolution. This Marxist proposition is absolutely irrefutable'. [V.I. Lenin, 'The Development of Capitalism in Russia,' *Collected Works*, vol. 3 (Moscow: Progress Publishers, 1960), p. 32].

 | HTTPS://DOI.ORG/10.1163/9789004765313-005

ductive forces of mankind, and revealed capitalism's transformation into an impediment to the development of productive forces, into a cause of their unprecedented collapse.

The decline in productive forces, the drop in the living standard of the proletariat and the army, the threat to the very existence of the masses, their revolutionary action – this was the basic mechanism of capitalism's disintegration and collapse.[2]

Basically, it was *world* capitalism, not Russian, that became an obstacle to development, a cause of the decline and destruction of the productive forces of Russia and of other countries. *In Russia*, though, this international historical breakdown in the development of world capitalism manifested itself in the disintegration and failure of *Russian* capitalism. And it could not have manifested itself in any other way, given the social structure of the era of finance capital, which was the prerequisite for the imperialist war itself; for in this era the main type of capitalist organisation was the capitalist *national* economy, which tended to transform itself more and more into a state-capitalist trust.[3]

Due to the specific peculiarities of the economic and social structure of Russian society, the nature and origin of which have been examined in the two preceding sections, the disintegration of Russian capitalism and of the Russian national economy organized by capital was quite different – both in form and tempo – from the disintegration of capitalism in other countries, and for this reason it culminated in the collapse of Russian capitalism. Nevertheless, in its essence, the mechanism of disintegration and collapse of Russian capitalism, despite all its specifically Russian complications, was completely identical to the mechanism of disintegration of capitalism in the other countries. Above all, this was about the disintegration and collapse of *capitalism*, and only secondarily of *Russian* capitalism.

In this way the Great Russian Revolution, for all its complexity, allows the essence of the social revolution of the proletariat to be revealed, it exposes the general mechanism of proletarian revolution.

All revolutions arise when the development of productive forces of society is impeded, and they lead to the elimination of this impediment. But not every impediment to the development of productive forces can become the start-

2 Comrade Bukharin outlines this process in his book 'The Economics of the Transition Period'. [Nikolai Bukharin, *The Politics and Economics of the Transition Period*, ed. Kenneth J. Tarbuck (London and New York: Routledge, 1979)].

3 This term 'state-capitalist trust' was coined by N. Bukharin. [N. Bukharin, 'Towards a Theory of the Imperialist State' in *Selected Writings on the State and the Transition to Socialism*, ed. by Richard B. Day (Armonk, NY: M.E. Sharpe, 1982)].

ing point for a revolution, only an impediment rooted *in society itself*, and this can thus only be eliminated by changing the structure of society. Moreover, not in every society will the structural change required to remove the impediment to the development of the productive forces lead to a revolution. This will happen only in an antagonistic society, in a society built on the alienation of the means of production from the workforce, built therefore on exploitation, i.e. on the appropriation of the social surplus product by a particular segment of society. It will happen, then, only in a *class* society. A social class (in our case the proletariat), which embodies the dynamic (changing) side of economic life, and which represents in potential (hidden) form the new (in our case socialist) mode of production, acquires, on the basis of a level of development attained through a particular (in our case capitalist) mode of production, a certain power grounded in the relations of production. This change in economic relations, which is expressed in the emergence of a new social class that is the bearer of a new mode of production and is gradually transformed into the – potentially – most powerful class in society, remains a potential (hidden) change in spite of the enormity of this turn.

This change in economic relations – the transition to a new mode of production – cannot come to pass as long as the old mode of production is preserved (maintained) by the political structure of society, as long as the dominant class under the old mode of production still has state power and controls the state organisation embodying it, as long as the class struggle plays out *within the framework* of the existing social order, and as long as it is forced, squeezed into this framework.

The new class – the master in the society the revolution will create – by dint of its very emergence and consolidation already changes the political life of society, but in the realm of political relations this change too remains hidden (potential). It is impossible for this change in political relations – the transition to a new political system – to find expression, while the old political system is maintained by the old (in our case capitalist) ideology which holds sway in the minds of the objectively revolutionary class; this ideology is imposed on it by the ruling class, which preserves the old society.

But changes occur in the ideology of the objectively revolutionary class as well,[4] and accelerate sharply in an era when the productive forces of society are in decline. A revolutionary overthrow (*perevorot*) begins in the realm of

4 Here too they happen latently over a long period, as the swelling masses of the revolutionary class become increasingly open to the revolutionary ideology of its vanguard, as their sympathy towards revolutionary ideology grows, and as they become more prepared to accept it.

ideology (viz. views on state power and the relationship with it) – at the upper reaches of the 'superstructure' over the economic 'base'. Revolution above all else wins over people [*liudi*] (a particular class, of course), and the very thing that sets them apart from inanimate objects, namely their *minds*. This *first phase* of revolution is focused in the ideological sphere, and the revolutionary party's basic task is to agitate for a *political overthrow*.

In the objectively revolutionary class (in our case, the proletariat), revolution in the ideological sphere destroys the power that maintains the old political system, the old ideological order, and the new revolutionary ideology of the now subjectively revolutionary class becomes the lever of political transformation. A revolutionary transformation takes place in the sphere of political relationships, *a political revolution* revealing the hitherto hidden changes in the political relationships of society. This is the *second phase* of revolution, which is focused in the political realm (political relations), and the basic task of the revolutionary party is to restructure [*perestroika*] political relations, to *destroy the old political system, and organise a new one*. The prerequisite for this second phase of revolution is essentially the completion of its first phase, the revolution in the realm of ideology. The prerequisite for the political revolution is *the presence of the revolutionary masses*, i.e. a completed revolution in the realm of ideology.

The political organisation of society, the state organisation of the ruling class – this is the specific institution of class society, a product of the antagonistic structure of the economy in this atmosphere of class struggle (a necessary consequence of the antagonistic structure of the economy); it is a means of imposing class collaboration (above all in the production process). It is in the political organisation of society, in the state organisation of its ruling class, that resistance to the development of society is concentrated; this obstacle to the development of productive forces is the starting point for revolution. This is precisely why political revolution becomes the concentrated expression of revolution.

Political revolution destroys the force preserving the old mode of production, the state organisation of the ruling class; it transforms the revolutionary class into the politically dominant class, namely the class monopolising in its hands all the means of organised coercion. This new organisation of the power of the revolutionary class becomes the lever of economic transformation: a revolutionary transformation of economic relationships, an *economic revolution* revealing the hitherto hidden change in the economic relationships of society.

The diverse economic relationships of capitalist society (and other societies) can be broken down *into two* basic types: relationships among members (or groups of members) of *one and the same* class, and relationships among members (or groups of members) of *different* classes. Relationships of the first type are for the most part – in whatever sphere – relationships *among* well-known social cells, relationships of the second type are *within* these social cells.[5] It is precisely the latter that are necessarily antagonistic in capitalist society.

The starting point of proletarian revolution is the antagonistic class structure of the capitalist economy. Economic revolution therefore leads primarily to the destruction of the antagonistic character of the capitalist economy, to the destruction of the power over the social worker [*obshchestvennii rabotnik*] wielded by the social productive forces, which are divorced from and in opposition to him, and embodied in the figure of the capitalist. It leads namely to the destruction of the command power [*komandnaia vlast'*] of capital in the economy, *to the integration of the social worker and his means of production, to the elimination of exploitation.* This *third* phase of revolution is concentrated in the sphere of *specific* economic relationships, when the basic task of the revolutionary party is to *destroy the old economic system and build a new one in the sphere of specific economic relationships*, and thus to change the most intrinsic social relationships, to reconfigure society's basic elements – *people*. Transition to this third phase of revolution requires the essential completion of its second phase – upheaval [*perevorot*] in the realm of politic – because the necessary precondition for economic revolution is the *power* of the new class *over society*, i.e. the completed political revolution.

The basic work of the third phase of proletarian revolution, of the economic revolution in the narrow, immediate sense of this term, is to destroy the old and build a new command power in the economy (a new economic adminis-

---

5 Relationships of the first type are analogous (but of course only analogous) to molecular interactions; relationships of the second type are analogous to atomic, intramolecular interactions. The former are more superficial, the latter are intrinsic, deeper. Before a class has taken shape as a class, its elements already exist as analogous components of different social cells (for example, before the proletariat took shape as a class, proletarians existed in individual capitalist enterprises).

Let us agree henceforth to call economic relationships between different classes and among members of different classes specifically economic relationships. On the one hand, it is precisely these that constitute the characteristic feature of a particular mode of production that is dominant in society and based on exploitation. On the other hand, unlike general economic relationships (for example, relationships among individuals of the same or different professions, etc) that arise from the struggle with nature (from technology) and although they themselves experience the effects of the class structure of society, their existence is not dependent on it. Specific economic relationships are rooted precisely in this historically transitional specific class structure of society, and they emerge and disappear along with it.

tration), just as the basic work of the second phase of proletarian revolution is to destroy the old and build a new command power in politics (a new state administration).

The antagonistic structure of the capitalist economy is not something foreign to it. This is why the crisis of the capitalist relations of production, as long as it lasts, is accompanied by a crisis in production. The painful nature of this crisis stems from the fact that capitalist society is distinguished from all other known class societies by its complex structure, which for its part is determined by the *role of the technical intelligentsia* [*tekhnicheskaia intelligentsia*].

The growing significance of the technical intelligentsia is an expression *of the increasing organic composition of* (social) *capital*, i.e. of a requisite process of capitalism: the growth in the basic part of fixed capital, the expression of the growing application of science in production, is necessarily linked with the growth in the technical intelligentsia which realises and embodies scientific methods of production and which is therefore the expression of the same process – of the growth of productive forces, but in the realm of living labour.

But the technical intelligentsia plays a *dual* role in capitalist production: it is not only the *organiser of production* but also the *organiser of exploitation*. This is why the elimination of capitalist exploitation necessarily becomes a temporary crisis in production, all the more painful (if all the briefer) the more significant the role of the technical intelligentsia, i.e. the higher the level of development already reached by the productive forces.

This third phase of the revolution is in essence the completion of the revolution, its *culminating* phase, for the destruction of the antagonistic structure of the economy brings with it the destruction of the fundamental *cause* of this obstacle to the development of the productive forces of society, which is the starting point of revolution.

But destruction of the forces holding back the development of the productive forces of society does not yet mean that this impediment has been completely overcome. The antagonistic (class) structure of the capitalist economy is not only reinforced by the capitalist state and capitalist ideology, it is itself the source of certain features of the economy (and technology) of capitalist society. These features complicate the development of the productive forces of society and do not suddenly disappear once the structure has disappeared: the class structure of society materialises in these features.

General economic relationships do not depend for their existence on the class structure of society; but in the concrete form they take in a given class society (in our case, capitalist society), they exist in this form because of the effect of the class structure of society upon them.

So the distribution of productive forces[6] according to various branches of production is a general economic relationship. In any societal structure (class or classless), productive forces are distributed according to various branches of production. But the kind of distribution of productive forces of society, when a large portion of them is concentrated to a certain degree in certain branches of production (in production of the means of consumption of capitalists), is a consequence of a particular class structure of society.

As far as there is, for instance, a demand for fine wines, the *fact* of their production is not tied to the class structure of society; but the *scale* of their production is determined precisely by this structure. Where the level of productive forces of society is the same, the scale of this production will be smaller in a proletarian than in a capitalist society.

The class structure of this society manifests in the distribution of the productive forces of capitalist society.

But the obstacle to the development of the productive forces of society, itself caused by capitalism, also manifests in it.

This is precisely why the internal structure of the productive forces of society (the degree of their concentration and centralisation) is a general economic relationship. But the precise degree of concentration and centralisation attained by the productive forces of society depends on its class structure. In a society with the same level of productive forces, their concentration and centralisation will be significantly greater in a proletarian than in a capitalist society. In other words, the capitalist structure of society holds back the degree of concentration and centralisation attainable by a given level of the productive forces of society, and the obstacle to the development of the productive forces of society caused by capitalism is revealed in this lower degree of concentration and centralisation.

The third phase of the revolution destroys the forces that have created and preserved these general economic conditions, or rather, those concrete manifestations of the general economic conditions which are typical of capitalist society and which, together with its specific economic relationships, constitute the capitalist mode of production; the new organisation of economic power of the revolutionary class becomes the lever of change for these general economic relationships within society. After the economic revolution has destroyed – fundamentally – the antagonistic structure of the economy, it sets about *reor-*

6 While the productive forces themselves are in the sphere of technology, their distribution, therefore their relationship, is at the same time also the distribution of the basic productive force of society, its labour force – it is therefore the relationship of people in the process of social labour, and thus an economic relationship.

ganising the general economic relationships of society. In their concrete form, these are the consequence either of the antagonistic structure of the capitalist economy directly (such as the aforementioned distribution of the productive forces of society), or of the level of technical-economic development at which capitalist society was arrested by the antagonistic structure of its economy and at which the revolution found it (also of relevance here is the aforementioned degree of concentration and centralisation of the productive forces of society, and thus also the degree to which the market has been overcome, something that occurs continuously under capitalism at the highest stages of its development, albeit in antagonistic forms). Society's productive forces are redistributed, and the character of its general economic relationships changes; this marks the transition to the next stage in overcoming the market, and – where the level of productive forces is high enough – the transition to overcoming the market completely, marking a new step in the direction (or in the latter case the transition) *away from the anarchy of production towards planned production*, away from the predatory production so wasteful of productive forces and, most of all, of the basic productive force of society, human labor (but also the resources of the earth, forests etc), towards the rational production that is mindful not only of tomorrow, not only of the day after, but of the more distant future.

This is the *fourth phase* of the revolution, and no longer a revolution in the true sense of the word, for it eliminates the impediments to the development of the productive forces of society, which are no longer rooted in the antagonistic structure of society but are just an echo of its former antagonistic structure.

This phase of the revolution is concentrated in the sphere of economic (and moreover *general* economic) relationships. The basic task of the revolutionary party is to *organise a new economic system* in the sphere of *general* economic relationships, and thus to change the more superficial (external) social relationships, to *regroup* the not yet individualised elements of society (people) within social cells, and the *cells* themselves. This fourth phase of the revolution requires the essential completion of its third phase – of the economic revolution in the direct and narrow sense of this word, for the prerequisite of the economic revolution in the sphere of general economic relationships is the *power* of the new class *over the economy*, i.e. a completed economic revolution (in the sphere of specific economic relationships).

In the broader sense of this word, the third and fourth phases together constitute economic revolution, the restructuring [*perestroika*] of the mode of production.

Once the fourth phase of the revolution is essentially complete, insofar as it is a revolution, i.e. insofar as it destroys those general economic relationships which do not correspond to the level of development attained by the productive forces of society, and whose disappearance was delayed by the antagonistic (class) structure of the economy, then the revolution penetrates down to the lowest level of social life, to the sphere of technology, but as a revolution it starts to fade away. Since the obstacles to the development of the productive forces have been removed, there is no impediment to their further development – the revolution, having been victorious and having achieved its ends, dies out. Its final task is to destroy those particular features in the technical relationships of society that are vestiges of its former antagonistic economic structure (e.g. the backwardness of certain branches of production, the goal of producing low-quality products, the use of technical methods harmful or unpleasant to the worker, and so on).

This is the *fifth* and final *phase* of the revolution, when the revolution has already ceased being a revolution. This phase of the revolution is concentrated in the sphere of technical relationships; this fifth phase of the revolution requires the essential completion of the fourth phase, for its prerequisite is the availability of certain *spare resources*. And these resources, at any given level of development of the productive forces, can be acquired only by realising the economic advantages of the new society, i.e. only if the resources of society can be expanded by reorganising its general economic relationships, or in other words only when the economic revolution (in the sphere of general economic relationships) has been accomplished.

Each subsequent phase of the revolution becomes possible only if the preceding phase has sufficiently advanced, although this phase can only be truly consolidated if the transition to the subsequent phase has taken place. So, for example, political revolution only becomes possible once the ideological revolution has occurred, but this latter revolution can only be consolidated when it has actually led to political revolution. But until one or another phase of the revolution is complete, the *old* relationships on the whole must be maintained in the remaining spheres. In particular, the transformation of technical relationships is not possible until all preceding phases of the revolution have been completed. The revolution takes place therefore on the basis of the *old* technology, the earlier methods remain essentially unchanged as the revolution unfolds. Of course, in the age of revolution (indeed in every age in general) all social relationships change, but the great bulk of the changes happens in each period in a particular sphere, and it is precisely in this sphere in each corresponding period that the creative destructive-constructive work of the revolution is concentrated.

This is the mechanism of proletarian revolution.[7]

But the Great Russian Revolution is an exceptionally complex social phenomenon, a proletarian revolution only in terms of its *basic* content. It is the first proletarian revolution and the first stage of world proletarian revolution, and this is its *global* significance. But it is not only an anti-capitalist revolution of the proletariat, it is at the same time an anti-feudal revolution of the peasantry, and this is its *national* significance, and this is crucial not only for world history but for the overwhelming majority of the population of Russia.

The mechanism of anti-feudal agrarian revolution is characterised by phases, analogous to the aforementioned phases of the anti-capitalist proletarian revolution. The peculiar feature of peasant revolution, which flows from the small-peasant economy that creates it, is the peasantry's inability, as a result of its scatteredness [*raspylennost'*], to undertake *on its own* the second, necessarily concentrated, phase of revolution, i.e. political revolution. All independent peasant disturbances [*vystupleniia*] known to history have always remained revolts [*bunty*], without becoming revolutions. In all agrarian revolutions known to history, control of society did not pass to the peasantry (which was never able to overcome its own atomisation [*razdroblennost'*] that was rooted in the economy and technology of the small-peasant household), but passed instead to another revolutionary class: in bourgeois revolutions to capital, in the Great Russian Revolution to the proletariat. In other words, for agrarian revolution to be accomplished, it must be *not only* an agrarian revolution; another revolutionary class, the hegemon of the revolution, must rise up alongside the anti-feudal peasantry, a class whose leadership the peasantry will follow and which in turn relies upon the peasantry. The political revolution of the peasantry is completed jointly with and under the leadership of this *other* class, on whose character the *essence* of the revolution also depends.

Modern warfare, i.e. war fought not by a small standing army but by the armed popular masses, plays a highly specific role in the preparation of agrarian revolution, and therefore also of the political phase of this revolution.

Modern warfare influences the preparation of proletarian revolution in two basic ways:

First, it functions as an enormous economic crisis, moving society from an era of expanding production (a boom in the productive forces of society) to an era of contracting production (a decline in the productive forces of society).

---

7 I outlined the basic features of this theory of the phases of revolution in Spring 1918 at the start of the revolution (see L. Kritsman, 'Ob ocherednoi zadache proletarskoi revolutsii,' in no. 5 of the journal 'Narodnoe khoziaistvo' for 1918). It was confirmed – in particular its final conclusion – by the entire later course of the revolution.

Specifically, war first and foremost strengthens capitalist ideology within the proletariat to an enormous degree (workers' patriotism, social patriotism), as a result of which any radical change in its ideological thinking as a result of economic crisis is *delayed*, occurring much later than in a peacetime economic crisis of similar magnitude; so the revolution takes place at a time when the productive forces of society are at a *lower level* of development. Second, it destroys the arms monopoly of the ruling class, making weapons the property of the broad masses of the proletariat.

Modern warfare influences the preparation of agrarian revolution in immeasurably deeper ways. It is experienced by the large mass of the peasantry not only as a huge economic crisis and not only because it puts arms into the hands of the peasantry, – modern warfare subjects the large mass of the peasantry in short order to similar treatment to that which capitalism subjects the proletarians: in organising the peasantry, it creates the fundamental basis for revolutionary action by the peasant masses (of course only where a revolutionary situation is at hand); it creates the basis for the development of social activism among petty producers, who have been set apart up to now by their mode of production.

This is precisely why the history of the Russian revolutionary movement underlines with the utmost clarity the importance of the union of *petty bourgeois* elements for the development of their social activism, something which is possible for the petty bourgeoisie, of course, only *outside of* production.

We are thinking of students here, who found their common cause in the university. Wherever a revolutionary situation was present for their class, the students became so socially active that the word student became synonymous with revolutionary.

Having graduated university, they stopped being individual members of the student body and became individual solitary workers; as a rule, these revolutionary students became common people [*obyvatel'*], i.e. they lost their social activism.

This has been touched on repeatedly in Russian literature and was usually attributed to the influence of age. The reality, however, was different as, on the one hand, even older students were no less active than the other students, and, on the other, young people from the ranks of white-collar workers who were socially close to the students did not display any special social activism.

This was all about *overcoming atomisation*, and, in the case of the peasantry, this role was fulfilled by modern war.

Modern warfare overcomes the atomisation of the peasantry, an atomisation that is rooted within its mode of production and that can therefore not be overcome in any other way than *outside of* production.

Wherever a revolutionary situation exists, modern war becomes a *simplified* yet *accelerated process for organising the cadres of the agrarian revolution.*

Of course, the transformation of the army, made up of peasants, into cadres for the agrarian revolution is tied to the destruction of the army as such, to its disintegration; the army does not become a directly revolutionary organisation, only a basis for it, as was the university for the students.

The process of organisation of the peasantry by modern war is not as deep-rooted as the process of organisation of the proletariat by capitalism, and it does not permit the bulk of the peasantry to create a *stable* revolutionary organisation on its own; it does, however, greatly facilitate, even create, the basis for the revolutionary organisational work of another class – the hegemon of the revolution, of our revolution – the proletariat.

The third phase of agrarian revolution entails the *destruction of feudal landholding* and of the feudal relationships of dependence connected with it, the destruction of the antagonistic character of the feudal economy, the elimination of feudal exploitation, and the integration of the individual worker-peasant with the basic means of his production – the land – from which he has been partially alienated up to now. The absence of a technical intelligentsia, analogous to the capitalist intelligentsia, makes this phase relatively easy. It transforms the feudal peasant into a petty bourgeois, a free, petty commodity producer, into a member of a simple commodity society.

The fourth phase is *revolutionary land reorganisation*, which destroys those general economic relationships in agriculture that formed as a product of the antagonistic economy of the feudal society, and that opened up the development of the productive forces of (small-scale) agriculture, and thus also its dialectical transformation into capitalist agriculture.

The fifth phase is the destruction of the technical features of (peasant) agriculture, the product of prerevolutionary land distribution (distant fields [*dal'nozemel'e*], strip-farming [*cherespolositsa*], etc); these features explain the backwardness of Russian prerevolutionary (peasant) agriculture.

It goes without saying that the aforementioned mechanism of proletarian revolution is the mechanism of a *pure* proletarian revolution, as it would be in an isolated, pure capitalist society (i.e. a society in which the vestiges of pre-capitalist economic formations have disappeared along with the social classes produced by them).[8]

8 The same must also be said about the aforementioned mechanism of peasant revolution. This is the mechanism of a purely peasant revolution, as it would be in a pure feudal society, so long as the external forces that helped the peasantry to stage its political revolution afterwards had no influence on the course of the revolution.

But the Great Russian Revolution is by no means either a pure proletarian (anti-capitalist) revolution or a purely peasant (anti-feudal) revolution; on the contrary it is an exceptionally complex social phenomenon.

This complex nature of the Russian Revolution derives primarily from the fact that the bourgeois revolution in Russia was delayed until the very moment of the outbreak of the proletarian revolution (we have already examined this previously), i.e. it derives from the historical *coincidence* of the anti-capitalist and anti-feudal revolutions.

But it not just about this *dual* nature of the Russian Revolution, it is also about the *specific ways* the anti-capitalist revolution (which would be a purely socialist revolution if it were not combined with an anti-feudal revolution) combined with the anti-feudal revolution (which would be a purely bourgeois revolution if it were not combined with a proletarian revolution).

Its first specific feature is that the combination of the anti-capitalist and the anti-feudal revolution was *not only* a *temporal* concurrence, *but also* a *geographic* concurrence. Insofar as the most developed capitalist countries for the most part[9] possess significant colonies, proletarian revolution in every such country will inevitably be accompanied by a peasant (and in some case also a bourgeois-capitalist) revolution in the colonies, by the liberation of the colonial peoples from colonial dependence.

But in these countries, the proletarian and peasant revolutions, while occurring at the same time, will be separated geographically. They will occur simultaneously, but spatially only in tandem: one – the proletarian revolution – will take place in the metropol, the other – the peasant revolution – in the colonies.

By contrast, in the Russian Revolution the proletarian revolution and peasant revolution coincided both temporally and geographically: instead of two parallel territorially separate revolutions, the proletarian in the metropol and the peasant in the colonies, one *complex* revolution occured in one and the same country.

In the era of finance capitalism, and thus in the era of the (unorganised) world economy, proletarian revolutions in individual countries are only stages in a *global* proletarian revolution that will inevitably bear a dual character, that of a complex revolution in which the revolution of the proletariat and the revolution of the (colonial) peasantry are intertwined.

The world historical significance of the Great Russian Revolution is therefore not only that it is the *first* proletarian revolution, and thus the *first* stage

9 But not all. Germany for example after the World War is still a highly developed capitalist state, even though it has been deprived of its colonies. Revolution in Germany, then, would be a proletarian revolution in the purest sense.

of the global proletarian revolution, but also that it is the *prototype* of the entire world revolution; for on a national scale it turns on its head (poses and resolves) the basic problem of the entire world revolution as a whole – the combination of the proletarian revolution and the peasant revolution.

The specific complication of the Russian Revolution is, however, not that it posed (and resolved) this problem, but that this problem confronted it in unusually *hypertrophied* (exaggerated) form.

This specific feature of the Russian Revolution comes from the fact that the Russian peasant economy was the agrarian appendage *not only of Russian but also of world*[10] (West European) *capital*. On the one hand, this gave the Russian proletariat the opportunity to act as liberator of the entire nation (primarily of the peasantry, 3/4 of the population) from the colonial exploitation that was threatening it, and, on the other hand, to an exceptional degree, it overburdened the proletarian anti-capitalist revolution with the anti-feudal revolution, forcing the Russian proletariat to resolve the question about the proletariat's relationship with the peasantry not only for itself, but also *for the West European* proletariat.

The combination of both revolutions, the proletarian and the peasant, in the Russian Revolution is complicated therefore not only by virtue of its special qualitative character, but also its special quantitative character.

Several consequences of these particular features of this combination and interaction of both revolutions, the proletarian and the peasant (predetermined already by the economy of prewar Russia), were touched on in the first part, and in part also in the second; we will now dwell below on several other consequences.

The complex character of the Great Russian Revolution is not exhausted by the above explanations. It derives not only from the combination of the two revolutions, the proletarian and the peasant, in its specific Russian context, but also from the fact that this national[11] (Russian) revolution did not occur in an isolated society at all, but, on the contrary, in an era when every individual national economy had already become part of the world economy.

In these circumstances, the Russian proletarian revolution could not be anything other than the first stage of a *world* proletarian revolution, a global revolution in content and national in form.

10 About 60% of the grain (its basic product) and 40–50% of all agricultural products exported from the Russian countryside went abroad.

11 In this case, national in the sense that it was accomplished within Russia's borders, in contrast to the world.

This contradiction between the global content and the national form of the Russian Revolution, that declared itself unambiguously in the form of intervention by foreign capital, inevitably had to complicate the course of the Russian Revolution even further.

On the other hand, there is no absolute distinction between the complex, territorially fused proletarian-peasant Russian Revolution and the territorially separate, parallel proletarian and peasant revolutions of the future in other countries.

Like the colonial empires of the highly developed capitalist countries, Russia was a *multinational* state. Like them, the dominant (Great Russian) nation was drawn into capitalist development to a greater extent than were the oppressed nations (with the exception of certain Western regions of the Tsarist Empire). This meant that the proletariat of Russia was predominantly Great Russian, and, alongside this, the oppressed nations – in comparison with the Great Russian – saw less capitalist development, and were almost entirely peasant in composition.[12]

Under these conditions, the peasant revolution had inevitably to take on a nationalist character, to be complicated by a struggle against nationalist oppression. And this meant a further complication of the Russian Revolution and a significant complication of the proletariat's basic task, namely the combination of the proletarian revolution with the – multifaceted because multinational – peasant revolution.

The complex character of the Russian Revolution inevitably led to a change (mostly complicating, but sometimes simplifying) in the course of each phase of the revolution.

12 An exception here, as mentioned above, were certain Western regions of the Tsarist Empire.

CHAPTER 2

The Development of the Revolution under the Influence of Internal Forces

1. The ease of the October overthrow and its causes. 2. The common work of the proletarian and peasant revolution. 3. The impetuosity of the peasant revolution and the restraint of the proletarian revolution. 4. The hegemony of the proletariat and its concessions to the peasantry.

The surprising speed and ease with which the October overthrow [*perevorot*] was accomplished, i.e. the transfer of power into the hands of the proletariat, an event of global historical significance with only one precedent that was but the hint of a precedent, the Paris Commune, can be explained by the presence of conditions highly beneficial to the first steps of the revolution. The delayed onset of the Russian bourgeois revolution meant that the Russian proletarian revolution, precipitated by the collapse of Russian capitalism, encountered relatively *minor ideological resistance* within the proletariat. Instead of a rigidly ossified ideological system (i.e. the old social order) filled with great inertia, it encountered a tense revolutionary atmosphere, which, as we have seen, had delayed the onset of the Russian bourgeois revolution. The significance of this factor (ideological opposition) became crystal clear in 1919–20 in Western Europe, where the ideology of its system (the ideology of the capitalist order in the proletariat, in proletarian minds) found its organisational expression and reinforcement in the form of present-day Social Democracy.

The revolutionary hegemony of the proletariat in the Russian bourgeois revolution was an ideological (although of course not only ideological) precondition of the Russian proletarian revolution, it was a bridge to it. The Russian revolutionary movement was victorious as a workers' movement, and the victorious workers' movement was transformed effortlessly into the revolutionary movement of the proletariat, into the proletarian revolution.

But the historical immediacy, the near concurrence, of the Russian bourgeois revolution and the Russian proletarian revolution meant that the latter encountered relatively *insignificant resistance* not only in ideological terms but also from the *state organisation*, for it was confronted not by a stable, long-entrenched machinery of bourgeois state violence, but rather by the half-destroyed apparatus of feudal state power (tsarism), whose partial transformation in a bourgeois sense had only just begun. The resistance that such a state

 | HTTPS://DOI.ORG/10.1163/9789004765313-006

organisation was able to muster was in fact not great. In the border regions [*na okrainakh*], this resistance of an already unstable state machinery was reduced to almost nothing by the *struggle* unfolding between February and October 1917 *by the oppressed* nations, which until then had been completely crushed by tsarism, for their own liberation; in Ukraine, prior to the October overthrow, the all-Russian state organisation had practically ceased to exist.

By forcing the peasantry to continue a war that was *alien* to it[1] and by revealing its counter-revolutionary stance on one of the fundamental issues of the bourgeois revolution – the agrarian question –, the government of the Russian bourgeois revolution guaranteed that the Russian proletarian revolution would have the support of the great mass of the population of Russia – its peasantry. It guaranteed the united revolutionary action of the proletariat and the peasantry. And at the same time, thanks to the historical situation, a powerful anti-revolutionary factor – foreign capital – was excluded from the ranks of active forces at the moment of the October overthrow.

The government of the Russian bourgeois revolution could not count on the aid of foreign bayonets: neither on German bayonets, because one of its main goals was to prosecute the war against Germany, nor on the bayonets of the Entente countries, because it was cut off from them.

Under these conditions, the first stages of the Great Russian Revolution were carried out before the eyes of the astonished capitalist world with a direct, truly fairytale-like swiftness. The fight against Krasnov for Petrograd lasted only one week; three months after the October overthrow, almost all of Russia from Gomel' to Siberia and from Archangel to Simferopol' had become Soviet. The decisive nature of the overthrow was underlined by the fact that the dissolution of the Constituent Assembly (on 5 January 1918) met with no response; its composition reflected a recent revolutionary past but one already lost in eternity.

The Russian Revolution was able to take its first steps so quickly because the anti-capitalist revolution and the anti-feudal revolution were pursuing a *common* cause.

The Russian bourgeois revolution, as we have seen, betrayed history. This is precisely why the *historically necessary work of the bourgeois revolution was carried out entirely by a revolution* that was, in its essence, a *proletarian* revolution.

It not only abolished all the legal institutions of the feudal state system, from the estate [*soslovnyi*] disfranchisement of the peasantry to the legal inequality

1 Subsequently, the Russian peasantry turned out to be capable within three years, the same length of time, of fighting – and winning – a battle against the landowners' [*pomeshchich'ii*] counter-revolution for the land handed to them by the revolution.

of women, it also obliterated the entire machinery of feudal state violence that had been built by tsarism over the course of two centuries and that the February Revolution had barely touched (and even then only at the upper reaches of government). The revolution destroyed the tsarist army, in which the February Revolution had changed only the upper command, and in fact this was a fiction, for all the tsarist generals were left in command positions; it shattered all the old bureaucratic apparatuses (administrative, legal, and so on), which, it has to be said, the February Revolution barely touched at all; it separated the church from the state and the school from the church. In short, the revolution, not just rhetorically but in practice, left unturned no stone of the entire edifice of tsarism, of the political dominance of feudal landholding, and of the state violence that had featured (become reified) in these apparatuses.

The October Revolution smashed not only the political rule of the feudal lords, but also the economic basis of feudalism – feudal landownership: only a memory remains of feudal landownership. In post-revolutionary Russia, there is not even a trace of the landlord [*pomeshchik*],[2] and the landlord way-of-life continues to exist today only in literature, where it is read about with the same interest as are descriptions of serfdom.

The agrarian revolution, as an anti-feudal revolution, was accomplished in its most complete, most finished form.

All land being worked by the peasants was transferred to them in usufruct *completely and free of charge*, without any kind of direct or hidden redemption payment [*vykup*].

In short, the historically necessary work of the bourgeois revolution was accomplished by the October Revolution with a speed unknown in human history, with consistency and finality.

In *this* work, the peasantry, as the lowest estate in feudal society, was an active but not a leading force alongside the proletariat; victory meant the destruction of feudalism and thus the elimination of the estates. Of course, the strongest effect of the peasantry was felt in the agrarian revolution.

The fact that the Russian bourgeois (anti-feudal) and the Russian proletarian (anti-capitalist) revolution coincided historically, that the historically necessary work of the former was carried out only after the victory of the latter, was because capitalist development coexisted with capitalist backwardness, a mark of the economy of prerevolutionary Russia. Thanks to this, however, alongside the three-million strong army of the modern capitalist proletariat, which was

---

2 For a long time, an exception were (and still are in part) the borderlands, such as Transcaucasia, Turkestan, where the vestiges of feudal relationships were preserved for a long time (and still are in Turkestan). We address this below.

organised in the most concentrated heavy industry, the majority of the population of the country, the tens of millions of peasants, continued to exist as a pre-capitalist peasantry.

But the common interests of the Russian proletariat and the Russian peasantry transcended the anti-feudal revolution because of the *semi-colonial* (and since the war, it can be said, colonial) nature of prerevolutionary Russia. International capital targeted not only the Russian proletariat, but also the Russian peasantry, from which it extracted a significant part of the surplus value it received from Russia, by drawing on its own financial muscle and by using the state apparatus of tsarism. The Russian proletariat acted as the liberator of the entire nation [*natsiia*] from the colonial exploitation that threatened it. The October Revolution led therefore to a sharp break in relations with the capitalist great powers, illustrated in the wake of the October overthrow by the *cancellation of all foreign debts*,[3] and by the steadfast refusal to pay any kind of tribute [*dan'*] whatsoever to international capital. Alongside the expropriation of foreign enterprises, this refusal to pay the interest on foreign loans and to pay off the loans themselves was one of the most important reasons behind international capital's stubborn pursuit of the politics of intervention. This was especially true for the predator state that 'suffered' most, France, the world's usurer [*rostovshchik*], which assumed the honourable role of Europe's gendarme from its thankfully deceased ally, Russian tsarism.

The Great Russian Revolution was also the liberator of the great mass of the population – the peasantry – not just from feudalism, but also from colonial dependence and from national oppression.

The Russian bourgeois revolution meant the inevitable struggle by the many oppressed nations of Russia for their own national liberation. The national limitation of the bourgeois revolution in such a multinational country as Russia led therefore to the start of an *era* of sharp *national conflicts*, which already made themselves felt in the short eight-month period between February and October 1917. But the very fact that the work of the bourgeois revolution was carried out by a detachment [*otriad*] of the world proletariat, by the Russian proletariat, and under its leadership, made it possible to overcome the national limitation of the bourgeois revolution and to realise the *simultaneous* national liberation of the numerous peoples inhabiting Russia. Only the proletariat was capable of carrying out *this* task of the bourgeois revolution, namely the elimination of *national* oppression in a *multi*national country.

---

3 Decree of 28 January 1918. Point 3 of this decree: 'Of course, all foreign loans are cancelled completely and without any restrictions'.

In this way, both the agrarian and the national questions were resolved decisively, completely, and consistently.[4] For each nation, the proletarian revolution recognised the unconditional right to national self-determination, the *right to secede* and form an independent state. The Soviet Federation was formed on this principle, uniting 33 Soviet independent and autonomous republics, autonomous communes and regions: Russia, Ukraine, Belorussia, Georgia, Azerbaidzhan, Armenia, the region of the Caucasus mountain-peoples, Dagestan, Abkhaziia, Adzharia, South Ossetia, Nakhichevan, Nagorno-Karabakh, Turkestan, Bukhara, Khivin, Kalmykia, Kirgiziia, Bashkiriia, Tatariia, Chuvash, Mariiskii, Votskii, Zyrianskii (Komi), Karelia, the Germans of the Volga region, Iakutiia, Crimea, Adygea, Kabardino-Balkariia, Karachaevo-Cherkessiia, Oiratskii, Buriat-Mongolia, all allied by treaty.[5] All institutions (People's Commissariats) responsible for popular enlightenment, health care, social security, internal affairs, agriculture, justice in all independent and autonomous republics were autonomous. In several of them, the institutions (People's Commissariats) responsible for food supply, inspection (supervision), and foreign affairs were also autonomous. The entire Federation shared (on the basis of treaties) the military institutions (Army and Navy) and economic institutions (industry, foreign trade, finance, transport, post and telegraph, labour). Only a memory remained of the old prison-house of peoples.

And yet the national question was one of the fundamental complicating factors of the Russian Revolution. Wherever the national bourgeois parties were able to draw upon external assistance, national anti-Soviet states arose on the territory of old Russia; their national form was but a mask for their active, counter-revolutionary, anti-Soviet content. Once external assistance disappeared, these states disappeared as well, and became Soviet states (Ukraine, Azerbaidzhan, Georgia, Armenia); but on Russia's Western border, where these states bordered directly on capitalist Europe, they continued to exist; they formed a solid curtain stretching from the Arctic Ocean to the Black Sea, separating capitalist Europe from the Russian proletarian revolution.

Destruction of the noble-landlord estate [*soslovie*], and by the same token of the estates and the estate system in general, and destruction of the basis of this

4 In more backward nations where the influence of the landowner-landlords of a given nation was strongest and where a pronounced class consciousness of the peasantry was absent, the resolution of the national question, the transfer of the fates of nations into their own hands, became an obstacle to the resolution of the agrarian question. This was the case in Turkestan, Azerbaidzhan, and for a time in Georgia.

5 For areas not covered by these national republics, a special agency – the People's Commissariat of National Affairs was tasked with eliminating the vestiges of national oppression and preparing for the creation of national republics.

system, landowner agriculture, in short, the destruction of *serfdom*; exit from the imperialist war and cancellation of old loans and old treaties, i.e. destruction of the *colonial* dependence on foreign capital caused by the imperialist war; finally, elimination of the *national* oppression weighing on all the nationalities (with the exception of the Belorussian) which were made up almost entirely of peasants – this was the essence of the anti-feudal peasant revolution, for which a broad and unobstructed path had been opened up precisely by the proletariat that had drawn on the peasantry's support.

This initial period of the Russian Revolution, as it developed under the almost exclusive influence of *internal* factors, was marked, on the one hand, by the rapid realisation of the tasks of the bourgeois revolution, by the precipitous intensification of the peasant anti-feudal revolution, which, immediately after the political overthrow, moved into the phase of economic revolution – to the destruction of feudal landholding, and, on the other hand, by the restrained development of the proletarian anti-capitalist revolution as it carefully felt its way.

The economic revolution developed quickly insofar as it was an anti-feudal revolution, and slowly insofar as it was an anti-capitalist revolution.

Capital, the unchecked master of the world, had until now not seen its dominance seriously challenged – either in word or deed. Capital viewed the capitalist system as the natural order of society, the only one fitting society's nature. In the eyes of capital and of the entire world under its hypnotic sway, the very first steps of the Russian proletarian revolution signified the destruction of all societal principles, a senseless collapse of the world. But between the October overthrow and the expropriation of large industrial capital, or rather of its proclamation (the decree of 28 June 1918 on the nationalisation of large enterprises),[6] was an interval of *about eight months*, i.e. the same interval as between the February and October revolutions. And had it not been for external factors, the expropriation of capital would not have happened in June 1918 either. If, however, we look at the Russian proletarian revolution not against the backdrop of the previously serene existence of capitalism, but compare this period with the subsequent period (from June 1918 to April 1921) and the simultaneous agrarian revolution, then we have to characterise the Russian proletarian revolution in this first period of its development as a revolution which lingered for a long time in its *second* phase (political revolution) without moving on to the next phase (economic revolution).

6 It took six more months to put into effect.

Once the rural revolution was unleashed by the jolt from the city, it outstripped the urban revolution; the revolution in the city – unlike the revolution in the countryside – remained a superficial political revolution, in which the *fundamental* task of this period was to organise a new *political* – soviet – system. At this time, even the dictatorship of the proletariat was very mild in character. *Sabotage* by all kinds of employees [*sluzhashchie*], who had abandoned their institutions, went unchecked, leaving behind only bare walls and furniture for the new proletarian government. Until July 1918, not only pseudo-socialist (petty bourgeois) newspapers were being published, but also bourgeois newspapers.

In economic terms, the victorious political revolution of the proletariat at this time meant primarily that the political power of the proletariat swept away the obstacles standing in the way of its economic revolution, it eliminated the resistance of the entire political edifice of capitalist society (the administration, police, courts, etc) to the class will of the proletarians to destroy capitalist exploitation. Now, in the event of a strike, a capitalist could call on neither the police nor the courts for help, and in this case it was not the proletarian but the capitalist who found himself behind bars. Stripped of its political moorings, capital hung in the air [*povis v vozdukhe*].

The destruction of all organs defending capitalist exploitation and their replacement with organs of proletarian dictatorship *unleashed* the hitherto suppressed class will of the proletariat and led to an *elementally chaotic* overcoming of capitalist exploitation, to *elementally chaotic* proletarian *nationalisation from below*. This was elementally chaotic not in the absolute sense of the term, but only in the sense of a lack of centralized unity here, in the sense of an independence of individual actions.

Among the most backward strata of the proletariat, which were close to the peasantry, and which had retained the vestiges of petty bourgeois (peasant) ideology, there was clearly a tendency to understand the slogan 'Factories to the Workers' as the need for every individual enterprise to be taken over by the workers of *that* enterprise, i.e. to transform it into a productive cooperative of a syndicate of its workers, to 'socialise' the factories just as the land had been socialised, whereby the land had passed into the usufruct of those peasants who worked it. However, this unique *cooperative-syndicalist*, anarcho-communist tendency, the manifestation of petty bourgeois influence on the proletariat, did not become dominant anywhere, and spontaneous nationalisation occurred at the local level as nationalisation, namely as the transfer of factories into the hands of the proletarian state and in its name.

But this spontaneous movement of the proletariat, and above all of a modern industrial proletariat which thus was a particular force in industry, was not initially supported by the central political power of the proletariat and was therefore restricted to scattered actions by individual proletarian groups. As long as the intensifying the civil war did not compel it to give up any efforts for gradual change, the dictatorship of the proletariat remained a tool not for immediate economic revolution, but only a tool *to blunt* capital as a counter-revolutionary force, and to *prepare* for future economic revolution.[7] At this time, therefore, the proletarian expropriation of the expropriators, leaving the bulk of productive (industrial) and trade capital intact, seized only the nerve centres and the circulatory system of the capitalist national economy, its credit and its transport organisation: on 14 December 1917, *private banks were nationalised*; on 26 January 1918, *the merchant marine was nationalised* (as is well-known, rail freight transport was already largely in the hands of the state before the revolution). Banking and transport were not only the 'strategic heights' permitting control over the national economy, they were also the most concentrated sectors of the national economy, and thus most prepared by capitalist development for socialisation. The monopoly of foreign trade, which was decreed on 23 April 1918,[8] cut off Russian capital from any contact with international capital; the cancellation of state loans and the nationalisation of the banks destroyed in one blow the dominance of finance capital. Nationalisation of the banks (of credit) and transport transferred the remaining capitalist industry and trade into the hands of the proletariat state, the monopolist of credit and transport. If capital had continued to function in industry and trade, if it had remained *qua* capital, i.e. a tool of exploitation of the proletariat, then it would have been forced to submit to regulation by the proletarian state and to return a portion of the surplus value to the proletariat in the form of taxes due to the proletarian state. In this way, not only the *rate of exploitation* would have been reduced, but capital would also in a certain sense have been *in the service of the proletarian state*, being bound to the latter by treaty (credit and the like) relations. The proletariat, using the reins of credit and transport, would have organised the national economy *with the aid of the services of capital.*

7 The very character of the revolution was, of course, beyond doubt. This was underlined especially starkly by the decree on the abolition of the law of inheritance of 1 May 1918 that opened with the following words: 'Inheritance, whether by law or by will, is abolished'. But this too was a measure that took effect only after death and not immediately; furthermore it appeared only six months after the October overthrow.

8 Para. 1 of the decree begins in typically laconic fashion: 'All foreign trade is to be nationalised'. See 'Sbornik dekretov 1917–1918 g'., Moscow, 1920, p. 24. [see James Bunyan, and H.H. Fisher, *The Bolshevik Revolution 1917–1918. Documents and Materials* (Stanford, California: Stanford University Press, 1961), pp. 617–618].

The tendency towards this kind of transitional organisation of the national economy, based on cooperation between capital and the proletariat on the ground and within the framework of the new proletarian social order (known as state capitalism, a clumsy term as the state here is not capitalistic), found its expression in the fact that for almost nine months after the October overthrow, industrial and trade enterprises were nationalised by the central power of the Soviets only as a punitive measure and only in individual instances. In the period from October 1917 to 1 June 1918, only 487 enterprises were nationalised (and confiscated), and in over 70 % of these cases they were nationalised for non-fulfillment of the decree on workers' control [*rabochii kontrol'*] or because the enterprises were closed arbitrarily by the owners; thus, only 20 % of these enterprises were nationalised and confiscated by the central authorities, the remainder by regional or other local organs of power.[9]

Industrial and trade capital were not expropriated, merely placed under *workers' control*. The demand for workers' control, the former slogan of the proletariat before the October Revolution, was realised by the law on workers' control that was passed on 14 November 1917.[10] For infringing on this law on workers' control, the capitalist was punished by confiscation of his enterprise.

This law threatened the holy of holies of capital, for point 7 decreed in laconic fashion typical of the proletarian revolution that 'commercial secrets are abolished'. Workers' control itself was an expression of a healthy proletarian aspiration to rein in the capitalists, who had until then run 'their' enterprises without any supervision and sabotaged production with impunity. But the very idea of workers' control that emerged from the uncertainty in that initial indecisive period of the proletarian revolution, namely the idea of first learning from the class enemy the art of managing all aspects of an enterprise – technical, administrative, commercial –, by supervising all his activities and thus observing all his habits, this was undoubtedly a utopian idea. In reality, the capitalist would not agree to take on the task of teaching the proletarians the art of managing an enterprise, nor would the organs of workers' control be able, within the context of the proletarian dictatorship, to restrict themselves to supervision. As a result of its half-heartedness, workers' control turned out to be an *unsuccessful* attempt at worker administration.

This same sign of half-heartedness also lay behind another failed attempt of this period – the attempt to organise joint share companies, in which the

9 See V. Miliutin, 'K voprosu o natsionalizatsii promyshlennosti,' in 'Narodnoe khoziaistvo' no. 5 for 1918.

10 [See Bunyan and Fisher, *The Bolshevik Revolution 1917–1918*, pp. 308–310.]

proletarian soviet state and capital (Russian and foreign) would invest as shareholders. Already in April 1918, negotiations took place in this direction between the Soviet government and wealthy capitalist businessmen headed by Meshcherskii,[11] who represented not only Russian but also foreign capital, indeed both Entente capital and German capital. The goal of these negotiations was the creation of an enormous metallurgical trust, which together with combined enterprises was supposed to incorporate almost all of Russia's heavy industry.

This tendency of proletarian power to accommodate capital on the basis of the *new* social order (the soviet, i.e. proletarian, order) was *utopian* at a time when capital, under threat of expropriation, was still fighting for dominance over society, when the battle was still being fought over the question of the very *system* of society. Only *after* expropriation was carried out and the reality of the new social system was beyond any doubt, could the question of class struggle *within the framework* of the new social system be raised; only then could proletarian state power become a tool for the forcible organisation of class collaboration of capital and the proletariat, i.e. giving this collaboration, insofar as it was necessary, forms that were most favorable to the proletariat.

But the proletarian revolution did not merely feel its way forward, it was forced from the very outset to make the most significant concessions and restrictions.

The presence of *two* revolutionary forces ensured that the *complex nature of the Russian Revolution* was inevitable.

The particular tasks, which the Russian proletariat had to and still have to resolve, are not only the result of the *dual* nature of the Russian Revolution, but also of the *peculiarities of the combination* of the anti-capitalist with the anti-feudal revolution briefly sketched out above.

The fact that in the beginning most of the revolutionary changes in terms of their scope (not in terms of their significance of course) unfolded not in Russia's large-scale economy, but in its small-scale economy. This explains the relatively slow, developmentally retarded course of the Russian proletarian revolution, which paved the way for the enormous spontaneity of the peasant revolution.

The victory of the revolution could be neither achieved nor consolidated without the *alliance* of both revolutionary forces. The external political expression of this was the coalitional form of the first Soviet government, which included Left SRs in addition to Communists. As a result of the revolution, the

11 See G. Tsiperovich, 'Sindikaty i tresty v Rossii', Moscow, 1919, pp. 164–7.

proletariat took control of industry and transport, and the peasantry took control of agriculture (this realised one of the main slogans of the revolution: 'Land to the Peasants, Factories to the Workers').

But the economy of the proletariat, as it is becoming socialist, and the economy of the peasantry, as it is turning to simple commodities production, despite all the differences between these modes of production, must remain bound by the strongest social bond of *material* connections, for the socialist mode of production cannot survive without grain, wool, leather, and so on, and the simple commodity society cannot survive without transport, textiles, nails, agricultural machinery and tools, and so on. Both therefore need the economic alliance of these two basic forces of the Russian Revolution. is therefore a necessity for both.

But just as necessary to both of them was a military political alliance as well. The peasantry, a majority of the population, inevitably constitutes the bulk of the revolutionary army; but it has never been the organising force anywhere; indeed it cannot be such a force given the amorphous nature of simple commodities production. The linchpin of the entire military and administrative apparatus of the revolution is the proletariat, whose organisational abilities overcome peasant atomisation.

The existence of two revolutionary forces, whose individual goals are not identical, requires that mutual *concessions* be made in the interest of achieving an alliance of these forces. Such concessions were made by both sides more than once in the course of the revolution, indeed very significant concessions. The proletariat made, above all, *significant concessions* on the issue that was most important to the peasantry, the *agrarian question*; the significance of these concessions derived from the aforementioned relationship between the anti-capitalist and anti-feudal revolution. Precisely because it was the hegemon of the revolution, the proletariat made the first significant concession. The very birth of the Russian proletarian revolution, the October overthrow, was tied to this concession, indeed it was made possible by it.

In the days of the October overthrow, the Russian proletariat did not propose a proletarian agrarian programme, but rather a peasant agrarian programme. There was a peasant, not a proletarian, expropriation of the expropriators in agriculture, *a partitioning* [*razdel*] *not only of the lands of the feudal lords, but also of capitalist non-peasant agriculture* (although not as private property, but as usufruct for the peasant petty bourgeoisie).

This very concession by the proletariat led to a *merger of the two revolutions*, the proletarian and the peasant. With this merger, the former got the support of the enormous majority of the population and the enormous majority of the army that it was missing, and the latter got the cohesion and leadership that it was missing. The revolution of the unorganised mass of the peasantry and the revolution of the organised proletarian minority of the population were fused into a victorious revolution of the organised masses.

This concession took legal form in *the decree on the nationalisation of the land.*[12] It is well-known that nationalisation of the land was the agrarian programme (and the duping of the peasantry) of the main party in the government coalition of the February Revolution, the Socialist Revolutionary Party, which before and after the October overthrow was the proletarian revolution's most damnable enemy. The party's policy of land nationalisation expressed both the historically progressive anti-feudal tendency of the peasant (agrarian) revolution and also its historically reactionary tendency, directed not only against capital but also against the large-scale economy [*krupnoe khoziaistvo*] in general. This latter tendency, which was very typical of petty pre-capitalist proprietors, being the independent commodity producers who did not exploit wage labour, was expressed in the principle of *levelling land-use* [*uravnitel'noe zemlepol'zovanie*] on the basis of the family household without utilising the labour of non-family members.

But the decline in the productive forces of the peasant economy during the war did not allow the peasants to become stronger, to take economic control of all the lands on which large-scale agriculture had been conducted before the revolution.

More than a year passed[13] before those lands that were not yet controlled by the peasantry began to see large-scale, not capitalist, but proletarian agriculture being restored – i.e. soviet farms, but on a much smaller scale than before. While even in 1916 privately owned sown land in European Russia amounted to 10½% of the total sown area (before the war it was undoubtedly more, possibly 15%), in 1919 in the Russian interior only 3% (in Ukraine only 4%) of the total suitable land[14] was in the hands of Soviet and collective farms (and significantly less in terms of sowing area); in other words, the potential scope of large-scale agriculture shrank to at least *a third*. The wretched state of this large-scale agriculture in 1919 (one and a half years after the upheaval of autumn 1917) was illustrated by the existence of only 10 per cent of the needed horse stock and a near complete absence of unspoiled dead

12 [*A Selection of Official Documents on Internal Policies*, ed. Mervyn Matthews (New York: Taplinger Publishing Co., Inc., 1974), pp. 317–320.]

13 The organization of Soviet farms on a statewide scale began in February 1919, see N. Bogdanov, 'Organizatsiia sovetskikh khoziaistv,' no. 6 of 'Narodnoe khoziaistvo' for 1919.

14 See N. Osinskii, 'Vosstanovlenie krest'ianskogo khoziaistvo v Rossii i nashi zadachi', Moscow, 1922, p. 5.

inventory [*ispravnyi mertvyi inventar'*].[15] In this way, the agrarian revolution destroyed large-scale agriculture, even if, given the special conditions under which this happened, it maintained the possibility of its *partial* reconstruction.

It is just as telling that the law on the nationalisation of the land makes no mention anywhere of *agricultural industry*, which it thus rejects de jure. Meanwhile, Russia had on hand a large-scale capitalist sugar industry of 600,000 desiatins of sugar plantations, producing about 100 million poods of sugar with a value in excess of 200 million roubles; i.e. $\frac{1}{25} - \frac{1}{30}$ of the value of all agricultural production (of European Russia) and $\frac{1}{8} - \frac{1}{10}$ of its total market production. This industry employed hundreds of thousands of agricultural seasonal workers, not to mention the other branches of agricultural industry. Agricultural industry hung by a thread, and only in 1918, six months after the law on nationalisation of the land was issued, was the sugar industry's right to exist strengthened. The connection between the other branches of agricultural industry and large-scale agriculture was severed.

The decree on nationalization of the land, which had realised all the demands of the peasantry on the agrarian question, was, together with the exit from the imperialist war, the basis of the political alliance between the proletariat and the peasantry, an alliance which secured the support of the peasantry for the proletariat in its conquest and subsequent consolidation of political power. But this law, in creating the initial and necessary precondition of the proletarian revolution – the transfer of power into the hands of the proletariat –, also meant the essential *limitation of the proletarian revolution*; in agriculture, large-scale enterprises were not nationalised but destroyed and broken up, and instead of the proletarian expropriation of capital there was a petty bourgeois (peasant) expropriation. This not only strengthened the material one-sidedness [*veshchnaia odnostoronnost'*], the economic incompleteness of the proletarian revolution, but also tangibly *limited the social basis of the proletarian revolution.*

Millions of agricultural workers disappeared, most of them having been turned into petty proprietors.[16] Ultimately, *the agricultural basis of industry*

15 See N. Bodganov, 'Organizatsiia sovetskikh khoziaistv,' article in no. 6 of 'Narodnoe khoziaistvo' for 1919.

16 In 1919, there were only about 54,000 permanent workers on Soviet farms. See the article by N. Bogdanov in 'Trudakh s.-kh. sektsii Inst. ekonomich. Issled'., NKF, Petrograd, 1921; S. Strumilin (see his article 'Sostav proletariata Sovetskoi Rossii v 1917–1919 gg.,' in the collection 'Dva goda diktatury proletariata', p. 14) gives the following figures for agricultural workers for European Russia (in thousands):

and town also shrank, because the most nationalised part of agriculture, where commodity production for the market was strongest – capitalist agriculture – turned into a small-peasant economy, more like a consumer economy; this loss of marketability [*tovarnost'*] alone must have amounted to at least one sixth of the entire agricultural production (by value) destined for the market.[17]

---

in 1917 2100
by 1919 34
so the latter had shrunk by 62 times over the former. According to data in the same article by Strumilin, agricultural workers as a portion of all workers were:
in 1917 30.8%
by 1919 1.3%
so a large portion of the proletariat had, practically speaking, disappeared.

17 If we assume a marketability of the peasant economy of 25%, and that of private ownership of 70%. On grain, see P. Popov, 'Proizvodstvo khleba v R.S.F.S.R. i federiruiushchikhsia s neiu respublikakh', 1921, p. 20.

CHAPTER 3

The Interference of External Forces and Its Consequences

1. The interference of global capital. 2. The prolongation and intensification of the Civil War. 3. The breaking of economic connections and its consequences. 4. Economic expediency and revolutionary necessity. 5. Expropriation of the owners. 6. The peasantry's concessions to the proletariat.

Despite these aforementioned limitations, however, the Russian proletarian revolution seemed to be guaranteed slow but unimpeded development: the exceptional concentration of industry (and of transport, two-thirds of which was already nationalised under tsarism), the explicitly proletarian and toiling character of the population due to the semi-colonial character of the country, the extremely weak resistance of the old ideology and the old political (state) organisation – this was all highly conducive to the unimpeded development of the proletarian revolution.

While this did not happen, while the Civil War, basically a stage of the political revolution, was dragged out for a full *three years* and attained an improbable degree of bitterness and tenacity, this was by no means due to the internal forces of the Russian counter-revolution. On the contrary, it became clear in its very first months that the proletarian revolution achieved complete and unconditional superiority over its internal enemies: by February 1918 all of Russia as far as Chita was Soviet.

The duration and intensity of the Civil War was a consequence of the relative persistence of capitalism not inside of Russia, but *outside of* it. *Foreign capital* stepped in as a powerful ally in support of Russia's ruling classes, which had been overthrown by the Russian Revolution. Foreign capital in all the large capitalist countries (all the great powers), all of *world capital*, stepped in. World capital's move against the Russian proletarian revolution, which included the deployment of German, Austro-Hungarian, French, English, Italian, American, Japanese, and other, armed forces against it, revealed the *world historical* character of the Russian proletarian revolution.

World capital joined the fight against the Russian proletarian revolution as a partner of the counter-revolution, but it was unable to stem the powerful revolutionary process, to extinguish the fire of proletarian revolution, because capital found itself in a double bind in this battle. First, it was hamstrung by

 | HTTPS://DOI.ORG/10.1163/9789004765313-007

the internal struggle going on among the capitalist great powers, which meant that they were only able to direct part of their forces to strangling the Russian proletarian revolution (even this part was not always put into action and not by everyone, because at times they saw the Russian proletarian revolution not just as their enemy, but also as the enemy of their enemies). Second, it was hamstrung by the widely spreading wave of universal proletarian sympathy for the Russian proletarian revolution and the enthusiasm for it that also captivated proletarians in soldiers' uniforms. This very soon led the capitalists to see that the Russian proletarian revolution had not only world-historical significance for capital, but also for the proletariat, that it was a revolution not only for the Russian proletariat but also for the entire world proletariat. Long before its own proletarian revolution, then, the world proletariat through its support of the Russian proletariat weakened the onslaught of world capital on the Russian proletarian revolution to such an extent that the latter managed to resist this onslaught. The clear revolutionary energy of the Russian proletariat and of the Russian peasantry organised by it – together with the formerly hidden revolutionary energy of the world proletariat – turned out to be stronger than the counter-revolutionary energy that the former ruling classes of Russia, which had been toppled by the Russian revolution, and world capital, could muster *inside Russia*.

But while world capital did not manage to turn the wheel of history backwards, it did strengthen to an extraordinary degree the resistance of the former ruling classes of Russia that had been toppled by the revolution. It was this resistance that forged the majestic period of the Civil War from 1918 to 1920, this heroic era of the Great Russian Revolution.

Above all, this resistance *prolonged* open civil war, transforming it from the short episode of the Krasnov march on Petrograd to an extended period of the Russian Revolution which lasted more than three years (from October 1917 to the destruction of the Wrangel' khanate in November 1920). The offensive launched by the German army in February 1918 did not only end Soviet power in Ukraine, turning the latter into a site of a most brutal civil war waged for the time being by the occupation regime, but also enabled both the Cossack counter-revolution (in the Don and Kuban regions) and the Volunteer Army to consolidate (strengthen), because it drew all the attention and all the forces of the young Soviet regime to the West and South-West. After the collapse of German imperialism, both the Ukrainian and the Cossack counter-revolution (in the Don and Kuban region) and also the Volunteer Army of Krasnov, Denikin, and Wrangel' relied for survival throughout on direct financial and military support (weapons and personnel) from the Entente; in the South, the Red Army fought against English, French, Italian, Greek, and Rumanian troops and the navies of all the Entente powers. The counter-revolution in the East began in May 1918 with the Entente-inspired armed uprising by Czechoslovak legions, which led later to the establishment of the Kolchak regime [*Kolchakovshchina*] that was not defeated until 1920. Kolchak, no less than Denikin and Wrangel', relied on direct support from the Entente.

The counter-revolution in the North began in August 1918 when English and American troops landed in Archangel (in July 1918, an Anglo-French landing party occupied Murmansk) and ended with their withdrawal. A counter-revolutionary 'government' in the coastal region of the Pacific survived (until 1922) only at the points of Japanese bayonets. Almost all the counter-revolutionary bonfires were lit, by the way, directly by foreign capital, and in all of them without exception the flames were fanned by the efforts of that same foreign capital, without which they would have been quickly extinguished.

In precisely the same way, the counter-revolution in the Western border regions of the former Russian Tsarist Empire, which led to the founding of a series of new states, relied initially on anti-democratic German imperialism and served as its direct instrument (at that time, Poland, Lithuania, Finland and others actively sought out suitable German princes for the new thrones being created); later they relied on the 'democratic' imperialism of the Entente powers (as a result of which the thrones were themselves replaced by the most democratic republics).

The longer the Civil War lasted, the clearer became the *internal weakness* of the Russian counter-revolution, and the more resolutely world capital shifted from supporting Russia's toppled ruling classes to using them as common mercenaries; ultimately, the national pride of the Russian landowners and capitalists had turned into the purest lackeyism [*lakeistvo*] vis-à-vis the 'Allies', until they had licked every 'Allied' boot, and until the only trace left of their nationalism was the permanent national betrayal of Russia, the sellout of its present, and the anticipated sellout of its future.

Intensification of the internal counter-revolution, however, not only prolonged the Civil War, it also *exacerbated* it. In a sentimental understanding of history – typical of those people who are extraordinarily sensitive to the cruelties of the proletarian dictatorship (although it was the lot of the proletariat to be the object of the cruelties of others) – this exacerbation can be seen in a comparison of November 1917, when imprisoned White Guard Officers and cadets (*iunkery*) and even General Krasnov were released[1] (and, of course,

1 In contrast, the educated and noble representatives of the landowning aristocracy, insulted

immediately went to the Don region to organise one of the major centres of the counter-revolution under the protection of German bayonets), and the Red Terror of the later period.

In sociological terms, the intensification of the Civil War was characterised by the coexistence on the territory of the former Russian Empire and even on the territory of Great Russia *of states which were differentiated exclusively from each other only by their class characteristics*: Red Russia of the soviets and White Russia of Kolchak, Denikin, and Wrangel'. The sharpening class struggle meant, therefore, that the *enemy classes of the same* (Russian) *society were organised as independent class states* (the Red and the White) with all the military and administrative apparatus and so on typical of a state. The struggle between the Red and the White Armies was but the military expression of this fact. The Red dictatorship of the proletariat, organised as the Soviet state, confronted the White dictatorship of the landowners and capitalists, organised as the state of the 'Supreme Ruler' [*verkhovnyi pravitel'*] Kolchak and his 'heirs'. This meant the political injustice of the exploiters in Red Russia against the political injustice of the exploited in White Russia; the Red Army against the White Army; shootings by the VChK against hangings by the White counter-intelligence forces; Red Terror against White Terror.

The state organisation of hostile classes, the organisation of states defined by class, also meant the *territorial demarcation* of class dictatorships, which were separated from one another by a flexible, highly mobile, but no less real line of fronts, a ring encircling Soviet Russia. From 1918 to 1920, the territory of Russia thus broke apart into a *terrain of revolution and a terrain of counter-revolution*. In the South and especially in the West, from the Black Sea to the Arctic Ocean, the territory of the purely class states was bordered by a belt of newly formed states and autonomous regions (Finland, Estonia, Latvia, Lithuania, Poland, Belorussia, Ukraine, Crimea, Georgia, Azerbaidzhan, Armenia), in which the class character of the Civil War was obscured for a more or less long time by the struggle for national liberation, which was exploited by the ruling classes and world capital for their own ends.

Acting as a counter-revolutionary force in the Russian Revolution, world capital thereby strengthened the counter-revolution far beyond the limits of its internal possibilities, prolonging and intensifying open civil war; this trans-

---

to the very depths of their pockets, and the representatives of capital, immediately unleashed merciless destruction upon the mob that had dared to rebel; it left it to the White Guardist socialist [*belo-sotsialisticheskie*] rhetoricians to express their indignation about the cruelties of the Red Terror. On this White literature, see e.g., Gul', 'Ledianoi pokhod,' among others.

formed the struggle for power into a *struggle for naked survival*, because world capital was seeking to make it impossible for the national economy of Russia to function at all.

Soviet Russia was transformed into a severely isolated economic region (an 'isolated state', although not in Thünen's sense). This isolation was expressed clearly enough in terms of foreign trade turnover:

	Imports (in millions of poods)	Exports[2] (in millions of poods)
1917	178.0	59.6
1918	11.5	1.8
1919	0.5	0.0 (109 poods)!
1920	5.2	0.7
1913 (for comparison)	936.6	1472.1

Even in comparison with 1917, isolation left a lot to be desired. World capital had managed to erect a complete and unconditional *blockade* of the proletarian revolution. When the defeat of the Russian counter-revolution was beyond doubt, world capital took pains to erect that wall of aforementioned 'independent' and 'democratic' republics from the Black Sea to the Arctic Ocean.

Soviet Russia's economic isolation (unlike its isolation during the imperialist war, this was *complete* economic isolation) led inevitably to a further *decline in the export sectors of the economy* – production of wheat, barley, flax, oil, timber and so on, and to a *supply crisis* in transport, industry, and agriculture affecting numerous materials which had been received from abroad during the imperialist war, if in significantly lower quantities than before the war (as a result of this, supplies of these materials had already been significantly exhausted even before the October Revolution).

Even more significant were the consequences of the *disintegration of Russia's economic territory* that Civil War brought to the territories of revolution and counter-revolution and the resultant dislocation of the economic organism of Russia. The Brest Peace, forced by German imperialism on a newborn and

2 Figures for 1917 from P. Kogan and I. Shenkman, 'Eksportnye vozmozhnosti Rossii,' p. 202; for 1918–1920 from the collection 'Mirovoe khoziaistvo,' p. 149.

thus militarily helpless Soviet Russia, and the worsening counter-revolution in the Cossack regions and the region of the Volunteer Army, had already inflicted extremely severe wounds on the economic organism of Soviet Russia. Russia was torn into two parts: Soviet Russia retained about two-thirds of the population, a large part of the metalworking industry, three quarters of the textile industry, but only 45 % of wheat production, 37 % of barley production, 8 % of sugar production, 10 % of coal extraction, 23 % of iron smelting, and 33 % of the production of metal products.[3] The loss of Baku and Groznyi deprived Soviet Russia of oil. The mutiny [*miatezh*] of the Czechoslovak legions cut Soviet Russia off from the Volga region, the Urals, Siberia, and Turkestan, thereby depriving it of what was left of the metallurgical industry, all cotton, Siberian cow butter, and, finally, of the most important remaining grain regions, which at the same time were producing agricultural raw materials.

The Civil War *completely crippled the economic organism of Soviet Russia*: Soviet Russia was a region carved out by the knife of the Civil War, a region in which metalworking and textile industries predominated, but with no mining and metallurgy, a region of small-scale agriculture and consumer farming with a developed culture of several trade crops (flax, hemp, and sunflowers) and a developed cottage industry, but a completely inadequate production of grain, sugar, and livestock products. These material shortcomings rendered the economy of Soviet Russia completely unviable. While the borders of this region were constantly changing, the above picture did not.

The dislocation of Russia's economy caused by the Civil War (with the strong support of anti-democratic German imperialism and the 'democratic' imperialism of the Entente powers) resulted in all kinds of completely unavoidable *supply crises* and consequently the use everywhere of *substitutes* for scarce products.

For White Russia, these crises were mitigated by the material support it received from world capitalism; for Soviet Russia, they were all the more severe and hopeless.

From a grain surplus of 775 million poods in pre-revolutionary Russia (not including Poland), only 87 million poods was in the territory of Soviet Russia in the period from 1918 to 1920;[4] as a consequence of the decline in agri-

---

3 See 'Biulleten' VSNKh,' no. 1, Moscow, April 1918, pp. 5, 7, and 8; and 'Trudy 1-go Vserossiiskogo S'ezda Sovetov Narodnogo Khoziaistva', Moscow, 1918, p. 24.

4 If we exclude Ukraine, the South East, and Siberia in Soviet Russia, but include all grain-producing regions of Great Russia, i.e. both the Volga and Urals regions, which were occupied by the Whites several times. The average figures for 1912–13 are taken from P. Popov, op. cit, p. 8.

culture during the imperialist war, Soviet Russia became a country *with a grain deficit.*

The extremely grave food-supply crisis (especially grain) required that food substitutes be sought (starting with feed grains: oats and barley). This led, on the one hand, to a catastrophic contraction of the urban population, to the *absorption of the cities* in the entire consuming region (in the non-black earth region from 1916 to 1920, cities lost more than 35 per cent of their population, even more in Central Russia, and about 27 per cent in the rest of Russia). Petrograd was most affected, losing 62 per cent of its population between 1910 and 1920 and being thrown back a half-century into the past (this decline was even greater when compared with 1917, when, as a result of the concentrated arms industry, the population undoubtedly was significantly larger than it had been in 1910). Moscow, in the three years between 1917 and 1920, lost 49 per cent of its population, shrinking to the population levels of 1897.[5] On the other hand, this crisis led to a noticeable *development of urban agriculture* (vegetable plots [*ogorodnichestvo*]).

The same thing happened in all factory regions. Grain was replaced by potatoes. According to P. Popov,[6] vegetable plots did not contract at all between 1913 and 1921 on average across the entire Republic, despite the aforementioned contraction of the cities, and thus grew in relation to the urban population, while agriculture in general shrank by one and a half to two times.

Equally significant was the growth of goat-raising in the cities.

The loss of the coal regions of the Don Basin and the oil fields of the Caucasus led to a critical *fuel crisis*, to a reduction of fuel shipments in 1919 and 1920 to less than a third of the levels of 1916, and mineral fuel was substituted with *wood fuel*, which until then had mainly been used for domestic heating. The scale of this shift can be seen from the following figures:

---

5 See N. Oganovskii, 'Ocherki po ekonomicheskoi geografii SSSR', Moscow, 1924, p. 72, and 'Stat. ezhegodnik 1918–20 gg'., Moscow, 1922, pp. 332 and 342. In reality, the losses of urban population were even greater, as the 1916 figures include only cities, while the 1920 figures include city and urban-type settlements.

6 See P. Popov, 'Tesizy doklada TsSU 4 – i sessii VTsIK', p. 3. In the collection, 'Na novykh putiakh', ed. V, 'Sel'skoe khoziaistvo', Moscow, 1922, in a special article by P. Shitt and I. Sokolov, 'Ocherki sovremennogo sostoianiia i vozmozhnykh perspektiv na blizhaishee budushchee dlia sadovodstva, ogorodnichestva I niogradarstva v SSSR', on p. 293 we read: 'vegetable plots for personal consumption spread widely everywhere and in the most diverse forms; and the RSFSR is, of course, indebted to them in its fight against the marauding enemy. It is unfortunately not possible to ascertain statistically how widespread these vegetable plots were. The agricultural census for 1920 did not include vegetable plots in the cities'.

Share of Fuels in percent[7]			
	coal	oil	wood
1916	67	19	14
1918	14!	12	71!
1919	3.5!!	5!	88!
1920	36	10.5	50

Two other (less significant) fuel substitutes were peat, and coal extracted in the Moscow region.

Rise in Peat Mining since 1918 in millions of poods[8]	
1913	80
1916	83
1917	71
1918	58
1919	67
1920	92

Rise in Moscow Coal Mining in millions of poods	
1912	13.8[9]
1914	19
1917	45
1918	24.4

7 For 1916, calculated according to figures for fuel shipments. See 'Plan elektrifikatsii RSFSR', pp. 26 and 61. For 1918–1920, calculated for fuel shipments taken from 'Russkaia promyshlennost' v 1921 g. i ee perspektivy', p. lxxiii.

8 See 'Russkaia promyshlennost' v 1921 g.', p. lxxi.

9 See 'Plan elektrifikatsii', p. 58.

(*cont.*)

	Rise in Moscow Coal Mining in millions of poods
1919	25.6
1920	35

The transition to wood fuel meant that the boilers of locomotives and in factories all over Soviet Russia had to be modified. Wherever liquid fuel had been used (e.g. in automobiles), gasoline was replaced with various mixtures of spirits, wood alcohol, and so on.

The supply crisis in oil products was so severe that when Baku once again became Soviet oil reserves remained (on 1 May 1920) less than 1% of the reserves on the same date in 1916 and 1917 and less than one half percent of the reserves on 1 May 1915, i.e. for all practical purposes they had been completely exhausted, and the same was true with kerosene and lubricating oils.[10]

To these two basic supply crises (grain and fuel), caused by the dislocation of the national economy of Russia, were added numerous others for the same reason: a hunger for metals, due to the loss of the metallurgical industry in the South and in the Urals, which led to the substitution of metal ores with scrap metal as the raw material for metal production; a hunger for raw materials in all their diverse forms (wool, oil, leather etc); a food crisis alongside the basic grain crisis (a hunger for fats, sugar, a meat and fish crisis, etc). Everywhere the supply crisis led to the search for substitutes: wool was replaced with rags [*ugary*], sugar with saccharine, etc. The idea of making use of everything that would normally be discarded even received its own organisational expression (so-called 'Centro-utility' [*Tsentroutil'*]).

But everywhere the substitutes were but a weak, partial *replacement, insufficient not only in quality but also in quantity*.

But it was not enough that Soviet Russia in economic terms was a living piece carved from the national economic body of Russia, the borders of this piece were changing constantly: like an amoeba, Soviet Russia expanded in the course of the Civil War – *hundreds and thousands of versts* – to the South, then to the East, then to the North, then to the West, and then it con-

10 See 'O neftesnabzhenii' in no. 11–12 of 'Narodnoe khoziaistvo' for 1920.

tracted again. Not taking into account the smaller advances and retreats, the White and Red Armies covered the journey from the Volga into the interior of Siberia *three times* and from Great Russia to the Black Sea *four times*, and while the population of Soviet Russia rarely fell below 60–70 million people, i.e. half of the total population of today's Soviet Russia, only one ninth of its current European territory with one sixth of today's population was *continuously* under Soviet power.[11] In Kiev, for example, Soviet power was established three times, in Odessa four times, and for the entire period of 1917 to 1920, Kiev experienced sixteen changes of power.[12] This resulted in complete *instability in economic relations*. It was best illustrated by the figures on the destruction of transport. During the Civil War, the following were destroyed:[13]

Railway bridges	3,672
Regular bridges	3,597
Railway tracks	more than 1,700 versts
Railway depots and workshops	381
Civic buildings	Ca. 5,000 totalling 117,000 square sazhen'
Telegraph wires	86,500 versts
Telephones wires	86,500 versts
Telephone apparatuses	10,896
Telegraph apparatuses	4,331

In 1918 and 1919, approximately 60 percent of the railway network was in the hands of the Whites, and in 1920 approximately 54,000 versts or about 80 per cent of it.

But apart from the extraordinary fluidity of the Civil War fronts, this war also differed from usual wars in that it was literally everywhere, that in hidden form it spilled across the entire territory of the country that had gone through revolution, flaring up in the least expected places; the Civil War, lasting an entire era, therefore led everywhere to an unparalleled *disintegration of economic infrastructure* (transport, post, etc).

The destructive consequences of this breakdown in economic infrastructure, quite unique in scale and duration, could be seen above all in *large-scale*

11 This includes the following provinces: Vitebsk, Vladimir, Vologda, Ivanovo-Voznesensk, Kaluga, Kostroma, Moscow, Nizhegorod, Novgorod, Rybinsk, Riazan', Severodvinsk, Smolensk, Tver', Cherepovets; population figures are from the 1920 census.

12 See 'Sotsialisticheskii vestnik', no. 11, p. 12.

13 See 'Piat' let vlasti Sovetov' published by VTsIK, Moscow, 1922, p. 427.

industry. This was precisely because the large-scale enterprise, both in terms of its supply of the means of production and the sale of its products, was connected with a large economic territory (often all of Russia and even a larger region than all of Russia, as was the case, for example, for many a giant Petrograd plant, which received metal from the Donbass, oil from Baku, coal from England, etc., and supplied its products perhaps to Siberia). For this very reason then, the larger the enterprise, the more likely it was to be brought to a standstill by the breakdown in economic infrastructure. By contrast, a small enterprise, and especially artisans or handicraftsmen working with local materials and for local consumers, remained less sensitive to the breakdown in economic infrastructure, reacting to the Civil War only if it impacted their location directly. This significant and extended breakdown of economic infrastructure, then, led to a relative *decline in large-scale industry* and a relative growth in small-scale industry.

An idea of the scale of this shift can be seen in a comparison of the value of gross production of large and small industry before the war and in 1920:[14]

14 See N. Vorob'ev, 'Izmeneniia v russkoi promyshlennosti v period voiny i revoliutsii' in no. 4–6 of 'Vestnik statistika' for 1923, p. 153, and 'Sbornik statisticheskikh svedenii po SSSR', Moscow, 1924, pp. 212–213.

The same phenomenon is reflected in a comparison of the average efficiency of active and inactive enterprises in 1920: for the former, it was 39.5 hp per enterprise, for the latter it was 43.3 hp, i.e. inactive enterprises had at their disposal on average 10 % *more* horsepower in their mechanical engines than active enterprises had; in short, *larger enterprises were more inactive* (according to data in 'Sbornik stat. svedenii po SSSR', Moscow, 1924, pp. 154–155).

In individual branches, things looked somewhat different, as can be seen from the following table:

		Average Efficiency (in horsepower)		
Branch of Industry	**No. of all enterprises (in thousands)**	**Active enterprises**	**Inactive enterprises**	**Difference (in percent)**
Food	78.5	1.17	13.3	+14
Mining, machine-building, cotton, and electrical works	3.6	565	449	-20
All others	9.0	82	90	+10

In those branches, then, where the choice was only among a few large enterprises, the larger enterprises continued to operate (due to efforts to concentrate production), although their work was very weak (see p. 254). Wherever there were both large and small enterprises, the small enterprises survived.

	Gross production in millions of roubles		
	1913	1920	Percentage ratio of 1920 to 1913 (1913 = 100)
Large industry	5620	1001	18
Small industry	1528 (in 1912–13)	660	43

In other words, large-scale industry contracted by more than five times, small-scale industry by only two times and its share of total gross production of industry, according to these data, rose from 20 to 40 percent, i.e. it almost *doubled.*

The war waged by the former ruling classes, which had been expropriated by the revolution, and by world capital against Soviet Russia was also a world war, *a war of annihilation.* Its main goal was not to defeat the army of the enemy, but to undermine its power, to destroy the base from which it could generate fighting forces; thus, it was about undermining and destroying the national economy of the enemy. And those signs of the decline and collapse of the economy, which we discussed above, show that the common efforts of the 'national forces' of Russian landowners and capitalists and the forces of global capital had not been in vain.

This was why the political struggle of the classes of Russian society took its ultimate *military* form, and the struggle of the revolutionary classes – the proletariat and the peasantry – was transformed into the bitterest fight *for the preconditions* of the new social order, above all *for an integrated* [*tselostnyi*] *economic terrain.* Wherever revolutionary power was established, it was transformed into a military dictatorship, forcing everyone to commit unreservedly to the principle of the new order, 'to the Soviet platform'.

The length and brutality of the Civil War, the fact that the second phase of the proletarian revolution (the political revolution) was *delayed* as a result of the interference of *external* forces, this all led to a unique change in the course of the revolutionary process, to a premature anticipation of the – inevitably distorted – future of the revolution, *to a concentration and deepening of the revolution*; the main features of the later stages of the revolution appeared in exaggerated and thus *sharply defined* form in the current, essentially political, stage of the revolution.

The essence of the political stage of the revolution was the smashing of the machinery of centralised class coercion, of the state machinery of the ruling classes (of capital) overthrown by the revolution, and the organisation of the state machinery of the victorious class, the proletariat.

Political power – the power of one class, as a class, over others – was not an end in itself, but only a *means* of consolidating the economic dominance of the class wielding political power, i.e. a *tool to destroy* the old economic relations and to *defend* the new.

If a revolutionary change in political power is always a prelude to a change in the economic organisation of societe – ahe political stage of revolution introduces its economic stage, then the pace of revolutionary transformation of the economy depends on the escalation of the class struggle at the political stage of revolution. The more tense this struggle for political power becomes, the more desperate is the resistance of those classes that have been overthrown and deprived of control, and the fiercer the civil war, the more formidable the threat of counter-revolution. All the more urgent becomes the political need to defeat economically the counter-revolution, the *revolutionary need to intensify economic revolution*, i.e. the increased use of political power as a weapon to destroy the old economic relations as the source of power (economic and political) of the ruling classes which have been overthrown by the revolution. Stripping the counter-revolution of its power, undermining its economic foundation, becomes a revolutionary necessity, and the stronger the resistance of the counter-revolutionary forces, the more *the economic politics of the revolution go beyond what is directly economically expedient*. Economic inexpediency becomes revolutionary necessity.

Only the insurmountable dimwittedness of the bourgeois and pseudo-socialist philistines (a sign that capitalism is already nearing its end) allows them to see in this an argument against revolution. When an army blows up a railway bridge or a quartermaster's store, if it 'trims away' forests and buildings in order to clear a path for its artillery barrage, then every bourgeois and even every pseudo-socialist sees both economic inexpediency and military expediency in these acts. But the philistine is unable to grasp that economically inexpedient actions can be revolutionarily expedient, as they undermine the power of the counter-revolutionary classes, for while he is able to understand that war is a societal phenomenon with its own logic, he is physically incapable of thinking of the proletarian revolution as a *logical* societal phenomenon, rather than merely as the obsession of an evil mind or as a nasty joke of musty old history.

The economic inexpediency of the deepening economic revolution that occurs under pressure of revolutionary need, is by no means absolute, but is just a result of the premature nature – and because of this the instability – of the changes that have occurred. It is a result of the fact that the revolution is taking (trying to take) its second and third step before it has taken its first, but does so precisely because this is the only way it can finish taking its first step.

The revolutionary process is not changing direction here, but the process does become *concentrated* to a certain degree; the following stage of the revolutionary process is pushed partially into the preceding stage, before this preceding stage is finished. The economic revolution is accelerated, and rather than being prepared by the political revolution, the economic revolution itself prepares the completion of the political revolution, and this of course *increases the costs of the revolution.*

The stability of capitalism outside of Russia, which prolonged and intensified the period of civil war (i.e. basically the political stage of the revolution), led, by the way, to an unusual concentration of the revolutionary process, to an unusually hypertrophied, ugly expression of *this* stage of the entire character of the proletarian revolution, and, at the same time, to a colossal increase in the costs of the revolution, as a result of the destruction of the transforming (changing), i.e. in this case capitalist, economy (consequently, the *large-scale* economy).

The essence of the economic stage of the proletarian revolution is that the productive forces of society, socialised by capitalism, cast off their *capitalist* shell. The replacement of the dictatorship of capital by the dictatorship of the proletariat (the political stage of the revolution) becomes the lever by which the proletariat *expropriates capital* and replaces the capitalist relations of production with socialist relations of production. At the same time this signifies the overcoming of capitalist antagonism between living labour and dead labour, between the working class and the means of production; it signifies the great *synthesis between the societal worker and the social means of production.* The capitalist means of production are replaced by new socialist means of production that are still just taking shape.

The decisive moment of the economic revolution comes when the *socialised* productive forces of society, i.e. large enterprises (in finance, industry, transport, agriculture, trade) *have ceased to serve as a means of exploitation*, and have passed from the hands of capital into the hands of the proletariat. The decisive moment is, therefore, the expropriation of *big* capital and the *transition* from the capitalist administration of large enterprises *to the proletarian administration* of them, the change in *large* enterprises from the command power of capital to the command power of the proletariat. Once this change has occurred, the economic revolution of the proletariat has taken place (although it is, perhaps, not yet consolidated). Middle and petty capitalists can continue to function as capitalists, large capitalists can have great riches at their disposal (palaces, piles of money, valuables, etc), commodity and monetary relations remain untouched, but once these great riches can no longer function *as big capital*, the economic revolution of the proletariat is carried out, for the proletariat has at its disposal the *fundamental* and crucial productive forces of society.

The proletarian revolution, however, is already in process when natural-capitalist [*natural'no-kapitalisticheskie*] relations are only just taking shape under the cover of *commodity* capitalist relations, and the latter still prevail. As a result of this, the transformative (reforming) work of the proletariat during its economic revolution comprises not only, and in fact not so very much, the organisation of the proletarian (socialist) management of production, but the organisation of social production as such in *open* form, i.e. in the replacement of *commodity* capitalist organisation of production by its natural-socialist organisation. But this extremely difficult work of the victorious proletariat is just a *result* of the proletarian economic revolution. The replacement of the capitalist by the proletarian management of production, being a true *turning-point* in the development of the management of production, which according to the level of development of capitalism is characterised by a growing contradiction between the command power of capital and the proletariat, is always reduced to the level of an inert productive force (*instrumentum invocale*); in contrast to this truly economic revolution, *the proletariat, in its efforts to build a natural-socialist planned economy, can only continue and complete the historic work of capital*, namely the overcoming of the market. For the latter, in the contradictory (antagonistic) forms characteristic of capitalism and within the framework of capitalism, also comprises the basic positive essence of capitalist development originating from a simple commodity society; it leads step by step through the individual enterprises first of trade capital (household workers), then of industrial capital (manufacturers and factories), through the syndicates and trusts of monopoly capitalism to the colossuses of finance and state (during the world war) capitalism of our 20th century.

Although the capitalist administration of production is replaced with the proletarian administration of production by the proletarian economic *revolution*, the replacement of anarchic commodity production with planned, natural production is but a *continuation of capitalist evolution* that has been interrupted by the proletarian revolution and continues in new proletarian (socialist) forms.

The economic revolution of the proletariat (in the narrow sense of this word) *does not mean* in itself that the anarchy of commodity production, and the costs of this anarchy, have been *overcome*. The anarchy of production is directly overcome only inasmuch as it is a consequence of the class struggle, and, moreover, only those aspects of this anarchy are overcome which are tied to the capitalist character of anarchic commodity production.

But while the continued existence of medium and petty capital, of private ownership in general and especially by large capitalists whose enterprises have been expropriated by the proletarian revolution, while the continued existence of the market and of commodity-monetary relations cannot by themselves change the achievements of the proletarian economic revolution, and even less negate them (reduce them to nothing), all this – both medium and petty capital, and private ownership by capitalists (particularly large capitalists), and the market with its commodity-monetary relations – are *sources of power* for large-scale capital (and of capital and the proprietary classes in general), and are thus also sources of *counter-revolutionary resistance.*

The prolongation and intensification of the Civil War inevitably, therefore, not only crucially accelerated the expropriation of capital, it also expanded the expropriation of the owners in two ways: first, it *expanded the ranks of the expropriated* to include both medium and petty capital, which was bound by inconspicuous links to the powerful independent commodity producers and elites of the new third estate (the technical intelligentsia), and it extended *expropriation to wealth* that did not function as capital but represented possible (potential) capital. Second, it destroyed the possibility of capital working to *strangle* the market *by force* and suppress commodity-monetary relations, since precisely these were the places which protected capital in the form of trade capital, and where trade capital ended up being the most difficult to seize.

The revolution, then, by not *limiting* itself to the economic ground prepared for it by the preceding capitalist development, and consequently by not limiting itself to economic expediency, *crushed* the counter-revolutionary resistance of capital, annihilating and destroying its economic foundation; this was not enough for dominance but was enough for the struggle for dominance. The proletariat, though, precisely because this ground had not been prepared by capitalism, was unable to get a firm foothold, and not being constrained by considerations of economic expediency inevitably carried within it the germ of partial failures and of a future temporary retreat.

In the atmosphere of heated civil war, any collaboration between capital and the proletarian dictatorship (workers' control, joint shareholding companies, etc) quickly turned out to be a fleeting utopia.

The intervention of world capital, which fanned the dying flames of counter-revolutionary resistance inside Russia, forced the proletariat to take a logical step – the merciless expropriation of large-scale capital and capital in general, the confiscation of the property of the ruling classes, the suppression of the market, and the all-encompassing proletarian organisation of the national economy, which was predicated on overcoming both exploitation and the market.

The basic stages of the expropriation of the owners were as follows:

Expropriation of state capital[15] – Decree on the Formation of the Soviet of People's Commissars [*Sovet Narodnykh Komissarov*] of 25 October 1917.[16]

Expropriation of property – Decree on the Socialisation of the Land of 26 October 1917.[17]

Expropriation of finance capital – Decree on the Nationalisation of Banks of 14 December 1917.[18]

Expropriation of transport capital – Decree on the Nationalisation of the Merchant Marine of 26 January 1918.[19]

Expropriation of loan (primarily foreign) capital – Decree on the Annulment of Loans of 28 January 1918.[20]

Expropriation of trade capital (foreign trade) – Decree on the Nationalisation of Foreign Trade of 23 April 1918.[21]

Expropriation of kulak capital (wealthy peasant capital) – Decree on the Formation of Committees of the Poor [*Komitety bednoty*] of 11 June 1918.[22]

Expropriation of large-scale industrial capital[23] – Decree on the Nationalisation of Large-Scale Industry of 28 June 1918.[24]

Expropriation of trade capital (domestic trade) – Decree on the 'Nationalisation' of Trade of 21 November 1918.[25]

Expropriation of cooperative capital – Resolution of the Presidium of VSNKh [*Vysshii Sovet Narodnogo Khoziaistva*] Depriving the Bourgeoisie of Voting Rights in Cooperatives of 30 November 1918.[26]

---

15 The taking of power [*zavoevanie vlasti*] by the proletariat meant the taking over by the proletarian state of the assets [*kapital*] of the former state of landowners and capitalists; this included also the state railways comprising the largest part of the Russian railway network.

16 [*First Decrees of Soviet Power*, ed. Yuri Akhapkin (Lawrence & Wishart, 1970), pp. 27–28.]

17 [See Bunyan and Fisher, *The Bolshevik Revolution 1917–1918*, pp. 673–685.]

18 [See Bunyan and Fisher, *The Bolshevik Revolution 1917–1918*, pp. 323–325.]

19 [See Bunyan and Fisher, *The Bolshevik Revolution 1917–1918*, pp. 611–612.]

20 [See Bunyan and Fisher, *The Bolshevik Revolution 1917–1918*, pp. 602–604.]

21 [See Bunyan and Fisher, *The Bolshevik Revolution 1917–1918*, pp. 617–618.]

22 [*Intervention, Civil War, and Communism in Russia, April–December 1918*, ed. James Bunyan (Baltimore: The Johns Hopkins Press, 1936), pp. 472–473.]

23 This same decree also nationalised private railways.

24 [*First Decrees of Soviet Power*, pp. 147–153.]

25 [*Intervention, Civil War, and Communism in Russia*, pp. 435–439.]

26 [*First Decrees of Soviet Power*, pp. 117–118; *Intervention, Civil War, and Communism in Russia*, pp. 439–440.]

The Decree on the Nationalisation of the Cooperative (Moscow National) Bank of 7 December 1918.[27]

And expropriation of small-scale industrial capital – Decree on the Nationalisation of Small-Scale Industry of 29 November 1920.[28]

After the initial eight-month period of the Russian Revolution with its indecisiveness and vacillations over the proletariat's economic revolution, the government of the Russian proletariat, under the pressure of the increasingly frenzied Civil War and the direct pressure of Imperial Germany's actions in defense of capitalist ownership after the Brest Peace, declared (proclaimed) by the decree of 26 June 1918 the expropriation of the expropriators, the nationalisation of all large-scale industry. That this declaration was forced at precisely this moment by the circumstances is clear from paras. 3 and 4 of the decree, according to which the owners of the enterprises under threat of the severest penalties were obligated to *remain* at the enterprises and *run them, as they had run them up till then*, until they could be organised by the state administration of nationalised enterprises.[29] The decree of 28 June 1918 immediately deprived capitalists only of their title to the property, leaving in their hands the legal administration of the enterprises and even the profits from them

27 Sobranie uzakonenii i rasporiazhenii pravitel'stva za 1917–1918 gg. Upravlenie delami Sovnarkoma SSSR (Moscow, 1942), pp. 1266–1267.

28 Sobranie uzakonenii i rasporiazhenii pravitel'stva za 1920 g. Upravlenie delami Sovnarkoma SSSR (Moscow, 1943), p. 502.

29 These points read as follows:

3. 'Until the Supreme Council of the National Economy issues a special ruling for each enterprise, the enterprises which have been declared by this decree to be the property of the Soviet Republic are considered in free rental use of the former owners. The boards of directors and the former owners shall continue to finance them according to former principles, and also shall receive income from them according to former principles'.

4. From the moment of the promulgation of the decree, the members of the administration, the directors and other responsible officers of the nationalised industries are responsible to the Soviet Republic both for the integrity and maintenance of the enterprise and for its proper functioning. If they abandon their posts without the explicit permission of the pertinent organs of VSNKh or if there are unjustified omissions in the management of the enterprises, the guilty parties will not only answer to the Republic for this with their entire property, but will also bear heavy criminal liability before the courts of the Republic.

These points drew the following humorous evaluation from the Berlin 'Vorwärts' (issue dated 16 July 1918): 'Sensationally, the decree meant that the Supreme Council of the National Economy of the Soviet Republic has only stipulated the formal right of ownership by the state, while the capitalists are restricted neither in their functions nor in their profits'. But 'Vorwärts' too understood that 'it would be very mistaken to suggest here that by this act the Bolsheviks had conceded and surrendered to the power of capital'.

(admittedly, this was highly problematic at the time). But this decree, of course, strengthened and accelerated the takeover of the enterprises by proletarian organisations. It still took, though, no less than half a year (till the start of 1919) before capitalists were replaced in most enterprises by worker administrations.

Subsequently, the process of expropriation of owners became a broad, unstoppable, all-engulfing torrent.

On the one hand, it encompassed property that did not function as capital. Innumerable regulations by local soviet authorities on confiscations, requisitions, revolutionary taxes and contributions, evictions, packings [*uplotnenie*], etc. turned the bourgeoisie into a unique lumpen-ex-bourgeoisie (a wandering, former bourgeoisie), into a class as deprived of economic influence as the lumpenproletariat had been in capitalist society. An idea of the extent of this process was the fact that even as of 15 March 1923 (i.e. after some buildings which had in fact passed into the hands of the state organs during the Civil War, but officially had been neither nationalised nor municipalised, had actually been returned to their former owners), in all of the cities of the USSR *almost half* (46.5 %) of the total number of brick dwellings were nationalised and municipalised; in the European part of the RSFSR it was almost *two thirds* (64.8 %); in Moscow 95 %; in Leningrad 98.3 %! Even of the non-brick (wooden) dwellings, about two thirds in the capital cities were nationalised as of 15 March 1923, 68 % in Moscow, 64 % in Leningrad. This was the scale of the expropriation of domiciles.[30]

On the other hand, the process of expropriation went beyond large-scale capital.

The decree of 11 June 1918 on the organisation and supply of the village poor [*derevenskaia bednota*] sent the signal *to expropriate petty rural capitalists* (kulaks).[31] In the towns, petty capitalists not affected by nationalisation were expropriated for the most part by local soviet authorities, in the form of municipalisation.

The actual scope of the expropriation of industrial capital was very broad. The 1920 census (carried out on 28 August 1920) revealed more than 37,000 state industrial enterprises with almost 2 million workers at a time when on 1 November 1920 VSNKh in its own report to the VIII Congress of Soviets listed only 4,547 nationalised enterprises with about 1,100,000 workers.[32]

---

30 See 'Narodnoe khoziaistvo SSSR v tsifrakh' published by TsSU, Moscow, 1924, p. 255.

31 Para. 3 of the decree reads: 'The scope of activity of district and village committees of poor peasants includes:…2. Support of local food supply organs by expropriating excess grain from the kulaks and rich peasants'.

32 See 'Narodnoe khoziaistvo SSSR v tsifrakh', published by TsSU, Moscow, 1924, and 'Otchet VSNKh VIII s'ezdu sovetov', Moscow, 1920.

The VSNKh report took account only of those enterprises which had been officially nationalised, i.e. by the highest organs, while the census counted all enterprises that were actually in the hands of the state and its organs. This expropriation of small capitalists was legally formalised by the decision of the Presidium of VSNKh on 29 November 1920, nationalising all industrial enterprises with more than 5 workers where a mechanical engine was present, and all those with more than 10 workers where no mechanical engine was present. But in actuality the expropriation of petty capitalists also included the smallest of capitalists.[33]

A (very incomplete) idea of the pace of the process of capital expropriation is provided by the following data:[34]

In Nationalised Enterprises

	No. of enterprises incl. in the count / No. of workers	On 1 October 1919	On 1 April 1920	On 1 November 1920
In the processing industry	6775 / 1,186,000	2522 / 751,000	4141 / 983,000	4420 / ?
In the raw-material industry	133 / 92,000	? / ?	? / ?	127 / ?
In all industry	6908 / 1,278,000	? / ?	? / ?	4547 / ?

(the numerator is the number of enterprises, the denominator is the number of workers)

The character of the cooperatives, having served as a haven for bourgeois elements, was changed decisively. The decree of 7 December 1918 nationalised the cooperative bank (Moscow National) and merged it with the State Bank, and shortly before this (on 30 November 1918) a decree by the Presidium of VSNKh stripped the bourgeoisie of the right to elect or to be elected to the leading organs of the cooperatives.

Finally, the decree of 21 November 1918 sanctioned the *expropriation of trade capital* and the elimination of free trade that had been broadly carried out by local soviet authorities.[35] The procurement and distribution of all products

33 Thus, according to the 1920 census, almost *one seventh* of the total number of state enterprises consisted of 'enterprises' with *one!* worker (see Naumov, 'Organizatsiia promyshlennosti' in the collection 'Narodnoe khoziaistvo Rossii za 1921–1922 g.', p. 325.

34 See 'Otchet VSNKh VIII s'ezdu sovetov', Moscow, 1920, p. 19.

35 Para. 5 of the decree reads: 'Requisitions and confiscations of wholesale commodity stores

for personal consumption and for the domestic household were proclaimed by this decree 'with the aim of eliminating the apparatus of private trade and ensuring the planned supply of the population with all products' of the People's Commissariat of Food, under whose supervision (by the same decree) the cooperatives were also placed.

The agreement to choke off the market and to ban trade was the *peasantry's fundamental concession to the proletariat*, the equivalent, so to speak, of the peasantry's petty bourgeois expropriation of capitalist agriculture.

The development of the agrarian revolution under the hegemony of the proletariat is a stark departure on this point from the course of agrarian revolutions which occur under the hegemony of capital.

In both cases, agrarian revolution ends feudal exploitation and transforms the feudal peasant into a petty bourgeois peasant. But at the same time as the feudal peasant, the bonded commodity producer, is transformed into a free commodity producer, the appearance of the peasant in the market is wholly and completely in the interests of capital at every moment of the bourgeois revolution, for the market is the foundation on which capital, like Antaeus, builds ever newer forces. The appearance of the peasant in the market, therefore, *clashes* with the interests of the proletariat, for the market is the refuge for the counter-revolutionary partner of the proletariat – for capital. To be able to strangle capital, the proletariat must pull the ground out from under it.

Small-scale production can only progress within a commodity economy; it requires trade, a market, commodity-monetary relations, and it inevitably reacts (responds) to their suppression (especially in the case of the incompletely specialised petty economy – the peasant economy) by *reducing the*

and nationalisation of the corresponding trade firms can only be undertaken by the People's Commissariat of Food....Requisitions, confiscations and the municipalisation of retail shops and firms are carried out only by local organs of the People's Commissariat of Food'. The decree thereby sets certain limits on the expropriation of trade capital; it restricts it. By the end of 1918, this was all carried out only by local authorities.

The pace of the process of destruction of free trade can be assessed to a certain degree from the number of state enterprises working in the free market:

Year	Total number of enterprises included in the count	Number of those working in the free market	As a percentage of the total number
1918	2541	242	9.5
1920	2487	19	0.8

(See 'Stat. ezhegodnik 1918–1920 gg'., 2nd ed., p. 354). In 1918, only a tenth of enterprises worked in the free market; in 1920, there were almost no enterprises of this kind left.

commodity surplus of its own production, and by shifting to a *consumer* (self-serving) type economy. The natural organisation of fifteen million small farmers is not feasible given their dispersed nature.

But the superhuman intensity of the Civil War made it imperative that the proletariat tightly control capital's access to the market it needed for survival, – proletarian power moved, therefore, to a total *ban* on trade, and to the compulsory *surrender* of all surpluses above a certain norm of personal consumption.

And the very complexity of the revolution meant that this necessity for the proletarian revolution also became a necessity for the peasant revolution. For the complex nature of the revolution and the complex nature of the counter-revolution were one and the same, two sides of the same social process.

The inability of the capitalist bourgeoisie to assume the leadership of the peasant revolution meant that the proletariat (*for the first time in the history of mankind*) took up this mantle. The revolutionary alliance of the proletariat and the peasantry caused a counter-revolutionary alliance of the capitalists and the landowners.

But the complex nature of the counter-revolution, for its part, meant that the class struggle of the proletariat against capital became a necessary element (a component part) of the anti-feudal revolution, and the suppression of the counter-revolutionary resistance of capital became *a necessary condition for the victory* of the anti-feudal revolution.

Suppression of the counter-revolutionary resistance of capital during the Civil War, i.e. when the very system of society was still unresolved, was impossible without suppression of the market. For, as already mentioned above, the market is the life-blood of capital, the source of its strength, and so also of its counter-revolutionary strength, and for capital, which has been stripped of the ownership of the means of production, it is the final well of its strength. To deprive capital of its market is to take away its oxygen, without which it cannot survive.

For this reason, the victory of the peasant revolution is impossible without the suppression of the market.

As long as the Civil War lasted – a war to eradicate not only capitalism *but also feudalism*, a war not only for factories for the workers *but also for land* for the peasants, the peasantry was by and large ready to *make this concession*, although in their successful spells Denikin and Kolchak illustrated not only the onslaught of global capital, but also the vacillations of the peasantry, which the ban on trade drove into the camp of the counter-revolution. Every such vacillation brought a sixth of the world (and indirectly even more) into play, because it reverberated in the advances of the White Armies, from the Black Sea, then from the depths of Siberia to the centre of Russia, and another time almost to Moscow itself. These vacillations underlined the importance of the peasantry's concession to the proletariat. For the peasantry's agreement with the suppression of the market meant nothing less than an albeit *temporary refusal to complete* the anti-feudal peasant revolution, namely to turn the peasant, entangled by feudal relations, into a free peasant, i.e. into a peasant who freely disposes of everything he produces. However, as soon as the counter-revolution revealed its seigneurial nature, the peasantry, realising that land was at risk, faced a choice – *concede the land to the landlords or reject freedom of trade* – and the peasantry chose the latter. The peasantry agreed to the hated demand to ban trade, to surrender their surpluses, if (and while) this was necessary in order to secure the land for itself.

The alliance of the proletariat and the peasantry in the Civil War era was based, on the one hand, on the transfer (practically of all) *of the land into the hands of the peasantry and on the proletariat's organisation of the armed defence of the gains of the agrarian revolution, and, on the other hand, on the transfer of political power to the proletariat, on the provision by the peasantry*, as we shall see below, *of the resources to conduct civil war, and on the elimination of the market.*

Of course, the ban on trade and the confiscation of surpluses by no means impacted the various class groups of the peasantry equally. For the poorest (proletarianised and pauperised) and middle strata of the village, the impact was small, for these strata (especially the poor peasants [*bedniaki*]) benefitted from the abolition of trade, because they received supplies of grain and industrial products that they would otherwise have been unable to purchase. For the large-scale capitalist peasantry, the impact in practice amounted to expropriation. Thus, the *anti-capitalist revolution, until then an urban revolution, was now extended to the peasant village*, namely, the class differentiation of the peasantry and a civil war between the various class groups of the peasantry: capitalist (kulak) groups on one side, and proletarian and pauperised (poor) peasants on the other, with petty toiling proprietors (middle peasants [*serednIaki*]) vacillating between the two.

This differentiation of the peasantry occurred along two lines. On the one hand, the industrial proletariat created (in Great Russia in summer 1918, in Ukraine and border regions significantly later) organisations of the village poor (the so-called Committees of Poor Peasants [*kombedy* and *komnezamozhi*]), which in every village became centres of anti-capitalist (anti-kulak) revolution, and rallying points primarily for poor peasants, and also for middle peasants, who followed their example.[36] On the other hand, the peasants of grain-

36 The Committees of Poor Peasants [*komnezamozhi*] still exist (in Ukraine). In the RSFSR,

consuming regions had lived in conditions of feudal exploitation before the revolution and were at the same time most closely bound with the proletariat, for the grain-consuming belt was the main region of the processing industry which drew its workforce from the peasantry which had been half-pauperised by feudalism; this peasantry, in the form of the Red Army and the military food detachments, which were recruited from workers and from peasants of the grain-consuming regions, was mobilised against the large-scale capitalist peasantry of the grain-surplus regions.[37] The grain-consuming region, a region of industry and feudal agriculture, became a *locus of revolution* with a (relatively) unwaveringly revolutionary peasantry; by contrast, the grain-producing border regions, where capitalist agriculture was relatively developed, became a *locus of counter-revolution*, primarily because of the peasantry's vacillations vis-à-vis the counter-revolution; this was a consequence of the preponderance of the large-scale capitalist kulak peasantry and their influence on the middle peasants (labouring owners).[38] In some border regions (in the West and in Ukraine), an additional beneficial condition for counter-revolution was the national factor, and everywhere the geographic possibility of support from world capital.

The class struggle in the countryside was primarily a *struggle for grain*: both the poor peasants and the peasantry of the grain-consuming provinces before and especially during the revolution did not sell as much grain as they bought. Some of the grain that was confiscated with the help of the Committees of Poor Peasants and the food requisitioning detachments [*prodotriady*] was supplied to the poor peasants and the peasantry in the grain-consuming provinces.

But this struggle was also a *struggle for land*. Large-scale capitalist (non-peasant) agriculture was, as we have seen, already destroyed at the moment of the anti-feudal agrarian revolution; as a result of the low level of development of the peasant economy, including the large-scale peasant economy, the anti-capitalist revolution played out in the countryside not in the form of

---

the Committees of Poor Peasants [*kombedy*] were dissolved by the decree of 2 December 1918, but the elections to the peasant soviets were carried out by the Committees of Poor Peasants, which made sure to exclude kulaks from the voting.

37 Here, a consequence of the capitalist backwardness of Russia, the worker's connection with the village, became a factor in the victory of the revolution.

38 The fact that regions of capitalist industry became loci of revolution, and that regions of capitalist agriculture became loci of counter-revolution throws into sharp relief the limits within which the anti-capitalist revolution had been directly prepared by the preceding capitalist development. In essence, capitalist agriculture, which was predominantly petty capitalist, had not yet exhausted its possibilities, and had not yet become an obstacle to the development of productive forces; hence its ability to resist.

proletarian expropriation (the agricultural proletariat had already disappeared before this), but in the form of petty bourgeois, *peasant expropriation* of the expropriators, the kulaks.

This undoubtedly *strengthened* to an extraordinary degree *the social reach of the anti-capitalist revolution*. From a revolution of an urban and industrial population of 20 million, it became a revolution of 130 million; from an urban and industrial revolution it became a genuine *people's* [*obshchenarodnaia*] revolution. If the city had until then been an arena of anti-capitalist revolution and the countryside an arena of anti-feudal revolution, now this demarcation between city and countryside was erased. At the same time, though, this meant that the anti-capitalist revolution had *gone beyond the bounds* of the terrain prepared for it by the preceding capitalist development: it destroyed not the capitalist shell, which had inhibited the development of the productive forces of the large-scale economy, as had been the case with large-scale industry, it *destroyed the large-scale economy* itself (the large-scale economy had only a relative meaning here) and consequently also the relatively high development of the productive forces associated with it. The anti-capitalist revolution in the countryside went beyond economic expediency, and was therefore *economically reactionary* and also utopian, inasmuch as it strove to change the economy. It *splintered the large-scale* peasant *economies* and enlarged the small, it *levelled out the peasant economy in general*, and transformed all peasants into petty bourgeois; this was a step forward for the feudal peasant and a step backward for the capitalist peasant, a return to his starting point.

	Of the total of peasant farms (the total equals 100):[39]			
	1917			1920
Farms with no sowing area	10.6			4.7 (7.5)
Farms with sowing of up to 2 des.	30.4	60.5	79.5	47.9 (39.2)
Farms with sowing from 2–4 des.	30.1			(31.6 (28.8)
Farms with sowing from 4–10 des.	25.2	28.9	15.8	15.3 (20.5)
Farms with sowing of over 10 des.	3.7			(0.5 (4.0)

39 See A. Khriashchova, 'Gruppy i klassy v krest'ianstve', Moscow, 1924, p. 53. The comparison refers to 32 (one and the same) predominantly grain-producing provinces and was undertaken on the basis of partial counts. It gives a sense of the character of the changes in the relationships among the groups, but not of the character of the relationships themselves,

So the percentage of farms with no sowing area *decreased by more than a half*; the percentage of farms with larger sowing areas *decreased by almost half* (to a seventh in the top group); the percentage of farms with smaller or medium sowing areas *rose* (from three fifths to four fifths of the total).

Comparison of the farms by horse count produced similar results (see ibid., p. 54):

	Percentage of farms			
	1917		1920	
With no draught animals	29.0		27.6	
With 1 horse	49.2	66.2	63.6	71.5
With 2 horses	17.0		7.9	
With 3 horses	3.4	4.8	0.7	0.9
With 4 horses and more	1.4		0.2	

i.e. a certain reduction in farms with no horses, a five-fold reduction of those with several horses, and an increase in the number of those with few horses.

But the anti-capitalist revolution in the countryside fulfilled its own revolutionary political task. The *expropriation of the kulaks destroyed the final social support of the counter-revolution*; alongside its defense of the land from the landowners, it gave a moral boost to the Red Army, made up of peasants, and secured the agreement of the peasantry for the ban on trade and the confisca-

as the figures in brackets show, which are calculated on the basis of bulk data about 48 provinces (ibid, p. 54).

Basically, these processes unfolded in the intervening period between 1917 and 1919, as can be seen from a comparison of the aforementioned data with data from 1917–1919 in other works by this author (see 'Krest'ianstvo v voine i revoliutsii', Moscow, 1921, p. 34, and 'Ekonomicheskoe rassloenie krest'ianstva v 1917 and 1919 gg'., p. 13), and also with the following data for 1917, 1919, and 1920 (see 'Pravda' of 1 June 1923, the article of V. Sokolov):

	Percentage of farms					
	1917		1919		1920	
With no sowing area	11.3		6.6		5.8	
With sowing area up to 4 des.	58.0		72.1		86.0	
With sowing area from 4–8 des.	21.7	30.7	17.5	21.3	6.5	8.2
With sowing area over 8 des.	9.0		3.8		1.7	

tion of surpluses, something that impacted the kulaks most of all. At the same time, the destruction of the capitalist large-scale peasant economy meant, like the destruction of large-scale capitalist, non-peasant agriculture, a further *contraction of the agricultural basis of industry and town* in general as a consequence of the transformation of the large-scale economy, which produced for others, into a small-scale economy, which was more of a consumer-type economy. Its economic effect was in all probability somewhat less than the effect of the destruction of the capitalist, non-peasant economy, which had occurred a year earlier.

CHAPTER 4

The Achievements of Socialist Construction

1. The essence of 'war socialism' and 'war communism'. 2. The basic principles of the new system. 3. The creation of a new labour discipline. 4. The creation of a new economic administration.

The immanent (internal) *tendencies of the proletarian revolution* were able to emerge freely because of this mutation of the revolutionary process: the intensification and concentration of the proletarian revolution; overcoming the limits of immediate, economic expediency under the pressure of revolutionary necessity; and the violent suppression of all capitalist and market relations after having eliminated all open resistance. Consequently, in 1918–1920 a completely unique *proletarian natural economic system* began to take shape. Insofar as the methods of the proletarian revolution here were applied to circumstances that had not been prepared by the preceding capitalist development and was therefore unsuitable (to petty bourgeois and petty capitalist economic forms), then the immanent (internal) tendencies of the proletarian revolution inevitably had to be realised not in a pure form but with certain *distortions*.

The quite, indeed one might say wholly, disparaging attitude of very quick-witted[1] individuals to the economic order of the period from 1918 to 1920 so popular at the moment, is, however, quite unjustified and extremely superficial; these people view this economic order as 'war communism', i.e. as a system that under the guise of a transition from socialism was merely organising the 'rear', and was therefore not organising socialism but only the war. In short, they saw a system, so to speak, simulating the transition to socialism – a completely unfounded and highly superficial view.

The very notion of so-called 'war socialism', i.e. of the economy of the capitalist states during the World War as a purely consumer economy, akin to that of a besieged fortress where consumer needs are simply rationed (distributed according to rations), is fundamentally and deeply incorrect.

The world imperialist war was not simply a war of armies, this was a *war of national economies*. Therefore, comparing a modern capitalist government par-

1 They include communist philistines [*meshchane*] whose enthusiasm blows like a weather-vane; they regard the weather-vane as the highest form of the dialectic.

 | HTTPS://DOI.ORG/10.1163/9789004765313-008

ticipating in the imperialist war (i.e. a state in which finance capital is master) and implementing so-called 'war socialism' (i.e. state capitalism in reality) to a besieged fortress is comparing the incomparable (if this comparison refers to anything more than just the fact of the blockade). In reality, a besieged fortress is above all not an organisation of production (and reproduction), because of its economic incompleteness: first, it lacks all extractive industry (and above all agriculture) and, second (due to the smallness of its territory representing an arbitrary portion of the larger economic whole), it lacks many branches of the processing industry as well. Under these conditions, economic activity within the besieged fortress in reality boils down basically to as rational a distribution as possible of the surplus supplies that were in the fortress at the beginning of the siege.

But it is ridiculous to see the economy of Germany from 1914 to 1918 in these terms. If, as is often heard, Germany's war economy from 1914 to 1918 had indeed come down to the best distribution of existing resources, Germany would not have even lasted for a few months. In reality, state capitalism in the years 1914 to 1918 did not only distribute existing supplies of coal, iron, grain, textiles, etc, but also *produced* these things; it was consequently first and foremost the *organisation of production and reproduction*,[2] and rationing consumption, along with other methods of the *capitalist natural economy*, which is a *higher form* of the capitalist economy than the capitalist commodity economy, was a means of organising production and reproduction (specifically, the reproduction of the labour force).

So in no way is the capitalist natural economy delivered unexpectedly by war, like a baby by a stork; on the contrary, it matures in the womb of the capitalist commodity economy and represents a further development of the tendencies of prewar capitalism accelerated by the war.

In capitalist large-scale industry, long before the war, judging from the continuing concentration of enterprises, market relations solidified among those enterprises, which had earlier been independent but which had partly transformed themselves into combined enterprises; one result of this solidification was the transformation of commodity relations into natural relations.

The coal from mines, which had become the property of the railways or metallurgical trusts, no longer reached the boiler of the locomotive or the blast furnace as a product acquired in the market, but as the product of one part of a combined coal-steel or coal-metallurgical enterprise.

2 For this very reason, the tendency towards state capitalism appeared also in the Entente countries, which were not in a besieged situation like Germany.

And finance capital, developing its own diverse activity leading to the actual, if still unfinished, formation of gigantic, combined enterprises, internally regenerated market relations and prepared the transition from a commodity economy to a natural economy.

The military crisis of world capitalism sharply accelerated this process. But it only accelerated it.

The process of consolidation of market relations reached a feverish tempo in comparison with the earlier tempo: compulsory deliveries and requisitions, forced syndicalisation, high prices, ration cards, a work obligation for proletarians. Finance capitalism was reborn – under pressure of military need – before everyone's eyes and with surprising speed as state capitalism. The internal regeneration of market relations, until then latent, was expressed in the explicit transformation of commodity relations into natural relations.

The clever ideologues of capital tend to portray so-called 'war socialism' (state capitalism) not as a development of immanent (internal) tendencies of capitalism, but rather as a happenstance of war. Indeed, it was even seen as a simple result of stupidity, and its senselessness and ridiculous failure became clear once the war psychosis subsided. But while the ideologues of capital, in professing such views, know whose eyes they are drawing the wool over and to what end, the representatives of the working class and its interests, by developing similar views, reveal not their cleverness but just the opposite.

It is well-known that capitalist production is the production of surplus value. The capitalist is essentially indifferent to what he is producing, whether insect powder or fine perfume or something else; whatever the sinful exterior of the product, the capitalist sees in it only its innocent golden essence [*dusha*], which even back in ancient Rome they said *non olet* (has no scent). Only this golden essence of the product exists for him; its exterior in itself has no importance for him. Capitalist zeal to materialise the golden essence of objects would make a spiritualist envious.

This fetishistic approach to reality nonetheless allows capitalism to be an economic form that creates the necessary conditions for developing the productive forces of society, but only as long as the *mechanism of competition* is effective, and the striving for profit is the driving force of technological progress and of the expansion of production. But as capitalism is transformed into *monopoly* capitalism, the engine of competition begins to turn more slowly; the entire complex mechanism that develops the productive forces of capitalism (even if bought at the high price of the costs of competition) fails. In place of the earlier means of generating profit – the expansion of production and the lowering of its costs – comes a third method that achieves goals far more simply and directly: *raise prices*, the direct generation of profit. All cartels (syndicates and trusts) employ this method, and it is a feature of the era of monopoly capitalism. With the onset of this victorious era for the capitalists, capitalism begins to lose its living revolutionary spirit, the spirit of technological revolution that has so transformed the globe over the past centuries. Capitalism, the historical task of which is to overcome the atomisation of mankind, to overcome the commodity economy, is *technologically reactionary* as far as it goes beyond the commodity economy. The era of technological stagnation sets in, the era of the rot of capitalism. The forms of the commodity capitalist economy come into conflict with the productive forces of monopoly capitalism, forces that have matured for the natural organisation of the economy and that were required by it; this is especially the case for its highest form, finance capitalism.

Capitalism was able to resolve this conflict between the forms of the commodity economy and the productive forces that transcended these forms only in the specific situation of the imperialist world war *within the framework of capitalism*.

The Great Imperialist War put every capitalist country at risk of military, and thus also economic, ruin[3] and by the same token it cast the national classes of capitalists out of their golden heaven down to the sinful earth.

In times of peace, a trust or a consortium of banks is just as willing to cut the production of coal and iron (e.g., as a result of a decline in demand resulting from an increase in price) as to increase it, depending on whether one or the other act promises more profits. If cutting production in the event of a corresponding price increase for the monopolist could bring victory in the fight for profits, then under the conditions of armed struggle for existence, and therefore, for the very *possibility* of the future production of profit, reducing (or even inadequately increasing) coal and iron production would mean military collapse and the end of any hopes of future profits.

Capital is forced to awaken from its golden stupor and turn from a spiritualist (fetishist) into a realist; it is forced to view production not as the generator of profit, but as the producer of commodities, as the producer of consumer value; it is forced to strive to expand and improve production, to develop productive forces directly. The Great Imperialist War restored the function of competition; it was however no longer the earlier (economic) competition – competition by means of price cuts –, but a new (technological) competition by means of increasing and improving the production of objects of military need and of everything connected with and required for it. The earlier competition

3 The reality of this threat is revealed by the fate of Germany.

expressed the technological superiority of the winning side *indirectly* – in the low price of commodities; the new competition did so *directly* – in the superiority of military technology.

But capital is only able to come to terms with this realistic approach to things in a completely *distorted* economic situation, when cannons, machine-guns, explosives, poisonous gases, tanks etc are the basic objects of value, and only while this distorted economic situation persists. Capital, it turns out, is incapable in the long term of overcoming, within the framework of capitalism, the contradiction between the forms of the commodity economy and the productive forces that outstrip these forms. This means that capitalism as an economic system became economically reactionary and was thus doomed to fail.

The interests of capital conflict with the demands of the development of productive forces. Capital does not need to repudiate the fetishistic approach to the economy beyond the context of global war. Global war is the only situation in which the decline in the production of commodities, even if accompanied by an increase in the production of profits, threatens the existence of the (national) class of capitalists. Usually (i.e. not in conditions of global war), the decline in the production of commodities means a decline in consumption and thus a deterioriation of the conditions of existence of the proletariat and petty bourgeoisie, but does not threaten the existence of the capitalist class; if this decline is accompanied by an increase in the production of profit, then this even means a growth in the power of capital. Beyond the context of global war, state capitalism (the natural capitalist economy) is, therefore, not a necessity for large capital.

While state capitalism is not economically necessary for large capital (other than in the context of global imperialist war), it represents a huge *social* danger for the magnates of capital. It lays bare the social character of capitalist production, by tearing away its deceitful mask of fetishistic monetary and credit relations; it sharply juxtaposes against the clique of capital magnates the grand mechanism of social production and of the proletariat belonging to it. The increasing organisational interconnectedness of social labour at the same time unmasks the dictatorship of capital to the concentrated power of the proletariat that has been organised by capitalist development. Capital can only resolve this under the pressure of extreme (military) need, only in the extraordinary atmosphere, created by the same imperialist war, of the deafness of the working class, of the decay and suppression of the class ideology of the proletariat, of the secured civil peace, i.e. of the collaboration of the proletariat with capital, their sacred patriotic union.

But state capitalism does not only cause capital to fear for the very stability of capitalism, it also triggers resistance from the mass (in number, not significance) of capitalists themselves, for it turns a small clique of capital magnates into the clear masters of the entire capitalist class. For this reason, the mass of capitalists, in pursuit of a phantom independence, comes out against state capitalism, but even the capitalist magnates show no desire at all to support the firm of 'state capitalism', in which they have to accept the capitalist small fry as shareholders.

State capitalism as such then could exist only while there was a global capitalist war, and it had to disappear along with it, creating the impression that it was a *creation* of the war, while in fact it was but the completion of internal tendencies of highly developed finance capitalism, and was merely unmasked by it.

Therefore, state capitalism, i.e. the *capitalist natural* economy, was replaced after the war by the capitalist commodity economy, even though the former represented a *higher* form of organisation of the national economy, enabling it, as the global war showed, to utilise the productive forces of society more completely and to develop them more efficiently. Capital returns to finance capitalism, being the *hidden* form of state capitalism, which has roughly the same relationship to finance capitalism as a trust has to a syndicate (it is superior to it). Capitalism by the way turned out to be incapable of realising its own progressive tendencies in the long run. This regressive step by capitalism showed incontrovertibly that society's progress can only be achieved by transcending the limits of capitalism, by overcoming capitalism itself.

The common views of state capitalism derive from the fact that capital cannot permit itself the luxury of being forthright about its need to take over the national economy by concealing the capitalist oligarchs and monarchs[4] behind a fog of monetary and credit relations. If, *for this reason*, the ideologues of capital portray state capitalism, i.e. the blatant dictatorship of the capital magnates during the war, as pure happenstance, then a similar kind of objection in the ranks of the representatives of the working class and its interests is undoubtedly the manifestation of bourgeois influence on the proletariat. The view, however, that the economy of Soviet Russia in the period from 1917 to 1920 was the economy of a besieged fortress, in which commodities were not produced but only distributed (if, I repeat, this comparison refers to anything more than just the stark reality of the blockade), revealed an even greater superficiality, an even more philistine mindset than analogous judgments of state capitalism in Western Europe.

4 After the war, finance capital made new huge strides in their efforts to take control of the national economy. The best illustration of this is the activity of Stinnes.

If state capitalism (so-called 'war socialism') in 1914–1918 was the organisation of capitalist production (and reproduction) under conditions of global imperialist war (and something that was but the completion of tendencies of prewar capitalism), then the organisation of the national economy of Soviet Russia in 1918–1920 (so-called 'war communism') was, insofar as it was facilitated by the war, the proletarian organisation of production (and reproduction) not in the conditions of war in general, but in the conditions of *civil war*. But civil war is nothing less than the climax of the revolution, in this case of proletarian revolution. Consequently, so-called 'war communism' was the proletarian organisation of production and reproduction in conditions of proletarian revolution, and indeed the most decisive period of the latter. It was therefore, in its essence, not something imposed on the revolution from the outside. The idea of it as the war-induced organisation of basic distribution alone is a mode of 'thinking' that uses simple words and the most superficial analogies to quietly equate civil war, i.e. revolution, with war in general, and a warring country, i.e. a national economy, with a besieged fortress. Both analogies are equally useless and no better than their originators.

In reality, so-called 'war communism' was the first major attempt at a proletarian natural economy, *an attempt to take the first steps of the transition to socialism*. In its basic thinking, it was not at all the delusion [*zabluzhdenie*] of individuals or of a class; it was an *anticipation of the future* – although not in a pure sense but with certain distortions, an intrusion by this future into the present (now already the past), and it was made possible by the specific conditions of development of the Russian proletarian revolution that have been discussed above.

Characterising the proletarian natural economic system that developed in 1918–1920 was complicated greatly by the fact that it was in *statu nascendi*, in a period of its tumultuous development, a period of incessant and abrupt changes. The following characterisation of this economic order refers to the end of the period of civil war, to 1920,[5] when its characteristic features were most visible, even though at this time it had by no means finished developing. But already at the start of 1921, as is well-known, the collapse of the proletarian natural economy and the return to the commodity economy had begun.

The entire social order of the era of this great Civil War bore the clear stamp of its creator, the proletariat. We were struck by the raw pathos of power-

5 This characterisation is the basis of my 1920 article 'Organizatsiia narodnogo khoziaistvo v Sovetskoi Rossii,' see Iu. Larin and L. Kritsman, 'Ocherk khoziaistvennoi zhizni i organizatsiia narodnogo khoziaistva Sovetskoi Rossii', Moscow, 1920.

ful revolutionary enthusiasm from this social order which the proletariat was building, and which, while still unfinished, was infused with an integrated completeness unknown to capitalism; it offered a premonition of the future amidst this chaos of the present.

This completeness, not yet achieved but anticipated, was felt directly in the iron, irrefutable consistency of the revolution, as logic given form; this *uniform nature* [*monizm*] of the emergent social order manifested above all in the destruction of the contrast, typical of the bourgeois system, between the abstract and therefore false political order, in which every citizen was considered an ideal individual, as atoms equal to each other, and the economic order, in which the real individual existed in real relations with the other individuals (these were above all the relations of class rule and class subordination).

In the emerging proletarian society, the political order and economic order were brought into complete harmony, and in such a way that the political order of society was restructured according to the image and the example of its economic order. The main principle of organisation of the new soviet state order differs sharply therefore from the principle of the state organisation of bourgeois democracy: it is the principle of *production*. The basic units of the soviet state order become the units of production – the enterprises: for example, the members of the Soviets of Workers' Deputies are elected by the enterprises, and thus the entire structure of the soviets is built upon them.

Labour relations in society became the relations that directly and openly determined the other relations in society.

And in the national economy, the production principle was put into effect completely and consistently, undistorted by any considerations beyond production: commercial, legal, or other.

The trade unions, of which the lowest basic units were the factory-plant committees, became *the basis of the entire organisation of the national economy* in this era. Not only were the state organisation of labour (worker power) and the state organisation of industry closely connected with the trade unions and to a significant degree built directly upon them, so too were the state organisation of the procurement of foodstuffs and raw materials, and the state organisation of distribution, finances, agriculture, and control. The state organisation of industry, with the exception of small industry which only had local significance, paralleled the structure of the trade unions: it was organised according to the branches of the national economy. In line with the general character of Soviet power, the trade unions played an important role in the construction of all apparatuses of Soviet power (and above all of its military apparatus: alongside the party mobilisations, the trade unions' mobilisation of their members formed the skeleton of the Red Army), but the significance of the trade unions in the organisation of the national economy was exceptionally strong.

Insofar as the individual apparatuses of the national economic organisation of Soviet power organised the activity of the proletariat in the production process, they were built directly upon proletarian organisations, the trade unions. But even where these apparatuses had no direct connection to the activity of the proletariat in the production process, the proletariat, organised in production by the enterprises and the trade unions, was closely connected with them. In this way, the middling classes [*promezhutochnye klassy*], and, of particular importance, the many millions of peasants, were organised around the proletariat, subordinated to its influence and leadership. This influence could be seen in the military and administrative apparatuses, but also in all national economic organisations. The productive activity of the peasantry was organised, inasmuch as it could be successfully organised at all, around enterprises which were united in their own centre. This was achieved by organising the work of the peasants in the agricultural industry, by organising the collection of raw materials in those branches of industry that processed agricultural raw materials, and finally by organising the food economy of the industrial proletariat. In all of these cases, the organs and bones of the organising process were proletarian. All former peasant organisations (the various types of cooperatives), if they still existed at all under the new conditions, were restructured little by little around the new proletarian centres.

The victorious advance of the production principle was the direct consequence of the victory of the proletariat, which had made the principle of the organisation of the proletariat into the principle of the organisation of society. The revolution of the proletariat handed the working class *power* over the entire national economy; the entire organisation of the national economy was *fused* with the organised proletariat.

This meant the *rebirth* of the organisation of the national economy, its transformation into its direct opposite – from capitalist to proletarian.

The revolution eliminated the basic contradiction of capitalist society, the contradiction between society's working force and its means of production, and it thus placed the uniform nature of the new society on the stable base of the uniform nature of its economy.

Precisely this *synthesis* of the previously antagonistic, although interdependent, *development of the organisation of the national economy and the organisation of the working class*, this penetration of the proletariat into the very pores of the national economy, this fusing of the national economy with the organised proletariat, was the most difficult but also the most majestic work of the social revolution of the proletariat in this era.

The difficulty and enormity of such a rebirth of the national economy was linked primarily to the unprecedented expansion of the organising activity of the working class, encompassing the *entire* national economy. Forced by capitalism, like a snail into its shell, to look after itself (politically and by unionising), the working class in the turbulent atmosphere of its own social revolution was compelled to deploy for the first time the full breadth of its organisational work and to take on the immense task of organising the national economy.

Completion of this titanic task, together with the work of organising the military and administrative apparatus of Soviet power, demanded an extraordinary concentration of efforts by the proletariat and a ceaseless and significant expansion of the cadres of active functionaries. And both were taken care of by the organised vanguard of the proletariat – the *Communist Party*.

The strength of any state apparatus depends on its ability to renew and consolidate itself continuously. But all states known to history recruited their administrative apparatus from a very narrow stratum. Soviet power drew directly on the proletariat and on the peasant masses close to it. The Communist Party became a colossal, historically unique *apparatus to recruit organising elements from the limitless mass of toilers* and to train them. The concentrated enthusiasm and steely, comradely discipline of hundreds of thousands of party members represented a force which, whenever it was directed at a particular focal point, was capable of radically changing even the most unfavourable correlation of forces. Kolchak and Denikin experienced this personally. The influence of this force could also be seen in the work of organising the national economy. The entire, active advance stratum of the Russian proletariat joined the Communist Party, whose members flooded into both the entire apparatus of state power (including the army), and the entire trade union apparatus, as well as all other worker organisations.

The growth of the Communist Party reflected the progress in proletarian construction. The members of the Russian Communist party numbered:

at the start of 1917	23,600 people[6]
at the start of 1918	115,000 people
at the start of 1919	251,500 people
at the start of 1920	431,400 people
at the start of 1921	585,600 people

6 See 'Vserossiiskaia perepis' chlenov RKP 1922 g.', Moscow, 1923, 4th ed., p. 32.

So the number of people drawn into active construction grew 25-fold in four years.

This growth was particularly strong at moments of extreme peril; these moments saw a high tide of proletarian energy and a strengthening of their will to victory. The highest increase in membership (180,000) was in 1919, when Iudenich was approaching Leningrad, and Denikin Tula.

An idea of the growth of Communist Party influence is offered by the data on the party composition of delegates to the All-Russian congresses of trade unions.

As a percentage of the total number of delegates:[7]

	Communists	Mensheviks	Other parties	Non-Party
at I Congress (January 1918)	66	16	10	8
at II Congress (January 1919)	80	6	9	5
at III Congress (April 1920)	75	4	4	17
at IV Congress (May 1921)	81	½	½	18

The role of the trade unions and the Communist Party sharply emphasises another basic principle of this era, that of the organisation of the Soviet state and the Soviet national economy, the *class* principle, which revealed most clearly the transitional nature of the era.

The entire social order of this era was permeated with the *spirit* of merciless *class exclusivity*. The expropriation of capital, the elimination of the possibility of using the means of production as a means of exploitation, removed the basic social contradiction of capitalism – between the social means of production and the social labour force – thereby placing the capitalist *outside of society*. The same thing happened to the feudal lords. The exploiter, the member of one of the former ruling classes, whether feudal lord or capitalist, was not only stripped of his former position of mastery, he was also pushed out of Soviet society to huddle in its backyard as a barely tolerated piece of dirt. The bourgeois was transformed into a despised outcast – a *pariah*, stripped not only of property but also of honour. He was deprived of all civil and political rights, including the right to elect or be elected to any public institution. He was also

7 See the article by V. Iarotskii, 'Professional'noe dvizhenie v Sovetskoi Rossii,' in 'Ezhegodnik Kominterna', Petrograd-Moscow, 1923, p. 446.

deprived of the right to join the military, the right to bear arms. He was destroyed, not physically but socially.

Just as in a society based on exploitation where everyone who wanted to have 'social' respect strove to prove his unimpeachable origins from the exploiters (from noble feudal lords or capital magnates), so too everyone who wanted to become an equal member of Soviet society strove stubbornly to prove his unimpeachable proletarian or peasant origins with all kinds of documents and evidence.

Neither title nor money, which became worthless, but designation as a proletarian and a toiler paved the way to social status. The stigma of belonging to the exploiter class could lead only to a concentration camp, a prison, and, in the best-case scenario, to those spaces left by proletarians who had moved to better homes.

This merciless class exclusivity, the social destruction of the exploiter classes, was the source of the enormous moral boost, the *source of the passionate enthusiasm* of the proletariat and of all of the exploited. It was a powerful appeal to all oppressed people, it was confirmation of their inner superiority over the filthy world of the exploiters.

The class principle was implemented with a merciless rigour in this period, permitting no exceptions, just as it was in the organisation of the national economy. After the transitional period (until summer 1918), access to all organs of the administration of the national economy was completely closed to all representatives of capital. The soviet organisation of the national economy was a strictly class proletarian organisation.

The character of the ruling class required that a third organising principle of the era be applied – the *work* principle. It found its sharpest expression in Article 18, section 2: 'The Russian Socialist Federated Soviet Republic considers work the duty of all citizens of the Republic and proclaims as its slogan: He who does not work shall not eat'.

And the work principle was not just the principle of organisation of the national economy, it permeated other spheres of social life; it thereby became the basic organising principle of the soviet school system.

The work principle – as the main feature of the *modern* proletariat – was asserted as the standard for the entire class and was applied to all of society. It lent the newly emerging economic and social order an aura of deep and serious gravity. In contrast to the simple-minded and shallow movements of the parasitic proletariat of old, the project to build a modern proletariat was a movement of the toilers. It was a movement of the hungry, but it was not a movement of the idle. The path to the empire of freedom [*tsarstvo svobody*] led through the acknowledgement of work as a necessity.

At the same time, this principle had a class significance, for, unlike the representatives of the formerly ruling classes of exploiters, it proclaimed itself to be the *rejection of parasitism* and to be based on the dictatorship of the proletariat.

The work requirement and the various obligations of labour took on a decidedly compulsory aspect because the material supply, particularly the supply of foodstuffs, was dependent on their fulfillment. These obligations intruded into the life of every individual, transforming it in ways akin to the harsh life of the toilers. The work obligation, which remained largely a purely formal requirement for the vast majority of toilers, i.e. it did not bring any significant actual changes, was a further step in the destruction of the owners' privileges. If the expropriation of wealth deprived them of all their possessions – in contrast to the masses of the dispossessed [*neimushchie*] – then the obligation to work impressed on them the fact that work up to now had been a distinguishing feature of the poor, but was now a general feature.

From the nature of the ruling class came the fourth organising principle of the era as well – the principle of *collectivity*. It found its deepest expression, of course, in the nationalisation of the means of production and of exchange.

As the particularly distinguishing feature of the proletariat, setting it apart from *all* other social classes, the principle of collectivity became in this era the most popular principle of construction, penetrating all spheres of social life.

Nothing was perhaps so typical of this era as the striving to root out individualism and instill collectivism. This appeared not only in the organisation of the administration (collegial administration), but also in the forms of payment for work (collective supply, collective rewards), in the forms of economic relations with the countryside (collective exchange of commodities), and in the attempts to replace small farming with large, collective units (agricultural collectives and communes,[8] the combining of traditionally independent craftsmen in shops, communal living quarters, and public social canteens, etc).

8 For the growth of agricultural collectives, see the following data:

Number of Collectives in the USSR	
in 1918	912
in 1919	6,186
in 1920	13, 607

Over two years, a fifteen-fold increase. In 1923, when the number of collectives in the RSFSR was the same as in 1920, four-fifths of the total comprised 276,000 people, i.e. more than a

On this principle, the system of *collegial administration* predominated in all administrative organs, including economic organs; all administrative organs were linked directly (in one or another form above all by elections) with the broad proletarian organisations, with trade unions; every possible organisation saw an enormous increase in membership. Each individual member of society was connected with society as a whole by ever newer pathways. In contrast to bourgeois society, which strives to set itself against the separate individual, in the emerging new society each of its members act everywhere as a member of one or another broader or narrower collective.

Finally, the fifth organising principle of the era was the principle of *rationalisation* [*ratsionalizatsiia*].

In a certain sense, every revolution exhibits a tendency towards rationalism, for it overthrows what has been traditional up till then, and brings the formerly unimpeachable before the court of revolutionary reason of the new class that comes to power.

The principle of rationalism also stamped the greatest of all bourgeois revolutions, the Great French Revolution, which fearlessly brought the entire former (feudal) society before the court of bourgeois reason.

> A mad God ruled the world,
> From now on Reason rules everything.[9]

So said the orator of the French Revolution in one of our works of Russian literature.

In the age of revolution, the existence of a social institution is no argument for its continued existence – other arguments are required deriving from reason (of course, the reason of a particular class). The principle of organic eras: 'It exists, therefore it is necessary', gives way to a different principle: 'It is necessary, therefore it will exist; it is not necessary, therefore it will be abolished'. The conservative principle of tradition gives way to the revolutionary principle of reason. This is how every revolution behaves, both the bourgeois and the prolet-

---

quarter million. See 'Na novykh putiakh', 5th ed, part I, Appendix III: 'Polozhenie kollektivov i ikh truda,' pp. 637–638.

9 [This appears to refer to a quotation from a poem by Nikolai Minskii from 1907: 'In the madness of the age, the universe was ruled by a mad god, Let Reason rule in the age of reason!' ['*V bezym'ia vek Vselennoi pravil bog bezumnyi, Pust' Razum pravit v vek razumnyi!*'], (Nikolai Minskii, *Russkie pesni i romantsy. Klassiki i sovremenniki* [Moscow: 'Khudozhestvennaia literature,' 1989]). It also resonates with Hegel's idea that 'Reason governs the world' (see G.W.F. Hegel, *Lectures on the Philosophy of History* (London: George Bell & Sons, 1894)].

arian. The demand that everyone display reason, and the fearless destruction of everything recognised as devoid of reason, was also very typical of our revolution in the Civil War era.

But this formal resemblance conceals a fundamental essential difference.

The rationalism of the bourgeois revolution did not penetrate below the 'superstructure'. Religion, morals, law, everyday life, the political system of society – it brought all of this before the court of reason which had to restructure everything anew. *But not the economy.* Here the bourgeois revolution proclaimed the principle of non-interference: *laissez faire, laissez passer*. Bourgeois social reason has no access to the economy – individual arbitrariness reigned there.

By contrast, the rationalism of the proletarian revolution penetrated deeper – it restructured not only the 'superstructure' of society, but also its deep base – the social economy.

A feature of the proletarian revolution was the transition to the *open* organisation of the national economy from the former fetishistically distorted one, the *elimination of fetishistic relations*, and the establishment of direct and immediate open relations among the various parts of the Soviet national economy.

This expressed itself in the then typical tendency *to abolish the market*, to abolish commodity-, monetary- and credit-relations, to abolish the commodity economy and thus also commodity fetishism, and to replace the commodity economy with a *natural* economy.

And this principle seized all spheres of social life: it manifested also in other spheres than the economy; in these, it expressed tendencies to abolish the law, and with it *legal fetishism* – to abolish the old law and its institutions: written law, the juridical estate, law faculties[10] – and to destroy religion, and with it *religious fetishism* – the struggle against religion in all its aspects.

The entire work of economic construction at this time was imbued with these principles. The foundations of the construction of the Soviet organisation of the national economy, as already mentioned, were the trade unions of the proletariat. The trade union movement of Soviet Russia was marked in this period above all by extremely intensive growth (this growth was by the way quite natural, for the workers were in power, and all obstacles to the devel-

10 The so-called revolutionary law of the civil war era was, it is true, authoritarian to a high degree, as the revolution itself is authoritarian, but it was founded not on an absolute (on ideas of eternal law) but on class interest, i.e. in its essence it was not law, and therefore (since it was explicitly founded on class interest) was devoid of legal fetishism.

opment of the trade unions had been swept aside). Trade union membership increased as follows:[11]

mid-1917 693,000
mid-1918 1,946,000
mid-1919 3,707,000
mid-1920 5,222,000

In three years, trade union membership increased by seven and a half times.

The sphere of activity of trade unions since the October overthrow became extremely broad: from the one-sided and therefore incomplete regulation of the market by the workforce, they moved not only to complete state regulation of the workforce (through the People's Commissariat of Labour), but trade unions also became the defining force in the organisation of both industry and the entire national economy in general. Paralleling the organisation of the national economy, the trade union movement created all-Russian associations in all spheres of labour. As the organisation of the national economy progressed, the number of All-Russian trade unions steadily fell, because native associations were merged: in 1920 there were more than thirty associations, and by the end of 1921 there were already only 22 encompassing some 9,451 trade union organisations.[12] The very nature of trade union organisations changed radically: from narrowly professional, shop unions, they were transformed into *production* unions, comprising all workers and officials of a certain branch of industry (or of another branch of the national economy) regardless of their profession. This clearly showed the trade union movement's adaptation to its new, overarching task.

At the top of the trade union movement stood the All-Russian Central Council of Trade Unions (abbreviated to VTsSPS), which was elected by its All-Russian Congress and led the activity both of the central committees of the individual all-Russian trade unions, and of the provincial councils of trade unions. The latter were elected by provincial congresses of trade unions and guided the activity of provincial boards of all-Russian trade unions and local trade union bureaus. The grassroots units were the factory-plant committees, which were elected by workers in the enterprises.

The entire Soviet organisation of the national economy, whose features we will describe below, was built upon the trade unions. The trade unions immedi-

11 See the article by V. Iarotski, 'Professional'noe dvizhenie v Sovetskoi Rossii' in 'Ezhegodnik Kominterna', Petrograd-Moscow, 1923, p. 445.

12 Ibid., pp. 446–447.

ately had to undertake the enormous task of creating a new proletarian labour discipline to replace the broken capitalist one.

This task in particular seemed absolutely insurmountable to the philistines. Corrupted by the parasitic nature of their own existence, the exploiters and their ideologues were saturated with mistrust and disgust towards labour; they were incapable of understanding how people could work if not threatened by the cudgel. Having turned labour into humanity's curse, they believed that this was the very nature of work itself.

But the real difficulty lay not in the natural properties of labour, but in the specific properties of capitalist wage labour. Precisely because the labour power of the proletarian was the only commodity not owned by capital, it was squandered under capitalist conditions in the most predatory fashion. Developed capitalism even invented an entire science of how to squeeze labour out of the worker – Taylorism; this system relied on a particular art, devised by the 'labours' of countless generations of capitalists and by the capitalist enterprise managers who replaced them like paper money replaced precious metal.

But capital exploited the power of the living worker as completely as it could (not in the sense of productivity, but in the sense of exhausting the workers), and consequently it also raised the demands on the workforce to its highest degree; for this reason, then, liberation from the yoke of capitalist exploitation has inevitably been accompanied by the striving if not to get rid of labour, but to reduce, to weaken the demands on it, something that was unknown before capitalism and was introduced for the first time by capitalism.

The established socialist society solved this problem by lowering the demands (or their duration) on labour and compensating for (balancing out) the associated loss in production by increasing the productivity of labour with new machinery and in general new technological methods.

In the revolutionary era, i.e. when productive forces have declined and when it is impossible to forego the *old* technology, the effort to alleviate the demands on labour become extremely intense as the living standard of the working masses deteriorates as a result of the decline in the productive forces and the enormous costs of the revolution. At the same time, it becomes more and more imperative to restore – temporarily – the earlier or roughly earlier demands on labour; for if the technology remains unchanged, then labour productivity depends directly on the level of the demands on it and on its organisation.

The revolutionary proletariat of Russia resolved this problem through class enlightenment and class coercion.

The trade unions became the organs through which a new attitude towards productive labour, a new conception of labour, was absorbed. This was not the petty bourgeois conception of productive labour as a field of activity of the free, creative forces of the individual, as a field of activity of man's creative personality. Such conceptions were tied to small production, indeed to insufficiently specialised small production.

In modern large-scale production, productive labour is in no way free labour, but on the contrary *necessary* labour; it is the mechanised fighting activity of the masses and demands the strictest discipline.

It becomes necessary, however, not as a result of the machinery: machinery only makes it a reality (reifies it); it makes it tangible by contrasting it with the living human being itself (a machine) as a materialised necessity. What gives productive labour its necessary character is the mutual connection between labour activity and the workers. The element of necessity emerges, therefore, wherever a link is created in the labour activity of individual workers. In a chain of workers passing bricks from the ground up to the top of a building (or a 'chain' of clerks, through whose hands 'paper' passes) or in a group of workers raising a heavy beam, the work of each is necessary work, because each is a necessary link, a necessary part of the shared task.[13]

But while a machine does not create the necessary character of labour in a large enterprise, it expresses and strengthens it by subordinating the worker completely to the iron logic of the motion of steel machinery. In a modern enterprise, blue-overalled people are lost amongst the mass of relentless machines that do not cease for a second. The more perfect the mute slaves – the machines – the more severe the strain on the attention of the worker. The development of machine production means, then, the transformation of the labour of every worker into an activity connected with the labour of others, it means a growing burden of labour that is ever more mechanised and demands not so much the entire physical energy of the worker, as his entire attention; it means ever stricter labour discipline enforced directly by the machines, the growing dependence of the worker on a machine which directly and strictly defines his actions and his psychology while at work, – in short, the worker's entire activity at work is transformed into a necessary activity imposed by a machine; it means that productive labour is strict, harsh, joyless, and necessary.

Modern productive labour is not a field of activity for the free, creative powers of human beings, it is not a pleasure in itself. In this respect, the proletarian revolution brought no fundamental change at all. On the contrary, insofar

13 Therefore, productive labour already took on all the features of necessary activity in the manufacturing period, and the negative sides of (excessive) necessary labour came out especially strongly precisely in the period of the dominance of manufacturing.

as it meant for the future that large-scale production would also be developed further, it consolidated the necessary character of productive labour.

The new attitude to productive labour is sustained by other sources.

Reinforcing the necessary aspect of productive labour is the converse of the growth in its productivity. And the growth in productivity of social labour means the possibility of freeing society more and more from necessary labour, of guaranteeing free leisure, which is all the greater, the more productive the necessary labour is, i.e. the stronger its necessity. Removing the elements of free creative activity from productive labour, generally speaking, does not mean eliminating them, merely setting them apart: to the extent that social productive labour becomes necessary, the preconditions are created (and precisely because of the growth in this labour productivity) for free creative labour, i.e. a period of free leisure guaranteed by the necessary labour. The liberation of necessary labour from the elements of free creativity means the liberation of free creativity from the shackles of necessary labour.

If the tasks of society boiled down only to productive labour, then man would have been transformed into a cog of the machine – into a cog of an automatic mechanism, into an appendage of the machine and, thereby, into a machine. But human society is faced not only with the task of productive labour, but also with the task of its further *development*. This task includes not only the further conquest and transformation of the external environment (technological progress), but also the future conquest and transformation of man's own nature (the perfecting of his organism, the organisation of his work and of his ideology) – this is a creative task. There is no space here for automatic, mechanical activity. This demands the utmost strain on the power of the *individual*, who, armed with all the achievements of society, treads *alone* the virgin soil of the unknown, and, feeling his way, making mistakes, and every minute turning one way and then the other, tries to penetrate the gloomy thickets of the uncharted. Here too collaboration exists, but it is the collaboration of people seeking a path through an impenetrable forest, and not the collaboration at the workshop benches that are set in motion by single engine. The individual is the product of society to the end. And in the realm of creativity, his work is social work (the work of the development of productive labour); but in this realm, *he* works as an individual, and not as a component of a mechanism. From this viewpoint, leisure itself, which is conditioned by productive labour, is a condition of the further development of productive labour; it is thus a field of *social* activity of immense importance, not necessary, like productive labour, but free, not automatic, but creative. To secure leisure for the masses means to secure the masses for creativity. *The creativity of the masses is the fundamental characteristic feature of communism.* For creativity in the realm of technology and the organisation of labour, and also in the realm of ideology, is available to every ordinary person, although of course not to everyone to the same degree.

Capitalism, however, severs the link between productive labour and leisure: it turns the productive labour of the proletarians into the leisure of the exploiters. By leaving necessary labour to the proletariat alone, it *separates* the proletariat in advance from the leisure guaranteed by the fruits of necessary labour, thereby rendering necessary work senseless and intolerable.

The proletarian revolution transforms necessary labour anew into a *means for securing guaranteed leisure*, restores the link between productive labour and leisure severed by capitalism, and thereby creates a powerful stimulus to raise the demands on labour. A pledge for the future here is the *eight-hour* (and in some branches of industry six-hour) *workday*, which has become the *enduring* gain of the victorious proletariat.

While capital transformed the enterprise into a mechanism, and did so in such a way that it severed the worker from the means of production, antagonistically set workers in opposition to each other, and killed in them any interest in labour and its product, the proletarian revolution, namely the synthesis (unification) of the social worker and social means of production, awoke in the worker a new attitude towards productive labour.

But capitalism did not just sever the link between necessary labour and leisure for the worker. As the most developed and most effective form of commodity production, capitalism transformed all branches of labour into the uniform production of money and every act of labour into (abstract) labour in general; it elevated to the highest degree the worker's complete indifference to the product of his labour, which was represented only as a disguised form of money, and to labour itself as a concrete act of labour producing certain products (of consumer value). The actual consumer qualities of the product were represented here as subsidiary, insignificant, essentially unreal. Within the context of capitalism, production remained for the proletarian the production of money, the production of his wage.

The proletarian revolution transformed production into a *social* activity for the proletarian. It directed the proletarian's attention to the utility of the product of his labour and to labour as a concrete phenomenon. And insofar as a proletarian *natural* economy emerged, which abandoned the fictions of commodity production, this economy, by restoring living colour to real things and by emphasising precisely their utility as products, became a new factor in the awakening and consolidation of the new attitude towards labour.

And so, in the same era when capitalism vainly fought against the catastrophic decline in labour activism (i.e. against the rise of laziness), which expressed itself in the collapse of capitalist labour discipline, a new attitude towards labour emerged in the ranks of the victorious proletariat, rising to a veritable labour enthusiasm in its advanced groups. This labour enthusiasm could be seen in the voluntary extension of the workday to 10 and 12 hours (wherever necessary to the interests of the new proletarian society) and especially in the so-called *subbotniki* (which appeared first in the railways to combat the transport crisis), i.e. voluntary unpaid labour after the usual workday for the benefit of the proletarian state. An increase in the demands on labour and a direct labour heroicism were witnessed on many occasions – and on a mass scale wherever food conditions were at least adequate.

A vivid expression of the new attitude towards labour was a feature typical of the new proletarian society, namely the peculiar *cult of the heroes of labour* in honour of labour jubilees of the rank-and-file workers who had devoted their energy and power to productive labour.

The enormous work of class enlightenment brought before the very eyes of the masses and into their midst this new definition of productive labour that followed the elimination of capitalist exploitation. Along with this explanatory work, along with the collective class approbation (e.g. honouring the heroes of labour), and in addition to leading by example (e.g. subbotniks) and so on, the trade unions also employed class compulsion, forcing the backward or inferior elements of the proletariat to raise themselves up and follow the example of the entire class. The trade unions did enormous work in the area of *normalising labour* (setting obligatory norms in production, etc).[14] One tool for supervising the fulfillment of these demands, which were set by the new proletarian labour discipline, were the worker-elected comradely disciplinary courts.

But the trade unions, i.e. the mass organisations of the proletariat, forged not only basic internal stability in the new proletarian economic system, namely the new proletarian labour discipline, they also created the very backbone of the new proletarian economic organisation and, first and foremost, of the new organisation of enterprise management and of the economy in general; they thus created not only the soul but also the bones of the new economic organisation.

The new organisation of economic management was not new in the sense that economic units were regrouped, but in the sense that their internal class structure was changed. This, together with the destruction of the old organisa-

14 Already at the start of 1918, the All-Russian Central Council of Trade Unions (VTsSPS) adopted the Decree on Labour Discipline, para. 4 of which reads: 'All trade unions must strictly oversee the observance of organisational and tariff discipline, having definitively recognised as a rule that for a certain, guaranteed work wage a certain norm of productivity must be guaranteed' (See 'Narodnoe khoziaistvo', 1918, no. 2 (April)).

tion of economic management, was the essence of the economic revolution in the narrow sense of the word.

The capitalist organisation of the management of the economy is characterised by the complete *separation* of the proletariat from the management of the enterprise: the unrestricted command power of capital contrasts with the complete absence of rights of the proletariat. While the entire social atmosphere of bourgeois countries has long been saturated with the ideas of freedom, constitution, republic, and popular sovereignty [*samoderzhavie naroda*], economic management under capitalism everywhere has always remained a realm where there could be no mention of these ideas, where the *absolutism of capital* [*samoderzhavie kapitala*] in its most unrestricted form held sway. Capital allowed no interference here, not even a visit. Already half a century ago, Marx wrote of the 'hidden abode of production, on whose threshold there stares us in the face 'No admittance except on business''.[15] This is the abode of factories, plants, mines, and generally those places where capital lavishly flaunts itself while exploiting worker power. Here is the holy of holies of capitalism. For capitalist countries, this still remains true today.

After a short transitional stage, after the unsuccessful attempt to enact *factory constitutionalism* in the name of worker control, which vainly sought to transform the capitalist from an unlimited autocrat into a constitutional factory monarch, after practical experience had convincingly shown that the capitalist did not want and was not able to be a constitutional monarch, that he, despite all his assurances, was always plotting high treason, i.e. continued sabotage, the proletarian revolution completely destroyed any kind of command power of capital in the factories, and established *proletarian absolutism in the factories* [*samoderzhavie proletariata na fabrike*]. Worker control itself, which was despotic [*despoticheskii*] after the October overthrow, was in essence a feature of only the first stage of worker management.

But proletarian absolutism in the enterprises reversed the former separation of the proletariat from the management of the enterprises, rendering the economic administration and the proletariat, i.e. the organised proletariat, practically *identical*. And this *identity* meant that the mass organisations of the proletariat, the trade unions, were welded tightly to the organisation of proletarian economic management, forming its backbone.

The close connection of the trade unions with the organs of economic management, and most of all the fact that the latter were permeated by the trade

15 [Karl Marx, *Capital. A Critique of Political Economy*, vol. 1 (Harmondsworth, UK: Penguin Books, 1976), pp. 280–281].

unions, is the defining feature of the organisation of economic management at this time. This process began even *before* the nationalisation of capitalist industry, when in the various regulatory organs (in the context of increasing civil war, these had inevitably become the organs of actual administration) there also emerged, alongside representatives of the capitalist organisations and representatives of the soviets (i.e. the general political organisation of the proletariat), representatives of the trade unions who quickly became the backbone of these organs. As a result of this, at the moment of nationalisation the organs of economic management were in practice formed by the corresponding trade union organisations: initially, they were in many cases elected by them; later, they were in part elected by the trade unions and in part appointed by the appropriate organs of Soviet power in agreement with the appropriate trade union organs.[16]

---

16 From a typical document, published in 'Ekonomicheskaia zhizn'' of 3 December 1918 and in the official 'Sbornik dekretov i postanovlenii po narodnomu khoziaistvu', Moscow, 1920, vol. 2, p. 343.

'From the Central Administration of State Combined Machine-Building Plants to all plant managements of state combined machine-building plants. Read out to all worker organisations and at general meetings in plants and departments.

...The Central Administration of State Combined Machine-Building Plants [GOMZ], organised by VSNKh, *consisting mostly of workers elected at the conference of comrades delegated by you* (my emphasis, L.K.), in agreement with the Department Of Metal of VSNKh, and having confirmed the plant managements of enterprises belonging to GOMZ, considers every plant administration the leader of the given enterprise and responsible for the economic conduct of matters before the RSFSR...'.

The 'Decision on the Management of Nationalised Enterprises,' adopted at the First Congress of Councils of the National Economy meeting from 26 May to 4 June 1918, reads (see ibid., 'Sbornik', Moscow, 1918, p. 315):

'§ 2. In every plant, factory, mine etc, which has become the property of the Republic, a factory-plant management is set up. Two thirds of factory plant managements are appointed by the Council of the National Economy..., whereby the Council of the National Economy has the right to propose...that the trade union association put forward half of the candidates. One third of the members of management is elected by trade union-organised workers of the enterprise'.

The resolution on the question of the management of nationalised enterprises, adopted at the Second Congress of Councils of the National Economy in December 1918, reads (see ibid., 'Sbornik', Moscow, 1920, vol. 2, p. 179):

'§ 3. ...The central managements must...be composed of a small number of people (7–13), a majority of whom are determined by trade union-organised workers and officials of the corresponding enterprises and the corresponding trade unions....The entire central administration is confirmed by the VSNKh'.

'§ 7. ...Group associations headed by corresponding managements, organised on the same principles as the central managements (see § 3)...'

If (in the respective branch of the economy) a more or less strong trade union organisation existed, the economic management of the enterprises of this branch and also of the branch of the economy itself was completely in the hands of the respective trade union; the composition of the economic management was in practice determined by the conferences and congresses of this trade union; this composition was then confirmed by the appropriate supreme organ of economic administration (sometimes with modifications after negotiations between the latter and the trade union). Any disagreements arising in this area were resolved by agreement between the appropriate people's commissariat (in particular the Supreme Council of the National Economy) and the central leadership of the trade union organisations (the All-Russian Central Council of Trade Unions).

Evidence of this trade union influence in the administration of the economy was the very extensive *staffing* of the organs of this administration *with workers* [*orabochenie*].

The aforementioned VSNKh report to the Eighth Congress of Soviets provides the following statistics characterising this process for nationalised industry and refers to the end of 1920:[17]

'§ 8. For the administration of individual plants and enterprises, plant managements of 3–5 people are formed, organised by group managements…together with the corresponding trade union association'.

In the official 'Report of the Supreme Council of the National Economy to the Eighth All-Russian Congress of Soviets,' compiled in December 1920, i.e. at the end of the period under consideration in the current chapter, the organisation of the management of industry is depicted as follows (see p. 13):

'The leading apparatus of the Supreme Council of the National Economy, the Presidium…is set up in agreement with the All-Russian Central Council of Trade Unions. The presidiums of the provincial councils of the national economy [*gubsovnarkhoz*], which are confirmed by the Presidium of VSNKh, are appointed by local executive committees [*ispolkom*] in agreement with the local provincial council of trade unions. The central administrations of production units, the main and central managements, are appointed by the Presidium of VSNKh in agreement with the central committees of the corresponding trade union, and in the event of disagreements with them – in agreement with the Presidium of the All Russian Central Council of Trade Unions. Regional managements of enterprises are proposed by the regional congresses of representatives of workers of the corresponding enterprises, and after agreement with the provincial department of their trade union are confirmed by the central administration of the corresponding branch of industry or by the provincial council of the national economy….The management of enterprises is nominated by regional (or by the main) administration after agreement with the corresponding trade union'. 'In this way, the report goes on, the administration of industry is founded on production trade unions'.

17 See 'Otchet', p. 14. We have adjusted the data on the boards of the central administrations (and thus also the totals) on the basis of more accurate data from a statistical question-

	Overall total	Total number of workers	As percent of total	Total number of specialists	As percent of total	Total number of clerical staff, etc	As percent of total
1. Leading apparatus of the Presidiums of VSNKh and provincial councils of the national economy							
	187	107	57	22	12	58	31
2. Boards of central administrations (departments, main committees, and centres)							
	184	48	26	72	39	64	35
3. Factory and plant administrations							
	1,143	726	63	398	35	19	2
Total	1,514	881	58	492	33	141	9

But the trade unions' role in creating the apparatus of economic management was much more comprehensive than is shown by the above statistics on the staffing of the apparatus with workers. Twenty six per cent of the total personnel of the boards of the central administrations [*glavki*] were workers; but 55 per cent of these were proposed for these posts by trade unions (it was these 76 of a total of 140 members who provided information; in total, there were 199 members on these boards). Of these, 10% were members of central committees of trade unions.[18]

The key question and main difficulty in organising the new proletarian management of the economy was the *question of specialists* ('spetsy').

The development of capitalism separates the capitalist from the enterprise and makes the running of the enterprise the profession of a particular category of wage-workers, the technical intelligentsia [*tekhnicheskaia intelligentsia*]; but this development, which replaces the capitalists with a particular category of wage-workers, *brings this latter group as organisers of exploitation into conflict* with the large mass of the proletariat, i.e. they are actual surrogates of capital and are saturated with *capitalist ideology*.

If the removal of the capitalists from large-scale industry was relatively painless, this was precisely because the capitalist's separation from production and his replacement in the management of the enterprises by the technical intelligentsia meant that all functions of the capitalist were reduced to the function of exploitation; so his removal merely meant liberation from exploitation. Things were quite different, however, with the technical intelligentsia. The economic phase of the proletarian revolution brought the tendency to remove the technical intelligentsia as well, and from both sides: the proletariat, having shaken

naire (see 'Narodnoe khoziaistvo,' 1921, April. Article by V. Gershgorn, 'Struktura i sostav glavkov i tsentrov', p. 49).

18 Ibid., p. 42.

off the yoke of capitalist exploitation, experienced the natural urge to rid itself not only of the capitalists, but also of the two-faced Janus of the technical intelligentsia (in particular its uppermost stratum, capitalist management). This Janus turned the face of a servant towards capital and the face of a master towards the proletariat, and even worse, the face of a servant playing the role of a master, giving himself the impression that in relation to the proletariat he was a master. The technical intelligentsia itself exhibited the same tendency; it saw itself as part of the ruling class (Besitz und Bildung, ownership and education), but saw the proletarian revolution as the end of the world (because in its eyes, as in the eyes of the capitalist, the capitalist world was the world in general, there was no other world, nor could there be).

But the attempt to remove the old technical intelligentsia could not but clash with the fact that this technical intelligentsia played a *dual* role: it was not only the organiser of exploitation but also the *organiser of production*. Moreover, in a certain sense, it held a *monopoly* in the organisation of production. In the age of revolution, an economic administration cannot function (act) without its participation. This monopoly of the capitalist intelligentsia (a monopoly of know-how and skills) – the obverse side of which is the lack of the appropriate know-how and skills of the proletariat, its generally inadequate cultural level – cannot be broken until a new proletarian intelligentsia is created in sufficient and self-sustaining numbers. But the creation of a new proletarian intelligentsia takes not only a long time (many years), not only large resources, but also selected proletarian cadres, who have been *freed up* from current work. This precondition could not be met while civil war was going on, a war that urgently required the mobilisation of all forces of the proletarian vanguard for the current task, the success of which was crucial to the fate of the revolution. But this meant that while civil war, i.e. the intensified period of the revolution, was going on, and for several years after, the monopoly of the capitalist intelligentsia could not be broken. In other words, the revolution inevitably took place *not only on the basis of old technology, but also under conditions of the necessary continued functioning (work) of the old capitalist intelligentsia.* So a completely inevitable marriage occurred; from the start, it was not a marriage of love but a marriage of convenience between the capitalist intelligentsia and the proletariat, one which produced a new proletarian economic administration. The capitalist intelligentsia was governed by para. 18, section 2 of the Soviet Constitution, but especially also by the system of ration card distribution [*raspredelenie po kartochkam*] set up on the basis of this paragraph, and by fear of the harsh dictatorship of the proletariat; it overcome its horror of the turmoil of the proletarian revolution and its disbelief in the possibility of creating and maintaining a new society, in which there was no master of its body and its soul, where there was no master – capital. The proletariat, though, overcame its own antipathy toward those whom it had only known until then as representatives of capital, and it not only permitted the technical intelligentsia to participate in the administration of the economy, but also reintroduced an *increased payment* for its work, which secured the necessary degree of affection for the arrangement.

Of course, this community of compulsory labour caused (and still causes) in part (i.e. in part of the old technical intelligentsia which will get larger over time) a complete transformation of this section of the technical intelligentsia from a capitalist into a Soviet intelligentsia. It is transforming from a link between the capitalist economy and administration of the economy, which mediates between the command power of the capitalist and the group of proletarians subordinate to him, into a link between the proletarian economy and the administration of the economy, which mediates between the command power of the proletariat as a class and the group of proletarians of a given enterprise (or groups of them) subordinate to this power. Individual representatives of the old intelligentsia become enthusiastic actors under these new conditions and align themselves closely with the proletariat. But the bulk of the capitalist technical intelligentsia functions not so much willingly as under duress.[19] This results in the *declining* productivity of their labour and the deteriorating quality of the work of the apparatus of economic administration, i.e. of the administration of production.

The class-conscious vanguard of the proletariat, the Communist Party, was clear from the outset that it was impossible to remove the old capitalist intelligentsia and that its participation in the new administration of the economy was a necessity, and so all of the 'Regulations on the Administration of Nationalised Enterprises' carefully emphasised the need for the technical intelligentsia to participate in the organs of the proletarian administration of the economy in numbers above a certain level (usually a third).[20]

---

19 This reveals itself not only in the (albeit concealed) antagonistic attitude to the new order, but also in the lack of belief in it, in an inability to adapt to it and work under the new conditions. As the dictatorship of the proletariat has consolidated itself, this lack of belief and inability has come to the fore.

20 Thus, § 2 'Regulations on the Administration of Nationalised Enterprises,' adopted at the First Congress of Councils of the National Economy, reads: 'one third of the factory and plant management must be made up of specialists from the ranks of the technical and commercial employees' (see 'Sbornik dekretov i postanovlenii po narodnumu khoziaistvu', Moscow, 1918, p. 315). In a resolution of the Second Congress of Councils of the National Economy on the same question, § 4 reads: 'The central management (according to § 3 it comprises 7–13 people, L.K.) must contain no less than two specialists with tech-

As we have seen, the technical intelligentsia (the specialists) was present in significant numbers in the organs of the proletarian economic administration (especially in the upper echelons that wielded command power and, as we see below, were the organs of the dictatorship in a particular sphere); in the factory and plant managements the share was 35 %, on the boards of all-Russian central administrations it was 39 %, and even in the presidiums of councils of the national economy (VSNKh and provincial councils of the national economy) it was 12 %. By the way, some of those specialists who joined the organs of proletarian economic administration were not part of the old capitalist intelligentsia. On the boards of the central administrations, workers made up 26 %, while Communist Party members made up 49 %, i.e. at least a third of the members of the boards of the central administrations, who were not workers, belonged to the Communist Party.[21]

Even more significant was the proportion of the technical intelligentsia in the subordinate (middle) links of the apparatus. Of the department heads of central administrations only 4 % were workers, 12 % were individuals with no middle-school education, and 10 % were Communist Party members and sympathisers.

Of the administrative staff of the departments of the Supreme Council of the National Economy, and in those departments not involved in production, 0.8 % were workers, 6 % were individuals with no middle-school education, and 13 % were Communist Party members.[22]

The author of the study cited here drew the following conclusion about the composition of the Supreme Council of the National Economy on 1 December 1920: 'If we now try to characterise in a few words the entire group we studied (about 900 individuals) of those employed in the most important positions of trust in the Supreme Council of the National Economy, then we would have to say that this group is made up of a *non-party (80 % non-party, 19 % communists), diplomaed intelligentsia (23 % engineers, 61 % with higher education, 87 % with completed middle-school education), with a small mingling of former workers (8 % of the total)*'.[23]

As we have seen, this conclusion derives from the predominance of the old technical intelligentsia in the *middle* ranks of the apparatus of economic

nical and commercial know-how'. And § 8 stipulates that 'plant management (according to the same point from 3–5 people, L.K.) must contain, alongside workers, also members of the technical staff' (see Ibid., vol. 2, Moscow, 1920, p. 119).

21 See V. Gershgorn, ibid., p. 52.

22 Ibid., pp. 53 and 54.

23 Ibid., p. 55 (author's emphasis).

administration; it refers mostly to these individuals, because in the organs which now no longer represent the command power of capital but rather the *command* power of the proletariat, the specialists and above all the non-party specialists, i.e. the capitalist intelligentsia, were a clear minority.

In terms of importance, this work of creating a new proletarian economic administration was, it can be said, the *fundamental* work of the proletarian revolution in this era (1918–1920, and especially 1919–1920). The work of installing a proletarian state political administration, a new state apparatus (a Soviet state) – an administrative, judicial, and military apparatus – was largely[24] completed in the first eight months of the proletarian revolution (from October 1917 to June 1918); that it lasted two and a half more years (not as a work of completion but as a work of rebuilding) was the result of the impact of *external* forces, which forcibly extended the phase of political revolution to three full years and compelled the revolution to reconstruct the state Soviet apparatus painstakingly and tirelessly whenever and wherever it had been destroyed by the merciless hand of the civil war that was sustained by global capital.

On the other hand, the work of creating a new organisation of the economy – not in the sense of changing the internal class structure of the administration of the economy, but in the sense of regrouping economic units and reorganising the connections between them, i.e. an organisation no longer in the realm of specific, but in the realm of general, economic relations – was fundamentally a work of the future; this work was similarly forced on the revolution at this stage by the impact of those same *external* forces, which meant that the intensification of the proletarian revolution was inevitable in order to undercut counter-revolutionary resistance.

By the way, while the work of creating the apparatus of state (political) administration was essentially a matter of bringing to completion past work, the work of creating a new organisation of the economy by regrouping economic units and reorganising the connections between them was an anticipation of future tasks; the work of creating a new economic administration, new in terms of its internal class structure (construction), was fundamental, and was therefore the irreversible work of the proletarian revolution in this era; this irreversible achievement is forever, and can never be taken away.

It was this work of creating a new proletarian administration of the economy that made ours a *proletarian* revolution, for precisely this work was the work of creating a new harmonious economic system free of exploitation in place of

24 This has to do, of course, not with the degree of completion of the Soviet state (especially military) apparatus, but with the fact of its *replacement* of the former apparatus.

the old antagonistic economic system that relied upon the separation of labour power from the means of production and thus on exploitation as well. It was this work that basically achieved the revolutionary transition *from an antagonistic to a harmonious organisation of social labour.*

The main stages of the creation and development of worker management of the economy were constitutional (according to its own programme) worker control before October; despotic worker control after October; forced participation of capitalists in the organs of state proletarian regulation until the decree on the nationalisation of large industry, and their forced allocation to enterprises before the formation of organs of worker management in enterprises (at the end of 1918 and the start of 1919); collective worker management; individual worker management. We will return to them again below.

Along with the creation of a Soviet state system, *the creation of a proletarian administration of the economy is the world historical achievement of the Russian Revolution, which created an organised form of transition to a future Communist society unprecedented (and thus most far-reaching in social terms) in the history of mankind.*

After the Paris Commune, which for the first time in the history of mankind created a proletarian state (political) administration (which in the Russian Revolution was developed further and completed in the form of the Soviet system), the creation of the proletarian administration of the economy also represents a new step forward in terms of principle, a step taken by the Russian Revolution.

The Paris Commune created the organisational form of the political dictatorship of the proletariat, the Russian Revolution created the organisational form of the economic dictatorship of the proletariat.

It is scarcely possible to overestimate the significance of this achievement.

CHAPTER 5

The Proletarian Natural Economic System (a Description)

1. The new organisation of the economic administration and the new organisation of the economy. 2. The Supreme Council of the National Economy and its organs. 3. Other economic commissariats.

The future course of development of our revolution showed beyond doubt that the enduring achievement of this period was the organisation of a new proletarian administration of the economy, i.e. the transition from an antagonistic organisation of production to a harmonious one. While this work of organising the new proletarian administration of the economy was without doubt the main task of the proletarian revolution in this era, the *characteristic* feature of this period of our revolution was something different: it was that the bulk of the work of the proletarian revolution unfolded, for reasons already discussed above, in anticipation of the future, above all not in the realm of specific, but in the realm of *general* economic conditions. This work was not limited in the main to regrouping the elements within the economic units and reorganising the relations within these economic units, it consisted rather of regrouping the economic units themselves and reorganising the connections among them. The new proletarian organisation of the management of the economy proved to be a lasting achievement of the revolution extending into its next phase, precisely because its creation was the fundamental work of this period of the revolution. On the other hand, the new organisation of the economy turned out to be ephemeral (short-lived), and it *did not carry over* into the following period, and precisely for this reason it is also characteristic of the period of the revolution under consideration here.

Viewed from the perspective of specific economic relations, the new economic system differed from the old system in that it was a *proletarian* system; from the perspective of general economic relations, the new, emerging (proletarian) economic system was marked by two basic features: it was (by tendency), first, a *natural* economy, and second, a *centralised* economy.

Of course, these two basic features were in no way the result of any kind of wishful thinking, they were in no way tendencies that were foreign to the preceding economic development, but on the contrary, they were the consistent

 | HTTPS://DOI.ORG/10.1163/9789004765313-009

and completed development of tendencies which characterised the preceding economic development that had taken capitalist forms.

The transformation of commodity relations in natural conditions (the germs of which appeared already in the era of capitalist monopolies; in the course of the struggle against them, these had produced the counter-tendency to form combined enterprises) had been broadly prepared by finance capital, and had, as such, emerged openly during the transition of finance capitalism into state capitalism.

The centralisation of the economy had already been broadly prepared in individual branches of the economy by the capitalist monopolies, and in the entire national economy by finance capital.

Under capitalism, these, however, were only tendencies in the actual development, which made their own way through the numerous vestiges of the old economic conditions. Now they became *the guiding principles* of proletarian economic construction. The latter was typically marked precisely by a striving to realise these guiding principles *completely* and to destroy everything that contradicted them.

The starting point for proletarian economic construction were the centralised economic organs of pre-October Russia, state organs: the ministries that were transformed into people's commissariats; the monopolistic organisations of the capitalists, the syndicates; and the state capitalist regulating organs that were created during the imperialist war, and which were transformed into the central administrations of industry (*'glavki'*).

Examination of the old and new centralised economic organs from the perspective of specific economic relations reveals that they have *nothing in common* with each other. On the contrary, the new are the direct, polar opposites of the old. Between the former and the latter stands the revolution. Some represent the command power of capital, which is the concentrated expression of the antagonistic nature of their specific economic relations (the separation of labour power from the means of production); others represent the command power of the proletariat, which brings about the transition to harmonious, specific economic relations (the merger, the synthesis of labour power and the means of production). But examination of the old and new economic organs from the perspective not of their specific but of their general economic relations reveals that the one is the *heir* to the other. The new economic organs created by the revolution (considered from this angle) are the expression of those same trends which took their own path, but – in contrast to the past – are now consistently striving to see it through to the end.

In the one sphere, the economic construction by the proletariat occurs *as revolution*, as a social rebirth of the mode of production, as a transition from one polar opposite to the other; in the other sphere, however, it occurs as the continuation of an evolution, as the continuation of the organised labour of the old social system, which has now assumed a hitherto unprecedented tempo.

The trend to create a centralised economic organisation was (before the revolution) furthest away from completion in industry. This is precisely why the *Supreme Council of the National Economy* was the signal creation of the proletarian revolution in the area of economic construction. It is barely worth mentioning its connection with the Ministry of Trade and Industry (which had existed before the October Revolution and for a while after it, and was later transformed into the People's Commissariat of Foreign Trade). In its most developed phase – that of the dominance of finance capital – capitalism led to the formation of a unified, state-capitalist trust. In the era of the dictatorship of the proletariat, the centralising impulse found expression in the Supreme Council of the National Economy. In a certain sense, the Supreme Council inherited and continued (in its unification of the national economy) the work of the organisations of finance capital (the banking concerns). It emerged from the unification of various organs of labour unions, symbolising the working class's transition from organising itself to organising the national economy. The Supreme Council of the National Economy was the authorised representative of the dictatorship of the proletariat in this realm; the same role was played by its organs, the production departments and the central administrations, in correspondingly narrower fields.

The central organ of administration and regulation of industry – the Supreme Council of the National Economy (abbreviated to VSNKh or Vysovnarkhoz) – was created at the end of 1917. By 1920, the functioning centre of the administration and regulation of industry was in practice the Presidium of the Supreme Council, consisting of 10–12 people (a broad, representative board – the plenum of the Supreme Council of the National Economy – had ceased functioning long before). It was elected at the All-Russian Congress of Councils of the National Economy which was composed of representatives of the largest enterprises, trade unions, central administrations of individual branches of industry and provincial councils of the national economy. The chair of the Supreme Council of the National Economy joined the Council of People's Commissars [*Sovet Narodnykh Komissarov*].

The organs subordinate to the Presidium of the Supreme Council of the National Economy were, at the centre, the production departments of the Supreme Council of the National Economy, and, at the local level, the provincial councils of the national economy. Each production department was led by a board of 5–7 people (its chair was the director of the department). The largest production departments were: the Department of the Metal-Producing and Metal-Processing industry (abbreviated to Metal Department), the Mining Council, the Department of the Electrotechnical Industry, the Department of the Chemical Industry (abbreviated to Chemical Department), and the Department of Processing of Food and Flavouring Substances (aside from these departments, at the end of 1920 only two other production departments existed: the Printing Industry and the Recycling [*utilizatsionnaia*] Industry). The boards of the departments were appointed by the Presidium of the Supreme Council of the National Economy in agreement with the Central Committee of the appropriate trade union, and – where disagreement arose – in agreement with the Presidium of the All-Russian Central Council of Trade Unions.

Each branch of industry was headed by the appropriate central administration, which was subordinated either directly to the Presidium of the Supreme Council of the National Economy (the largest central administrations such as, e.g., the central administration of the textile industry, the central administration of the leather industry, and several others) or else to the board of the appropriate production department. In all, there were (at the end of 1920) over 40 central administrations (abbreviated to *glavki*):

		Abbreviation
1	Central administration of locomotive and wagon-building plants	Gomza
2	Central administration of nail and wire plants	Glavgvozd'
3	Central administration of copper-processing plants	Glavtsvetmet
4	Central administration of the goldmining industry	Glavzoloto
5	Central administration of aircraft plants	Glavkoavio
6	Central administration of automobile plants	Avtozavody
7	Central administration of the salt-extraction industry	Glavsol'
8	Central administration of the coalmining industry	Glavugol'
9	Central administration of the peat-extraction industry	Glavtorf
10	Central administration of the oil industry	Glavneft'
11	Central administration of the shale industry	Glavslanets
12	Central administration of the ore-mining industry	Glavruda
13	Central administration of the textile industry (with departments of cotton, linen, wool, silk, etc)	Glavtekstil'
14	Central administration enterprises of the clothing industry	Glavodezhda
15	Central administration of the elemental chemical industry	Khimosnov

(*cont.*)

		Abbreviation
16	Central administration of the rubber industry	Glavrezina
17	Central administration of the match industry	Glavspichka
18	Central administration of the glass and ceramics industry	Glavsteklo
19	Central administration of the cement industry	Tsentrotsement
20	Central administration of the slate industry	Tsentroshifer
21	Central administration of the chamotte and brick industry	Tsentroshamot
22	Central administration of the paint and varnish industry	Glavkraslak
23	Central administration of the coke and benzene industry	Glavanil
24	Central administration of the dry distillation of wood	Khimdrevpravlenie
25	Central administration of the chemical-pharmaceutical industry	Glavfarmazav
26	Central administration of the stationery industry	Glavbum
27	Central administration of the forest committee (running the logging and wood-processing industry)	Glavleskom
28	Central administration of the leather industry (including shoe production)	Glavkozh
29	Central administration of the fur industry	Glavmekh
30	Central administration of the bone processing industry	Glavkost’
31	Central administration of the bristle industry	Tsentroshchetina
32	Central administration of the fat (and soap) industry	Tsentrozhir
33	Central administration of the tobacco industry	Glavtabak
34	Central administration of the distilling industry	Tsentrospirt
35	Central administration of the starch industry	Glavkrakhmal
36	Central administration of the sugar industry	Glavsakhar
37	Central administration of the flour and cereal industry	Glavmuka
38	Central administration of the confectionery industry	Glavkonditer
39	Central administration of the coffee and tea industry (production of surrogates)	Glavchai
40	Central administration of the canning industry	Glavkonserv
41	Central administration of the dairy industry	Tsentromoloko
42	Central administration of the oil milling (vegetable oils) industry	Glavrasmaslo

Each type of central administration was led by a board, which was appointed by the board of the appropriate production department (or by the Presidium of the Supreme Council of the National Economy if the central administration was directly subordinate to it) in agreement with the Central Committee of the appropriate trade union. Often the composition of the central administration was proposed beforehand by the All-Russian Congress of the appropriate trade union.

In those branches of industry where for one or another reason no independent center of administration and regulation in the form of a central administration had yet been created, this work was carried out by the appropriate production section of the production department, whose activity to a great extent was devoted to creating the preconditions for the organisation of a central administration. In contrast to the central administration, the production section worked not only under the general leadership of the production department, but all of its ongoing work was supervised contantly by this department. Examples of these production sections include the agricultural machine-building section of the Department of Metallurgical Industry; the earth- and mineral-colour [*moskotil'naia*] section of the Chemical Industry; the technical reprocessing of fruits and vegetables section of the Department of Processing of Food and Flavouring Substances, among others. By the end of 1920, only five or six of these sections remained. Each section was headed by the usual director.

Both the Supreme Council of the National Economy, and its production departments, and also the central administrations of the industrial branches had a number of functional organs (i.e. organs which took over a certain part of the field of activity of their institutions), such as the Departments of Finance, Accounting, Material Supply, Distribution, Technical, sometimes Agronomical Departments, and others.

All enterprises in the Republic were divided into three categories: the first category comprised all of the most important enterprises which bypassed the local economic organs and were directly subordinate to the central administrations or even to the production departments of the Supreme Council of the National Economy. Other less important enterprises, but whose importance was by no means purely local, worked according to plans, which were confirmed by their central administration, but were also organisationally linked with the provincial councils of the national economy. Finally, the third category comprised enterprises of purely local significance, and were subordinate exclusively to the provincial councils of the national economy, which drew up work plans for them (the urban economy of large towns was also in their hands). By 1 November 1920, a total of 6908 enterprises were divided up as follows:[1]

1 See *Otchet VSNKh VIII S'ezdu Sovetov*, p. 20. According to the census of 28 August 1920, there

first category	2,374	i.e. 35%
second category	3,450	i.e. 50%
third category	1,084	i.e. 15%

It must be noted here, though, that only a small portion of the enterprises in the third group were included in the data.

The provincial councils of the national economy (abbreviated to gubsovnarkhozy) were the local organs of the Supreme Council of the National Economy, although in reality they were only loosely connected with it. Their leading organs – the presidiums – were composed of 3–7 people and were appointed by local soviet power in agreement with the provincial councils of the trade unions and confirmed by the Presidium of the Supreme Council of the National Economy. They numbered 68 by 1920.[2] The county soviets of the national economy that had existed earlier were closed by 1920. In the counties, only organs with an auxiliary function existed, namely the economic departments of county Soviets of Worker and Peasant Deputies, which were subordinated to the provincial council of the national economy. The urban economy of smaller settlements was administered by communal departments.

The district administrations of enterprises of a particular branch of industry were provisionally nominated by district congresses of representatives of workers of these enterprises and confirmed in agreement with the provincial department of their trade union either by the central administration of the appropriate branch of industry or by the provincial council of the national economy, depending on whether the enterprises belonged to the second category or the third. In accordance with this, the district administrations were either completely subordinated to the provincial council of the national economy, or they were set up under them but worked according to the plans of their central administration.

---

were more than 37,000 state industrial enterprises; the overwhelming majority of them (small enterprises) undoubtedly belonged to the enterprises of the third category, so that the total number of enterprises (not just the large enterprises) was distributed among the individual categories as follows:

first category	6–7%
second category	9–10%
third category	83–85%

2 See *Otchet VSNKh VIII S'ezdu Sovetov*. This official (!) report numbers the local organs at 81, including five regional councils of the national economy, the others being provincial councils. However, in the table *on the opposite* page (p. 17) in this report, all local organs are listed by name; it turns out that there are not five, but six regional councils and 68 provincial councils, a total therefore of 74 and not 81.

Various central administrations formed associations of similar enterprises (or trusts); the leadership of these formations was set up in the same way as the district administrations; these trusts comprised a group of enterprises which shared a production technique, e.g. so a semi-finished product of one plant could be finished in a second and sometimes even in a third enterprise of the trust.

A large number of such trusts existed in the textile industry and in the metallurgical industry, etc. By 1920, these kinds of associations (trusts) numbered 179 (46 of which were in the textile industry, 46 in the food industry, and 20 in the metallurgical industry). These trusts comprised a quarter (25%) of all the plants that were included in the statistics and over half (52%) of the workers employed in them (in those plants which had provided data on the number of workers employed in them). These trusts were set up almost exclusively between 1 October 1918 and 1 July 1919; four fifths of all the trusts (existing in 1920) were set up during this period.[3] The largest of these trusts, especially in the metal industry – for example, the Central Administration of Heavy Industry of Southern Russia (abbreviated to Tsepti), the Mal'tsovskii region, the State Association of Moscow Metallurgical plants (abbreviated to Gomomez), the district administrations of plants in the Urals, and others – were directly subordinated to the appropriate production department of the Supreme Council of the National Economy.

The enterprise administrations were appointed by the district (or main) administration in agreement with the appropriate trade union. The enterprise administrations were initially just boards, but later were either a board (usually of three people) or an individual. The factory and plant committee was only an organ of the trade union, and not an organ of the management, in which it did not interfere.

Subordinated to the People's Commissariat of Food were also industrial-type organs: the Central Administration of the Fishing Industry (abbreviated to Glavryba), which in the first period was a joint organ of the People's Commissariat of Food and the Supreme Council of the National Economy, and the Central Administration of Refrigeration Units (abbreviated to Tsentrokholodoboinia), which originated in the Supreme Council of the National Economy. Both of these administrations were organised in exactly the same way as the central administrations of the Supreme Council of the National Economy (the boards were appointed in agreement with the central committee of the trade union of workers of the food industry). There was no absolute

---

3 See *Otchet VSNKh VIII S'ezdu Sovetov*, pp. 23 and 24.

demarcation of responsibilities between the Supreme Council of the National Economy and the People's Commissariat of Food either in the food industry as a whole or in its individual branches (dairy, fruit and vegetable processing, etc).[4]

The Council of the Armaments Industry (abbreviated to Promvoensovet) was set up almost exactly the same way as the production departments of the Supreme Council of the National Economy. It was subordinated to the Extraordinary Plenipotentiary for the Supply of the Red Army in the Council of Defense (a post filled by the same individual who chaired the Supreme Council of the National Economy). The Council of the Armaments Industry, which had several central administrations under it, included the purely military plants which had until then been subordinated to the People's Commissariat of Military Affairs: its activity prepared for the later incorporation of the arms industry into the general organisation of industry.

According to the general direction of the economic policy of Soviet power, small and artisanal shops and enterprises (whose owners, in contrast to the big bourgeoisie, were not expropriated but nonetheless in many cases preferred to hide behind a screen of 'labour' production artels [*trudovye arteli*]) were regulated not from any kind of special centre but by the central administrations of the appropriate branches of industry.

The Artisanal-Cooperative Administration (abbreviated to Glavkustprom), in charge of specific matters of small and artisanal industry, was at this time more a functional than a production department.

State buildings came under a particular body, which had been set up after the October Revolution – the Main Committee of State Construction [*Glavyi Komitet Gosudarstvennykh Sooruzhenii*] (abbreviated to Glavkomgosoor). This had its own provincial organs, was in charge of all of the largest building projects, and regulated all other building activity at the local level. It included the administration of railway construction, the administration of waterway construction, the administration of roadways, the administration of electrical stations, the administration of shipbuilding, the administration of urban and rural construction (also in charge of the construction of worker settlements), the administration of industrial construction, and so on. On completion of construction, they were handed over for use by the appropriate institutions. The Main Committee of State Construction was a department of the Supreme Council of the National Economy and was organised like the other departments

4 Consequently, two more central administrations, Glavmuka and Tsentromoloko, were added to the People's Commissariat of Food.

(its board was appointed in consultation with the Central Committee of the Trade Union of Construction Workers).

The People's Commissariat of Transport (the former Ministry of Transport) was initially an administrative organ of rail transport, and an organ of exploitation. Like all the people's commissariats, it was headed by a board which worked with the support of the All-Russian Trade Union of Railway Workers. The People's Commissariat of Communication Routes (Narkomput') was set up on completely different principles than the Supreme Council of the National Economy, and its organs had a great deal in common with the organisation of the Red Army. Its organs were not run by boards but by individual heads. Most of them were specialists, who were from non-revolutionary circles. Earlier, a commissar (a communist) had been placed alongside each specialist, just as commissars had been placed alongside the important military experts; the commissars had the right to overrule the orders of the experts. By 1920, the institution of the commissars both in the army and in the railway system began to die out (the commissars, who were specialists in their fields, took over the leadership duties). Like the main political administration of the Revolutionary Military Council of the Republic (of the Red Army), there was also a main political administration of the People's Commissariat of Transport (abbreviated to Glavpolitput') with the same functions. It conducted Communist Party work among the railway workers and deployed and directed communist workers in the railway system according to the demands of the moment. Like the Supreme Council of the National Economy, the People's Commissariat of Transport was also the sole organ of administration of railway (and later waterway) transport in the entire territory of the Federation.

The deep crisis in rolling stock demanded extraordinary repair measures. This was the task of the Extraordinary Commission for the Repair of Rolling Stock (abbreviated to Komrem) in the Supreme Council of the National Economy; this commission had special powers over those enterprises and railway workshops responsible for the repair of rolling stock in the railways.

The Central Administration of Marine Transport (abbreviated to Glavod) was created after the revolution when the state took over transport on the waterways. It originated as a department of the Supreme Council of the National Economy and was organised exactly the same way as the central administrations of the branches of industry; by 1920, the Central Administration of Marine Transport became part of the People's Commissariat of Transport, which combined control of both railway and marine transport, and later also local transport. The Central Administration of Marine Transport was responsible not only for the entire merchant navy (i.e. those vessels not belonging to the military navy), steamers and sailboats, passenger ships, cargo ships, and ships for special purposes, but also for all ports, canals, and waterways in the entire territory of the Federation. At the local level there were district administrations of marine transport.

Draft animal transport in industry and the administration of warehouses and of the haulage societies taken over by the state came under the Transport and Materiel Department (abbreviated to Tramot) of the Supreme Council of the National Economy, and it had its own provincial organs at the local level. This department was also responsible for the entire matter of evacuation, which took on enormous significance during the Civil War, when huge swathes of land changed hands between the Whites and the Reds multiple times. Closely linked with the Transport and Materiel Department, which was also only created in the revolutionary period, was the Extraordinary Commission for Ownerless Property and Spoils of War, which played a significant role for the same reason. Draft animal transport and warehouses were not completely centralised, and the economic national commissariats (of food, etc) had their own transport departments, although they did not have any general functions.

The People's Commissariat of Post and Telegraph (the former Ministry of Post and Telegraph) was responsible for the entire communications service in the entire territory of the Federation. Its board was closely linked with the Central Committee of the Trade Union of Postal and Telegraph Workers. All postal, telegraph, telephone, and radio-telegraph agencies of the republic were subordinate to the People's Commissariat of Post and Telegraph (abbreviated to Narkompochtel').

The People's Commissariat of Labour (the former Ministry of Labour, which was set up after the February Revolution during the Kerensky era) was the supreme state organ on questions of the distribution of the labour force and on labour protections. It was closely linked with the All-Russian Central Council of Trade Unions, which proposed the makeup of the board of the People's Commissariat of Labour. The departments of the People's Commissariat of Labour (abbreviated to Narkomtrud) worked closely with the appropriate departments of the All-Russian Central Council of Trade Unions, and the provincial departments worked closely with the provincial councils of trade unions, which also proposed the makeup of the boards of the provincial departments of labour.

For the labour mobilisation of the dispersed masses (mostly peasants) for special tasks, the Main Committee for Compulsory Labour (abbreviated to Glavkomtrud) was set up. It carried out mobilisations for logging work, construction work, sugar beet cultivation, etc.

The scale of the use of compulsory labour can be judged, from incomplete figures, from the fact that for the first half of 1920 5,800,000 people and 4,160,000 horses were mobilised in fulfillment of the wood fuel removal obligation [*toplivo-guzhevaia povinnost'*] (decreed in November 1919); from May to December 1920, about 10 % of the preparation and removal of wood was carried out using compulsory labour.[5]

The policy of labour mobilisation was carried out by all organs of Soviet power: the People's Commissariat of Internal Affairs provided labour detachments to perform various kinds of difficult and unpleasant work; these detachments were made up of individuals who had been imprisoned in concentration camps (they were predominantly members of the former ruling classes). The Central Committee for the Assistance of Prisoners and Refugees formed labour detachments from prisoners and refugees for use predominantly in agricultural labour. There were also attempts to make some use of the labour of invalids and juveniles.

Raising the level of qualifications of the labour force was the task of a particular institution – the Main Committee for Professional and Technical Training. In this way, the People's Commissariat of Enlightenment also mobilised its forces to the same ends as did other organs of Soviet power.

All scientific and technical activity in Soviet Russia fell under the Scientific-Technical Department of the Supreme Council of the National Economy, which was responsible for all laboratories and special scientific-technical institutes and authorities, as well as for all inventions. Also affiliated to the production departments of the Supreme Council of the National Economy were the scientific-technical institutions, which worked under the general leadership of the Scientific-Technical Department.

The economic relations between the proletarian state and the peasantry were not only restricted by the fact that it served as a reservoir of labour power and as producers of agricultural products; the proletarian state also sought, to a certain extent, to regulate the economic activity of the peasantry directly. The People's Commissariat of Agriculture (the former Ministry of Agriculture), in addition to its earlier tasks, had to run the enormous process of land distribution, and worked to promote the development of collective forms of agriculture (public cultivations, agricultural artels and communes). One of its most important tasks was the distribution of agronomic forces. Ukraine had its own People's Commissariat of Agriculture.

5 See the collection *Lesozagotovitel'naia politika v obshchei sisteme narodnogo khoziaistva*, 1921, pp. 65–66. The incomplete nature of these data is evident, for example, from the fact that these figures show that 114,000 were mobilised in Kaluga province, but later more complete data show it to be about 268,000 (ibid., p. 66). This same source attests that 'up to 60 % of the population of forested provinces capable of working took part in these mobilisations for wood preparation and removal work'.

A completely new institution created by the revolution was the Department of State Farms [*sovkhozy*] in the People's Commissariat of Agriculture (abbreviated to Glavsovkhoz), which emerged from the proletarian expropriation of the expropriators in agriculture, i.e. the expropriation of landowners without redistribution of their lands and without the destruction of large-scale farming. The Department of State Farms was by definition a central administration of state farms and sought the support of the Trade Union of Agricultural Workers. At the local level, there were provincial departments of state farms, which were subordinated to the central department but linked with the local organs of the People's Commissariat of Agriculture as a whole – the provincial departments of agriculture.

A significant number of state farms were associated with the industrial proletariat. These state farms were led by the Central Administration of Agricultural Farms of the industrial proletariat (abbreviated to Glavzemkhoz), which was a department of the Supreme Council of the National Economy. State farms were assigned to enterprises or associations (central administrations) by a special Committee for Worker Support for the Creation of Agricultural Farms of the industrial proletariat; this committee was composed of representatives of trade unions and set up under the People's Commissariat of Agriculture. These state farms were closely linked with the enterprises, which were interested both in the maximum productivity of the state farms assigned to them, because their products ended up in the food supply stores of the enterprise, and also in ensuring that they were well-appointed, as they were also used as places of relaxation.

In addition to these state farms, which served nutritional purposes, there were also state industrial farms, which produced raw materials for appropriate branches of the agricultural industry (the sugar beet, distilling, tobacco, dairy industries, etc); these were also connected with the Central Administration of Agricultural Farms and served mostly as model farms or to raise valuable seed; an exception here was sugar beet production, which by area made up almost half of all state farms and was subordinated to the main administration of the sugar beet industry.

To promote the cultivation of vacant or neglected lands, the Committee for the Organisation of Sown Area (abbreviated to Orgasev) was set up under the People's Commissariat of Agriculture. A significant part of these lands was made up of farms of former landowners, which peasants had been unable to manage in view of inadequate inventory or for other reasons.

With the exception of the sugar beet industry, agricultural products were procured to an enormous extent not from state farms but from small producers – peasants. This procurement was carried out by various soviet organs, the most important of which was the People's Commissariat of Food Supply (the former Ministry of Food Supply). Agricultural products were procured by two departments of the People's Commissariat of Food Supply: the Administration for Perishable Goods (abbreviated to Zagotosel'), responsible for the procurement of potatoes and other vegetables, as well as meat, game, butter, honey, etc; and the Administration for Grain and Feed (abbreviated to Khlebofurazh), responsible for the procurement of grains, hay, etc. Both administrations had their own provincial organs, which were subordinated to the provincial food supply commissars, representatives of the People's Commissariat of Food Supply at the local level.

Some agricultural products procured from the peasants were subject to a state monopoly (the most important were grains, potatoes, cattle, etc), and while the monopoly was extended with time to ever newer products, other products were not subject to a state monopoly (game, many vegetables, cottage cheese, milk, honey, etc). The latter were bought by organs of the People's Commissariat of Food Supply or by other organisations under their control. Monopoly products were surrendered by peasant associations according to quotas [*razverstki*] set by the People's Commissariat of Food Supply. Where the quantities established by quota were not surrendered, the missing quantities were taken by force by military food detachments. These detachments were formed by a special military food-supply bureau under the All-Russian Central Council of Trade Unions from the ranks of individual workers, trade union members, and from the poorest peasants of the grain-consuming regions, i.e. those regions without a secure food supply. In their procurement work, the food supply organs relied on the poorest part of the local peasant population and its organisations (at one time the special Committees of Poor Peasants), as this part of the population (the poor peasants) was socially close to the proletariat and was thus inclined to support it; moreover, the peasantry had a direct interest in the successful procurement of foodstuffs, for satisfaction of its demands (redressing its lack of grain) was directly related to successful procurement.

Failure to deliver the quantities called for by the quotas led not only to the threat of confiscation of the grain that was being kept back, it also meant that the peasant population did not receive the products due to them from the state supply, as these products (industrial products, such as manufactured goods, crockery, matches, etc, or products procured elsewhere) were released to the peasant community only on fulfillment of their share of the quota.

Procurement of agricultural products and agricultural raw materials was carried out by many organs of the Supreme Council of the National Economy. Apart from sugar beet, which was procured in a particular way, various central administrations of the Supreme Council of the National Economy were responsible for the procurement of flax, tobacco, hemp (exclusively for these products), oilseeds, potatoes (in part, alongside organs of the People's Commissariat of Food Supply) and other products. The procurement methods in 1920 did not differ significantly from those used by the People's Commissariat of Food Supply. The differences came down to an increased specialisation of the procurement apparatus, to a connection with the industry interested in collecting the raw materials and with the proletariat employed in this industry, and finally to a specialisation of the state product exchange stock (the People's Commissariat of Food Supply had a common product stock for all its procurement actions).

Procurement of wood was handled organisationally in much the same way as the above procurements and was carried out by the Main Forestry Committee of the Supreme Council of the National Economy and its local organs – the provincial forestry committees. Procurement was carried out by peasants in their capacity as seasonal workers (by agreement). The concentration of efforts to procure wood and the utilisation of nature's abundances (textiles, salt, etc.) offered something of a solution to the fuel crisis, which was threatening to cripple the entire economy.

Agricultural cooperatives played an important role in the procurement actions (although their significance in this period declined). Most of all, the lowest ranks of the agricultural cooperatives (and in the beginning their central sites as well, which were later abolished) served as the contractors of the food supply and industrial organs carrying out the procurements. Some procurements were already taking place by 1920 without any participation from the cooperatives (the procurement of sugar beet, tobacco, tree resin, and other products).

The People's Commissariat of Food Supply was not only the organ in charge of carrying out the most important procurements but also the organ in charge of supplying the population. Two departments of the People's Commissariat of Food Supply were responsible for this: the Administration of General Distribution in charge of the distribution of the majority of products procured by the organs of the People's Commissariat of Food Supply (some products were distributed by the Administration of Perishable Products) and the Central Administration of State Product Exchange (abbreviated Glavprodukt) responsible for the distribution of industrial products; the latter's board included a representative of the Supreme Council of the National Economy.

Distribution was carried out according to a card system, which functioned mostly in large cities. The entire population was forced to organise in cooperatives. In every town, one united consumer cooperative existed; these cooperatives were united in the centre by a Central Union of Consumer Societies (abbreviated to Tsentrosoiuz) and at the local level by their provincial unions (all other types of cooperatives were subordinated administratively to the Central Union).

Distribution cards were allocated according to several categories. While children received special cards, all adults were divided into three categories: the first category comprised predominantly factory and plant workers, the second comprised members of their families and other labourers with their families, the third comprised representatives of the former ruling classes.[6] Supplies to this latter group were very meagre (many products were not given out at all to them). In the beginning, when the public distribution of commodities was not yet regulated and the bourgeoisie had all kinds of commodities at their disposal, their dwellings, furniture, utensils, clothing etc were confiscated and distributed among the proletarians. Peasants received products according to special norms, smaller than the norms of the first two urban categories. Those workers who performed heavy physical labour received an additional card. In Leningrad, additional bread cards were distributed only for days actually worked (the work ration).

In the large cities, numerous communal dining halls were set up (in Leningrad in 1920 the entire population frequented them, in Moscow about half of the population). For children, a free meal was provided at school; moreover, children received free clothing and, of course, teaching materials. Mothers who were breastfeeding received special distribution cards. Family members of Red Army soldiers also received special cards (additional so-called 'Red Star' cards).

Supplying provisions to workers fell under a special organ of the People's Commissariat of Food Supply – the Department for the Supply of Food to Factory and Plant Workers and Fuel Production Workers (abbreviated to Prodfaztop), which had its own provincial organs. Special organisations were responsible for supplying food to railway, waterway, and construction workers. A special commission was responsible for supplying workers with the necessary work clothing – the Special Commission for Work Clothing (abbreviated to Prozodezhda) under the All-Russian Central Council of Trade Unions. Work clothing, both general (work overalls) and specific (depending on the task) was free to the workers, but only when in use as they were part of the enterprise's inventory. In addition to clothing (which included footwear and headwear),

6 From the end of 1918, ration sizes were proportioned amongst the three categories as follows: 4:3:1, i.e. the bourgeoisie were to receive a fourth of what the workers received. See N. Vishnevskii, *Printsipy i metody organizovannogo raspredeleniia* etc, Moscow, 1920, p. 37.

soap and hand towels were also handed out to the workers, also at no cost. Supplying workers with accommodations was the responsibility of the Land and Housing Departments of the Soviets of Worker Deputies.

Supplying the Red Army with food was the responsibility of a special organ of the People's Commissariat of Food Supply, the Administration of Food Supply of the Red Army (abbreviated to Glavsnabprodarm), which had its own organs at the fronts.

Supplying the Red Army with uniforms and other military equipment, as well as military provisions and any kind of military materiel, was the responsibility of the extraordinary plenipotentiary of the Council of Defense for the Supply of the Red Army (Chusosnabarm), to which all supply organs of the Red Army were subordinated, and many of which retained their own prerevolutionary organisational structure. By 1920, the task of supplying the Red Army fell predominantly to the organs of the Supreme Council of the National Economy, which had assumed many functions that until then had been fulfilled by military institutions.

Supplying industry and distributing its products was the responsibility of several poorly interconnected institutions. The distribution of fuel of any kind – wood, charcoal, coal, and oil –

was the responsibility of the Main Fuel Committee (abbreviated to Glavtop) of the Supreme Council of the National Economy, which also had provincial organs: provincial fuel committees. The committee also distributed lubricating oils and many lighting materials. The distribution of metals and many metal products was the responsibility of a special organ of the Department of the Metal-Producing and Metal-Processing Industry of the Supreme Council of the National Economy–the Committee for the Purchase and Distribution of Metals (abbreviated to Prodrasmet), which also had its own provincial committees at the local level. The distribution of many kinds of chemical materials and products was the responsibility of the Supply Subdivision of the Department of the Chemical Industry (abbreviated to Khimsnabzhenie) of the Supreme Council of the National Economy. As appropriate distribution organs were lacking, many products were distributed, on the basis of demands and orders received, by the central administrations of the enterprises that manufactured these products. Finally, widely used items were distributed by the Central Administration of Product Exchange, an organ of the People's Commissariat of Food Supply. Special items of various kinds were distributed by the appropriate institutions (e.g., medications were distributed by the People's Commissariat of Health).

Legal domestic trade almost ceased to exist and was replaced by the apparatus of state distribution; foreign trade (also barely functioning at this time due to the enforcement of the total blockade of Soviet Russia by the capitalist countries of the Entente) was the monopoly of a special organ of the Soviet state – the People's Commissariat of Foreign Trade (abbreviated to Narkomvneshtorg), which emerged historically from the Ministry of Trade and Industry. This People's Commissariat had a Council of Foreign Trade, which included representatives from institutions involved in import or export. Under the Supreme Council of the National Economy was a special commission on foreign product exchange, which determined the import needs of industry and the export resources.

The People's Commissariat of Finance (the former Ministry of Finance) underwent significant changes at this time. After nationalisation of the state banks, and later of all private banks, the administration of the entire banking system was transferred to the People's Commissariat of Finance (abbreviated to Narkomfin). Only the cooperative bank existed for a relatively long time as a separate institution. By 1920, all banks were merged with the State Treasury in a single accounting apparatus of the Soviet Republic, and even the very term 'bank' was abolished (19 January 1920). The accounting of monopoly products was transferred to the appropriate organs of the Supreme Council of the National Economy and the People's Commissariat of Food Supply.

Money gradually lost any kind of significance. There was no obligation (even a formal one) to exchange credit money against gold; the newly printed bank notes were simply just accounting marks for the Soviet Republic (and not credit money). By summer 1920, the state recognised a drop (in fixed prices) in the exchange rate of banknotes by sixty to a hundred times; prices on the free market had risen by a thousand to ten thousand times by summer 1920 and continued to rise, something that was largely explained (aside from the basic cause – the issuance of banknotes [*emissiia*]) by the growth in moneyless (natural) exchange.[7] The devaluation of money made it necessary to make natural payment for labour, and for the state to make a natural exchange of products with the peasants. The state strove to introduce accounting among state institutions without using accounting marks by means of simple mutual accounting practices. In this way, the tax system also died out, being replaced by public distribution (the allocation of certain quantities of each product for the needs of the army, of hospitals, shelters, schools, for children, state employees, etc).

7 From the data of S. Fal'kner for the first quarter of 1920, the cost of the food ration in free prices rose (in comparison with 1913) by 2,103 times; in hard prices, the costs of the same ration rose fifty five times by April 1920. See S. Fal'kner, *Problemy teorii i praktiki emissionnogo khoziaistva*, Moscow, 1924, pp. 150–151.

Early on, contributions were levied on the bourgeoisie; property and income continued to be taxed.

All financing of industry occurred through the Finance and Accounting Department of the Supreme Council of the National Economy; this department was also responsible for the work of uniform reporting in all enterprises and their associations. The existence of a special fund at the disposal of the Presidium of the Supreme Council of the National Economy lent a certain flexibility to the financing of industry. Enterprises operated according to draft plans, and their income (in fact, by no means all of it) flowed into the state coffers. Draft plans were confirmed by a special Calculation Commission [*smetnaia komissiia*]. Production departments and central administrations had their own financial organs, which were subordinate to the Finance and Accounting Department of the Supreme Council of the National Economy (and also their own Calculation Commissions).

All statistics were the responsibility of the Central Statistical Administration.

The People's Commissariat of Worker and Peasant Inspection (the former State Control Office) supervised the activity of all institutions of the Republic, including the economic institutions, especially in questions of finance, supply, and distribution. The Worker and Peasant Inspection was supported by the trade unions; its lowest organs were factory and plant cells. The experience in the economic organs accrued by proletarians in their capacity as collaborators in the Worker and Peasant Inspection acquainted them with the work of the economic organs and prepared them for later administrative and economic activity. The activity of industrial enterprises and organisations was supervised by the Department of Inspection under the Supreme Council of the National Economy, the organ of the Presidium.

As the huge mass of the peasantry, and also the artisans and handicraft workers, were small producers, a significant quantity of products was not taken account of by state organs, but went 'free', i.e. into the speculative market. Moreover, the new labour discipline was weak among state employees (i.e. the employees of the Soviet state), and occasionally, counter-revolutionary elements engaged in conscious sabotage of work. Even among workers, instances of infringement of labour discipline were observed. Soviet power fought the free market by using military food detachments to confiscate the products being kept back, and by using blocking detachments to confiscate the products being transported above the permissible norm, as well as by launching raids on markets, etc. The struggle with speculation, sabotage, bribery and so on was the responsibility of the All-Russian Extraordinary Commission for Combatting Counter-Revolution, Profiteering, and Corruption (abbreviated to VChK) and its local organs. In the economic sphere, this struggle was led by a special inter-agency commission composed of representatives of the Supreme Council of the National Economy and the economic national commissariats.

These were the main features of the new organisation of the national economy, which the proletariat was building.

CHAPTER 6

The Anarchy of the Proletarian Natural Economic System

1. The lack of planning. 2. The anarchy of distribution and the anarchy of supply. 3. Sales crises and supply crises. 4. The market and 'urgency'. 5. The new economic system as a distortion of the transition to socialism.

The organisation of the national economy, which we described above as a *proletarian natural economy*, was in many respects the direct opposite of the capitalist organisation of the national economy. This was the case not only in the realm of specific economic relations, where the replacement of the capitalist economic administration with a proletarian economic administration had brought a transition from antagonistic relations to harmonious relations, but also in the realm of general economic relations, which saw a transition from capitalist *fragmentation* to proletarian *centralisation* and *from* a capitalist *commodity economy* to a proletarian *natural* economy, i.e. from production for the market to production for the direct satisfaction of public needs. It is true that while the transition from antagonistic to harmonious relations signified a *change in the direction* of development, a break in the very trends of development, on the other hand the transition from fragmentation to centralisation and from a commodity economy to a natural economy was not a change but a *preservation* of the former direction of development; indeed it accelerated and therefore strengthened it. But precisely for this reason, here too the new proletarian economy was the direct opposite of the former capitalist economy.

A big shift occurred in *quantitative* relations, as a result of which the new organisation of the economy turned out to be *qualititatively* different from the former. If earlier, in spite of all the successes of the centralising processes, the economy was still largely dominated (although not of course in terms of significance) by its non-centralised part, then now the centralised part had achieved qualitative predominance. If commodity relations had decisively predominated earlier, now natural relations had become predominant. In short, then, a break occurred not in the tendencies of development, but in the character of the *predominant* (general economic) relations. And these predominant relations, which were typical of the new proletarian organisation of the national economy and which set it apart from the preceding capitalist organisation,

 | HTTPS://DOI.ORG/10.1163/9789004765313-010

were undeniably *socialist* relations. For socialism too will be a centralised and natural organisation of the economy.

And yet this new proletarian natural national economy *was not a socialist economy*. It is true that a socialist economy is a centralised and natural[1] economy, but for a centralised, natural economy to become a socialist economy, it still has to become a *planned* economy. This means that under socialism the activities of all individual economic units cease to be determined by the economic units themselves, that the social division of labour is replaced across the board by the technical division of labour, and that the social economy as a whole becomes a conscious [*soznatel'nyi*] undertaking, run according to a particular schedule, according to a previously devised plan.

It was precisely this, however, that was missing in the natural economy of the civil war period outlined above. Not that the plan here was imperfect and unfinished; *no such plan existed*, i.e. no schedule of who (i.e. which organ) should produce, and what should be produced, and in what quantities. Nor did an organ exist to devise and carry out a national economic plan: *it did not exist because no corresponding function existed*. Of course, every Soviet economic organ had its own economic plan; but each capitalist enterprise also had its own economic plan, even every handicraft shop. The very existence of many mutually independent economic plans meant that a single, national economic plan did not exist, i.e. that planning was absent. In accordance with the centralised character of the proletarian national economy, the economic plans of its economic organs were distinguished by their very broad scope. But this was a quantitative difference from the plans of capitalist enterprises, a difference which could become qualitative only once the many economic plans of the individual economic organs were replaced by a single national economic plan. This was not the case, however, and so the aforementioned difference was not qualitative, but remained only a quantitative difference between our proletarian natural economy and the capitalist economy, and was a qualitative difference between this proletarian natural economy and the socialist organisation of the national economy.

So the new proletarian natural organisation of the economy we have described above is characterized by the fact – and this is no less a defining trait than the others we mentioned above – that, as well as the socialist features distinguishing it from the capitalist organisation of the economy, i.e. as well as its centralised and natural character, it also had certain features in common with

1 And, of course, a classless economy. But here we are speaking of general economic conditions.

capitalism, features which set it sharply apart from the socialist organisation of the national economy, namely the lack of planning.

If we take the entire economy as a whole (both the specific and general economic relations), then we come to the conclusion that our proletarian natural economy overcame *exploitation and the market without overcoming the anarchy of economic life*.

The first steps of the true transition to socialism were taken, but not the final, crucial step. The transition to socialism remained unfinished – an anticipation of the future – incomplete and therefore distorted.

This statement might seem paradoxical, but this does not stop it being true. The commodity economy is well known to be an anarchic economy. It would be wrong, however, to conclude from this that a non-commodity economy, i.e. a natural economy, must by definition be a non-anarchic economy, i.e. a planned one. A natural economy can be a planned economy, but it can also be an anarchic economy, although in a natural economy the anarchy will inevitably manifest in different ways than does the anarchy in a commodity economy. For an economy to be anarchic, multiple (independent) economic subjects are necessary and sufficient.

The anarchy of the commodity economy is the *anarchy of distribution*.[2] This anarchy is a precondition for potential capitalist crises; as is well known, the deep roots of these crises lie in the antagonistic nature of the capitalist means of production. As the producer of profit, capitalism has a tendency towards unlimited expansion of production. At the same time, however, this gives rise to the limitations of consumption (the limitations of solvent demand): the proletarian condition of the masses, and the barriers, created by capitalist accumulation, to the growth of the personal consumption of the capitalist class. The manifestations of this contradiction (even if it is not the contradiction itself) between the growth of the productive forces and the limitations of the solvent demand of capitalist society are produced by the anarchy of distribution.

The very nature of the commodity economy (and also the capitalist commodity economy) inevitably means, first, that every individual enterprise is independent and, insofar as it has access to resources, can freely acquire everything that is on the market, and second, that such an enterprise is an organised economic unit and therefore only acquires whatever is expedient. For this reason, it is a feature of the commodity economy that supply is organised within it.

2 Distribution means above all the distribution of the conditions of production and therefore only one moment of production itself. The term 'distribution' here is taken to contrast not with production but with supply.

But this very nature of the developed trade economy, which produces for the market, also means just as inevitably that the future fate of products produced by an individual enterprise is of interest only in terms of how much they yield (their price), and not in terms of the rational satisfaction of public needs. Consequently, in the commodity economy, distribution (sales) is not organised. Each enterprise (so long as it does not cease production) will surely buy what it needs, even at high prices; but it will surely sell at the highest prices, even if its products reach those who – from the viewpoint of public production in general – need them least, while those who need them most are left empty-handed. In short, each enterprise will buy (will supply itself with) what it needs and sell (offload) at higher prices.

And so, in a developed *commodity economy* (i.e. also in a capitalist society) *supply is organised, but distribution is not organised. The typical anarchy of a commodity economy is the anarchy of distribution.*

By contrast, the anarchy in the proletarian natural economy we have described above was an *anarchy of supply*. In contrast to the capitalist (and petty bourgeois) enterprises, the (state) economic organs of the proletarian natural economy have not raised the question of prices (as a rule, this question could not even be raised here, as in the beginning, as a rule, fixed prices were paid for products, but later any kind of payment at all was generally suspended). But a given product was delivered only after an explanation of why the consumer needed the product, and whether it was really needed in the requested amount. Any decision on delivery took into account the importance of the consumer's stated purpose and the availability of a given product (stocks of the items and anticipated deliveries), and made every effort not to exceed them. As we see, the proletarian natural economy we examined was characterised by the fact that distribution within it was organised.

But precisely this, given the multiplicity of independent (state) economic organs distributing their own products, inevitably meant that each economic organ could receive the products it needed from *various* organs only in the quantities they had at their disposal. And so *each* distributing organ was guided *by its own* considerations; the organ taking delivery could never, therefore, get everything it needed in the *requisite* amounts. Consequently, in the proletarian natural economy examined by us, supply was not organised. Each economic organ distributed the products of its production (or procurement) according to the public need for them (as far as this could be determined), but it did not receive the products it needed in the requisite quantities.

And so, in the *proletarian natural economy examined by us, distribution is organised but supply is not organised. Its anarchic feature is the anarchy [anarkhiia] of supply.*

We see that the anarchy of the natural economy in this case indeed takes different forms than the anarchy of the commodity economy; moreover, it is by its very nature the diametric (complete) opposite of the anarchy of the commodity economy.

But the anarchy of the proletarian natural economy is still anarchy and leads to no fewer crises than does the anarchy of a commodity (capitalist) economy. Therefore, for the most important manifestations of anarchy in the capitalist commodity economy there are corresponding manifestations of anarchy in the proletarian natural economy: they are opposite in form but analogous in content.

In the commodity economy, the individual parts are connected through the market. This connection is based on an equivalence in the act of buying and selling products. The producer of the commodity brings it to market. It is not certain that he will offload his product, and this uncertainty brings into play the anarchy of the commodity economy (and of the capitalist commodity economy). Nor is it certain how much the producer will receive for the product he sells, and this too brings into play the anarchy of the commodity economy. Only when the producer has received a certain sum of money for his product does he then have the possibility of acquiring – within the limits of this sum – the commodities he needs.

The transition to natural economic relations means the rupturing of commodity relations. The producer places his product at the disposal of the state distributional organ, sells it, but this circumstance does not mean by itself that he can acquire the products he needs. This only becomes possible once other producers have also delivered their products to the distributional organs; once these have carried out this distribution, our producer can receive the products he needs. It is not certain that he will receive the product in question and, moreover, in sufficient quantity, because production and supply happen not according to a predetermined calculation (according to a plan), but spontaneously, i.e. by many organs, some of which depend on whether materials for production are available or anticipated, and others on whether the finished products needed for distribution are available or anticipated. This is where the anarchy of this kind of natural economy comes into play.

As no unified economic centre, or unified economic plan established by it, exists, the national economy represents a *federation* of independent *authorities* (central administrations), which are essentially only contractually connected with each other, and so the replacement of commodity exchange with product exchange does not eliminate the anarchy – *anarchic commodity exchange is replaced with anarchic product exchange*.

It is well-known that the anarchy of economic life ensures that products, which society as a whole needs, nonetheless end up not being consumed and are left unused. In the capitalist commodity economy, this happens in such a way that consumption (solvent demand), which is hemmed in by the limitations placed on it by the nature of the capitalist economy, is not sufficient to absorb everything that has been produced; the surplus products begin to accumulate *at the producers* (the original owners of the commodities), and at the same time the demand for these products grows among those who do not have a particular product or enough of it.

But essentially the same phenomenon exists in the proletarian natural economy too – namely, the impossibility of utilising (consuming) the existing products needed for society as a whole. In this case, though, it takes the opposite form: surpluses of products start to accumulate not with the producers, but *with the consumers*. It is impossible for surpluses to form with the producers, unless a given product is absolutely superfluous; after all, if such a surplus forms, it will immediately be distributed as soon as a need for this product becomes clear. But given the multiplicity of distribution organs and their independence from each other, it is unavoidable that, for example, an organ needing lamps gets a full complement (100%) of lamp glasses from one economic organ, 60% of the bases from another, 50% of the wicks from a third, and 20% of the burners from a fourth: in this case, then, four fifths of the lamp glasses, two thirds of the bases, and three fifths of the wicks turn out to be superfluous, and sit unused in storage. After a month, however, another organ that needs lamps has burners, of which the first lamp consumer does not have enough, lying unused in storage. This is inevitably the same story with fuel, raw materials, and various kinds of auxiliary materials.[3]

3 One typical example shows how far the independence of the individual distribution organs went and the extent to which each of them acted according to their own considerations. A report on an extraordinary review undertaken in 1918 reads: 'The Tambov provincial food supply committee has several departments, and in each department several official instances [*stoly*] "count" the population of the province, and each official instance "counts" "in its own way". The population count in the province of Tambov is as follows:

1	Count re distribution of salt	4,100,000 people
2	Count re distribution of fuel and kerosene	3,823,000 people
3	Count re distribution of wood chips	3,890,000 people
4	Count re distribution of metallurgical products	3,510,000 people
5	Count re distribution of textiles	3,807,000 people
6	Count re distribution of leather goods	4,000,000 people
7	Count re distribution of household items	no information'

The author, who quotes this, adds: 'Seven official instances, which by the way are in the same room, give six different numbers, ranging from 3,510,000 to 4,100,000, i.e. they differ by 20% … But that is not all. In the same provincial food supply committee, the Department of Account-

This is also true for labour power. In a capitalist commodity society, where labour power is one of the commodities, the anarchy of economic life means that labour power is left unexploited by its original owners, the workers: unemployment grows.

In a proletarian natural economy, labour power is left unexploited by its consumers – like unemployment, the downtimes and interruptions to the work process are highly typical of this system, as is the furloughing of workers as a result of interruptions in the supply of enterprises or of workers. Here too we see the same phenomenon, but expressed in opposite forms.

All of these (and many other) signs of the breakdown of economic life accumulate, and lead, both in the capitalist commodity economy and in the proletarian natural economy to *general crises* in production (and exchange). Production and transport are reduced, and exchange and consumption are squeezed – in short, the crises are in substance precisely the same in both instances, although they take directly opposite forms.

In a capitalist commodity economy, characterised by the anarchy of distribution (and consequently of sales), the crisis manifests *as a crisis of sales*, as an inability to obtain the products the producer possesses. In the proletarian natural economy, characterised by the anarchy of supply, the crisis manifests, on the other hand, *as a crisis of supply*, as an inability to obtain the products needed for consumption.

In other words, in a capitalist commodity economy, the crisis in production manifests *as a crisis of overproduction*, in the proletarian natural economy it takes the opposite form, *as a crisis of underproduction*.

In a capitalist commodity economy, the breakdown of economic life, the sign of economic anarchy, manifests as an overall *surplus*, and in the proletarian natural economy as an overall *deficit*. In both cases, this does not mean that it is completely impossible to consume the surplus products or produce the deficit products. There is nothing natural about this impossibility, it is societal: it is rooted not in the nature of things but in the nature of a given society. A surplus in the one case, a deficit in the other, are only apparent causes, surface phenomena.

---

ing of Provincial Products numbers the population of the province at 3,660,000–a seventh number. The Bureau of Accounting under the Provincial Food Supply Committee, from whose figures the volume of the grain surpluses is calculated, starts from a figure of 3,506,000–an eighth number, and, finally, the main production department gives a new, ninth, number of 3,620,000'.

See N. Fidelli, 'Ocherk istorii kartochnoi sistemy 1915–1917 g.g.,' in *Prodovol'stvie i revoliutsiia*, nos. 7–12, Moscow, 1923, pp. 152–153.

When there is a product surplus in a capitalist commodity economy, there is an unsatisfied demand for these products, i.e. a shortage of these products, but this demand cannot be satisfied, because it cannot take the form of a solvent demand; and it cannot take the form of a solvent demand, because for this it lacks the means of payment resources because it was impossible to realise (sell) certain items of production, i.e. because a surplus had developed.

When there is a product deficit in a proletarian natural economy, i.e. when there is an unsatisfied demand (unmet sales) for these products, there are unutilized quantities of (the same) products, i.e. there exists a surplus of them; but these products are not utilised, because the corresponding production process cannot be put into operation at the required scale; and this production process cannot operate at the required scale, because it does not have access to the necessary materials for production, having not received them during distribution, i.e. because a deficit had developed.

In this way, in a capitalist commodity economy a surplus of products leads to the formation of a deficit of them, while in a proletarian natural economy a deficit of products leads to the formation of a surplus of them. In one case, a surplus of products, in the other a deficit of products, appears as a cause of the breakdown of economic life.

Due to these anarchic features of a proletarian natural economy, supply difficulties are just as constant as sales difficulties in a capitalist commodity society – if, in the latter, periods of stagnation and crisis are interspersed with periods of boom times, so, in the former, supply difficulties constantly crop up now here, now there, sometimes deteriorating into a general crisis.

These kinds of crises shook the economy of Soviet Russia several times during the short three-year period of civil war, and for a final time after it had ended, already during peacetime, at the end of 1920 and start of 1921; this crisis served as the prelude to a rupture [*perelom*] in the revolution, to a return to a commodity economy.

The regulating factors in economic life, which enabled it nonetheless, even with interruptions and retreats, to make progress in spite of the anarchy, are also completely analogous in content and directly opposite in form.

In the capitalist commodity economy, the market is just such a regulating factor, its tool – market prices. Overproduction leads to a drop in prices, and this drop in prices leads to a curtailing of production and the elimination of the overproduction; by contrast, wherever there is a shortage of products, prices rise, and production expands, eliminating the shortage of products. In actuality, this result is achieved only after constant fluctuations in opposite directions; but it is, on the whole, achieved (even if at the expense of great losses).

In the proletarian natural economy, an analogous regulating factor was so-called 'shock work' [*udarnost'*] (which became very popular in 1920). The shortage of certain products led to a declaration of 'shock work' in their production. In distribution, the needs of those branches of production, which were declared for 'shock work', were met first. As a result, those branches of production expanded. By contrast, other branches of production, whose needs were met only after the 'shock work' branches had been supplied, shrank.

And so here we see that the content is completely analogous, while the form is diametrically opposed: in the capitalist commodity society, economic life is regulated by market prices, which are established spontaneously in the market behind the backs of the producers; in the proletarian natural economy, they are set by the conscious actions (decrees) of the central organs of the national economy.

And here too we are confronted no less by the unmistakable dominance of the anarchy of economic life, because the designation of certain branches of industry for 'shock work' was not the result of socialist planned foresight, but rather the result of the unforeseen blows of the anarchy of economic life, a result as automatic as the rise in market prices in a capitalist trade society.

The 'shock work' economy of 1920, therefore, was the most complete form of the proletarian natural-anarchic economy.[4]

The proletarian natural economy, which we have described here, thus possessed a number of the most important traits of a socialist economy, but it was not yet a socialist economy. Looking at it in terms of its general economic relations, we come to the conclusion that the proletarian natural economy, which differed in many essential ways from a capitalist commodity economy, was still similar to it on the most important point: it was still an anarchic economy;

---

4 In December 1920, I wrote the following about this:

> What does our 'shock work' economy boil down to? One or another branch of production is declared for shock work. 'All hands to the pumps [*Vse na imia rek*]'. Things go well. But as soon as they make great efforts to poke out their 'shock work' nose, it turns out that their 'non shock work' tail is still stuck. The tail is immediately declared for shock work and the story starts over. Don't these shock work stories remind you, dear readers, of something very familiar? Of course they do. The price of one or another product rises (a sign that it is in short supply). The market declares it for shock work. Its production expands at the expense of others. Then (even if there is no absolute surplus production of the 'shock work' product), the price of other products (now the market declares them for shock work) begins to rise, and capital flows into a different area. And the story starts over.
>
> We see that the 'shock work' economy is the usual anarchic economy, i.e. unplanned, and while proletarian, it is by no means communist.

See L. Kritsman, *Ob edinom khoziaistvennom plane*, Moscow, Gosizdat, 1921, p. 6.

while it was also similar in many main ways to a socialist economy, it was still (we are referring here to *general* economic relations) sharply distinct from it on this most fundamental point.

The centralised and natural character of the socialist economy is a mark of the most developed form of the economy, because it provides the means to overcome the anarchy of economic life and the resultant huge waste of productive forces of society. As long as it is unable to provide the means to overcome the anarchy of economic life, and this was the case in the proletarian natural economy we described above, it is unable by itself to create the most developed form of the economy.

The proletarian natural economy was an *anarchic* natural economy; it was thus a transitional economy to socialism but an economy of *distorted transition*. It was easier to see its transitional nature, than to see its distortions. Production for the direct satisfaction of public needs, natural relations, centralisation of economic organisation – all these features that capture the essence of the current economic system are of a kind that are abundantly apparent every time. And all of these features are common both to the proletarian natural economy we have described above and to socialism.

On the other hand, it is not always easy to see whether a particular economic system is planned or anarchic; the anarchy is revealed by signs that surface from time to time – by crises.

The anarchy of the proletarian natural economy made it a non-socialist system. But you would have to be hopelessly blind[5] not to see that the proletarian natural economy was the result of a powerful and majestic spontaneous effort by enormous social forces *in the direction of socialism*. You would have to be a Communist petty bourgeois [*kommeshchanin*], a Communist philistine [*komfilister*], not to feel in this heroic work of creating the proletarian natural economy the fevered pulse of history, burning with the enthusiasm of creativity, merely to point out with a cool smug grin the flaws of this still formless, raw, but grand enterprise, an enterprise not yet complete, but permeated with that marvellous unity that is a sign of all great things.

The petty bourgeois (and the Communist petty bourgeois is no exception here) tends to notice only the petty things; he cannot bring himself either to truly criticise its significance or to feel its greatness. He is capable of seeing what has been achieved, but is blind to what is in the process of being achieved.

5 An affliction that is widespread in our ranks, for we live in a country in which the petty bourgeoisie predominates in overwhelming numbers.

This striving for socialism derived not from any kind of external circumstances, but from the very nature of the proletarian revolution. But the product of labour is determined not only by labour itself, but also by the material situation and its conditions. The roots of the *distorted* nature of the proletarian natural economic system created by the revolution can be found here, i.e. in the material situation and conditions that have gradually exhausted the creative forces of the proletarian revolution,[6] after these forces, due to a combination of peculiar historical conditions, had suddenly been unleashed, like an explosion.

The proletarian natural economic system created by the proletarian revolution was a system *of transition to socialism*, it was the product of the social nature of the forces that had created it; these were the forces of the proletarian, i.e. the socialist, revolution. But this was only a distorted transitional system, because of the unfinished nature of the work its forces had carried out.[7] The creative forces of the proletarian revolution in this realm (in the restructuring of general economic relations) exhausted themselves completely before their work was completed. The economic system created by them turned out to be centralised and natural, but not planned.

The fact that the work of the proletarian revolution remains unfinished was itself the result of the peculiarities of the material situation, and of the conditions under which and through which the revolution operated, i.e. a result of the resistance that the creative forces of the proletarian revolution had to overcome.

But even unfinished, this work represents one of the greatest achievements of mankind. In the realm of general economic relations, the proletarian revolution did not solve the task confronting it, but – *for the first time in the history of mankind* – it took on that task, and it did so in the way it had taken on its own tasks of revolution, i.e. as a practical matter. Despite the greatest strain on its resources, it exhausted them without having solved the task confronting it. But while its resources turned out to be exhausted at *this particular* historical moment, the resources of the proletarian revolution as a whole were not. 'Mankind', says Marx, 'thus inevitably sets itself only such tasks as it is able to solve'.[8]

6 In this very area, this had gone far beyond the limits of what had been prepared by history.

7 This contradiction between the socialist, social nature of the driving forces of the proletarian revolution and the result of their work (in the realm of general economic relations) inevitably produced the tendency – the more the character of the anarchic proletarian natural economy created by the revolution comes to light – to complete the socialist character of the created economic order. We consider this tendency below.

8 [K. Marx, *A Contribution to the Critique of Political Economy* (Moscow: Progress Publishers, 1977), p. 21.]

Therefore, the very fact that the task had been set, served as a pledge to solve it in the future.

Our proletarian natural economy described here was grandiose in scope and until now the only attempt in the history of mankind to make the transition to a socialist economy. This attempt was not interrupted by external forces, it exhausted all of its own available (under the given conditions) internal possibilities. The revolution was not defeated, it retreated. This was the first serious foray by mankind into the foggy terrain of its future.

The organisational forms, the forms of construction – these are just as much the tools of labour as are actual work tools. They never come into being in finished form. But their appearance, even in their most unfinished form, is a great achievement and a cause of great celebration for mankind; it is an achievement that is worth the sacrifice – even a great sacrifice – for without it there is no path to the future.

History usually tries out new organisational forms repeatedly, it shapes them, bends them, grinds them down, until they are fit for purpose.

The contours of the political organisation of the new proletarian society, the new proletarian state, originated in 1871, more than half a century ago, in the form of the Paris Commune. As the fruit of the unparalleled heroism of the selfless pioneers of the future, the proletarians of Paris, it emerged in its most unfinished form and was plunged back into the furnace of history. In 1905 it showed up again in Petersburg (now Leningrad), only to disappear once more. Only in 1917 did it appear in a sufficiently complete and finished form, in the form of the Soviet state, which has become the final form of the political organisation of the new society, and will exist until the remnants of the old have been rooted out.

As enduring an achievement of the proletarian revolution as the Soviet state is the proletarian organisation of the administration of the economy, which has been created by many years of revolutionary work and after numerous modifications and improvements.

By contrast, the form the proletarian organisation of the economy took in the Civil War period was but the first rough draft – a tool, which was not yet fit for purpose and therefore needed modifications. *But this organisation did emerge*. Everything that until then had existed only in the realm of the possible, now appeared in the realm of the real. The hidden tendency had materialised. A crack opened up into the realm of the future. Indeed, the developmental tendencies were realised the first time in distorted form. But they were realised!

The non-existent now existed. Now the unfinished has to be finished. However great this historical task might be, it is less than what has already been achieved.

CHAPTER 7

The Separation of the Economy into Legal and Illegal Realms

1. Transcending the limits of the large-scale economy. 2. The illegal economy and its relationship to the legal economy. 3. Bagging [*meshechnichestvo*] and the 'Sukharevka'. 4. Issuance of paper currency [*emissiia*] as the umbilical connecting both spheres of the economy. 5. The fundamental contradiction of the economy of the Civil War.

It was not at all by accident, however, that the internal tendencies of the proletarian revolution, i.e. the transition to a new society, took on a distorted form in the realm of general economic relations. It was not by accident that our revolution created a proletarian state and a proletarian management of the economy fit for purpose, and yet a proletarian organisation of the economy in a distorted form.

Of course, this distinction is not an absolute one. Distortions – and quite serious ones – exist in the proletarian state and the proletarian economic management as well. But the revolution sustained the proletarian state and the proletarian economic administration, but destroyed the proletarian natural organisation of the economy.

Consequently, the former were generally suited to their purpose, the latter was not.

To understand the reason for this, we must examine the specific historical circumstances under which our proletarian natural economic system emerged. It arose, as we have seen, as a result of the deformation (modification) of the revolutionary process, a deformation brought about by the effect of external forces on it, by the intensification and consolidation of the proletarian revolution, and by the brutal suppression of all capitalist and market relations; this allowed the internal tendencies of the proletarian revolution to express themselves. However, despite the fact that all capitalist and market relations were brutally suppressed and that the internal tendencies of the proletarian revolution were able to express themselves freely, these tendencies were unable, as we have seen, to realise themselves completely; they did not lead to the creation of an even incomplete socialist economic system, but rather a rough draft of one. The reasons for this lay, however, as noted above, not in the tendencies themselves, but in the conditions of their realisation.

 | HTTPS://DOI.ORG/10.1163/9789004765313-011

Under the pressure of revolutionary necessity, the proletarian revolution did not limit itself to concerns of economic expediency in two ways.

Spatially, it stepped outside of the economic territory laid out by the preceding capitalist development; it did not restrict itself to large-scale capitalist production, but drew in both small capitalist and petty bourgeois enterprises. As a result, to a significant extent the material needed for revolutionary economic construction, in so far as this included small capitalist and petty bourgeois enterprises, turned out not to be ready for this act of construction.

Temporally, it did not restrict itself to own immediate, still unsolved tasks, but instead grappled prematurely with future issues by restructuring the general economic relations, even though the basics of restructuring the specific economic relations were not yet finished, and even though the struggle (the Civil War) to establish new political relations was still continuing (and, as we have seen, the revolution took on these tasks precisely because of the resistance encountered during the restructuring of the latter): as a result, the revolution itself turned out not to be ready for this task.

Of course, only by not being restricted to concerns of direct economic expediency was the revolution able to prevail, although here too lay the roots of the distorted nature of the proletarian natural system created by the revolution.

By not limiting itself to large-scale production (and to the large-scale economy in general), the work of economic construction expanded enormously. One of the first stages of taking control of the large-scale economy, namely the creation of partial economic associations (agglomerations, trusts), was basically completed only by mid-1919 (and had begun at the end of 1918). But the process of taking over small capitalist and petty bourgeois enterprises had already spread far and wide in 1919 and especially in 1920. On 29 November 1920, the Presidium of VSNKh announced the nationalisation of all industrial enterprises with more than 5 workers and a mechanical engine, and of enterprises with more than 10 workers where there was no mechanical engine; this validated the local seizures of enterprises that had already occurred. This measure meant that all small capitalist enterprises were immediately drawn into the orbit of the organisation of the proletarian natural economy. It turned out to be impossible, however, to assimilate and take organisational control of this mass of small enterprises in reality. On 28 August 1920, the census registered 37,226 industrial enterprises belonging to the state with almost two million workers, and, in spite of this, on 1 November, i.e. two months *after* the census, VSNKh reported only 6,908 enterprises in all three categories (i.e. including the enterprises of local importance) with almost 1,300,000 workers; of these 6,908 enterprises, according to VSNKh on 1 November 1920, only 4,547 were nationalised.[1] So more than 30,000 small state-owned industrial enterprises (with an average of 20 to 25 workers per enterprise) were not even included in the VSNKh numbers.[2]

No less revealing is the following comparison. On 1 November 1920, according to VSNKh, there were, as stated above, 4,547 nationalised enterprises; a year later (at the start of 1922) 7,113 nationalised enterprises were put up for lease, i.e. *one and a half times more*; these were small enterprises (by 1 September 1922, 3,874 of them with almost 70,000 workers, i.e. on average only 18 workers per enterprise)[3] were put up, but this is exactly why their inclusion in the general organisation of the economy in addition to the 4,500 large enterprises increased the total number of workers (and thus also of production) by some 6%; the number of enterprises, however, increased by more than two and a half times, as did the difficulties of organising them.

But the real expansion of the scope, and thus of the difficulties of organization, was more significant than can be seen from the above figures on industry. With the constant increase in the number of products being declared by the state to be monopoly products,[4] i.e. as trade was being progressively elimin-

---

1 By the way, the Central Statistical Administration (TsSU) itself, on the basis, as it says in its footnote, of partial results compiled by the current censuses of 1918 and 1920, provided tables which in its words 'give an idea of the numeric composition of state institutions…on 31 August 1918 and by the end of 1920,' and discovered only 3,833 state enterprises, i.e. even less than the VSNKh numbers. See *Stat. ezhegodnik* for 1918–1920, vol. II, p. 352.

2 Of 37,226 state enterprises, 'enterprises' with one (!) worker were 13.9% of the total number of enterprises and 0.3% of the total number of workers; enterprises with 2–15 workers were 53.7% of the total number of enterprises and 5.6% of the total number of workers; and enterprises with more than 16 workers were 32.4% of the total number of enterprises and 94.1% of the total number of workers (see Naumov, 'Organizatsiia promyshlennosti,' in the collection *Narodnoe khoziaistvo Rossii za 1921–1922 g.g.*, p. 325).

And so the transfer to the state of enterprises with 1–15 workers increased the number of state enterprises by more than three times, while their production (judging by the number of workers) rose by barely 6%.

The 7,000 enterprises examined by VSNKh, i.e. less than a fifth of the 37,000, concentrated two thirds of the workers employed in these 37,000 enterprises, i.e. the inclusion (judging by the number of workers) of a third of industry increased the number of state enterprises by more than five times, and even more so the organisational difficulties.

No less revealing is also the fact that of 37,000 enterprises belonging to the state over 18,000, i.e. almost half, had no mechanical engines at their disposal.

(see *Sbornik stat. svedenii po SSSR*, Moscow, 1924, pp. 154–155).

3 See V. Miliutin, 'Arenda predpriatii,' in *Na novykh putiiakh*, Moscow, 1923, vol. III, p. 70.

4 On 26 November 1918, the resolution of the Presidium of the VSNKh and of Narkomprod was published, and read: 'a state trade monopoly is declared on the following items and products: galoshes, leather and rubber plates, products of factories of yellow tobaccos, shag, cigar, and cigarette tube; saccharin; products of starch and syrup factories; products of confectionery

ated and replaced by state distribution, all the remaining small capitalist and petty bourgeois enterprises were drawn de facto into the state organisation of the economy, supplying the state organs with the items they produced and receiving from the state supply the products they needed. This meant that the proletarian natural organisation of the economy took on the work of taking over hundreds of thousands of handicraft and so-called artisanal enterprises, and millions of peasant households.

This meant that many hundreds of thousands of trade enterprises (storage facilities, warehouses, shops, etc) were immediately transferred into the hands of the state (its organs). At the same time, hundreds of thousands of structures (living accommodations) were taken over by the state (its organs); indeed on 15 March 1923, almost 430,000 nationalised and communalised structures were counted.[5]

In short, the influx of small (small capitalist and petty bourgeois) enterprises into the realm of the proletarian natural economy meant that the number of enterprises involved was soon *no longer in the thousands, but in the hundreds of thousands and millions*.

---

factories; tea, coffee, and cocoa and their factory substitutes; salt; matches; products of textile factories; sewing threads; factory-produced shoes; kerosene; lubricating oils from crude oil production; factory production of nails, horseshoes, and horseshoe studs; all kinds of iron; factory-produced candles; agricultural implements and machines; factory-produced soap; products of sugar and sugar-refining plants; writing-, note-, wrapping- and cigarette paper; powder for hunting rifles, and other products imported from abroad for the personal use of the population'.

Before now, a trade monopoly had been declared on gold and platinum, cotton, leather, oil seeds, rice, coffee, pepper, and spices. On 13 May 1918, the trade monopoly on grain, which had already been introduced by the Provisional Government on 25 March 1917, was confirmed.

(See *Sistematicheskii sbornik dekretov i rasporiazhenii pravitel'stva po prodovol'stvennomu delu*, vol. 1, pp. 279, 316, 294, 33).

Fixed prices were introduced for pharmaceutical items, barrels, paper, knitting wool, cotton wool and rags, peas, grits, buckwheat, coal, potatoes, leather goods, processed and unprocessed skins, groats, large cattle, sheep, beef, mutton, animal fats of all kinds, corn, flax, linen threads, yarns, woven materials of all kinds, butter, plant oils, oil seeds, agricultural machines and implements, metals, shag, fur, bags, bast, soap, footwear and semi-manufactured commodities in the footwear industry, petroleum and petroleum residues, threads, hemp, hemp fabrics, belts, products of the rubber industry, sugar, straw, salt beef, sausage, salt products, hay, alcohol, cloth, matches, cheese, tobacco products, harnesses for peasant carts, beans, cotton, bread, cement, tee, lentils, cast iron, wool, eggs, etc. Most of these measures were introduced already in 1918.

(See *Sbornik dekretov i postanovlenii po narodnomu khoziaistvu*, vol. I, II, III, covering the period to 1 September 1919).

In practice, legal trade in any products whatsoever was impossible.

5 See *Narodnoe khoziaistvo SSSR v tsifrakh*, Moscow, Izd. TsSU, 1924, p. 255.

This process of drawing the small-scale economy into the orbit of the general proletarian natural economy was only codified into law by the end of the civil war period. In November 1920 (on 29 November), the Presidium of the VSNKh decreed the *general* (universal) *nationalisation of all small-scale industry*, and in December 1920 the VIII Congress of Soviets resolved '*to declare it an obligation to the state to sow a plot of land, the size of which is set by the state sowing plan*, ...to charge the provincial sowing committees [*gubposevkomy*], under the leadership and control of Narkomzem, to issue *binding regulations* governing the principal methods of mechanical cultivation of the fields, of improving meadows, of sowing, and of preserving the natural fertility of the soil..., to require that the rural district executive committees [*volispolkomy*] and village soviets, with the participation of the Peasant Committees for the Improvement of Agriculture, *establish* in the rural districts the *correct utilisation* of livestock and agricultural implements through the mutually beneficial labour of the peasants'.[6] If we keep in mind that the most important agricultural products were subject to a state monopoly, and that the peasants were obligated to surrender them (minus what was retained for private consumption) to the organs of the state, and that the land itself was state property, then this decree inevitably meant – de jure – that 18 million peasant households had been brought into the realm of the general proletarian natural organisation of the economy.

The enormity, the gigantic, immeasurable scope of the proletarian natural economy, which was the result of its class exclusivity, the result of its striving to eradicate capitalist and trade relations *completely*, meant that it went far beyond what preceding capitalist development had already prepared for the anti-capitalist revolution. Drawing innumerable (hundreds of thousands and millions) of small enterprises into the orbit of the proletarian natural economy meant extending the work of the proletarian revolution into areas that were unready and difficult to deal with, it meant working under colossal, insurmountable resistance from these areas.[7]

---

6 Re § 6, 12, and 16 of the decree, see N. Osinskii, *Vosstanovlenie krest'ianskogo khoziaistva v Rossii i nashi zadachi*, Appendix II (text of decree), pp. 62–65. Author's italics in the citation. The introduction to the decree reads: 'Worker-peasant power...declares the correct management of the agricultural economy to be the great state duty of the peasant population....Worker-peasant power...demands that all agricultural workers tirelessly sow their fields and to cultivate them correctly according to the demands of the state' (my italics).

7 This resistance is best characterised by the complete failure of all attempts to perform an accounting of the small enterprises, and especially of the peasant economy. It might seem to be harder to hide land than it would a cat in a bag. And yet the peasants contrived to hide millions of desiatins of crops. So, according to data cited by S. Strumilin (see his article 'K reforme urozhainoi statistiki' in *Ekonomicheskoe obozrenie*, no. 9–10, 1924) from the figures

of the Central Statistical Administration and its calculations based on these figures, in 1920 over 9 million desiatins of crops of the most important grains were concealed; 58.2 million desiatins were counted, but in reality, according to the calculations of the Central Statistical Administration, the area of crops was 67.5 desiatins. Here, S. Strumilin believes that in reality even more was concealed: if it is assumed that half of the missing harvest yield must be attributed to the missing crop area, but the other half must be attributed to the small yield figures per desiatin, then about 14 million desiatins of the 72 million, i.e. one fifth of the total crop area, would turn out to have been concealed.

As far as the gross harvest of the seven most important grains is concerned, in 1920 no less than a third of the total yields turned out to have been concealed – about 900 million poods from a total of about 2700 million poods. If we consider that in every case no less than two thirds of the grain production must be consumed in the producing peasant households themselves, then we must conclude that the peasantry concealed in their numbers all the production that they were able to hold back, and even more.

These conclusions are derived from a comparison of statistics provided for the harvest with the statistics provided for consumption: and indeed it turns out that consumption (all kinds) exceeded crop yield by more than one and a half times. And this is the reason to assume (S. Strumilin uses this reasoning) that consumption figures are also too low.

'The rates of lying, writes S. Strumilin, as we see, are not at all humorous. Reading the statistics on crop yields for grains,' he writes ironically (this is about the years with good harvests), 'all the uninitiated could do nothing other...than be amazed at the vitality of the Russian peasants, who had so far still not perished under such a catastrophic decline in our agriculture'. The small-peasant economy put up such resistance to all attempts to capture its production statistically, and also to any attempt to bring them into the system of the proletarian natural economy.

The fact that S. Strumilin's calculations were not at all exaggerated is shown by a detailed investigation of the Boritsk rural district in Tver' province (see A. Bol'shakov, *Sovetskaia derevnia za 1917–1924 g.g.* Leningrad, 1924), the author of which comes to the following conclusion (see p. 5, point 6 of the theses): 'in 1920 with the complete (!) actual sowing of the entire crop area of the rural district, a fictitious under-sowing of 33% (!) of the land area is cited, which corresponds to the actual stock from which the peasantry of the rural district covered all the needs of domestic economic daily life'.

No less telling is the following report of an eye-witness:

The 'elegance' of the 'lying' was often expressed by the fact that they did not just lie, they lied while making 'honest' gestures, as if it was not a lie at all.

This was achieved in a quite original way. The entire land of the community within the limits of each field was divided into partitions according to the quality of the soil. The soil of a certain higher quality was set as one unit, the medium quality counted as $1\frac{1}{2}$ and the poorer quality as 2 units.

So a householder received, let's say, 10 provisional sazhens of land and this was entered into the contract on the distribution of land without the word 'provisional'. In fact, these ten sazhens could mean the following in provisional sazhens: 5 sazhens of the best land, 2 sazhens of the medium land, and 3 sazhens of the worst land, and in reality this is 5 + 3+6 = 14 sazhens. In this way, in our concrete example, about 30% of the entire plowing and crop area was hidden from the eyes of the authorities.

The 'art' of lying, which is strongly reminiscent of the 'art' of the gypsy peddler who foists a sick horse off on you while claiming it to be a thoroughbred, appeared on God's earth specifically in clashes with statisticians and other accountants. To determine the quantity of arable land and crop land, the statistician was presented with the judgment on the partition of the land, with figures meant specifically 'for external use'; and then, according to the rule that 'attack is the best form of defence,' the assault began, not on the statistician, but on the chairman of the village soviet (he 'was expelled as chair precisely because of this'), who carried out the partition and drew up the judgment; in doing so, he messed things up terribly – never had there been such a large arable area as appeared in the judgment, and they simply had no idea how the chairman had come up with such a figure, etc.

And the statistician sees in the figures in the judgment that a good half of the arable land that should have been present had disappeared; after a heated argument, and having expended all of his store of energy (already severely depleted in all the preceding communities), he secures a 'dazzling' victory, by forcing the community to recognise the figures in the judgment with a reduction of 1–2 sazhens, or sometimes as a whole, and they then go their separate ways.

On the one hand, the statistician came away with the feeling that the 'little peasants [*muzhichki*]' had taken him for a fool and had made fun of him, and would make fun of him tomorrow when chatting in their courtyards; on the other, the representatives of the community had the feeling that they had not only defended everything they had hidden beforehand, but also that they had also grabbed an extra sazhen' per head.

On the following day comes the questioning in the individual courtyards, when, under the vigilant gaze of the 'specialists' in leading the authorities by the nose, unrestrained lying starts about the sowings of individual crops, etc. And when some village patriarch or other, who cannot and does not want to lie, begins to tell the truth, then the 'moral censors,' the defenders of the unified peasant front, begin to make assurances that this intelligent and honest individual standing in front of you is in fact a fool, who is not in charge of any farm, and who has never even seen his own field, etc. The 'specialist,' who knows all the farms, corrects with lightning speed all of the bewildering testimony of the fellow villager who is well aware of his duty of discipline before the commune [*mir*] – and the numbers that correspond to the sowing norms set by the entire community win out and are left untouched.

(see Vishnevskii, *Statistika i sel'sko-khoziaistvennaia deistvitel'nost'*, Moscow, 1922, pp. 34–35).

'We are governed by decree and we live by secrecy,' so goes a saying that the same author cites and that he first heard in 1919 in the Narovchatsk county, Penza province.

In addition to this, we cite a highly typical excerpt (from the report of the Simbirsk province for 1919–1920), corroborating and explaining the summary numerical figures given above: 'The peasantry was not only able to conceal the actual figures for average yields based on sample threshing, but even the land area turned out in natura to be greater than the figures from the land partitions, in spite of the redistribution of the land per head recently carried out. During the sample threshings, the peasants tried all possible measures to conceal the true quantity of threshed grain: for example, by hiding the best fields; by shaking the sheaves during transport from the fields to the threshing floor; by threshing with strong blows, so that the grain was scattered around; and simply by stealing the grain by hiding some in their pockets etc. If we add to this the fact that the peasants of Singeleev county re-threshed the straw that was left over after the sample threshing, and threshed up to 7 poods more, then it becomes clear why the average yield in desiatins fluctuated from 12 to 40 poods.…Initially objecting to the accounting, the peasants understood very quickly all its benefits, and they themselves began to insist on the accounting…to mobilise all their forces

Under these circumstances, the exclusionary dominance of the proletarian natural economy inevitably took on a certain formal, abstract character. The resistance from the small-scale economy to being drawn into the proletarian natural economic system was overcome, but only partially. Suppression of capitalist and commodity relations led to their partial elimination, although it also partially caused them to move underground from the surface of economic life, from being legal to being illegal.

The national economy of Russia in the Civil War period of 1918–1920 is marked by the progressive *division of its economy into a legal economy* (a proletarian natural economy) and *an illegal economy* (a simple commodity and capitalist commodity economy).

As if in a gigantic centrifuge, two layers separated out in the vortex of revolution: on top, the visible, official, proletarian natural economy, and beneath it, the hidden, underground, commodity and capitalist commodity economy.

---

and to throw themselves into this new accounting. This was tried in Buinsk county….The first attempt never goes well: the best instructor, a peasant, who had his own farm, and threshed at home about 72 poods per desiatin, received in a similar threshing for the accounting only 38 poods per desiatin, but then a sample threshing yielded 42 poods….The statistical department of the Provincial Food Supply Committee [Gubprodkom] knew no more than I did: we knew there was grain, we just did not know how much and where it was. The precise area of land cultivated by the peasantry, the area of various cultivations, the yields, the inventory of livestock, i.e. we did not know what we needed to know for our day-to-day work'.

See the article by Kaganovich, 'Uchet izlishkov ili razverstka,' in the collection *Prodvol'stvennaia politika*, Moscow, 1920, pp. 181–183.

The impotence and powerlessness in the accounting of small-scale farming is highly typical here.

Not only petty bourgeois, but also small capitalist (sometimes not very small), enterprises slipped through the accounting process. So, an extraordinary investigation conducted in 1920 in Leningrad (!) province revealed the following: 'In the counties, a number of *active* (the italics here and in future are mine. L.K.) plants were uncovered, which had never been registered before and produced products for the private market. In this way, many leather factories were discovered with a significant quantity of raw material, semi-fabricated products, and finished leather. In Iamburg county, Osminsk district, a large, well-equipped leather factory was registered for the first time, and it had large basins with 400 skins, and there were finished products with chrome leather and calfskin. In the same district, a second factory of this kind was discovered, somewhat smaller, but nonetheless with a large supply of raw materials and tanning materials. At the same time, in Gdovsk country, Loiazvolovsk district, two leather factories were discovered. Finally, in Luzhsk county, Kotorsk district, in the village of Nen'kovo, a large leather factory was discovered, in which 422 tanned skins were found, some of which were sheep skins of varying quality'.

See I. Amosov and A. Savich, *Problema material'nogo ucheta v sotsialisticheskom khoziaistve*, Petrograd, 1921, p. 98.

As the proletarian natural economic system took shape, as it grew, its indelible shadow also spread. As the regular, legal market was being destroyed, on the one hand the natural economy of the proletariat grew at the same time, and on the other hand so too did the illegal market, which had already emerged during the imperialist war of 1914–1917 as a supplement to the regular market, but subsequently became the sole market.

The illegality of the underground economy and the poor statistics on the legal economy, so unavoidable under civil war conditions, made it very difficult to determine the quantitative relationship between them. Without a doubt, however, the illegal, underground economy played a highly important role, for as the large-scale economy transitioned to a natural economy, its share of the entire national economy fell; by contrast, the share of the small-scale economy, which sustained the illegal market, grew.

On one of the primary fronts, the grain front, the relationship in 1918–1919 was such that of 136.6 million poods of grain reaching the consumers, 40% (i.e. 54.4 million poods) was delivered by state distribution organs (Narkomprod) and 60% (82.2. million poods) by illegal, 'free trade'.[8] According to these figures, the urban population received from the state organs only a little over 42% of the grain they consumed, the rural population received about 35% of the grain that did not come from their own consumer economy.

According to the findings of a Central Statistical Administration investigation into the food supply conditions of the urban population, the percentage of products which were acquired with cards and from state and cooperative stores was as follows:[9]

In worker families				In non-worker families			
Bread	Flour	Potatoes	Total	Bread	Flour	Potatoes	Total
In March–April 1919 (112 towns and urban-like settlements in 29 provinces) (Russia)							
51	24	4	–	47	19	3	–

8 See A. Lositskii, 'Potreblenie khleba i miasa v 1918–1919 godakh,' in *Vestnik statistiki*, no. 1–4, p. 70. A. Lositskii cites the figure of 64.4 instead of 54.4 million poods, an arithmetic error made when adding 22.3 + 18.1 + 14.0. This mistaken figure of 64.4 is repeated in N. Kondrat'ev, see *Rynok khlebov*, p. 139.

9 See *Statisticheskii ezhegodnik* for 1918–1920, vol. I, Moscow, 1921, pp. 8, 16, 24, 32. Percentages rounded off by me.

(*cont.*)

In worker families				In non-worker families			
Bread	Flour	Potatoes	Total	Bread	Flour	Potatoes	Total
In July 1919 (25 provincial towns)							
		Cereals					Cereals
56	22	14	36	53	21	11	33
				(in families of civil servants)			
In December 1919 (31 provincial towns)							
67	38	26	47	67	40	29	47
In May 1920 (28 provincial towns)							
70	53	42	59	71	56	34	59

These figures show that up to and including the summer of 1920, state distribution of the most important products of mass nutrition, grain, did not achieve a preponderance even in provincial towns. But at the same time it was in this area (grain supply) that the state concentrated the bulk of its efforts.

If we look at food supply as a whole, then the picture looks like this:[10]

	Percentage of products allocated by cards for average monthly food supply	
	In provincial towns	In county towns
in January 1919	19	27
in April 1919	31	32
in June 1919	22	20
in October 1919	21	19
in January 1920	20	24
in April 1920	29	25

Consequently, if we look at food supply as a whole, being the main item of the domestic budget of the masses, the decisive share even in the cities came from the free market (from two thirds to four fifths of the total food supply).

10 See Prof. Fal'kner, *Problemy teorii praktiki emissionnogo khoziaistva*, Moscow, 1924, p. 152. The figures are in calories; percentages rounded off by me.

In the countryside, the situation was, of course, even worse. According to an investigation into the food supply of the rural population from September 1919 to January 1920, of the total number of products acquired by the peasants in three provinces, state organs supplied from 7 to 13.5%, on average 11%.[11]

It is true that food supply products were the main area where the illegal, free market played such a role, as things were different of course in the other most important areas of personal consumption (living accommodation, clothing, etc) and even more so in the area of productive consumption.

So, of the total worker budget, averaged for all of Russia, including apartment etc, supply from the state in natura accounted for:[12]

in 1918 41%
in 1919 63%
in 1920 75%

i.e. by 1920, the free market accounted for one *quarter* of the worker budget. But this was not a negligible percentage, as the share of the free market was much higher among the other strata of the urban population. Whatever the case, the picture sketched out above of the role of the free market in such an important area as food supply for the masses illustrates well enough the importance of the underground layer of the economy in the Civil War era.

A *large* part of the population was involved in the illegal (free) market; thus, these are the percentages of people who resorted to buying grain on the free market:[13]

	Of workers	Of non-workers
in January–May 1918 in Moscow	85%	77%
in March–April 1919 in the capitals	75%	74%

11 Ibid., p. 155. These were the provinces: Novgorod (13%), Vladimir (7%), and Simbirsk (13.5%).

12 Calculated according to data in the article by S. Strumilin, 'Zarabotnaia plata v russkoi promyshlennosti za 1913–1922 g.g'. in the collection *Na novykh putiakh*, vol. III, p. 112. It is interesting to note that in 1917 the share of natural supply amounted to only 5%.

13 Ibid., p. 8 and N. Kondrat'ev, *Rynok khlebov*, p. 197.

The numerous and thus ineradicable agents of the illegal market were the so-called 'baggers' [*meshechniki*]. Their numbers can be determined from the results of a questionnaire by the Kaluga Commissariat of Food Supply, covering the period from 1 August 1917 to January 1918, which revealed that of 627 participating villages 94% confirmed bagger activity in their districts and the total number of baggers was estimated at about 187,500, i.e. about 40% of the population; even taking into account that some were counted multiple times, this is still a very imposing number.[14]

Even the severest measures were not able to eliminate bagger activity.[15] Moreover, the government of the working class found itself forced from time to time (at moments when the food supply situation had worsened) to legalise bagger activity and to permit legal conveyance (of usually 1½ poods of foodstuffs). In September 1918, these 'one-and-a-half-pooders' [*polutorapudniki*] bought up and conveyed to the capital over 4½ million poods of grain, double what had been set for the capital by Narkomprod (indeed, Narkomprod was unable in this month to fulfill even half of its plan[16]).

It would be wrong to attribute everything to the shortage of grain in the country, to the reality of the cruel food-supply crisis. On the contrary, essentially a significant part of the existing grain surpluses (i.e. that part of the grain which was not consumed in the economy of the producers) could not be procured in any other way than *by commodity methods*, even though it was so dangerous and difficult to use them. The small-scale economy defended its trading methods with insuperable stubbornness.

This inability to eradicate the market, even though it had become illegal, was rooted in a failure to eliminate the small-scale economy, and this was not only evident from the bagger activity.

---

14 Ibid., p. 198.

15 On 16 February, the Council of People's Commissars set up the All-Russian Extraordinary Commission for Protection of Roads. § 5 of the decree reads: 'Protective duties include in particular the struggle against speculators and against proscribed commodity trade'. On 19 February, this commission issued the resolution 'On the Struggle Against Bagger Activity'. §§ 1 and 3 of this resolution read: '§ 1. Local soviets, railway committees and all organisations on railway lines have the obligation to conduct the most resolute struggle against bagger activity, as the most malignant form of speculation, which is destroying transportation and food supply.… § 3. In the event of resistance, the bagger must be arrested and handed over to the people's courts. In the event of armed resistance, the bagger must be shot at the scene of the crime'. See *Sistematicheskii sbornik dekretov i postanovlenii pravitel'stva po prodovol'stvennomu delu*, vol. I, pp. 130–131.

16 See N. Kondrat'ev, *Rynok khlebov*, p. 199 and *Statisticheskii ezhegodnik 1918–1920 g.g.*, vol. I, p. 8.

The illegal economy, in addition to petty bourgeois relations, also involved capitalist relations, and not only in the realm of trade. In one official publication, for example, we read: 'the majority of these institutions[17] had no logging machinery at all for conducting procurements in a profitable way: they had long been accustomed to using permanent *large contractors*....These private procurers were now brought in by them *covertly* as 'plenipotentiaries' or as 'specialist practitioners' who received a 'commission'.' The Main Forestry Committee [Glavleskom], – it goes on, had been forced to permit this departure from the economic mode of procurement. 'The results of drawing into the procurement process the consumers themselves (i.e. precisely those institutions which resorted to help from contractors) justified to a certain extent the hopes placed in them; the second half of 1918/19 saw a significantly higher percentage of procurements than the period up to the foundation of the Main Forestry Committee. Up to January 1919, only 24.1% of the anticipated amount had been procured and 10.3% had been transported; and for the next six months, 75.9% had already been procured and 89.7% had been transported'.[18]

Here too we see that the scale of work, which could not be achieved by the methods of the proletarian natural economy, could be achieved (in that area which essentially knew no modern large-scale production) by the methods of the trade-capitalist economy. In 1920–1921, according to the same source, 'private entrepreneurship fulfilled approximately 15% of the overall total of procurements'.[19] And this was by no means an overestimate; quite the contrary.

The persistence of the market was rooted not only in the fact that the division of labour *within small-scale production* (the internal relations of the various branches of crafts, agriculture, so-called handicraft trades) could not be satisfactorily organised using the methods of the centralised natural economy. Nor was it because the mutual relations between the small-scale and large-scale economy and above all between the town and the countryside could not be satisfactorily organised using these methods. The inability to eliminate the market was rooted in the anarchy of the proletarian natural economy itself. We have already noted above how every consumer had a surplus of certain products and a shortage of other products at the same time, while with other consumers the opposite was the case, namely that there were products that could only be used

17 Institutions which produced firewood and forest materials.

18 See the collection of the Main Committee for Political Enlightenment (Glavpolitprosvet) and the Main Forestry Committee, *Lesozagotovitel'naia politika*, 1921, p. 77.

19 Ibid., p. 79.

as such if they changed their location. As this was a question of already distributed products, this change in location could only occur through *barter*. In other words, the anarchy of the proletarian natural economy created *potential products*. It produced simultaneously the need for demand and the possibility of supply.

In this way, the anarchy of supply helped sustain the (illegal) market.

On a broad scale, this was the case for products and items of personal consumption. As soon as they were distributed to the population on the basis of cards, these products turned up on the market (especially textiles, footwear, sugar, coffee, herring, etc).

But also as far as objects of technical consumption were concerned, the threat of an interruption of production due to a shortage of (sometimes quite small amounts) of various auxiliary materials often forced these enterprises also to turn to the market.

The symbol of the inability to eradicate the illegal commodity economy and the commodity capitalist economy was the 'Sukharevka', an enormous market square, constantly black with dense crowds of people, in Moscow, the very centre of the severe proletarian dictatorship. There was an extremely intensive trade here in all possible products, and especially in products under state monopoly control. It was underground trade with furtive glances; a trade interrupted from time to time by noisy raids, accompanied by shots in the air, shouts, confusion, which merely caused the trading to relocate temporarily, often simply to a different part of the very same enormous Sukharev Square. The power of the working class, which organised the proletarian natural economy, was forced to put up with the 'Sukharevka', this huge outlet of illegality, into which the market had been driven.

The lifeline that connected these two mutually exclusive spheres of the economy – the official proletarian natural economy, which had laid claim to exclusive control of the entire economy, and the underground, commodity and capitalist commodity economy, which hid away in fear – this lifeline was especially evident in the issuance of paper currency [*emissiia*] that continued unabated for the entire period of the Civil War.

Indeed. While the proletarian natural economy, which was being built by the working class, had not yet rid itself of the external form of commodity-monetary relations, i.e. while fixed prices[20] were still being paid, then the paper

20 The general system of fixed prices (and in the Civil War period fixed prices were quickly established for more and more products) retained only the appearance of a commodity economy, but eliminated its essence, the unorganised character of market relations. In essence, it is a natural economic system.

currency issued under proletarian state power would appear as a source of payment for products on the basis of these fixed prices. But to the extent that this appearance was discarded, to the extent that products, both for production and for personal consumption, began to be distributed at no cost, to the extent that transport, living accommodations, the use of communal services all became free of charge, – in short, to the extent that all demands were being satisfied at no charge, and satisfied by the organs of the state (i.e. by the proletarian natural organisation of the economy[21]), *then to that extent the issuance of paper currency became a means for the economic and other organs and the workers of the proletarian state to pay for purchases on the illegal market that was banned by the very same state.* The issuance of paper currency in a moneyless proletarian natural economy could have no other significance. The money that the state provided to its organs and its civil servants could have no use within the framework of a moneyless economy, only *outside of* it. The issuance of paper currency was the legal lifeline that connected the official proletarian natural economy with the underground commodity and capitalist commodity economy, with the illegal market.

The role played by this legal-illegal connection between the legal and the illegal economy can be assessed with some justification by comparing the results of grain requisitions (the earlier kind of connection between the small-scale and large-scale economy) and the results of the issuance of paper currency.

21 'In Spring 1920, the value of an apartment and the value of what an average worker family receives in food, clothing and others services from the state, amounts to less than 5% of their financial budget, even though the state in general covered no less than half of all their needs'. See Iu.J. Larin, 'Ocherk khoziaistvennoi zhizni Sovetskoi Rossii,' p. 53 in the book by Iu. Larin and L. Kritsman cited above.

Of the total financial expenditures for food, the following amounts in percent went to pay for products received from the state:

	In provincial towns	**In county towns**
in January 1919	6.0	8.5
in April 1919	5.1	5.5
in July 1919	2.0	2.1
in October 1919	1.8	1.6
in January 1920	1.0	1.1
in April 1920	0.7	0.8

(Calculated from data in S. Fal'kner, *Problemy teorii i praktika emissionnogo khoziaistva*, p. 153).

	The value of procured products comprised (in millions of prewar roubles):[22]	
	Via requisitioning	Via issuance of paper currency
in 1918–19	127	523
in 1919–20	253	390
in 1920–21	451	200

To appreciate the relative significance of these two kinds of connection between the large-scale economy and the small-scale economy – the legal, natural economy (requisitions) and the legal-illegal economy (issuance of paper currency) – it should be noted that the figures in the second column were essentially three times higher. For the issuance of paper currency served, first, product turnover in the natural economy (payment of fixed prices, which initially still had the significance of payment, even if a reduced one[23]), whereby this product turnover took place both within the large-scale economy and between it and the small-scale economy; second, the issuance of paper currency served the legal market; third, it served the illegal market. Only in 1920 did the size of the latter component begin to approach the total. In any case, in 1920 the legal-illegal connection played a very powerful role.

At the same time that the legal-illegal connection grew, so too did the purely illegal sale of products of the large-scale economy or the moneyless exchange of these products for products from the small-scale economy.

The above data also provide a sense of the interconnection between the natural and commodity relations between the large-scale and the small-scale economy. But this comes with even greater caveats. Firstly, the increase in the numbers in the first column overestimate the extent to which the small-scale economy had been drawn into the proletarian natural economic system, for as

22 See E. Preobrazhenskii, *Finansy v epokhu ditatury proletariata*, Moscow, 1921, p. 28. The author took the procurement year (from autumn to autumn) for the requisitions, and the calendar year for the issuance of paper currency.

23 Assuming the value of a food ration of 2700 calories, free prices exceeded fixed prices by the following:

In the first quarter of 1919	by 7 times
In the second quarter of 1919	by 12 times
In the third quarter of 1919	by 14 times
In the fourth quarter of 1919	by 23 times
In the first quarter of 1920	by 46 times

Calculated from the data of Prof. Fal'kner, op. cit., pp. 150 and 151.

requisitioning grew, the state supply of industrial products to the peasantry fell, because this supply contracted sharply; secondly, the numbers in the second column underestimate the commodity connection between the large-scale and small-scale economy, because the small-scale economy, under the pressure of the devaluation of the paper currency forced on them, moved more and more *from monetary turnover to moneyless turnover*. Thus, from September 1919 to January 1920, according to data covering three provinces, of the total number of products acquired by the peasant population, 54% were bought at 'free market' prices, 35% were acquired without money (through barter, etc), and 11%[24] were received from organs of the state, i.e. moneyless turnover was only slightly behind monied turnover.

The separation of the entire economy into two separate and at the same time inextricably linked spheres – the official, proletarian natural economy and the underground commodity and capitalist commodity economy – *was the basic contradiction in the economy of the Civil War era,* a contradiction which grew inexorably as the above proletarian natural economic system took shape. In essence, it was a contradiction between the large-scale and the small-scale economy, which found its clearest expression in the form of a contradiction between the city and the countryside. The city had a centralised large-scale economy, each industrial branch of which was run according to the production plan for that particular branch, and which extended its feelers (railways, soviet products, agricultural enterprises) also into the countryside; the countryside had a diffuse and levelled out production chaos, run through its own albeit half-strangled and crippled market, and which extended its feelers ('artisans' and speculators) also into the city.

---

24 Ibid., p. 155. Elimination of the highest form of product exchange, monetary product exchange, is also illustrated by the data on the drop in purchasing power of the entire quantity of money in circulation. This purchasing power amounts to (in rounded out numbers):

before the war	2,335 mill. roubles
1 January 1916	3,930 mill. roubles
1 July 1917	2,570 mill. roubles
1 January 1918	1,315 mill. roubles
1 July 1918	487 mill. roubles
1 January 1919	371 mill. roubles
1 July 1919	153 mill. roubles
1 January 1920	93 mill. roubles
1 July 1920	63 mill. roubles

i.e. in comparison with the prewar period, with freight transport shrinking to a fifth, the purchasing power of all money in circulation shrank to a fortieth (ibid., p. 186).

The city delivered all of the products it produced to the distribution organs, the only exceptions here being those lost to theft; the countryside delivered its products to the market, even though it had been driven underground. The large-scale economy, having discarded the capitalist forms that had impeded the development of its productive forces, sought, as a function of the specific historical conditions, to impart a *universal* character to the new economic system it was creating, to force the entire economy as a whole into the new economic forms. *The conflict between the natural organisation of the economy and the small-scale economy* had earlier been very significant, and had even grown a great deal during the revolution, and it *was the basis of the contradiction* that tore apart the economy of this era, ultimately sabotaging the system of the proletarian natural economy.

CHAPTER 8

Soviet Bureaucratism

1. The formal universality of the proletarian natural economy. 2. The roots of Soviet bureaucratism. 3. The resistance of the ideology of the intelligentsia.

The universal (exclusive) *character of the proletarian natural system of the economy* could be realised and *was realised under these circumstances only by external means*. Its universality was only a *formal* universality, which hid the actual division of part of the economy, the actual separation of the small-scale economy from the large-scale economy.

The fact that the small-scale economy was forced to adopt organisational forms that contradicted its very nature inevitably reflected both on the small-scale economy and on the proletarian natural organisation of the economy itself, and exacerbated the decline in the productive forces of Russia's national economy. Going beyond considerations of immediate economic expediency – as a result of external forces – had inevitably to be paid for with an increase in the costs of the revolution.

For the small-scale economy, this contradiction meant a degradation in market relations – destruction of credit, replacement of monetary relations with direct exchange of products, reduction in the qualifications of the trading apparatus (baggers in place of the earlier merchants), enormous costs and risks of market transactions that had become illegal, and finally, extreme one-sidedness and incompleteness of the market, which, having gone underground, became almost exclusively a market for items of personal consumption. The forced nature of the natural connections between the small-scale economy and the large-scale (state) economy and the constriction of its commodity relations destroyed any interest from small entrepreneurs, killing their initiative for production of anything that went beyond satisfaction of their own personal needs.

'Personal initiative' is a favourite mantra of the bourgeois economy. Tossing this catchphrase around when speaking about large-scale production is a sign of the dimwittedness and hypocrisy of bourgeois economists, who use it to conceal from other people the basic fact that with the development of capitalism the influence of so-called personal initiative on the development of productive forces becomes more and more *indirect* and acts directly only on an ever-narrower circle of individuals. ULtimately, this personal initiative takes on, like everything else in the world of monopoly capitalism, *the features of a monopoly*, because apart from a clique of monopolists everyone else acts

 | HTTPS://DOI.ORG/10.1163/9789004765313-012

not according to their own personal initiative but according to the personal initiative of the monopolists, i.e. they do not in fact act according to this famous 'personal initiative'. In the *small-scale* economy, however, a weakening of the personal entrepreneurial initiative of the small owner further destroys the connections between the small-scale economy and the national economy, and in particular the connections between the city and the countryside. This leads to a decline in the productive forces of the small-scale economy and the entire national economy as a whole.

On the other hand, the proletarian natural economic system turned out be *incomplete in economic terms*, for in practice it lacked some of the most important branches of the national economy, which had not been included in this system; it turned out, therefore, to only appear to be a complete economic system. The attempt to draw the small-scale economy into the proletarian natural economic system helped create an underground market, and it not only constantly ate away at this system, turning its officials through bribery into agents of the underground market, it also caused *the internal relations* within this system *to become distorted.*

The *fundamental distortion* of the internal relations of the proletarian natural economy *was* its *bureaucratism* [*biurokratizm*].

One of the roots of this Soviet bureaucratism was that the system had gone beyond the limits of the large-scale economy, that the proletarian natural economic organisation had been overloaded with an enormous number of small-scale enterprises, making it impossible to establish a real – and not just a paper – connection with the individual economic units. This led therefore to a purely clerical approach to matters, because of the enormous number of issues to be tackled and the impossibility of resolving these issues without intimate knowledge of them, without a detailed analysis of each of them.

Another root of Soviet bureaucratism was that the revolution had not restricted itself to the immediate unresolved tasks it faced, that the task of restructuring the general economic conditions had been taken on prematurely at a stage of the revolution when the restructuring of the specific economic conditions and even the political conditions were basically still unfinished. We have already noted above that the revolution inevitably occurred not only on the basis of the old technology, but also under conditions that required the old capitalist intelligentsia to keep functioning (working). This was primarily because it was impossible during the Civil War to train a new proletarian intelligentsia, because all those who might be suitable material for this work were being consumed completely and ceaselessly by immediate current tasks. Inevitably, many years will pass between the initial efforts to train a new proletarian intelligentsia and the moment when it will be ready for work.

The old capitalist intelligentsia, however, is of course an intelligentsia with a *capitalist* ideology, and especially so during the restructuring of specific economic relations, i.e. when the old economy is collapsing and a new economic administration is being created. Meanwhile, the restructuring of *general* economic relations, i.e. restructuring the very organisation of the economy, *presupposes* that an economic administration already exists, and that the intelligentsia has already taken up its place in it, that the intelligentsia is already on the ground in the new order. It presupposes therefore that the restructuring of the specific economic relations is essentially already complete. But because general economic relations were being restructured *prematurely*, at a time when specific economic relations had basically not yet been completely restructured, a sharp *contradiction arose between the role of the intelligentsia and its ideology*, which was expressed in the forced, soulless nature of the intelligentsia's work, in its disgust towards this work being done under duress and towards those people whom this work was supposed to serve; – in short, it found its expression in bureaucratism. They did not work in order to achieve results, but to somehow just to not do the work.

The mood of the employees (*the intelligentsia*) displayed real nuance under these conditions: from apathy and a lack of belief in the fruitfulness of their labours to the most malicious sabotage.

Highly revealing of the mood of the intelligentsia was a unique questionnaire, compiled in summer 1922, when the anti-Soviet sentiments of the intelligentsia had already subsided. Its results were published in *Pravda* (no. 127).[1] This questionnaire (produced, of course, not from completed question-sheets, but from conversations with acquaintances, etc) included 270 engineers who worked in trusts and other state organs in Moscow and held responsible positions (board members, directors, etc). The respondents were then divided into two groups: the first included those who had occupied a prominent position in the capitalist hierarchy *before* the revolution, the second had been ordinary engineers before the revolution.

Asked whether they sympathised with Soviet power, 9% of the first group and 13% of the second responded in the affirmative. The overwhelming majority, then, were still antagonistic to working-class rule in summer 1922.[2]

1 These are resulted are cited by Iu. Larin, *Itogi, puti, vyvody novoi ekonomicheskoi politiki*, 1923, pp. 78–79.

2 Numerous legal trials (employees of Nobel' and many others) have documented the links between some (predominantly high-level) employees and their former masters and the direct sabotage of production.

Asked whether they considered their own work to be useful, 30% of the first group and 75% of the second answered in the affirmative. So almost three-quarters of the first group and a quarter of the second were still working in 1922 without any interest in their work. One question about whether they considered bribes to be absolutely impermissible was highly revealing of the work ethic of the capitalist intelligentsia: 25% of the first group and 30% of the second answered this question in the affirmative, i.e. that they considered bribes to be impermissible.

Three quarters of both groups, then, did not see their labour as social labour, but saw it as 'foraging in the enemy camp'. One can imagine how 'economic construction' was viewed by these principled and unprincipled heroes of bribery, who believed that they, and only they, were continuing the heroic traditions of the Russian intelligentsia.

The work of the old intelligentsia (we are speaking here, of course, of typical cases and not of individual people, and moreover of typical cases in *this* period), and consequently also the work of the institutions they inhabited, was marked on a daily basis under these conditions not only by a pen-pushing approach to matters, but also by inattentiveness and hostility towards the representatives of the labouring masses, those whom the divinely inspired prophet of capitalist boorishness, Mr. Merezhkovskii,[3] had long ago called, with his prophetic foresight, 'the *forthcoming* boor'.

But the pen-pushing attitude to matters and the inattentiveness and hostility to the 'simple people', combined with the lackey's obsequiousness to authority, which in the conditions of a harsh dictatorship naturally inspired great reverence – this is bureaucratism.

Of course, this mood of the old intelligentsia (the civil servants) was not at all accidental: it was an expression of the very same *resistance* of the old capitalist *ideology* of the technical (and other) *intelligentsia*, especially its elites. This resistance is to a more or less inevitable consequence of the changed socioeconomic function (role) of the technical intelligentsia, when its role changes from that of a transmission link in the organisation of capitalist production and of capitalist exploitation to a transmission link in the proletarian organisation of production, where there is no exploitation. The hostile attitude of the civil servants, especially the higher-ups, is thus an inevitable consequence of the crisis in the relations of production.

The dictatorship of the proletariat meant the *material defeat* of the technical intelligentsia (and of its elites directly), as one of the *privileged* classes

3 [D.S. Merezhkovskii, *Griadushchii kham. Chekhov i Gor'kii* (St. Petersburg: Izd. M.V. Pirozhkova, 1906)].

of capitalist society. It lost not only its specific functions as the organisers of capitalist exploitation but also the *high remuneration* that went along with these functions. The intelligentsia's loss of this remuneration is a direct result of the loss of these functions, for clearly the remuneration for the elite of this technical intelligentsia (and this remuneration is the irrepressible goal of its middle strata as well, and dominates their ideology), insofar as it is not the price of its labour power, represents part of the surplus value and flows to them as the organisers of capitalist exploitation. At the same time, the threat to the future also grows, the threat to the monopoly of knowledge, a result of the *weakening of the monopoly on education*. The *obligation* to serve the new regime becomes nakedly apparent, as the destruction of capital means that service to the proletarian state becomes the *sole* source of existence.

The intelligentsia took a long time to recognise *that its material collapse was also its ideological collapse*, that its material collapse was the result of its objectively incorrect evaluation of the direction of societal development, and that its former capitalist ideology was a result of the fact that it was bound to capital by the golden chain (and more often by the golden dream) of its share of surplus value and of its collaboration in the organisation of exploitation. And in contrast to capital, whose personnel (at the highest levels) remained outside of production, the technical intelligentsia is a productive force, whose importance grows with technical progress (or to put it in the language of capitalist relations – with the growth of the organic composition of capital), as it was not thrown out of production like capital but remains within it; ultimately, then, its ideology begins to adapt to the changing economy.[4]

Until this adaptation has taken place on a sufficient scale and until the end of the monopoly on education has created enough cadres of a Red technical

4 This is illustrated very clearly by the data from the aforementioned questionnaire. If the responses to the following two questions are compared: 1) whether the respondents sympathise with Soviet power, and 2) whether the respondents consider Soviet Russia to be moving in the direction of a Communist system, then it turns out that they answered affirmatively to both questions in the following percentages:

	Question 1	Question 2	Ratio of responses in both categories
First group	9%	13%	1:1½
Second group	13%	33%	1:2½

i.e. many of those who had come to understand that the collapse of the intelligentsia was also an ideological collapse were nonetheless unable to overcome their hostile feelings towards the new system – their capitalist education proved stronger than their intellect. For data, see Iu. Larin, op. cit., pp. 78–79.

intelligentsia from the ranks of the proletariat, the problem of the specialists will inevitably remain one of the most difficult problems for the dictatorship of the proletariat.

The anti-Soviet mood of the civil servants was sustained and nurtured further by the fact that the burgeoning of the bureaucratic Soviet apparatus (the causes of which we will address below) was caused to a significant degree by the influx of large numbers of the former ruling classes, of those strata close to them, and, above all, *of members of their families*, whom the revolution had expropriated and deprived of any means of existence. This created a specific type of young Soviet lady [*baryshnia*], many of whom were distinguished not only by the anti-Soviet sentiments they brought with them from their families, but also by their very low levels of qualifications for the work, due to a lack of any kind of training.

A specific complication of our revolution was, however, not this mood of the intelligentsia per se, as, generally speaking, this is unavoidable at a certain stage of the revolution. The revolution begins, as we have seen above, with a breakthrough in the ideology of the proletariat, the mass of which moves from a capitalist ideological order to a proletarian ideology dedicated to overthrowing this order. The dialectical nature of revolution means that the growth of the revolutionary ideology of the proletariat inevitably signifies a growth in the counter-revolutionary ideology of capital and the intelligentsia (*Besitz und Bildung*, the owners and the educated).

But since the intelligentsia, unlike capital, represents a productive force, then it too inevitably experiences an ideological breakthrough, a transition from capitalist ideology to a recognition of the new Soviet system. But the intelligentsia does not experience this breakthrough in the first phase of revolution (the ideological phase) like the proletariat, but in its third phase (the economic phase in the realm of specific economic relations).

And this specific complication of our revolution also meant that because the fourth phase of the revolution (the economic revolution in the sphere of general economic relations) encroached into the third phase (the economic revolution in the sphere of specific economic relations), economic construction was carried out with the aid of the intelligentsia, which had *not* yet experienced the ideological breakthrough it needed for its participation in this construction.

The basic roots, the essence, of Soviet bureaucratism, then, are as follows: the *overwhelming* of the proletarian natural organisation of the economy with an enormous number of small-scale enterprises and the resultant clerical approach to affairs; the *premature nature* of the transition to economic construction, the resultant contradiction between the ideology of the intelligentsia and its role in economic (and state) construction, and the associated hostile attitude to the work itself and to the labouring masses served by this work; and finally the *low* cultural level of the leaders and the led, a product of the capitalist backwardness of prerevolutionary Russia.[5]

A manifestation and consequence of this bureaucratism was, *alongside* the endless *red-tape*, the *innumerable commissions* with their endless meetings that were typical of this period. These commissions were the direct result, on the one hand, of the anarchy of the economic system of this era and, on the other, of its tendency to rationalise social relations. The absence of planning, and the concomitant lack of forethought, meant constant contradictions among the many economic organs; but while, in the conditions of the commodity economy, these contradictions take the form of competition in the market, in the conditions of the proletarian natural economy, which is its own kind of federation of authorities and central administrations, these contradictions necessitate agreements among the appropriate organs (the notorious 'coordination'). With the tendency of the proletarian natural economy to introduce rationality, to destroy fetishism, *the anarchic chaos of commodity relations crystallises in the form of commissions*; it becomes explicit, but without ceasing to be chaotic.

As the proletarian revolution was not confined by concerns of direct economic expediency, a result both of the victory of the revolution and of the associated interference by external forces, the efforts of the proletarian revolution to create a socialist economic system were incomplete and thus distorted. This proletarian natural economic system realised a number of basic principles of the socialist economy – synthesis of the social labour force and the social means of production (the elimination of exploitation), *establishment of natural relations* (production not for the market but for direct consumption), and *centralisation of the economy. At the same time, however, it was also marked by a particular kind of anarchy of the economic system, by a formal exclusiveness and a real* (actual) *incompleteness, a result of the division of the overall economy into official and underground sectors, with all of its economic relations permeated with bureaucratism.*

---

5 To a certain extent, Soviet bureaucratism was just growing pains, unavoidable when building a colossal mechanism with colossal tasks encompassing the entirety of social life, and which was establishing and defining competencies in a long and torturous process. But Soviet bureaucratism took on such proportions that the congress of the governing Communist Party felt a need to define the Soviet state in Russia as a dictatorship of the proletariat with bureaucratic distortions, and this cannot be seen as simple growing pains but as a consequence of specific features of the Russian Revolution.

CHAPTER 9

The Decline in Productive Forces

1. In agriculture. 2. In small-scale industry. 3. In large-scale industry. 4. In the national economy as a whole.

The long duration and the intensification of the Civil War – a result of the relative stability of developed capitalism *outside of* Russia – led to an extraordinary deepening and concentration of the proletarian revolution at the political stage of its development, and to the encroachment of the economic stage of the revolution onto its political stage, which could only be accompanied, as we have already emphasised several times above, by a sharp *increase in the costs of revolution.* As a result of this, the entire revolutionary process was happening against the backdrop of a quite extraordinary decline in the productive forces of the country.[1]

According to the most reliable (still very approximate) calculations of N. Vishnevskii, the sown area (in the present territory of the USSR, not including Turkestan, Transbaikalia, and Transcaucasia) comprised 93.6 million desiatins in 1917 and 86.1 million desiatins in 1920, i.e. a reduction of 8% or one twelfth over the three years of the Civil War. This was almost *double* the reduction during the three years of the imperialist war; in the years from 1913 to 1917 (according to calculations by the same author), then, the sown area was reduced by only 5% (from 98.4 to 93.6 million desiatins). The overall reduction compared with 1913 comprised 12.5% in 1920, i.e. *one eighth* of the total sown area.[2] To grasp the full significance of these figures, it is necessary to bear in

1 Statistical information from the Civil War period is extremely unreliable. The objective causes of this unreliability are the economic destruction, the instability of social relations, and the population's interest in distorting the information they were conveying. But there is also a subjective cause: the carelessness (enough said) of those who are the first to circulate the information. Evaluating and correcting all this information is a matter for future collective efforts. However, this information can, for the most part, be used to provide a picture of general trends of development. In the present book, we do not offer in each individual example a caveat about the inaccuracy of the data, and we use them insofar as the general picture of the comparisons we are making, in our view, would not change if we were to replace available inaccurate data with accurate data, were the latter available.

2 See N. Vishnevskii, *Statistika i sel'sko-khoziaistvennaia deistvitel'nost'* (Moscow, 1922), p. 69. These figures (recognised as the most probable by the State General Planning Commission) diverge sharply from the official statistics of the TsSU (which do not, as S. Strumilin points out, take into account the 'rate of lying'). According to these figures, the sown area (for the

 | HTTPS://DOI.ORG/10.1163/9789004765313-013

mind that the peasantry consumed up to three quarters of the grain they produced in their economy, so a reduction in the sown area by one eighth in itself already meant a reduction of a third in the surpluses of the peasant economy, i.e. of the amount left over for consumption by the towns, army, etc, after large-scale agriculture had been eliminated.[3]

But at the same time, there was a sharp drop in crop yield. According to the estimates by the same author, it comprised, as a percentage of the average yield for the decade before the war:[4]

in 1917	93%
in 1918	89%
in 1919	80%
in 1920	70%

Here too, the reduction in harvest yield in the three years of the Civil War exceeded significantly – by more than *three times* – the reduction in harvests for the three years of the imperialist war. As a result, the total harvest shrank catastrophically. According to the calculations by the same authors:[5]

same territory) comprised 79.5 million desiatins in 1917 and 63.0 million desiatins in 1920. The difference is almost 21%, and compared with 1900–1913 (83.1 million desiatins) an even higher 24%. See *Sbornik stat. svedenii po SSSR*, Moscow, 1924, publ. by TsSU, p. 123. N. Vishnevskii leveled withering criticism at these numbers in the cited work. In any case, the extent of reduced sown area noted in the text is not an exaggeration.

3 This is a rough and very approximate estimate: before the war, 29.5% of the harvest went to crops and cattle-feed, 46.5% was consumed by the rural population, and the rest (24%) went to the cities and for export (see P. Popov, *Proizvodstvo khleba v RSFSR*, 1921, p. 19). If a reduction in sowing (and yield) by an eighth also assumes a reduction by an eighth in production costs (for seed and for cattle-feed), then we get 87.5% of the yield, 25.75% of the production costs, 46.5% for rural consumption, and surpluses of 15.25% instead of 24%, i.e. a reduction of about a third.

4 See N. Vishnevskii, op. cit., p. 79. According to official statistics (see the above-cited *Sbornik*, p. 128), the harvest as a percentage of the average harvests from 1909–1913 comprised for the main grains:

in 1917	91%
in 1920	71%

5 See N. Vishnevskii, ibid., pp. 71 and 72; the figures for 1917 are calculated by us on the basis of Vishnevskii's aforementioned data on the sown area and the yield. According to official statistics (see the above-cited *Sbornik*, p. 131), the grain harvests comprised:

on average for 1909–13	3,850 mill. poods
on average for 1917	3,350 mill. poods
on average for 1920	2,082 mill. poods

During the civil war years, then, the harvest shrank by 38%, and in comparison with 1909–1913 by 46%, which is unlikely because, were this the case, the year 1920 would have brought

before the war	4,774 mill. poods
in 1917	4,217 mill. poods
in 1920	2,944 mill. poods

And so for the civil war years the harvest was reduced by *almost a third* (by 30%), while during the years of the imperialist war it was reduced by not quite 12%, i.e. the reduction during the Civil War, then, was two and half times greater than the reduction during the imperialist war. Compared with the prewar period, the harvest was reduced by 37%, i.e. *more* than the amount of surpluses from agriculture in terms of the prewar norms of peasant consumption. Russia became a country of absolute and thus significant grain shortage.

No less catastrophic was the decline in the other major branch of agriculture, animal husbandry. Taking the number of each kind of livestock in 1916 to be 100, then in 1920 the ratios were as follows:[6]

Horses	75% (81)
Cattle	79% (78)
Sheep and goats	55% (61)
Pigs	72% (76)

The contraction in animal husbandry was even more catastrophic than the contraction in agriculture. But if the decline in agriculture was already catastrophic in itself, it was especially so from the viewpoint of industry and the city in general.

So, at the same time as the area of grain cultivation was shrinking from 1916 to 1920 by 23%, i.e. shrinking by almost a quarter (and in comparison with 1913 by 29%), intensive crops for the same period were reduced by 56%, i.e. *by more than half*.[7] Several intensive crops were almost destroyed here.[8]

death by famine to millions of peasants, like the terrible year 1921. In any case, the data cited in the text do not exaggerate the scale of the reduction in the harvest.

6 See the official 'Trudy Zemplana,' N. Kondrat'ev, N. Oganovskii, *Perspektivy razvitiia sel'skogo khoziaistva SSSR*. Moscow, 1924, vol. I, p. 83. In brackets are the official statistics of the TsSU. Data from the above-cited *Sbornik*, pp. 136–137. As the reader will notice, only the figures for cattle coincide.

7 Ibid., p. 81. The actual reduction in sown area for grains was, as we have seen, significantly less (almost half). We are using the data of Prof. N. Oganovskii, who states (see ibid., p. 88) that they represent a *relative* decline in various crops.

8 Ibid., p. 81. It is necessary to note that Prof. Oganovskii's table, whose absolute figures we have partially used, has been compiled very carelessly, with a multitude of *arithmetic* errors in the calculation of the percentages. This is how incorrectly the percentages have been calculated:

in comparison with 1916:

- for potatoes Prof. Oganovski has 29%; according to his own data, it should be 38%
- for hemp Prof. Oganovski has 61%; according to his own data, it should be 54%
- for cotton Prof. Oganovski has 89%; according to his own data, it should be 88%

in comparison with 1913:

- for sugar-beets Prof. Oganovski has 45%; according to his own data, it should be 94%
- for cotton Prof. Oganovski has 79%; according to his own data, it should be 87%
- for all intensive crops (total) Prof. Oganovski has 66%; according to his own data, it should be 56%

Consequently, the reduction in the sown area of intensive crops was from 9,036,000 desiatins in 1913 to 4,005,000 desiatins in 1920 (66%) and from 9,026,000 desiatins in 1916 to 4,005,000 desiatins in 1920 (56%), which is clearly impossible (calculations based on arithmetic principles give in the first case a reduction of 55.7% and in the second case a reduction of 55.6%, the difference being only one-tenth of a percent).

But many of Prof. N. Oganovskii's figures are simply not accurate.

Thus, Prof. Oganovskii's figures on tobacco showed a twenty two-fold reduction in sown area from 1913 to 1920 because it was comparing the incomparable: his figures for 1913 covered the total sown area of tobacco, but for 1920 only Great Russia and Ukraine.

In both cases, we included only Great Russia and Ukraine (see *Russkaia promyshlennost' v 1922*, p. 383). If Kuban', Crimea, and Transcaucasia are added, we get a little less than an eight-fold reduction from 1913 to 1920.

The same applies to sugar-beets. Prof. Oganovskii calculated a reduction from 1913 to 1920 from 701,000 desiatins to 39,000 desiatins, i.e. an eighteen-fold reduction (as a percentage, an arithmetic error turned it into little less than a two-fold reduction, to 45%); but once again this was only because for 1913 and 1916 data for the USSR were included, but for 1920 only data for Great Russia, i.e. again comparing the incomparable.

The negligence extends not only to miscalculated percentages, but also to issues of substance (the comparability of data). It is very revealing to compare three works by the same author: the first edition of *Ocherki po ekonomicheskoi geografii*, which appeared in 1923, p. 128 (see column I); the above-cited article in *Perspektivy*, which appeared in 1924, pp. 67 and 81 (see column II); and the second edition of *Ocherki*, which came out recently, p. 188 (see column III).

Here is the comparison (in thousands of desiatins):

	I	II	III
Area of sugar-beets in 1913	701	701	697
Area of sugar-beets in 1916	613!	479!	613!
Area of sugar-beets in 1920	180	39!	39.2

The comparison for cotton produces similar results:

	I	II	III
Area of cotton in 1913	498	785!	785
Area of cotton in 1916	714	855!	714!
Area of cotton in 1920	102	102	102

As the reader can see, the figures largely conform. For cotton, this is because the numbers in *Ocherki po ekonomicheskoi geografii* only cover Turkestan, the numbers in *Perspektivy* only cover Turkestan for 1920, but they also include Transcaucasia for 1913 and 1916. Once again this is a comparison of the whole with one part of the whole.

Fodder grasses produce a similar comparison:

	II	IIIa	IIIb
Area of fodder grasses in 1915	917	997	997
Area of fodder grasses in 1916	1,706	1,620	1,705
Area of fodder grasses in 1920	367	367	

IIIa and IIIb are two consecutive pages of work III, i.e. the second edition of *Ocherki*.

And here is the comparison for corn:

	II	IIIa	IIIb
Area of corn in 1913	827	827	828
Area of corn in 1916	895	900	934
Area of corn in 1920	891	860	1,043

In the first edition of *Ocherki*, then, we have *no change* from 1916 to 1920, in *Perspektivy* we have a reduction, and in the second edition an increase in sown area. All possibilities have been exhausted.

The book has the following title-page:

R.S.F.S.R.

People's Commissariat of Agriculture

Works of the Land Planning Office [Zemplan]

Prof. N.D. Kondrat'ev

Prof. N.I. Oganovskii

Long-term prospects for the development of agriculture in the USSR

Under the general editorship of I.A. Teodorovich

In the figures for potatoes, there is an irreconcilable contradiction between Prof. Oganovskii, the head of statistics for the People's Commissariat of Agriculture, and the statistics of the Central Statistical Administration. They comprised the following:

	Sown Area (in thousands of desiatins)			Yield (in millions of poods)	
	1913	1916	1920	1913	1920
From *Ocherki po ekon. geografii*	2,797	2,323	1,454	1,245	242
	(1909–1913)			(in 1909–1913)	
From *Sbornik stat. svedenii po SSSR*	2,626	2,310	2,250	1,212	1,142

According to Prof. Oganovskii, then, the sown area is one-and-a-half times less and the har-

1920	Compared with 1916	Compared with 1913
Area of hemp declined to	54%	60% (by more than half)
Area of flax declined by	58%	50% (by half)
Area of peas and beans declined by	42%	61% (by more than half)
Area of grasses declined by	79%	60% (by more than half)
Area of sugar-beets declined by	71%	74% (by almost three-quarters)
Area of cotton declined by	88%	87% (by almost a seventh)
Area of tobacco declined by	90%	90% (by almost a ninth)

At the same time as this reduction in sown area, there was also a decline in productivity, and, consequently, an even stronger decline in harvest yield.

This was the yield per desiatin in poods:[9]

	1913	1920
Flax	29.7 (in 1915)	12.5, i.e. a 60% reduction
Tobacco (in Great Russia)	150	87.0, i.e. an almost 50% reduction

vest is four-and-a-half times less than the figures given by the Central Statistical Administration. And lest there be any doubt that this is his claim, Prof. Oganovskii calculates that the potato yield had fallen between 1913 and 1920 by 81%. According to the Central Statistical Administration, the yield fell by 6%.

The difference, as this comparison shows, is not small.

Regarding cotton, the following must be noted: the figures in I carry the following note: 'The figures for the crop in 1920 and 1921 do not include Khiva and Bukhara, where in 1913 92,000 desiatins were cultivated, and in 1916 136,000 desiatins'; the figures in II have no such note; the figures in III have a different note: 'The sown area of cotton for 1916–1922 does not include Khiva and Bukhara, where in 1916 136,000 desiatins were planted'. And so, in I, 714,000 desiatins was the sown area of cotton in Turkestan together with Khiva and Bukhara; in III, 714,000 desiatins was the sown area of cotton in Turkestan without Khiva and Bukhara. Let us limit ourselves, however, to these comparisons.

9 For data on the flax harvest, see *Syr'evye problemy tekstil'noi promyshlennosti*. Moscow, 1923, p. 68. Data on the tobacco harvest is calculated from data in *Russkaia promyshlennost' v 1922 g.*, p. xxix. The data for Ukraine are also cited here, but they are clearly incorrect: from 1913 to 1920 there is a twenty-fold reduction in sown area and a little more than a three-fold reduction in yield, i.e. the increase in productivity is six times greater, up to 950 poods per desiatin. These

A sense of the reduction in the yields of intensive crops can be obtained from the following data (in percentages relative to 1913):[10]

	1913	1916	1920
Yield of hemp	100	–	10
Yield of flax	100	–	25
Yield of sugar-beets	100 (1914)	71 (70)	15 (7)
Yield of cotton	100	160	11
Yield of tobacco (in Great Russia)	100	–	10

If we also add the reduction in sheep-breeding by 50% (and of fine-fleece sheep-breeding by at least 93%),[11] then we must conclude that the decline in the production of agricultural raw materials for industry was quite extraordinary.

Such an extraordinary decline in intensive crops was caused not only by the transition of the peasants to an economy geared to their own consumption, but also by the decline in intensive crops as work-intensive crops; just like the imperialist war, the Civil War drained the life-blood from the peasant economy by stripping it of its workforce and working livestock.[12]

---

awkward numbers are used twice: in the introductory article by Prof. Kafengauz (p. xxix) and in the article on the tobacco and shag industry (p. 383). They are borrowed from an article by S. Narkir'er, which appeared in *Narodnoe khoziaistvo Rossii za 1921–1922 g.*, published by the editorial board of the newspaper *Ekonomicheskaia zhizn'*, p. 514.

10 See N. Oganovskii, *Ocherki po ekonomicheskoi geografii RSFSR*, part I, Moscow, 1923, pp. 130, 133, 134; and *Russkaia promyshlennost' v 1922 g.*, p. xxix. While the sown area was shrinking (apart from tobacco) by 2–4 times (and of tobacco in Great Russia by 5–6 times), the yield fell by 4–10 times. The figures in brackets on the sugar-beet harvest are from *Russkaia promyshlennost' v 1921 g.*, p. lxxix; for 1920, the difference is in all 100%, even somewhat higher.

11 See *Syr'evye problemy tekstil'noi promyshlennosti*, Moscow, 1923. There, in an article by B. Liadovskii, 'K voprosu o vosstanovlenii ovtsevodstva' on p. 90, we read: 'In 1912 Merino sheep numbered 2,100,000, in 1922 there were at most 150,000,' i.e. a 14–fold reduction. In the introductory article of the same publication, A. Nol'de, 'Problema syr'ia v russkoi tekstil'noi promyshlennosti' on p. 18, we read: 'Fine-fleece sheep breeding has died out completely: of 2,500,000 sheep before the war, barely 100,000 were left,' i.e. no less than a 25–fold reduction. Finally, in *Russkaia promyshlennost' v 1922 g.*, p. 273, we read: 'Only 2.4% of the prewar number of Merino sheep were left,' i.e. a 42–fold reduction. The situation of Merino sheep breeding in 1920 was about the same as in 1922.

12 The Red Army alone by mid-1919 numbered 1,500,000 people and 250,000 horses; by 1920

But in the main branch of the production of foodstuffs (and of fodder) as well, the production of grains, things looked similar: crops destined for the city (and for export) were particularly reduced. So the reduction in sown area comprised:[13]

	compared with	
	1916	1913
Wheat	-24%	-34%
Barley	-33%	-38%
Rye	-20%	-28%
Oats	-30%	-31%
Millet	+26% (an increase)	+17%
Buckwheat	-3%	+2%

If we put in one group those crops that are less important for the market (such as rye, oats, and millet), and in a second group those that are very important for the market (such as wheat, barley, buckwheat, and corn), we see that in 1920 the sown area declined as follows in comparison with 1916 and 1913:[14]

it already numbered 5,300,000 people, and of course considerably more than 250,000 horses. See *Piat' let vlasti Sovetov*, p. 157. At the same time, in the Civil War horses had to be changed in the army considerably more often than in the world war.

13 Calculations are from the aforementioned *Trudy zemplana*, pp. 66 and 81. See also footnote 7.

14 Ibid., pp. 66–67 and 81; the third column is calculated from Prokopovich (see his Opyt, pp. 71 and 75). The numbers in brackets are comparable with the third column (excluding cotton and grass that were not included in Prokopovich); the percentages of market production for individual crops according to Prokopovich are as follows:

For rye	10.6%
For millet	19.1%
For oats	25.9%
For barley	32.0%
For corn	32.2%
For wheat	45.2%
For buckwheat	46.0%

Prokopovich's data refer to the 50 provinces of European Russia, the data in *Trudy zemplana* to the USSR, but this distinction cannot have any great influence. Despite all the distortions in *Trudy zemplana*, the fundamental logical traits in these distorted figures become apparent.

	Compared with		As a percentage of the production for the market in
	1916	1913	1909–1913
In the first group	-20%	-26%	16
In the second group	-25%	-32%	41
In the second group, together with intensive crops	-31% (-29%)	-37% (-36%)	45
In intensive crops	-56% (-45%)	-56% (-56%)	52

This was also the case with livestock-farming. If we compare the per cent reduction in livestock from 1906 to 1920 and its marketability (the percentage of the production of a given branch of livestock farming destined for the market), we find the following:[15]

	% reduction from 1916 to 1920	% of marketability in 1913
Large cattle	-21 (ca. -22)	19
Pigs	-28 (ca. -24)	27
Sheep	-45 (ca. -39)	37

The nature of the changes in both agriculture and livestock farming is perfectly clear from these figures: the greater the contribution of a given branch of agriculture to the market, the greater its decline. The peasant economy became a *self-sufficient* economy for its own consumption and withdrew from the national economy. As a result, agriculture as the base for industry and city in general (and as the food-supply base of the army) *was reduced to naught.*

15 The figures in the first column are from ibid., p. 83; the bottom figure (45) refers to sheep and goats together. The figures in brackets are from the official statistics of the TsSU (see the above-cited *Sbornik*, pp. 136–7). The figures in the second column are from Prokopovich's statistics, see his *Opyt*, pp. 76–78. The calculations of market production of livestock in Prokopovich do not include skins; this would increase the first figure (19) to 21–23. No calculation was made for horses, since they are basically used as working livestock.

It is very difficult to determine even approximately the extent to which agriculture functioned (acted) as an agricultural base for the city. Apparently, the countryside delivered to the city and army only about a third of what it supplied (to the city and for export) before the war.[16]

Apart from the reduction in agricultural production and, of course, the even greater reduction in the surpluses from agricultural production, the scale of the surpluses was reduced significantly because of the change in the internal structure of the economy, a result of the shift to a small-scale economy due to the peasant expropriation of capitalist (non-peasant and large-scale peasant) agriculture. This all sharply narrowed the agricultural base of industry and city, and this base had already been restricted for a time by the agrarian (anti-feudal) revolution and by the temporary disruption of the peasant economy (during the transitional period). Moreover, the ban on commodity- and money-trading on the market meant that some of the surpluses remained in the peasant households themselves.

The decline in productive forces in small-scale industry was even more significant. A comparison of its condition in 1920 with its condition in 1912 offers the following picture:[17]

---

16 The head of the Central Statistical Administration, P. Popov, in vol. III of *Na novykh putiakh* (see p. 194) writes that in 1921 the national economy received agricultural products in the amount of 866,6 million gold roubles as against 2,000 million roubles before the war, i.e. about two fifths.

17 See *Sbornik stat. svedenii po SSSR*, Moscow, 1924, pp. 212–213. It is noteworthy that the 1920 census counted only 855,000 people with a total production (in finished products) of 193 million roubles (see the article by the head of the Central Statistical Administration, P. Popov, in the collection *Na novykh putiakh*, Moscow, 1923, vol. III, p. 188). P. Popov is of the view that underreporting of production of small-scale industry (in 1922) was less than 5% (20 million roubles out of 415 million roubles). Consequently, according to this calculation the entire production of small-scale industry comprised ca. 202 million roubles. One year later, the number of people employed in small-scale industry was determined by the Central Statistical Administration to be 1,678,000 people. Their production amounted to 660 million roubles, of which more than 640 million roubles went to finished products (see op. cit., Sbornik, p. 221). In other words, the 1920 census, according to the Central Statistical Administration's own data, counted approximately half of those employed in small-scale industry. The production of this industry was underreported not by 5%, but in the best case by 25% (if from the 640 million we subtract a full 350 million roubles for the raw materials used in processing foodstuffs, which includes in part the customers' grain, which apparently has not been taken into consideration in the first count). In reality, the difference is undoubtedly even higher.

The following observation by V. Morgenshtern, then, is completely justifiable (see *Narodnoe khoziaistvo Rossii za 1921–1922 g.*, Moscow, 1923, p. 533): 'Coming to these conclusions, it was necessary to acknowledge that this section of the industrial census of 1920 was not successful. Nor could it have succeeded. The conditions of 1920 encouraged petty com-

	1912–13	1920	1920 as percentage of 1912–13
Number of employed persons	3,706,000	1,578,000	43%
Gross production	1,528,000,000 roubles	660,000,000 roubles	43%
Net production	283,000,000 roubles	97,000,000 roubles	34%

In other words, the decline (compared with the prewar period, no data are available for 1917) was 2½–3 times. Especially severe was the decline in metal-processing (gross production fell by almost seven times) and in textile-processing (by four times).

The decline in large-scale (licenced) industry is illustrated by the following figures:[18]

modity producers to hide from the census, and in village settlements … this was extremely easy to do'. As we have seen, relatively large enterprises also worked illegally in the countryside (see p. 199n7).

18 See N. Vorob'ev, 'Izmeneniia v russkoi promyshlennosti v period voiny i revoliutsii,' in No. 4–6, *Vestnik statistiki*, for 1923, p. 153; and also *Kratkii otchet Gosplana*, Moscow, 1924, p. 239. The official statistics of the Central Statistical Administration fluctuate here too:

	Re *Stat. ezheg. 1921 g.* (vol. I, p. 110)	Re article by head of TSSU P. Popov in collection *Na novykh putiakh*, vol. III, p. 180	Difference	Re *Vest. Statistiki*, no. 4–6, 1923, (article by N. Vorob'ev, p. 153)
	Millions of roubles			
Value of finished products in 1912	3,721	3,721	–	–
Value of finished products in 1920	501	518	+17	–
Value of finished products in 1921	566	585	+19	–
Value of semi-finished products in 1912	2,339	2,338	-1	–
Value of semi-finished products in 1920	299	318	+19	–
Value of semi-finished products in 1921	270	285	+15	–

	1913	1917	1918	1919	1920
No. of employed persons in thousands	2,599	3,024	2,486	2,035	1.585
Gross output in millions of roubles	5,620	4,344	1.941	1,448	1.001
Value of finished products in millions of roubles (1912)	3.721		–	–	518

If, then, we take the production in 1913 as 100, we obtain the following:

for 1917 77
for 1918 35
for 1919 26
for 1920 18

i.e. for the years of the Civil War, large-scale industry shrank by *four* times, and in comparison with the prewar level by more than *five-and-a-half* times, and for finished products even by *seven* times.

(*cont.*)

	Re *Stat. ezheg. 1921 g.* (vol. I, p. 110)	Re article by head of TSSU P. Popov in collection *Na novykh putiakh*, vol. III, p. 180	Difference	Re *Vest. Statistiki*, no. 4–6, 1923, (article by N. Vorob'ev, p. 153)
	Millions of roubles			
Gross production in 1912	6,061	6,059	-2	5,620 (in 1913)
Gross production in 1920	800	836	+36	1,001
Gross production in 1921	836	870	+34	1,189

Consequently, according to *Vestnik statistiki* (the organ of the Central Statistical Administration), the gross production in 1913 was 440 million roubles (7–8%) less than according to *Stat. ezhegodn.* in 1912 (although, as is well-known, 1913 was still a boom year, and before this from 1900 to 1912 the annual growth in gross production was approximately 9%; see ibid., p. 154), but in 1920 and in 1921 according to *Vestnik statistiki* it was 201 and 363 million roubles (25% and 43%) larger than according to *Statisticheskii ezhegodnik*.

However, these contradictions do not affect the basic character of our comparison.

The drop in basic branches of large-scale industry was no less significant; for individual branches, the figures are:[19]

(in millions of poods)	1913	1918	1919	1920
Coal extraction	1738	731	511	467
Iron ore extraction	579	1.7	–	10.1
Iron smelting	256.8	31.5	6.9	7.0
Martin steel production	259.3	24.5	12.2	10.0
Steel rolling	214.2	21.8	10.9	12.2
Cotton yarn production	16.0		1.0	0.8
Sugar production	82.9	20.3	4.9	5.5

The scale of the decline in large-scale industry is characterised by the following figures:[20]

Production for 1920 as a percentage of production for 1913	
Peat extraction	97.7%
Petroleum extraction	42.7%
Tobacco production	42.5%
Leather production	38%
Production of cables	38%
Production of linen yarn	38%
Salt production	30%
Production of wool yarn	27%
Coal extraction	27%
Production of hydrochloric acid	26.7%

19 See the collection *Za 5 let*, Moscow, 1922, pp. 404–6 (according to the statistics of VSNKh). In the collection, the yield of iron ore for 1913 was cited wrongly as 57.9 million poods instead of 579 million poods.

20 See *Russkaia promyshlennost' v 1921 g. i ee perspektivy* (report to the IX Congress of Soviets), p. xiii. Calculation was in natural units (poods, items, etc). Here too we find crude contradictions: on the cited page, the production of caustic soda for 1920 is given as 2,352 poods and it is carefully noted that this comprises 0.1% of the production for 1913. But on p. 246 of the same book, we find that the production of caustic soda for 1920 is given as

(cont.)

Production for 1920 as a percentage of production for 1913	
Production of paper and cardboard	25%
Production of hemp yarn	23%
Production of shag	20%
Production of sulphate	17.3%
Production of low-current devices	16.3%
Production of locomotives	14.8%
Production of matches	14%
Production of ploughs	13.3%
Production of batteries	12.5%
Production of lightbulbs	10.1%
Production of sulphuric acid	9.0%
Production of soda ash	7.2%
Production of sugar	6.7%
Production of vitriol oil	5.9%
Production of electrotechnical machines and high-current devices	5.4%
Production of cotton paper yarn	5.1%
Production of nitric acid	4.4%
Production of wagons	4.2%
Production of vegetable oils	3.0%
Production of cement	3.0%
Iron smelting	2.4%
Production of fireproof brick	2.2%
Production of red brick	2.1%
Extraction of ores	1.7%
Copper smelting	0.0%

So the decline comprised (not including peat extraction) 60–98%, and production sometimes even ceased completely.

The general condition of the national economy (the scale of the decline in the forces of production) can best be characterised by the data on the work of the railways.

93,560 poods, i.e. forty times higher, not 0.1%, but over 4%. It is interesting that not even numbers on two neighbouring pages (245 and 246) agree with each other; it is true that these pages are not facing each other but are on opposite sides of the same sheet.

Freight transport comprised the following, in comparison with the corresponding territory in 1913:[21]

In 1919	30%
In 1920	20%

i.e. a four-fifths reduction by 1920.

For the most important types of freight, transport on the railways and waterways in 1920 as compared with 1913 was:[22]

All types of grain	12.5%
Coal	11%
Petroleum and its products	33%
Iron and pig iron	17%
Textiles	14%
Lumber	17%

If we wanted to make a rough and very crude estimate of the national income in 1920, then, keeping in mind the aforementioned figures for the most important branches of the national economy, we must conclude that national income in 1920 was no more than 40% of the national income in 1913, i.e. it declined by at least *two and a half times*, and, probably, by a full *three* times.[23]

---

21 See *Statisticheskii ezhegodnik* for 1918–1920 g.g., vol. I, p. 26. The situation was similar with transport on the waterways as well, which comprised as a percentage of the prewar numbers:

In 1913	100%
In 1917	62%
In 1918	19%
In 1919	9%
In 1920	3!%

See *Sbornik stat. svedenii po SSSR*, p. 442.

22 Ibid, pp. 452–466. An exception here – for understandable reasons – is wood, of which 97% of the amount in 1913 was transported.

23 We made this very rough evaluation in the following way: income from grains took up 62.5% of the income for 1913; from intensive crops, 44% (this is undoubtedly exaggerated, because while the area maybe did not shrink so much, we did not see here the highly significant reduction in harvests that we saw with flax and tobacco crops, and so the harvest of intensive crops was undoubtedly less than 44% of the harvest for 1913; for individual crops, it comprised from 10 to 25% of the prewar volumes). From livestock farming, it was 74% (calculated from the individual branches of the industry). For the other branches of agriculture (which furnished only 1/12 of the total income from agriculture) the reduction was

in relative terms as large as the reduction for the main branches of agriculture; the income from small-scale industry is 43%, from large-scale industry – 18%, from transport – 20%, from construction – 3%, from forestry – 40% (corresponding to the transporting of wood and timber), from fishing – 31% according to the figures on fish catches in 1920 (see *Stat. ezhegodnik* for 1918–1920, vol. I, p. 13, and *Stat. ezhegodnik* for 1921, vol. III, p. 363), from trade (which, according to Prokopovich, took up about 1/12 of the national income) – 20%, in accordance with the changes in freight turnover.

This rough (and overestimated) evaluation, which is in no way a precise calculation, comprises therefore about 43% of the national income for 1913, as Prokopovich calculates it for 50 provinces of European Russia. If the decline in income from trade is seen as a proportion of all the remaining part of the national income, this comes to a little more than 43%. This 43% is an overestimate largely because we are looking at the decline in national income from each branch of the economy proportionally to the decline in gross production; in reality, however, when production is falling, net production falls much more quickly than gross production.

This accelerated decline in net production, when production falls, can be illustrated to a certain extent by comparing gross and net production of the Donbass (net production equals gross production minus the mines' own coal consumption).

	(in millions of poods)			(as a percentage of 1913)		
	Gross	Own consumption	Net	Gross	Own consumption	Net
1913	1,543	126	1,417	100	100	100
1917	1,510	203	1,307	98	161	92
1918	541	152	389	35	121	28
1919	338	126	212	22	100	15
1920	273	134	139	18	106	10

(See *Stat. ezhegodnik* for 1918–1920, vol. II, p. 219).

Consequently, when the gross production was reduced by 5½ times, personal consumption was not reduced at all, and net production was reduced by 10 times, i.e. twice as much as gross production.

We see the same result when considering railway traffic.

	Total freight transport as a percentage of 1913	Percentage of economic freight transport	Commercial freight transport (minus economic freight) as a percentage of 1913
1913	100	11	100
1919	30	25	19
1920	20	28	15

Here too, the decline in commercial freight transport is significantly faster than the decline in overall freight transport. Moreover, like the reduction in coal yield or railway traffic, analogous manifestations occur not only in relation to private consumption of coal or economic traffic, but also in relation to other production costs, which also decline more slowly than does production.

To appreciate the full significance of this fact, it is necessary to keep in mind that the surplus product in prewar Russia was (according to our rough evaluation in part I) about half of the total national income. Consequently, the decline in the productive forces of Russia during the Civil War period was so great that it led *to the complete disappearance of surplus product*, i.e. social production, even at the cost of giving up everything that went beyond the simple reproduction of the labour force, was no longer able to guarantee this reproduction.

Such a decline in the productive forces not of a small community but of a large hundred-million strong society – a decline caused by the unheard-of worsening and deepening of the Civil War caused by the powerful support of the counter-revolutionary resistance from without – is without parallel in human history.

Nothing shows us the full power of the revolution as clearly as the *fact* that it was successfully able to survive such a test.

In small-scale industry when gross production was declining to 43% of the prewar level, net production was declining to 34% of the prewar level. Accordingly, it can be assumed that total national income declined to about 33%, i.e. to one third of the prewar level. Such an assumption would not be far from the truth.

CHAPTER 10

The Causes of the Extraordinary Decline in Productive Forces

1. The unavoidable costs of the revolution. 2. The influence of the deformation of the revolutionary process. 3. The military deformation of the national economy. 4. The specific features of the Civil War. 5. The scale and significance of the costs of the Civil War. 6. The influence of the Civil War on the organisation of the national economy. 7. The demobilisation and remobilisation of the national economy. 8. The effect of the destruction of the imperialist war.

A temporary decline in the productive forces is the unavoidable outcome of revolution, if it is truly a revolution, i.e. the struggle between classes taken to its most extreme degree. But this decline in productive forces is by no means the outcome of the new social order; it is the outcome of the *transition* to this new order and all the more so where the resistance to this transition is strong and still being overcome. In itself, the new (political and economic) social order, once it has been established, can be used to produce an *upswing* in the productive forces. But it must first be created and consolidated (established), and, before this process of emergence and transition can be used to produce an upswing in the productive forces of society, it unavoidably becomes a cause of their decline.

But the sheer *depth* of this decline described above was caused not by revolution itself in general, but by the specific features of the Russian Revolution. The direct and therefore, generally speaking, unavoidable costs of the revolution are connected with a crisis in social relations, and with *a crisis in the relations of production* in particular. Production activity demands a *specific* organisation of production, *specific* relations of production. The period of crisis in the means of production, and the replacement of the old capitalist production relations with new socialist relations, is inevitably a period when capitalist production relations are disintegrating and socialist ones are still emerging, a period when specific production relations do not yet exist.[1] The replacement of the capitalist administration of enterprises with a workers' administration is therefore a serious temporary factor in the disintegration of the economy, which is aggravated

1 See N. Bukharin, *Ekonomika perekhodnogo perioda*.

 | HTTPS://DOI.ORG/10.1163/9789004765313-014

significantly by the spontaneous and thus unorganised nature of this transformation. This transformation takes place at the same time everywhere in all capitalist units from top to bottom (from banks and syndicates to plants, factories, and workshops).

However, these inevitable costs of the revolution can in no way alone explain the extraordinary *scale* of the decline in Russia's productive forces in the Civil War era.

Only the impact of a number of additional powerful factors could cause such an extraordinary decline in Russia's productive forces.

A significant increase in the costs of the revolution was already inevitable because the bourgeois and proletarian revolutions occurred at the same time, and consequently their effects did not only coincide with each other, but *compounded each other*. As a result of this, the disintegration of the large-scale economy caused the additional disintegration of the small-scale economy, and vice-versa. And this coincidence of revolutions was necessary because the bourgeois revolution had been delayed in Russia. This delay was a feature of prerevolutionary Russia and was essentially, as has been described above, a consequence of the advanced development of capitalism outside of Russia.

A further increase in the costs of the revolution was caused, as we have seen in part II, by the fact that the revolution took place when the level of Russia's productive forces had already been *depressed* by the imperialist war and especially by its long duration, a product of the influence of advanced capitalism outside of Russia.

An even more acute increase in the costs of the revolution was caused by the afore-mentioned deformation of the revolutionary process, being, as we have seen, a consequence of the interference from external forces. This deformation of the revolutionary process – the intrusion of its final phase into the still unfinished preceding phase – increased the costs of the revolution in various ways.

Going beyond the framework of what had been prepared by the preceding development, the expansion of the anti-capitalist revolution to small-scale capitalist and petty bourgeois economic forms, and, consequently, the contradiction between the nature of the revolution and its scope, all meant that the costs of revolution increased along with its increase in scope. Even more, the process of transformation was more difficult for those economic forms that were unprepared for it, and the resistance it faced was far greater. This expansion of the scope of the revolution made its activity more complicated, even in its main sphere of activity, the large-scale economy.

On the other hand, the contradiction, springing from the same source, between the old ideology of the intelligentsia and its new function (work) fostered the bureaucratic nature of this work, i.e. further deterioration and, consequently, an increase in the costs of the transition to the new order, i.e. an increase in the costs of revolution.

Finally, the forced inclusion of the small-scale economy in the system of the proletarian natural economy led, first of all, to the incomplete extraction of product surpluses from the small-scale economy (compared with the quantities that could be extracted using the methods of the commodity economy),[2] and consequently the already sharply reduced productive forces of society could *not be fully utilised*; secondly, it led to the suppression of economic stimuli in the small-scale economy, thereby inhibiting its development; for both reasons, the costs of the revolution increased further.

But all of these causes of the increase in the costs of the revolution, including the deformation of the revolutionary process, however significant the influence of the latter, cannot explain the extraordinary depth of the decline in the productive forces of society that occurred during the Civil War.

The most powerful factor in the increase in the costs of revolution was a different consequence of the impact of external forces, namely the fact that as a result of this impact the revolutionary class struggle took *the form of a protracted civil war*. The three-year duration of the Civil War, its intensification, and the expression of this intensification – the military organisation of the fighting classes by the state – meant that the entire national economy of Soviet Russia inevitably had to be put on a *war footing*, i.e. the basic *needs of the Red Army* were prioritised and had to be, and were satisfied above all other needs, and the *production of resources needed by the Red Army* became the most important determinant of all production.

This unproductive (military) consumption and the associated reallocation of the productive forces of society (the deformation of the economy caused by the war) were an additional enormous factor in the decline in productive forces, whose harmful effects were felt more and more as the productive forces declined. As surplus product disappeared, military consumption could take place only at the expense of a restriction of necessary consumption (at the expense of the reproduction of the labour force) and at the expense of the reconstruction of the technical basis of the national economy, i.e. only by destroying it. This additional and extremely powerful factor in the decline in productive forces was a necessary consequence not of the revolution per se, but of its intensification, which, as we have seen, was the result of interference by *external* forces, a result of interference by global capital.

2 If the same quantity of products needed by the state had been acquired not by requisitioning but through taxes (even if natural taxes).

The Civil War lagged behind the imperialist war in terms of scale. While the army in the imperialist war already numbered 5,600,000 at its start, rising to 11,400,000, the Red Army reached 5,300,000 only by the end of the Civil War.[3] Until then, the combined total of the Red and White armies did not reach this figure.

And yet the destructive effect of the Civil War was undoubtedly no less than the effect of the imperialist war. In our examination of the imperialist war (see Part II), we singled out, from among the characteristic features of this war from a national economic perspective, its geographic concentration at the front line, as a result of which a colossal apparatus encompassing millions of people was concentrated on a relatively small strip of land, where the immediate activity of this apparatus was focused on direct military destruction.

Unlike this extraordinarily geographic concentration of the imperialist war, the Civil War was characterised by extraordinary *dispersion* – it was being fought everywhere. It lagged far behind the imperialist war in terms of the concentration of enormous masses of people and its capacity for destruction, in terms of the scale of direct military action and, as a result of all this, in terms of its destructive impact in certain areas – the theatres of war. But it was truly all-pervading and omnipresent. Deep in the rear (and especially in Russia given its enormous distances), the imperialist war was known only by hearsay; the Civil War, however, was experienced firsthand by the entire 130 million-strong population of Russia. For unlike the imperialist war, the Civil War *knew no rear*; its mobile fronts tore like whirlwinds across the entire country, returning several times to many places, drawing everyone in, and leaving no one untouched.

In particular, this feature of the Civil War completely *destroyed any continuity* of economic life, causing constant disruptions in work and shutdowns of enterprises; and this was all the more frequent the larger the enterprise and the broader the network of its economic connections.

And so, although the direct (battle) *losses* of material resources and people in the Civil War were *less* than in the imperialist war, the *disruption* it brought to all economic life (and to the general life of society) *was far greater*; and therefore, taking into account the entirety of the destruction it wrought, both direct and indirect, the destruction in the Civil War was greater.

This is confirmed by the calculation (by S. Strumilin) of Soviet Russia's military losses in the imperialist war and in the Civil War.

These losses comprise (in millions of years of working capacity):[4]

---

3 See *Piat' let vlasti Sovetov*, Moscow, 1922, p. 157.

4 See the article by S. Strumilin, 'Trudovye poteri Rossii v voine,' in the December issue of *Narodnoe khoziaistvo*, for 1920, p. 105.

	In the Imperialist War	In the Civil War
Losses of the army	*55.5*	*21.7*
incl. mobilised	24.8	5.0
incl. killed and deceased	15.8	5.3
incl. war invalids	14.9	11.4
Losses in the civilian population	*96.6*	*232.0*
incl. premature deaths	22.1	137.0
incl. unborn	74.5	95.0
Total losses	*152.1*	*253.7*

Consequently, direct (battle) losses in the Civil War were two to three times *lower* than in the imperialist war, but indirect losses were two to three times *higher* (and if unborns are not included, almost seven times greater); as a result, all losses, both direct and indirect, were almost 70% *higher* (and if unborns are not included, then *two times* higher).

Furthermore, the Civil War took place with a significantly lower level of productive forces than the imperialist war. As a percentage of the prewar volume, we get the following:

	At the end of the imperialist war	At the end of the Civil War
Grain harvest	88%	62%
Gross production of large-scale industry	77%	18%
National income (rough calculation)	ca. 85%[5]	less than 40%

So even the direct costs of the Civil War, although lower in absolute terms, represented an incomparably heavier burden, and led to an even greater decline in productive forces, than the costs of the imperialist war.

It is very telling that, according to data from medical experts, the average loss of working capacity of invalids was 36% in the imperialist war, and 43% in the Civil War, i.e. a fifth greater (see ibid., p. 104).

5 See Part II (according to S. Prokopovich's data).

In summer 1920, the Red Army received the following percentages of the total volume of products destined for distribution (on the basis of distribution plans, which covered the total consumption of the country, insofar as it was served by state organs[6]):

Flour	25%	Fats	40%
Cereals	50%	Soap	40%
Grain feed	40%	Tobacco	100%
Fish	60%	Matches	20%
Meat	60%	Cotton fabrics	40%
Dried fruits	90%	Other fabrics	70–100%
Sugar	60%	Men's footwear	90%
Salt	15%		

The distribution plans for many of these products indeed encompassed almost the entire consumption (these products reached the 'free' market only after distribution). It must also be kept in mind that those distribution plans affecting the Red Army were fulfilled to a greater degree than for the other consumers.

Military transports took up 24% of total railway traffic in 1919, and 18% in 1920.[7]

By the way, although the army in the Civil War was significantly smaller in size than in the imperialist war, the magnitude of the deformation (change) of the national economy caused by the war was greater in the Civil War than in the imperialist war. As we saw with a range of products (sugar, fish, footwear, textiles, soap, fats, tobacco), about a half and even more than a half of all products served the needs of the Red Army, which, of course, would not have been pos-

6 See *Prodovol'stvennaia politika*, Moscow, 1920, p. 236. Highly typical are the data on footwear production by state industry.

The following were produced (in millions of pairs):

	in 1919	in 1920
Army footwear	4.6	5.8
Civilian footwear	2.1	1.8

So the production of footwear for the civilian population (including women and children) comprised in 1919 only 31%, and in 1920 only 24% of overall production.

(See *Narodnoe khoziaistvo SSSR v tsifrakh*, Moscow, 1924, p. 163).

7 See *Statisticheskii ezhegodnik* for 1918–1920, vol. I, p. 29; and *Stat. ezheg.* for 1921, vol. II, p. 137. The following is noted here in the explanations to the tables (vol. I, p. 66): 'The statistics for free travel (for army personnel) are not recorded accurately'.

sible during the imperialist war. With the contraction of industry from 1917 to 1920 by 82%, even an army that was two to three times smaller and more poorly supplied, but supplied completely from internal resources, inevitably led to a further intensification of the military deformation of the national economy.

The entire organisation of the national economy in the Civil War period bore the clear stamp of war need. As the Civil War unfolded, this became crystal clear. The entire organisation of the national economy came under the organ of the military dictatorship – the *Council of Defense* [*Sovet Oborony*] *and its organs*: the Extraordinary Plenipotentiary of the Council of Defense for the Supply of the Red Army (this position was filled by the chair of the VSNKh) had dictatorial powers [*diktator*] over the fulfillment of all orders to supply the army and the war industry with everything they needed, apart from foodstuffs; the Central Administration of Food Supply of the Red Army under the People's Commissariat of Food played a similar role in the supply of the army with foodstuffs. All distribution organs took care first and foremost of the needs of the Red Army and of the war industry. Several products went completely and exclusively to meet the needs of defense,[8] while others were guaranteed ('reserved') for the Red Army in certain quantities that could be used for no other purposes.

The structure of the national economic organisation in the Civil War period was thus defined by two moments, by the extreme exacerbation and intensification of the revolution, i.e. of the class struggle, and by the fact that this struggle took *the form of war*. The combination of these two moments also determined the aforementioned forms of organisation of the national economy in the Civil War period, and the nature of the distribution of productive forces realised in these forms. Revolution and war – these were the two roots of the concrete system of economic organs, in which the organisation of the proletarian natural economy took shape. The fundamental principles, however, which permeated and characterised this organisation, were not the product of war, i.e. of the form the revolution had taken, but of the revolution itself, of which war was but one manifestation.

The destructive effect of the deformation caused by the war was greatly intensified by the proletarian revolution's urge for external peace, a peace which could open up the opportunity for creative labour at home. In this respect, the great proletarian revolution in Russia was the direct opposite of the great bourgeois revolutions, such as the French. The characteristic proletarian urge for productive labour found its expression in the rapid shift to

8 For example, for a time, all tobacco (see above) and castor oil was supplied to military aviation etc.

peacetime labour, a shift that was often far too premature, and which the Soviet state rushed ahead with in the faintest hope of an end to military operations: immediately after the October overthrow [*perevorot*], after the defeat of Kolchak, after the defeat of Denikin, and, finally, after the war with Poland and the defeat of Wrangel'. The national economy of Soviet Russia, then, had to experience *several* attempts to shift from a wartime to a peacetime economy and from a peacetime back to a wartime economy, from demobilisation to remobilisation, and again to a new demobilisation and a new remobilisation.

The scale of these vacillations, which inevitably must have exacerbated the decline in the productive forces of Soviet Russia, can be seen in the fact that the army, which numbered 11 million people in the second half of 1917, fell apart so quickly and to such an extent that, even after several months of efforts to organise the Red Army, the latter still only numbered 350,000 by October 1918.[9]

No less significant was the scale of the demobilisation of industry. Thus, in the centre of the armaments industry in Petrograd (in enterprises with over 100 workers), the workers numbered 403,000 on 1 January 1917 and 124,000 on 1 December 1918, i.e. a more than *three*-fold decrease.[10] Metal-processing experienced a five-fold decrease (from 248,000 workers on 1 January 1917 to 49,000 on 1 December 1918).

The pace of remobilisation (a new mobilisation) can be seen in the fact that for the month of December in 1918, the Red Army grew from 372,000 people to 435,000, i.e. almost by a quarter, and by mid-1919, it already had 1,500,000 members, i.e. it had more than tripled in six months; in 1920 it had 5,300,000 people, i.e. it had almost quadrupled again.[11]

One attempt to try to mitigate these transitions from a war footing to a peace footing and back again were the so-called labour armies [*trudovye armii*]. The transformation of part of the Red Army into a labour army meant a redistribution of roles within these units: the workers (communists) and technicians came to the fore, while the military specialists receded into the background, but this was done in such a way that everything could be put back as it was before at short notice. The large and small military units performed their tasks, while remaining subordinate to the military authorities in military matters. In addition to the partial use of the material resources of the Red Army (its engineering, technical, transport and other materiel) and of the personnel in its ranks (technical personnel, including skilled workers, and administrative

9 See *Piat' let vlasti Sovetov*, Moscow, 1922, p. 156.

10 See *Statistika Truda*, no. 104 for 1919, p. 5. As a result of demobilisation, the number of workers turned out to be even less than before the war (cf. 194,000 on 1 January 1913).

11 See *Piat' let vlasti Sovetov*, pp. 156–7.

personnel, predominantly worker communists) in various industrial and transport enterprises, labour armies created the opportunity to utilize large masses of unskilled workers for mass projects.

Labour armies were used most widely for logging, for maintaining railway lines, and for construction and other similar work. Labour armies put to work large numbers of peasants, who were organised and led by advanced workers for other (military) purposes, but maintained their own organisation on the field of work. But labour armies could not, of course, be anything other than a forcible attempt to use the army, i.e. an organisation created for other purposes, for the purposes of labour, an attempt to mitigate the severity of the transitions from a war footing to a peace footing and back again, which were increasing the Civil War's impact on the already disrupted national economy of Soviet Russia.

As we have seen, the depth of the decline in Russia's productive forces during the Civil War can be explained neither by the direct costs of the proletarian revolution, nor by the direct costs of the agrarian revolution, nor by the sum of these costs, nor even by the *combined* effect of the proletarian and the agrarian revolutions which sharply increased the costs of both. It can instead be explained by the fact that new costs were added to these inevitable costs of revolution. These new costs accrued both from the deepening and intensification of the proletarian revolution caused by the intervention of global capital, an intervention which prolonged and intensified this civil war and, therefore, the accompanying deformation of the national economy caused by it.

Furthermore, this Civil War era was not only a time when all of these factors became a reality, but also *a time when the destruction wrought on Russia's national economy by the imperialist war of 1914–1917 became apparent.* The deterioration of fields, the destruction of technical resources of the entire national economy (transport, industry, agriculture) happened (as shown in Part II) during the imperialist war as well, – but the full force of their consequences were felt only later. Before October 1917, this destruction, despite the fact that its full impact had not yet been felt, was masked by the material support from the powerful coalition of highly developed capitalist countries of the Entente. Even more, this (hidden) destruction took on colossal proportions precisely because of this artificial external support, which prolonged the imperialist war that had placed such a strain on Russia's national economy. This destruction caused by the war became ever more apparent once this support was cut off as a result of the October overthrow, and was replaced not only by the most severe blockade of Soviet Russia, but also by military attacks from the newly created states on Russia's Western border, above all Poland, and by direct military and material intervention by global capital on the side of White Russia against Red Russia.

CHAPTER 11

The Effect of the Decline in Productive Forces on the National Economy

1. The 'separation' [*razmychka*] of city and countryside. 2. Extra-economic coercion. 3. The destruction of the technical apparatus of the national economy. 4. The decline in the living standards of the masses. 5. So-called consumer communism. 6. The decline in the productivity of labour. 7. The disappearance of unemployment. 8. The growth of the bureaucratic apparatus.

This enormous decline in productive forces, which led to a contraction of agriculture by more than one-and-a-half times, transport by five times, industry by five and a half times, and total national income by not less than two-and-a-half times – inevitably had a deep and comprehensive effect on the entire national economy of Russia and on the ways in which the complex revolutionary process played out.

Highly relevant here was the fact that this decline did not occur uniformly across all branches of the national economy. Large-scale industry and transport experienced the largest decline, for reasons we have already described above, while on the other hand the decline in small-scale industry and in agriculture was comparatively smaller. This means, however, that *the decline in productive forces also meant the destruction of economic connections*, a regression in the division of labour in the national economy. The contraction of railway traffic alone speaks to the scale of this regression in the division of labour. This contraction was such that freight transport as a percentage of the prewar volumes in 1919 and 1920 comprised the following:[1]

	1919	1920
All freight	30%	20%
All freight excl. military need	23%	17%
All freight excl. military and domestic need	17%	12%

1 Commercial freight [*khoziaistvennye gruzy*] is the railways' own freight. The percentages are

 | HTTPS://DOI.ORG/10.1163/9789004765313-015

By the end of the Civil War, the freight transport serving the national economy contracted to an *eighth*.

But the rupture of the economic connections between the two main spheres of the national economy – industry and agriculture, and thus between city and countryside – was yet more significant and led to a full-blown economic *rupture* between the city and the countryside. The unprecedented collapse of large-scale industry (a more than 80% decline in 1920), together with the fact that in the same year about half of industrial production was consumed by the Red Army (40% of cotton, 60% of sugar, etc), meant that the longer the Civil War raged on, the less the city was able to supply to the village.

If we compare, on the one hand, the delivery of grain by the peasants through requisitioning, and, on the other hand, the state supply of the village population with textiles, then we get the following figures:[2]

	Procurement of grain and forage	**Supply with textiles**	**Ratio (arshins of textiles for one pood of grain)**
1919	108 mill. poods	325 mill. arshins	1:3.0
1920	212 mill. poods	ca. 180 mill. arshins	1:0.85

This comparison is, of course, incomplete in two ways: firstly, it does not take into account state procurements of agricultural products other than grain and feed, or state supply of the village population with products other than textiles;[3] secondly, it does not take into account the illegal exchange of products between the city and the countryside. But this comparison does give a sense of the general scale of the national economic connections between the city and the countryside, and of the direction in which these connections were

calculated from data mentioned in chapter 9 in footnotes 21 and 23. In 1913, commercial freight transport was about 11% of total freight transport, the percentage of military freight transport was 1%. See *Sbornik stat. svedenii*, p. 440.

2 See *Prodovol'stvennaia politika*, Moscow, 1920, p. 232, and *Sbornik stat. svedenii po SSSR*, Moscow, 1924, p. 424. Since the supply of the rural population was carried out according to the fulfillment of allocations, we have used the procurement years 1918/19 and 1919/20.

3 According to calculations by Iu. Larin (see his article in the cited book of Iu. Larin and L. Kritsman, p. 19), considered in fixed prices, about 4/5 of the state procurements were grain products and about 2/3 of state supply were textiles. Consequently, the cited figures cover a major part of the legal exchange of products between city and countryside.

changing. This comparison shows, first, a colossal contraction in the supply of textiles to the agricultural population (and it was no different with other products), a decline which in 1919 was two-thirds to three-quarters and in 1920 four-fifths to five-sixths of prewar levels; so the comparison reveals a sharp and developing rupture in the economic connections between the city and the countryside.[4] It shows, second, a growing inequality in the economic relations between the city and the countryside that led *to the economic parasitism of the city*.

It is necessary to keep in mind here that even these figures understate the scale of the rupture in economic connections between industry and agriculture. This is so, firstly, because peasants received a significant portion of the products from the state not as producers of agricultural products but as proletarians who supplied the state with their own labour in logging, sugar-beet plantations, etc. Of the 180 million arshins of textiles which the agricultural population received in 1920, more than 30 million arshins fell into this latter category. Secondly, in terms of state supply, more industrial products were received by those groups of peasants (the poor peasants) which supplied fewer agricultural products, or none at all.

One specially examined rural district in 1920, therefore, revealed that the following amounts of grain and potatoes were delivered:[5]

	per head of population	per desiatin
Households with a sown area less than 1 desiatin	7.8	33.3
Households with a sown area from 1–2 desiatins	11.4	41.5
Households with a sown area from 2–4 desiatins	15.8	45.4

From the state, each head of population received:

4 If we assume, from the data of Prof. Grinevetskii, that up to half of the products of the textile industry went to the countryside, then the demand of the rural population before the war must have amounted to one and a half billion [*milliard*] arshins, and over a billion arshins on the territory of Soviet Russia.

5 See *Prodovol'stvennaia politika*, Moscow, 1920, p. 88. The table contains arithmetical errors (for footwear, 0.026 instead of 0.008); these errors have been corrected in the text.

	Textiles (arshins)	Salt (pounds)	Footwear (pairs)	Nails	Agricultural appliances (items)	Household commodities (items)
Households with no sown area	1.5	1.07	–	–	–	–
with a sown area, but delivering nothing	1.4	1.03	–	–	–	–
with a sown area, delivering less than 50 poods	1.4	1.00	0.007	0.20	0.10	0.024
with a sown area, delivering from 50–100 poods	1.4	1.00	0.008	0.09	0.06	0.013
with a sown area, delivering more than 100 poods	1.4	1.04	0.009	0.07	0.06	0.008

Consequently, product exchange by the state was not so much an exchange between industry and agriculture as an exchange of industrial products for services performed by poor peasants in securing products from the economy of the well-to-do strata of the village.

It must be emphasised that the economic rupture between city and countryside was not just a separation of industry from agriculture, i.e. a rupture of the *economic* connection between the proletariat and the petty bourgeois (and bourgeois) peasantry; it was no less, indeed perhaps even more so, also an economic separation of the urban proletariat from the proletarian (and semi-proletarian) strata of the countryside.

The contraction of large-scale industry and transport to a fifth and lower, the almost complete cessation of construction work, and the reduction in logging work led to a sharp decline in the proletarian activities of the peasantry, its so-called non-agricultural income-producing employments [*nezemledel'cheskie promysly*]. Unfortunately, pertinent statistical data are very scarce; however, the existing data clearly show this process. Thus, the percentages of households with such employments comprised:[6]

6 See *Ekonomicheskoe rassloenie krest'ianstva v 1917–1919 g.g.*, Trudy TSU, Moscow, 1921, p. 22. These 'employments' of the overwhelming majority of the peasants were the sale of their own labour power. It must be noted that already 25 years ago comrade Lenin branded the use of the term 'employments' in our statistics as a 'barbarous misuse of words,' and declared that employers and wage-workers were 'the minimum number of economic types without discriminating between which economic statistics cannot be regarded as satisfactory,' but this (as comrade Lenin declared already at the end of the 19th century) 'glaring anachronism' continues to exist untouched in our statistical literature and now, six years after the October overthrow. And now the basic fact is ignored completely that such employments are diverse,

	1917	1920
In Kostroma province	40	18
In Novgorod province	36	28
In Iaroslavl' province	31	21

i.e. the households with 'employments' were reduced by a quarter to a third and even by half.

At the same time, then, as the political connections between the proletarian and semi-proletarian strata of the countryside with the city were getting stronger, their economic connections, which had earlier played such a strong role, were disappearing.[7]

that there are employments and there are employments. See the aforementioned publication of the Central Statistical Administration, and also L. Litoshenko, *Krest'ianskii biudzhet v 1922–1923 g.*, Moscow, izd. TsSU, etc. [V.I. Lenin, *The Development of Capitalism in Russia*, in *Collected Works*, vol. III, 4th Edition (Moscow: Foreign Languages Publishing House, 1961), p. 95.

7 So the loss of labour time on non-agricultural employments as a percentage of the total labour time of the peasantry before the war comprised:

Khar'kov province	6(34)
Smolensk province	6(23)
Viatka province	19 (48)
Vologda province	21 (31)
Kostroma province	23 (15)
Penza province	25 (16)
Moscow province	28 (13)

(see L. Litoshenko, op. cit., p. 18). The figures in brackets show the amount of labour time spent on agriculture. In many provinces, most activity of the peasants was not petty bourgeois (and feudal) agriculture, but (predominantly proletarian) industry.

But these are the average figures of the narodniks, which 'distribute' the wage labour of the proletarianised and semi-proletarianised peasants between them and the bourgeois peasantry.

Among the bottom groups of the peasantry, their 'employments' played an even greater role. For example, Lenin cited figures for, e.g., Saratov province, where the percentage of households with employments changed from group to group as follows:

group with 5 head of working cattle and more	47%
group with 4 head of working cattle	59%
group with 3 head of working cattle	55%
group with 2 head of working cattle	62%
group with 1 head of working cattle	71%
group with no working cattle	91%
On average	66%

Of course, this aforementioned unevenness of economic interrelations between the city and the countryside can be attributed to a great extent to the fact that the burden of the Civil War, which was not only a war against capital but also a war against the landowners, weighed far more heavily on the city than on the countryside, and so the destruction of industry was, as we have seen, far more significant than the destruction of agriculture; above all, industry bore the direct brunt of the costs of the war, because it delivered *up to a half* of the gross production of its most important branches to war needs, at a time when agriculture was not giving up even one tenth of its production.

But, as we shall see, although it was not the petty bourgeois village but the heroic proletarian city that bore the heaviest sacrifices during the Civil War, the near complete disappearance of surplus product in the city meant that most of the resources to conduct the Civil War could only come, and indeed came, from the village.

The alliance between the proletariat and the peasantry during the Civil War rested not only on the fact that the peasantry, even though it vacillated, was in agreement with the proletariat's assumption of political power and the destruction of the market, but also on the fact that it was ultimately ready to *provide the resources* for conducting the Civil War under the guidance of the proletariat; under this leadership, the peasantry received land, and the proletariat organised the military defense of the gains of the agrarian revolution.

The peasantry did this because, after all kinds of vacillations, it nevertheless took the side of Red Russia against the Whites. This demanded heavy sacrifices from the peasantry too, all the more so as the burden of the Soviet costs of the Civil War fell on a relatively small territory.

During the Civil War, most of the grain-surplus regions were outside of the borders of Soviet Russia the entire time, and so its agricultural base was grossly disproportionate to its urban, industrial and military superstructure. This is precisely why it was a matter of life and death that *all* the surpluses, and in

---

(see V. Il'in, Razvitie kapitalizma v Rossii, Moscow, 1923, p. 40).

And the income from personal industries as a percentage of the total income, according to the data from peasant budgets in Voronezh province for the same groups, comprised:
8%
11%
7%
15%
20%
31%
an average of 12%, i.e. semi-proletarians (those with a single horse) and proletarians (with no horse) exceeded the average by 2–3 times (calculated from the data, ibid., p. 89).

general the minimum required for the city and the army, be procured. As the agricultural base narrowed, *pressure on it inevitably increased*, and this was a further cause of stability in the food supply politics of Soviet power during the Civil War. Despite the decline in the grain harvest (gross yields fell from 1917 to 1920 by at least 30%, and net yields by even more), which led to the disappearance of grain surpluses, grain requisitioning brought in the following quantities:[8]

in 1916–1917	212.5 million poods
in 1919–1920	180.5 million poods

i.e. a decline of only 15%. During the Civil War, it grew tangibly:

from 27 million poods	in 1917–1918
to 108 million poods	in 1918–1919
and 180.5 million poods	in 1919–1920

Under these conditions, the resources needed to conduct the Civil War could be extracted from the peasant economy only *through force*. The most extreme economic method of coercion was the issuance of paper money. But to the extent that this method too stopped working, *extra-economic force* became the only way.[9]

The significance of this factor was made abundantly clear by the official theses on the food requisition army [*prodarmiia*], which were published in the collection *Prodovol'stvennaia politika*. We read there:[10] 'All these circumstances create the need to organise persistent and systematic work to establish and apply the armed force, *on which much of the success of requisitioning depends*'. This should not be taken to mean that armed force was the be-all and end-all of this. 'In an examination of which factors had the greatest influence on delivery', writes the author of another article in the same collection, 'armed force, agitation, or product exchange, I came to the conclusion that they were all equally critical to delivery, and that each of them in isolation was no more important than the other'. 'It was very important for the agitation work of the members of the food supply detachments [*otriadniki*] that they be accompanied by a

8 See *Stat. ezhegodnik za 1918–1920 g.g.*, vol. I, p. 2. For 1916–1917, the same requisitioning territory for 1919–1920 is assumed.

9 This coercion was necessary under these conditions regardless whether the resources needed by the state were obtained via requisitioning or by taxes.

10 p. 248 (my italics).

small armed unit. The several armed individuals in the gatherings and in daily life silenced the kulaks and the open counter-revolutionaries, but they quickly found sympathy among the poor and middle peasants and had a great influence on them. It is telling that wherever agitation work took place without any armed presence but just with individual agitators or a single unarmed detachment, it had no influence'.[11] In short, it was not just a matter of armed force, but *without* it requisitions could not be carried out.

A direct consequence of the extraordinary decline in productive forces was not only the absolute impossibility of foregoing the old technology, not only the very rapid and merciless collapse of all premature projects, such as the construction of the Volga-Don canal, irrigation in Turkestan, the transfer of Leningrad's industry to the Urals, the railway link between the Kuznetsk Basin and the Urals, the development of petroleum in Ukhta, the construction of the oil pipeline and railway to Emba, universal electrification, the construction of the Northern rail line and many other plans, but also the impossibility of simply maintaining the existing technical apparatus of the national economy.[12]

---

11 Ibid., article by Kaganovich, pp. 254–255.

12 In spring 1918, I wrote the following about these projects: 'Russian public life, and especially revolutionary life, has never suffered from a dearth of projects. There are now more than enough. What has not been proposed in order to get the national economy of Russia out of this dismal situation into which it has fallen thanks to the exhausting imperialist war, capitalist sabotage during the revolution, and the violence of German imperialism! These projects include shifting the centres of economic life, creating new industries, developing untouched natural resources, utilising new sources of power (electrification and others), constructing new transport routes, etc etc. All of these projects suffer, however, from an unforgivable deficiency – *a lack of any long-term prospects.*

Unfortunately, this is not simply a matter of timing, not just that these measures are unable to solve the crisis of the moment, they cannot even contribute to a solution; they do not account for the fact that the most important preconditions for their success do not yet exist…

The goal and meaning of the socialist overthrow (as of any revolution) is the development of productive forces, *changing man's attitude towards nature* with the aim of increasing man's control over it, in short a *technological revolution*. But this revolution assumes *a change in the relationship between people in the production process*, without which a true technological revolution is impossible. It presumes an *economic revolution*.

Of course, the proletariat faces technological tasks now, but these are not the tasks of a technological revolution. Until a revolution occurs in the realm of economics, the proletariat, in the realm of technology, remains wholly and completely *bound by the technology bequeathed to it by capitalism*.

The immediate technological tasks of proletarian power include, therefore, the *repair*, i.e. the complete *restoration* of the prewar technology of capitalism; this is, of course, not a technological revolution at all'.

(See L. Kritsman, 'Ob ocherednoi zadache proletarskoi revoliutsii v Rossii,' No. 5, *Nar-*

In the national economy, production *continued to be restricted*; it fed on its own substance, i.e. production did not only not expand (as shown by the near total *cessation of construction*), but repairs of worn machinery were not sufficient to sustain basic production. Furthermore, it turned out to be impossible and impractical to undertake major overhauls of existing machinery, and *any attempts at major overhauls* had to be abandoned in favour of *running* repairs.

This was particularly evident in the railway industry. The locomotive- and wagon-building plants had to move from building new locomotives and wagons to doing major overhauls of them; railway workshops had to abandon major overhauls and concentrate on running repairs.

Here are the statistics on major overhauls and running repairs of locomotives as a percentage of 1913 figures:[13]

	Major overhauls	Running repairs	Ratio
1918	90	80	10:9
1919	50	70	10:14
1920	50	90	10:18

We see an absolute decline in major overhauls; in running repairs, we first see an absolute decline, and then an absolute growth; major overhauls are constantly being squeezed out by running repairs (an unbroken relative growth of the latter). Just how catastrophic this decline was both in construction and repair work can be seen in the near complete cessation of production of construction materials, fluctuating for various materials in 1920 by 2–3% of the prewar production. The result was a sharp acceleration in the destruction of all basic production resources (all kinds of buildings, engines, etc).

Every enterprise, from a technical perspective, is very much like an organism. It has a continuous metabolic process – the destruction and reconstruction of factory (or plant) equipment, which does not happen at the same rate for its various components.

Maintaining the enterprise and its functioning (its suitability for work) is achieved by establishing a balance between the processes of destruction (wear and tear) and reconstruction (repair) of factory equipment. Disrupting this

---

odnoe khoziaistvo, 15 July 1918).

The further course of events fully justified this view.

13 See *Stat. ezhegodnik 1918–1920 g.g.*, vol. I, p. 37.

balance (inadequate repairs compared to wear and tear) causes the gradual breakdown of the plant itself.

The extent of this destruction and development can be seen in the example of railway transport, where the percentages (as a percentage of the total) were as follows:[14]

	Percentage of damaged locomotives
1913	17
1918	41
1919	52
1920	57

i.e. more than half of the locomotives were therefore out of service; the percentage of damaged locomotives was more than *three times* greater than before the war.

Another example is the state of the steam boiler industry in the Donetsk Basin, where in 1921 functional heating surface comprised only 51%, i.e. half was out of service.[15]

But not only the buildings and machinery of industry and transport were destroyed, everything else was too. In 1924, the value of housing stock in Moscow was only 2,015 million roubles compared with 3,300 million roubles before the war, i.e. about 40 per cent of the housing stock had been destroyed (of which 30% was due to the decline in housing stock and about 10% to the deterioration of the remainder).[16] This destruction, we must assume, continued unabated from 1918 to 1920.

Another consequence of the decline in productive forces was an equally catastrophic *decline in living standards* of the masses of people.

In the grain-consuming belt, the consumption of grain products (unmilled grain in poods per head) was as follows:[17]

14 See *Narodnoe khoziaistvo SSSR v tsifrakh*, p. 232 and Obzor sostoianiia i raboty transporta k 1921 g., p. 78.

15 See the collection *Na novykh putiakh*, vol. III, article, 'Polozhenie Donbassa,' p. 58.

16 See *Zhilishchnoe tovarishchestvo*,' no. 5 for 1924, p. 14.

17 See *Narodnoe khoziaistvo SSSR v tsifrakh*, pp. 121 and 124 and the article of A. Lositskii, 'Potreblenie khleba i miasa v 1918–1919 godu,' in *Vestnik statistiki* for January–April 1920, p. 69. The figures in brackets are from the latter source.

Before the war	14.7 (14.2)
1918–1919	(11.0)
1919–1920 (January–February)	11.4
1920–1921 (November–December)	12.1
1920–1921 (February)	11.9

i.e. a reduction of 18–25%.

Consumption by the urban population comprised:

Before the war	(14.0)
1918–1919 (March–April)	9.4 (incl. in producing region (11.0), in consuming region (8.2))
1919–1920 (first six months)	11.6
1920–1920 (second six months)	11.8
1920–1921 (first six months)	10.6

i.e. a reduction of 17–33%, and for the grain-consuming belt even up to 42%, i.e. almost half.

Furthermore, during the war, consumption in the lowest economic group (i.e., those who did not have enough to eat) was 13.7 poods in the city, and 13.0 poods in the countryside. Even the starving peasants in the prewar period had 11–12 poods per head – government assistance alone amounted to 9 poods per head per year.[18] Consumption by peasants in the grain-consuming belt and consumption by urban-dwellers during the Civil War, then, did not exceed the consumption by *starving* peasants in the prewar famines, and for long periods *it was even significantly lower*. World capital was strangling the insurgent workers and peasants with the 'bony hand of hunger'.[19]

It is highly typical of the *proletarian* dictatorship that in relation to the hungriest but also most proletarian city – Leningrad, the author of a study of the food situation of the Leningrad population in those awful times was able to

18 See N. Vishnevskii, op. cit., p. 74.

19 [Trotsky used this phrase at a public meeting in Moscow in June 1918, see Leon Trotsky, *How the Revolution Armed: The Military Writings of Leon Trotsky*, vol. 1, 1918, p. 81].

write the following lines: 'the entire population (not including non-working elements, which are not included in our table) is sharply divided into two parts – adults and children…; children are guaranteed 60% and 100% more than a significant part of the adult population engaged in light and heavy labour, and 40% to 70% more than the adult population engaged in medium labour'.[20]

Where and when did the starving bourgeoisie give up their bread to workers' children to ensure that their situation was 40, 60 or 100% percent better than their own? Where and when did the full, sybaritic bourgeoisie do that? And yet the starving Leningrad workers, who were dying from hunger, gave up part of their hunger rations every day even for the children of the bourgeoisie. Supervision of rationing often led to a reduction in workers' rations and an increase in children's rations.[21]

At the same time that the masses in the towns and villages of the grain-consuming regions were experiencing this terribly reduced consumption of basic food supply, the peasantry in the grain-producing regions was suffering no shortages at all.

Its consumption comprised the following:[22]

Before the war	17.0 (16.1)
1918–1919 (Jan.–Feb.)	(16.5)
1919–1920 (Nov.–Dec.)	16.3

i.e. up to and including 1920 it remained as high as before the war, perhaps even higher. Inevitably, this led to the bitterest struggle for grain, which we discussed above, and which was a direct struggle for existence for urban workers and poor peasants (and middle peasants) in the grain-consuming belts.

20 See N. Vishnevskii, *Printsipy i metody i.t.d.*, Moscow, 1920, pp. 52–53.

21 Ibid., p. 43. Changes in the rations at the end of 1918 led to the following:

for workers, a reduction of	24%
for children from 3–12 years old, an increase of	52%
for children up to one year old, an increase of	106%
for children from 1–3 years old, an increase of	204%

i.e. to a tripling of the former ration.

22 See footnote 17. Only the failed harvest of 1920 and the even worse harvest of 1921 changed the situation.

Given this extraordinary contraction of grain consumption (by 40% and more in the towns), the overall drop in the living standards of the broad masses of the urban population in particular was on a scale completely unheard of. Indeed, the average monthly wage of a worker in Russia (real wage in commodity roubles) comprised:[23]

1913	22.0
1918	10.5
1919	8.5
1920	8.3

In the Civil War years, wages consequently fell *by two and a half times* in comparison with prewar wages (and in comparison with wartime wages which were relatively close to prewar wages). It should be kept in mind here that this insignificant sum has to cover all the worker's needs, including an apartment, which during the war became not worse for the worker, but better.[24] Thus, the total average monthly living costs of a Russian worker, not including housing, comprises:

1913	20.0
1918	8.5
1919	6.5
1920	6.3

So if we ignore housing (but include heating and lighting), the living standard of the Russian worker in 1919 and 1920 fell by at least *two thirds* in comparison with the prewar period. These dry figures show more clearly than anything else the extraordinary heroism of the workers' revolution. These figures conceal hunger and cold, disease and death, children starving to death before the eyes of their loved ones.

The following are figures on the spread of one of the worst epidemics – typhus. The number of those who fell ill (in European Russia) comprised:[25]

---

23 See S. Strumilin, Zarabotnaia plata i proizvoditel'nost' truda v Russkoi promyshlennosti v 1913–1922 g.g., Moscow, 1923, p. 33.

24 The price for an apartment according to S. Strumilin, in his aforementioned calculation of real wage, did not change between 1913 and 1920 and was equivalent to 2 roubles, ibid., pp. 24–25.

25 See D. Pletnev, *Sypnoi tif*, Moscow, 1922, p. 20. And in those cases where doctors are kee-

1914	83,000 people
1915	90,000 people
1916	102,000 people
1917	88,000 people
1918	180,000 people
1919	2,105,000 people
1920	3,114,000 people

In two years, more than *five million* people suffered from typhus, a thirty seven-fold increase between 1914 and 1920! In 1920, about 4% of the population of European Russia fell ill with typhus, and in Nizhnii Novgorod province, for example, *more than 20%*!!! And typhus was not the only epidemic. In 1920, for example, the total numbers suffering from various diseases (around the USSR) were as follows:[26]

Typhus	3,303,000 people
Typhoid fever	627,000 people
Relapsing typhus	1,406,000 people
Indeterminate typhus	244,000 people
Smallpox	151,000 people
Scarlet fever	83,000 people
Diphtheria	42,000 people
Cholera	25,000 people
Malaria	431,000 people
Total	6,312,000 people

Premature deaths from 1 January 1918 to 1 July 1920 can be estimated at more than *seven million* people, i.e. 7% of the entire population covered by these figures.[27]

---

ping statistics, there are misunderstandings with the numbers. In D. Pletnev, those who fell ill in 1921 total 4,993,030, at the same time that his figures for the individual provinces total about 500,000. In his work too, the zero is evidently in the wrong place.

26 See *Stat. ezhegodnik*, 1921, vol. II, pp. 90–100.

27 See S. Strumilin, 'Trudovaia poteria Rossii v voine,' in the December issue of *Narodnoe khoziaistvo* for 1920, p. 104. For 1914–1917 (also years of war), the number of premature deaths was estimated to be 2.5 million, i.e. in relative terms, at least, *six* times less. The calculation is based on a population of 100 million; if the entire 130-million strong Soviet Russia is taken into account, the number would be more than *nine* million. In particular, mortality in the cities increased as follows:

The more protracted and bitter the Civil War turned out to be, the worse was the disintegration of the productive forces, and the worse this disintegration, the worse were its consequences – the declining living standard of the masses threatened the existence of millions with from starvation, cold, and disease; the more merciless the Civil War became, the more stubborn the revolutionary process became. World capital drove the masses to extremes, and rendered impossible any other methods than the most extreme ones.

The working class and the urban population in general (and partly also the poor peasantry in the grain-consuming belt), which found themselves in a hopeless situation, poured into the villages, mainly in the grain surplus region. Thus, already in 1919 the number of industrial workers shrank by a million people (from 3 to 2 million), and cities in the grain-consuming belt lost almost half of their population, the capitals even more. In the countryside, this flight from the cities led to the return of 'missing' households, 60–80% and more of which returned between 1917 and 1919 in the various provinces.[28] But this movement met resistance from the peasantry. 'The rest of the peasantry', wrote comrade Iu. Larin (referring to farmhands [*batraki*], although the same applies even more so to the urban-dwellers returning to the village), 'did not immediately open up their ranks to the new claimants to the land, livestock, and inventory. The land organs of rural district peasant soviets and their county associations (agricultural departments [*zemotdely*]), for the entire first six months of Soviet power in Russia, put all possible obstacles in the way of efforts by former agricultural workers to become independent farmers. An intriguing historical document in this connection is the book *The Composition of the Population Which Has Been Allotted Land* [*Sostav nadeliaemogo zemlei naseleniia*], a compilation by the People's Commissariat of Agriculture of reports and resolutions of agricultural departments from this period on the basis of statistics from 36 different provinces of Soviet Russia'.[29]

---

	in Moscow	in Petrograd
1913	2.40%	2.14%
1917	2.37%	2.89%
1918	3.49%	4.37%
1919	4.61%	7.26%!
1920	3.78%	5.06%

(See *Ezhegodnik Kominterna*, Moscow, 1923, p. 296).

28 See Iu. Larin's article in his and L. Kritsman's book, p. 18.

29 Ibid., p. 13.

However, outmigration to the countryside could not be a way out for the entire industrial proletariat and urban population. So-called *consumer communism* was the inevitable result of the terrible decline in the living standards of the proletariat, a decline which threatened its physical existence; it was a means of preventing this destruction. Only the expropriation of capital and indeed only of large capital is a necessary element of the proletarian revolution, by no means, however, the expropriation of the means of consumption. But consumer communism, the expropriation of housing, furniture, utensils, bedding (blankets, etc), clothing, linen, etc through evictions, confiscations, and one-time seizures (in-kind taxation) was, in the context of this catastrophic decline in productive forces, a *means of preserving* the most vital productive force of society and a means of preserving the driving force of the revolution – *the proletariat*.

This expropriation necessarily had a mass, class aspect to it, but not a personal aspect, just as, whenever capitalist society threw proletarians out into the street during a crisis or physically destroyed proletarians during the imperialist war, it is not personal but class in nature: capital does not ask about the individual proletarian's personal guilt.

But consumer communism was not only a means of preserving the proletariat, it was also the highest expression of the dictatorship of the proletariat, the highest expression of the proletarian revolution. The essence of this revolution consisted, of course, in the expropriation not of the means of consumption, but of the means of large-scale production. But while it is not the essence, the relationship of the members of the different classes *in everyday life* [*v bytu*] on a day-to-day basis, is the clearest, most striking, most concrete manifestation of class dominance and subordination, and is experienced continually every day. Security, luxury, the privileged customs of some, uncertainty about tomorrow, poverty, and humiliation of others – this is what everyone experiences directly, even the most backward and undeveloped elements, as the expression of class differentiation. This differentiation, however, has now been eliminated. *Consumer communism was a revolution in everyday life*. Immediately and in practice it destroyed the outrageous luxury, crushed the smug security, broke the privileged customs of the former ruling classes, toppled – a method which the most backward, undeveloped proletarian could appreciate – the members of the former ruling classes from their social pedestal, and created in the proletariat and its affiliated social groups the feeling of true liberation, the sense of true upheaval, and powerful, revolutionary enthusiasm.

This destruction of class inequality is best illustrated by data on the change in the distribution of housing. From 1912 to March 1923 in Moscow, apartment occupation density changed to such an extent that the number of inhabitants per 100 apartments was as follows:[30]

	1912	1923	Change
in apartments with 1 room for living	621	408	−213
in apartments with 2 rooms for living	376	260	−116
in apartments with 3 rooms for living	274	208	−66
in apartments with 4 rooms for living	221	196	−25
in apartments with 5 rooms for living	181	200	+19
in apartments with 6–9 rooms for living	130	206	+76
in apartments with 10 or more rooms for living	108	257	+149

In 1912, population density in the largest apartments was almost a sixth of that in the smallest apartments; in 1923 it was 40% smaller. Population density in apartments with two rooms was in 1912 almost four times greater than in the largest apartments; in 1923, the density was *equal*. The luxury that had existed alongside the misery was destroyed not only in words but in practice.

However, given the aforementioned appalling decline in productive forces, even the scale of production and consumption that occurred would have been impossible, had production been the only source of resources. With such a decline in productive forces, existing *supplies* had inevitably to be *distributed*. In themselves, these supplies, which for the most part had been distributed during the imperialist war, were not large. But given the contraction in production to a fifth or a sixth, then even a third of the old supplies represented a huge supply stock. The role of supplies can be seen from the following table:[31]

Type of raw material	Amount procured for 10 months of 1920	Supplies on 1 October 1920	Ratio of supplies to procured amount
Cotton	847,000 poods	7,500,000 poods	9:1
Flax	2,044,000 poods	5,700,000 poods	3:1

30 See *Zhilishchnoe tovarishchestvo*, 1924, no. 5, p. 3. These changes occurred mainly prior to 1920.

31 See *Otchet VSNKh VIII S'ezdu Sovetov*, p. 42. For the normal (prewar) course of production, supplies, e.g., of cotton would have lasted for four months; with the scale of production that occurred in 1920, it would have lasted *for five years*.

(*cont.*)

Type of raw material	Amount procured for 10 months of 1920	Supplies on 1 October 1920	Ratio of supplies to procured amount
Hemp	1,400,000 poods	2,000,000 poods	1.5:1
Wool	2,417,000 poods	3,850,000 poods	1.5:1
Large hides	1,190,000 items	on 1 Sep. 318,000 items	0.25:1
Small hides	1,435,000 items	on 1 Sep. 2,710,000 items	2:1
Tobacco	417,000 poods	on 15 Nov. 550,000 poods	1.5:1
Shag	300,000 poods	on 15 Nov. 1,250,000 poods	4:1

Even the standard of living (more accurately the standard of dying), which we have described above, could not have been maintained given an over 40% contraction of agriculture and an over 82% contraction of industry, even if construction had not ceased, and even if basic replacement of disbursed production resources, amortisation of the main production resources, and replenishment of the disbursed raw material and material supplies had taken place.

An immediate consequence of the steep decline in the living standard of the toiling masses was a most severe *decline in labour productivity*.

According to rough calculations by S. Strumilin, the gross output of a Russian worker changed as follows:[32]

32 See S. Strumilin, *Zarabotnaia plata i proizvoditel'nost' truda*, p. 5. By the way, different numbers can be found with the same author:

	Gross output per head	
	in roubles	as % of 1913 level
In 1913	2,163 (2,163)	100
In 1917	1,436	66
In 1918	781	36
In 1919	711	33
In 1920	694 (631)	32 (29)

(see *Kratkii otchet Gosplana*, Moscow, 1924, p. 239). The figures in brackets are from G. Krzhizhanovskii, *Tovaroobmen i planovaia rabota*, Moscow, 1924, p. 36. The general character of this comparison is not affected by these discrepancies.

The gross output per worker is, strictly speaking, a measure of labour productivity only within the production of a particular product. Where there is a sharp change as a result of the numerous relationships among the various branches of industry, the comparison of gross output per worker, and the attempt to use it to determine the change in labour productivity, can lead in unfavourable cases to completely false conclusions. For example, from a detailed examination of the data on small-scale industry (see *Sbornik stat. svedenii SSSR*, pp. 212–213), we get the following:

	Gross output per head		
	1912–1913 (in roubles)	1920 (in roubles)	Difference
Extraction and processing of minerals	136	110	-26
Extraction and processing of metals	386	179	-207
Extraction and processing of wood	153	154	+1
Extraction and processing of food products	1,454	1,116	-338
Extraction and processing of leather and other materials originating from animals	450	348	-102
Extraction and processing of fibres	251	156	-95
Extraction and processing of other products	366	345	-21
Total	412	418	+6

This completely ridiculous result – an increase in average gross output by 1½% during a decline in it of 6%, 20%, even 54% in individual branches of industry, and an increase by not even 1% in one individual branch is a consequence of the fact that the specific weight of an branch of industry with the largest gross output per head (the processing of food products) was double in relation to the total number of workers from 1912–1913 to 1920 (from 12 to 24%). An accurate calculation, taking into consideration this circumstance, reveals that the average gross output from 1912–1913 to 1920 did not rise by 1½%, but sank by 28%.

We are using S. Strumilin's calculations for large-scale industry here, because they do not have these unfavourable conditions (for the calculation), and because the movement of gross output approximates the movement of labour productivity. This can be seen from these data for individual branches (see S. Strumilin, ibid., pp. 86–87):

	Production per worker in 1920
	As a % of 1912 level
Coal industry	26
Petroleum industry	50
Salt industry	41
Ore mining industry	9
Gold and platinum industry	23
Silicates industry	19
Paper industry	26
Food industry	12
Chemical industry	16

	Gross output per head		
	in roubles	as % of 1913 level	as % of 1917 level
In 1913	2,372	100	–
In 1917	2,023	85	100
In 1918	1,044	44	52
In 1919	512	22	25
In 1920	616	26	30

This was a four to five-fold decline over the prewar level, and a three to four-fold decline over the 1917 level.

It would, of course, be completely wrong to imagine that the decline in labour productivity came from a decline in its intensity, from a decline in the *will to work* because capitalist slavery had been abolished, and thus capitalist labour discipline along with it. On the contrary, only proletarian management of enterprises had made it possible – under the conditions of revolution – to create new proletarian labour discipline and, even more than this, labour enthusiasm. The proletariat, especially its communist vanguard, was truly heroic in its striving to keep alive the exhausted plants despite their horrendous working and living conditions. This heroism was most clearly on display on Communist Saturdays [*subbotniki*].

But labour productivity is not determined only by the will to work. Labour requires an expenditure of energy, which a human being receives from out-

(*cont.*)

	Production per worker in 1920
	As a % of 1912 level
Leather industry	17
Textile industry	32
Electrical industry	8
Metallurgical industry	10
Tobacco-shag industry	25
Total	26

As a function of the total number of workers, the average output per worker is not 26% but about 23%, i.e. a figure that is not too far from the average.

side. The potential expenditure of energy is directly dependent on the worker's standard of living and, especially, on his intake of food.

To maintain the life of a worker, an average 2000 calories of energy are needed, which are received from food; these 2000 calories cannot be used for work. Therefore, any deterioration in food intake must cause a significant drop in labour productivity. Here is an example of this calculation:[33]

	Nutrition per day (in calories)	Labour energy (in calories)	As a % of 1913–1914 levels	As a % of 1916–1917 levels
1913–1914	4,000	2,000	100	–
1916–1917	3,520	1,520	76	100
1917–1918	3,100	1,100	55	72
1918–1919	2,680	680	34	47
1919–1920	2.660	600	30	39
1920–1921	2,600	600	30	39

So, as a result of the deterioration in food intake alone, labour productivity in 1919–1920 had to fall to 30% of the prewar level.

But the deterioration of other living conditions had to reduce labour productivity even further. Inadequate heating in the enterprises and apartments and poor clothing inevitably meant that some of the energy that could have been utilised for work went to maintaining the bodily heat of the organism. Furthermore, workers walked around half-naked, and apartment temperatures sometimes fell below zero.

While the worker's nutrition in 1919–1920 had declined by 40% in comparison with the prewar status, and while, consequently, labour productivity inevitably had to fall to 30% of the prewar level, the total wage of the worker in 1920, as we have seen, declined not by 40% but, if we do not include living quarters, by more than two thirds. This factor alone had to cause labour productivity in 1919–1920 to drop significantly below 30% of the prewar level.

But the productivity of labour is determined not only by factors linked to the capacity for work, but also by factors independent of that capacity or in any case on factors not dependent on the worker. These include, in addition to the reduction in the qualifications of the labour force (in part a result of changes

33 Data from S. Strumilin, ibid. pp. 50 and 51.

in the makeup of the proletariat caused by the war), also the effect of wear and tear on equipment (also a result of the imperialist war), the deteriorating quality of materials, and *interruptions in the continuity of production.*

Interruptions in the continuity of production are themselves in part a product of the decline in labour productivity, because these interruptions are caused by worker absences from work for various reasons.

Thus, on average a worker was absent from work for the following number of days in each year:[34]

1913	12.6
1917	22.7
1918	29.0
1919	68.4
1920	71.0

i.e. a *six-fold* increase in absences by 1920. This increase in absenteeism, which was both open and hidden, took on enormous proportions, and was caused to a large extent by the workers' trips to the countryside in search of food provisions.

But breaks in the continuity of production were caused to a greater extent by factors that had nothing to do with the workers. The isolation of Soviet Russia from the world market and the economic crippling of its territory led to constant crises in food supply; industry was disrupted by its demobilisation and remobilisation; on top of this came the transport crisis. In short, all of this – this completely unstable economic situation – inevitably led to incessant interruptions in the continuity of production, the result of inadequate raw materials, inadequate fuel supplies, and inadequate materials, and also of the overflowing factory supply stocks caused by the disruptions to transport.

Plants were idle (in days per worker per year) as follows:[35]

1913	6.4
1917	24.5
1918	42.0
1919	51.2
1920	15.7

34 Ibid., p. 44.

35 Ibid., p. 44. In the individual months of 1920, almost half of worker time was unutilised (45%), *see Russkaia promyshlennost' v 1921 g.*, p. xxxvi.

This is an *eight-fold* increase by 1919 over 1913. Idling enterprises meant, of course, a sharp decline in labour productivity.

For all these reasons, labour productivity should have fallen far more significantly than could be explained by the worsening food situation of the worker alone. The fact that this did not happen, that labour productivity turned out to be only slightly below the level corresponding to the nutrition level of the worker (and according to other data it was slightly above this level), is evidence of that heroic will to work displayed by the working class in times of unheard-of deprivations, when they were tormented by the cruelest hunger and cold. This fact revealed (at times in hidden form) the creative potential of the new social order.

In small-scale industry, which was less prone to the influences of non-local conditions, and which was more simply organised and which operated in the illegal market, the decline in labour productivity was not as great. According to calculations in *Russkaia promyshlennost' v 1921 g.* (p. 484), output per worker in 1920 in large-scale industry was 39% of prewar output, and in small-scale industry it was 67%.[36]

The decline in workers' living standards led not only to a quantitative deterioration (reduced output per worker), but also to a qualitative deterioration – a horrendous *deterioration in the quality* of industrial products, so that every manufactured product was turned into its own substitute. One example of this deterioration in quality was 'non-burning coal' – i.e. coal mixed with a large quantity of rock and thus very difficult to ignite.[37]

A direct consequence of this sharp decline in labour productivity was a paradoxical feature of this era: this most severe industrial contraction was accompanied by a near-total *disappearance of unemployment* and even an apparent shortage of workers.

In 1920, therefore, there were 128 to 246 positions for 100 job applications (per month): the number of job applications was therefore significantly *higher* than the number of positions.[38]

This paradox can be explained by the fact that when production contracted to a fifth, not only the number of workers contracted by 40–50% (due to the flight to the countryside etc), but also labour productivity fell by more than 70%, and so workers were in short supply. The disappearance of unem-

36 A similar result, i.e. 72% of prewar productivity, was also obtained in our calculation. See footnote 32.

37 Typical of this era is one of the slogans of so-called production propaganda: 'Miner! Coal is the Bread of Industry! Don't deliver rock instead of bread!'

38 See *Stat. ezhegodnik 1918–1920 g.g.*, vol. II, p. 166.

ployment was in this case not a result, as is usually the case, of an increase in production, but on the contrary a result of its contraction, a simple expression of the decline in labour productivity.

The shortage of workers was felt in all branches of labour, and applied to both skilled and unskilled workers. A shortage of skilled workers was felt particularly acutely whenever the administrative and especially military-administrative apparatus absorbed a significant number of primarily skilled proletarians who took up positions as commissars, etc. To a certain extent, this transfer of proletarians from production to the bureaucratic apparatus is an inevitable consequence of the transition of power into the hands of the proletariat, because this transfer can take place in actuality, not just in words, only when proletarians appear in these administrative positions.

In Russia in 1918–1920, however, the ranks of skilled proletarians were truly decimated.

This was a consequence, on the one hand, of the disparity between the numerical strength of the industrial proletariat and the size of the administrative apparatus, which was servicing not only the city but also the immense, pre-capitalist countryside, i.e. a consequence of Russia's backwardness; and, on the other hand, it was a consequence of the numerical growth of the Red Army, i.e. the intensification of the Civil War, and thus a result of the intervention by world capital.

The full significance of this factor is clear from the fact that of 34.6 days of absence (in a year) per worker in 1920–21, 10.2 days[39] were spent on activity in organisations, i.e. almost a *third* of the absences, and it was a small number of mainly skilled workers who missed work due to these organisational commitments.

The scale of the shortage of skilled workers is illustrated by figures on the number of open positions per 100 job offers among metalworkers – in 1920, it fluctuated from 174 to 649 (on average, as noted above, only from 128 to 246).[40]

But the shortage was also felt with unskilled workers. Thus, for labourers [*chernorabochie*], the number of open positions per 100 job applications in 1920 was 141 to 292.[41] In this category of workers, flight to the countryside was particularly strong. One of the attempts to supplement the missing unskilled workforce were the labour armies

One consequence of the decline in labour productivity during the general contraction of production was a growth in the number of workers not occupied

39 See S. Strumilin, op. cit., p. 47.

40 See *Stat. ezhegodnik*, 1918–1920, vol. II, p. 166.

41 Ibid., p. 166.

in directly productive labour (i.e. direct extraction or production of a particular product).

The contraction of production inevitably leads to the *under-utilisation* of production capacity both of individual enterprises and of the national economic apparatus as a whole. This leads, however, to a change in relations between those workers performing direct productive labour and whose number is directly dependent on the scale of production, and those workers performing auxiliary tasks for direct productive labour. The numerical strength of these categories of workers depends less on the scale of production than on the scale of the existing material structure (the technical apparatus) of production. So, for example, when production contracts in one or another factory, the work of guards or clerical staff changes comparatively little, or in any event comparatively less than the contraction of labour of those engaged directly in production. In a general decline in labour productivity, the accompanying increase in the number of workers means that workers in the first category (those engaged in directly productive labour) see a smaller decline in their number than the decline in production, while workers in the second category (not performing directly productive labour) often see an *overall increase in their number.*

In an individual branch of industry, for example in coal-mining, this led to an absolute growth in the number of surface workers, and to a fall in the number of face workers [*zaboishchiki*] and underground workers in general. The following calculations are from the Don Basin:[42]

42 Calculated from data in the article by V. Bazhanov, 'Donetskii Bassein v 1920 g,' in no. 1–2 and 8–9, *Narodnoe khoziaistvo* for 1920. We have taken for 1914 the same percent ratio as for 1913, which is undoubtedly not far from reality.

For large-scale industry as a whole (although unfortunately only for part of the period under consideration), this same phenomenon can be seen in the following data on the number of employed workers. (See N. Vorob'ev, 'Izmeneniia v russkoi promyshlennosti,' in no. 4–6, *Vestnik statistiki*, for 1923, p. 145):

	Engaged in production	Engaged in other work
1913	87%	13%
1918	82.5%	17.5%

The percentage of those engaged in other work rose by a third. Those engaged in other work were distributed as follows:

	Repairs	Auxiliary work	Other work
1913	5.3%	6.5%	1.3%
1918	6.8%	9.6%	1.1%

	All workers	Surface workers	Underground workers	of which, face-workers
1913	168,000	51,000	117,000	35,000
1920	114,000	63,000	51,000	16,000

And so the total number of workers shrank while the number of *surface* workers *grew*; the number of underground workers, including face-workers, declined even more strongly. In 1913, the correlation of the number of surface workers to the number of underground workers was 1:2¼, but in 1920 it was reversed at 1¼:1.

In industry as a whole, this led to a decline in the total number of individuals engaged in industry at a time when the number of clerical staff was growing, and thus to an even greater *decline in the number of workers*. A compilation of data on 2,029 enterprises revealed the following:[43]

	All employees	Clerical staff	Workers	Change among clerical staff	Change among workers
1913	914,000	58,000	856,000	–	–
1918	885,000	78,000	807,000	+20	−49

So the number of clerical staff increased by one third as the total number of those employed declined.

Industrial clerical staff as a percentage of the total number of individuals engaged in industry changed as follows:[44]

Especially strong (by almost 1½ times) was the percentage increase in those engaged in auxiliary tasks. By 1920, this process undoubtedly increased.

43 See *Sbornik stat. svedenii po SSSR*, p. 185.

44 This is true for the first three years; for 1920, according to data on all of industry from the 1920 census, see *Narodnoe khoziaistvo SSSR v tsifrakh*, p. 127. In reality, this percentage for large-scale industry (if we exclude enterprises with no clerical staff) would have to be even higher. Thus, for Petrograd we have the following:

1913	6.4
1917	6.8
1918	8.9
1920	13.5

In the transport industry, something similar occurred – while the number of workers employed in transport, i.e. the direct provision of transport services, remained constant, there was an overall increase in the rest. Thus, if those engaged in transport are divided into three groups: transport personnel, track personnel (which partly includes workers directly servicing transport, and partly others) and other services, then we get the following:[45]

	Number engaged in transport	Number engaged in track work	Number engaged in other services
1913	222,000	242,000	352,000
1920 (on 1 January 1921)	222,000	422,000	585,000

When transport was reduced to a fifth, the number of those involved in the transport service remained unchanged, but the number of others increased to 75%.

	No. of workers and clerical staff	No. of clerical staff	% of clerical staff
1918	144,000	14,000	9.9%
1920	108,000	17,000	15.6%

(See S. Iugenburg, 'Vserossiiskie perepisi 1920 g. po g. Petrogradu,' cited re *Materialy po statistike truda rabotnikov transporta*, Moscow, 1924, vol. I, p. 11). If the percentages cited in the text are for all of large-scale industry, then we would get the following (p. 153):

	Number of workers	Number of clerical staff
1913	2,599,000	178,000
1920	1,585,000	245,000

i.e. the number of workers was reduced by more than a third, and the number of clerical staff increased by more than a third, while industry overall contracted to less than a fifth.

45 See *Obzor sostoianiia i raboty transporta k 1921 g.* (*Materialy k dokladu IX s'ezdu sovetov*), Moscow, 1921, p. 15.

Finally, in the entire national economy as a whole, this meant that the *number of transport workers grew and especially in the bureaucratic apparatus (clerical workers), while the number of those employed in the industrial sector decreased.*

Comparison of (officially registered [*tsenzovaia*]) industry and railway transport gives the following numbers of those employed in them:[46]

	Large-scale industry	Railway industry	Ratio
1913	2,599,000 (2,777,000)	815,000	3½: 1
1920	1,585,000 (1,820,000)	1,229,000	1½: 1

When the number of those employed *in industry shrinks* by 40%, then we see a *growth* in those employed *in transport* by 50%.

More complete comparisons are highly dubious. For clerical employees of institutions, we have the following figures:[47]

1917	1,000,000 (European Russia)
First half of 1921	2,444,000 (USSR)

46 See footnotes 44 and 45. The numbers in brackets are presumably together with (industrial) clerical employees.

47 The first figure is S. Strumilin's estimate (see his article, 'Sostav proletariata Sovetskoi Rossii v 1917–1919 g.g.,' in the collection *Dva goda diktatury proletariata*, Moscow 1919). The second figure represents the number of employee trade union members (see *Sbornik stat. svedenii*, p. 246). According to S. Strumilin's data in the article, the number of employees in institutions in Petrograd in 1900 was 6.8% of its population, in 1910 it was 6.7%. if we this percentage refers to the number of employees in relation to the entire urban population of the territory of the USSR (and in the provinces, the percentage of employees in 1913 was less than in Petrograd), then we get the following number of employees: in 1913–about 1,500,000 (this figure is exaggerated for the above reason), in 1921 – 2,444,000.

The we would get the following table:

			As a percentage of the total	
	1913	1920	1913	1920
Number working in industry (official)	2,777,000	1,820.000	55% (60)	33%
Number working in transport (railway)	815,000	1,229,000	16% (18)	22%
Number working in bureaucratic apparatus	1,500,000 (1,000,000)	2,444,000	29% (22)	45%

If in 1913 for every clerical employee in industry there was not even one in other branches, in 1920 there were already two.

The predictability of this phenomenon can be illustrated by the following rough scheme. Let's say, for example, that about 55% are engaged directly in productive labour, and 45% in other labour. Let's say that production has contracted to a fifth, and let's assume that in the other branches of industry for half of the workers the scale of work is not dependent on the scale of production, and that for the other half it changes according to changes in the scale of production (as, e.g., is the case in the railway industry).

Let's say that labour productivity fell to a third.

Then, the workload of those engaged directly in productive labour is about 11% of the total earlier scale of national economic activity, and they comprise 33% of the earlier number of all those working. For the others, the workload for the one half is 4.5%, for the other half 22.5%, and overall 27% of the earlier scale of the national economic activity, and their number is 81% of the earlier number of those working. Our example, then, shows, first, a 14% increase in the total number of those working, and second, a change in the internal distribution of those working:

	Engaged in directly productive labour	**Others**
Before contraction of production	55%	45%
After contraction of production	29%	71%

According to the above data, the total number grew by 8% and the correlation changes as follows:

Total 55% and 45% before contraction of production
33% and 67% after contraction of production

The general nature of the changes is clearly the same.

If, however, we take the number of employees, according to S. Strumilin, to be 1 million, then we get, as is easy to calculate, an even more complete coincidence of results: the calculated increase in the total number is 8%, and the correlation of the two main groups is 33% and 67%, i.e. precisely the figures above.

If we take all branches, except for agriculture, we get the following numbers of those working:

	In industry (incl. construction)	**In transport (of all forms)**	**In other branches (except for agriculture and household)**
1917	3,317,000	1,400,000	2,000,000
1921 (first half)	3,141,000	1,617,000	3,000,000
As a percentage of the total			
1917	49	21	30
1921 (first half)	40	21	39

The statistics for 1917 are from S. Strumilin, op. cit., p. 14 and relate to European Russia. Statistics for the first half of 1921 are from *Sbornik*, p. 24 and relate to the USSR. The figures in other branches for 1921 include domestic employees, but only to the tune of several tens of thousands, and they are not able to influence the result. The comparability of these figures, as S. Strumilin stresses in his similar calculation for 1917–1919, is highly relative.

This enormous growth in the number of clerical employees during a contraction in the number of workers, this growth in bureaucracy [*biurokratiia*], was also *a growth of bureaucratism*. Precisely here can be found one of the roots of Soviet bureaucratism [*biurokratizm*] (in addition to those considered above).

It would be wrong, however, to attribute the growth in the number of employees to the expansion of the state bureaucratic apparatus. The number of state employees did indeed grow, but only because the former employees of the zemstvos, towns, associations, and private enterprises became employees of the state. On its own, making state employees of the former zemstvo, city, public and private institutions and enterprises (warehouses, shops, schools, hospitals, etc) did not lead to an increase but rather to a *decrease* in the total number of employees, because similar plants were merged (concentrated) and superfluous plants were closed. But this tendency towards a decline in the number of employees was far exceeded by a countervailing tendency, which, however, was caused not by the transformation of employees into state employees, but by the decline in the productivity of their labour.

The drop in living standards of employees was especially sharp. Thus, industrial employees received on average the following:[48]

1913 394% of the average wage of a worker
1917 179% of the average wage of a worker
1920 100% and less of the average wage of a worker

i.e. the drop in living standards from 1913 to 1920 was *four times more severe* than the drop in living standards of workers.

The living standard of the other employees, though, dropped even more significantly than that of industrial employees.

Given the inevitable counter-revolutionary mood of the mass of employees during this period under study, the extreme drop in their living standard led not only to a sharp decline in their labour productivity, but also to their extraordinary bitterness towards the regime of the proletarian dictatorship. They increasingly took the view that everything was permissible vis-à-vis this regime, as long as there was no risk of being exposed and falling foul of the strict regime of dictatorship. A telling illustration of these moods are the aforementioned data on the employees' attitude towards bribery. Of course, the influence of these moods facilitated an unprecedented blossoming of red-tape [*volokita*], and of

---

We are making this comparison only to show that the general character of this phenomenon occurs with complete clarity in all cases.

48 See S. Strumilin, *Zarabotnaia plata i proizvoditel'nost' truda*, p. 37.

hostility towards the toiling masses they served, and in general a burgeoning bureaucratism.

This was the general picture of the effects of the decline in productive forces on the national economy of Russia. The colossal scale of this decline in productive forces exerted, as we have seen, a deep and comprehensive effect on the entire national economy of Russia. It was unavoidable that the economic construction of the revolution would also feel its effect.

CHAPTER 12

The Effect of the Decline in Productive Forces on Economic Construction

1. Proletarian dominance of the economy and its organs. 2. From training to management. 3. From horizontal organisation to simple and complex vertical organisation. 4. The 'Centre' and the 'Periphery'. 5. Dismantling the VSNKh. 6. The tendency to revert to commodity relations. 7. The petty bourgeois degradation [*pererozhdenie*] of large-scale industry and of the proletariat. 8. The significance of the decline in productive forces.

In its initial stage, the economic construction of the proletarian revolution was a direct continuation of the class struggle that had been led by the proletariat before it gained the opportunity to take up the work of economic construction. At this stage for the proletariat, organisation of the national economy meant the direct organisation of its class struggle.

Like every process of economic organisation, the process of proletarian organisation of the national economy began at the surface of economic life, in the realm of circulation, with the organisation of supply to the workers and enterprises and the distribution of products. The struggle against sabotage by capital led to attempts to create a proletarian organisation of the supply of enterprises, and this led inevitably to the organisation of a system of state distribution and to one product after another being withdrawn from market circulation.

When it received a demand for any product, every state distribution organ asked the following question – for what purpose? (instead of the earlier question, at what price?). This meant above all this: will the product be used by the organs of the proletarian state and organisations of the proletariat or will it fall into the clutches of capital? The distributive organs (and in the first period of the revolution all state organs and to a certain extent also all proletarian organs – central and local – and proletarian organisations were distributive organs) were at this stage a means of providing proletarian class supervision over the use of material resources.

Furthermore, even the attempt to regulate distribution led just as inevitably to the proletarian organisation of production.[1] But the economic organs cre-

1 It would be wrong, however, to assume that the process described in this text was the result

© 2026 KONINKLIJKE BRILL BV, LEIDEN | HTTPS://DOI.ORG/10.1163/9789004765313-016

ated by the proletariat were at this stage designed above all *to assert control over the economy*, to take control of production and of material resources (supplies of raw materials, materials, manufactured goods).

The signature institution of this period was the Supreme Council of the National Economy (VSNKh). This was the central organ of control of the national economy, the all-powerful organ of the dictatorship of the proletariat in the economic realm.

The decree on it is clear and concise:[2]

1) 'The Supreme Council of the National Economy is the economic department of the All-Russian Central Executive Committee of Soviets...
2) The Supreme Council of the National Economy regulates and organises all production and distribution and is in charge of all enterprises of the Republic'.

The Supreme Council of the National Economy was created to be the sole economic centre, a proletarian successor to finance capital, and gradually to unite and absorb *all* economic authorities: financial, food supply, means of communication, agriculture, etc.

In the beginning, however, the proletariat had neither the experience nor the organisations for this work. After all, capitalism by definition meant that the proletariat was kept away from the running of production and of the economy in general. Of course, in one key area, i.e. where it operated as the seller of its labour power, the proletariat had created its own economic organisations, namely the trade unions, which exhibited their own tendencies – constantly suppressed by capital – to intervene in the economy. The dictatorship of the proletariat had smashed the capitalist barriers and turned trade unions into the engine of the proletarian organisation of the economy. But this does not change the fact that the trade unions in themselves were not set up to organise the economy.

---

of the naked fact of struggle; it is not a matter here of the logic of struggle in general, but of the concrete nature of this particular struggle, of the struggle against sabotage by capital, and consequently, of the class struggle between the proletariat and capital. The logic of this struggle led to the proletarian natural economy, because it was a struggle between the proletariat and capital, a proletarian revolution. Had the struggle been between the feudal lords and the bourgeoisie, then the logic of struggle would have led to the confiscation of the lands of the feudal lords and to their division or sale, i.e. to a transition to a petty bourgeois or capitalist economy.

The logic of the struggle determines the result. But the precise nature of this result depends on which classes are participating in a given struggle. The struggle does not produce this result, which is determined by its content, but merely reveals it, breaks open the shell concealing the internal tendencies of development.

2 See *Sbornik dekretov 1917–1918 g.g.*, Moscow, 1920, p. 101.

So in the beginning, the Supreme Council of the National Economy was something contrived, theoretical, abstract, and especially so when compared with the simultaneous process, unfolding spontaneously, of enterprises being seized by worker organisations, of capitalists being dispossessed and replaced with worker managements. This spontaneous process was of course accompanied by the rupture of the old economic connections and often led to enterprise shutdowns. At this time, the work of the economic organs of Soviet power consisted largely of introducing the principle of planned organisation into the tubulent activity of revolutionary spontaneity.

Under these conditions, the Supreme Council of the National Economy was not in a position to lead economic activity, for the economic organs it needed to do so did not yet exist. Its activity, then, could only, and in fact did only, consist *of creating* various economic organs.[3]

Both the central organs created by the Supreme Council of the National Economy, the so-called central administrations (the central administrations of the individual branches of the national economy), and the emergent 'local' (i.e. not set up by a directive 'from the centre') economic organs of Soviet power, the so-called 'local councils of the national economy' [*sovnarkhozy*], were, like the Supreme Council of the National Economy, primarily *organs to assert control over the economy*, but in a correspondingly narrower sphere.

Within their particular branches, the central administrations were the same sovereign organs of the proletarian dictatorship as the Supreme Council of the National Economy was for the entire national economy as a whole. The central administrations were by no means simple economic institutions, although they were large, they were sovereign *organs of power*, whose orders (insofar as they pertained to that branch of the economy run by a given central administration) were *binding* for all state organs and for the population.[4]

---

3 In *Otchet VSNKh VIII S'ezdu Sovetov*, p. 22, this situation was characterised in the following way: 'It was necessary above all to carry out an accounting of the enterprises in each branch, of their machine equipment, of their required labour force (technical personnel and workers), to take control of this complicated apparatus, to supply it with the necessary raw materials, fuel, etc and to guide the entire work of the hitherto fragmented production units on the basis of a general, previously devised plan. Therefore, central, responsible boards were set up with the requisite staff of employees (central administrations and centres) which were to carry out the aforementioned tasks'.

4 Thus, for example, § 3 of 'Regulation of the Central Administration of the Tea Industry (Tsentrochai)' reads: 'All orders of Tsentrochai pertaining to tea and all other products listed in § 2 of the present order are, in accordance with the instructions in § 2, binding, and they must be consistently carried out both by private enterprises and individuals and by public and government organisations'. (see *Sbornik postanovlenii i dekretov po narodnomu khoziaistvu,*

This was how the process of organising and implementing the economic dictatorship of the proletariat unfolded. As, on the one hand, the Supreme Council of the National Economy created its own organs in the form of the central administrations, and, on the other hand, the process of combining local economic organs moved forward, the Supreme Council of the National Economy's remoteness from economic life disappeared, and the working class moved from taking possession of the national economy to managing it.

The open class struggle *within* society became more and more a thing of the past: on the one hand, it transformed into a military struggle between Red and White Russia, and, on the other, it disappeared from the legal veneer of public life inside Soviet Russia. The institutions (central administrations) created by the Supreme Council of the National Economy initially took on small numbers of representatives from enterprise associations of the corresponding branch of the economy, but they were included *by force* – any All-Russian association of capitalists of a given branch was akin to an association of feudal lords who were responsible to the organs of the proletarian dictatorship (the central administrations) for carrying out its orders (so-called forced proletarian syndicalisation and trust formation). From the moment nationalisation occurred, the capitalist representatives were thrown out of the central administrations, although the capitalists remained, as we have seen, associated with the enterprises. From the moment proletarian administration was organised in the enterprises, any kind of legal nexus between capital and the economy was destroyed. And this removal of the capitalists, as we have seen above, went far beyond the confines of the large-scale economy, and, moreover, the new centralised organisation of the economy (the central administrations) also went beyond the confines of the large-scale economy, intent as they were on acquiring a universal (general) character.

The use of state power to expropriate owners also became a thing of the past. With the successes of nationalisation, municipalisation, and other forms of proletarian socialisation of the economy, the rationale disappeared both for taxing the owners and for their expropriation, which was carried out with the aid of the printing press by suppressing the purchasing power of money to a thousandth and ten thousandth part of its original purchasing power, i.e. in effect, by eliminating accumulated hoards of money.

In connection with this, the economic organs began to take on a quite different character: from fighting *within these organs* against its class enemies,

---

vol. II, p. 26). The central administrations had the right to issue binding orders, to requisition, to confiscate, and to seize individual products and materials, etc.

the proletariat moved on to positive tasks, to *setting in motion* the new proletarian organisation of the national economy. This was no longer a direct class struggle, although it created the basic precondition for success of the proletariat's struggle against its underground, domestic enemies and especially against its external enemies – namely, its economic base. This is why this sphere of proletarian activity was often called 'the economic front'.

The very organisation of the national economy was transformed from a field of battle waged between the proletariat and capital for dominance of the national economy into a proletarian organisation of the economy. The processes that took place in the proletarian organisation of the economy could be explained to a significant extent by the transition to the fulfillment of the tasks of economic construction and revealed the transition of the proletarian organisation of the national economy to the higher stages of its development.

One of these processes is the transition from *collegial to individual administration*. Initially, administrations at the centre, at the local level, and in the enterprises were headed by broad and numerous collegiums [*kollegii*].[5] This resulted from the need to include representatives of the authorities in them, so that all issues could be resolved on site without red tape, and also from the proletarians' natural mistrust of the administrative technical personnel and officials [*chinovniki*] (the representatives of the authorities), who had to be diluted by double the number of proletarians (mainly, representatives of the trade unions). While representatives of the capitalists joined economic organs (Unions of Enterpreneurs [*Soiuz predprinimatelei*]), the aforementioned reasons for this had an even stronger effect. But as the running of a particular economic organ really became concentrated in the hands of the respective collegium, the representatives of the authorities became superfluous. Some of the workers became so familiar with matters, that they could actually ran things, and the administrative technical personnel was selected little by little in such a way that (in many cases) it was no longer steeped in the earlier mistrust. Alongside these changes, there was also a transition from broad representative collegiums (which for the proletarians were a training ground for management, and which fulfilled this task) to narrower working collegiums (whose staff became smaller and smaller), and at the enterprises also to individual management.

By the end of 1920, this process was almost complete: of 2,051 enterprises in the first category (large-scale enterprises under the leadership of the central organs), which had provided information, 1,783, i.e. 86%, already had an

5 For example, the plenum of the VSNKh numbered 60 people, the plenums of the central administrations each numbered 20, 30, 40, even 66 (Central Administration of Leather). See *Sbornik dekretov i postanovlenii po narodnomu khoziaistvu*, Moscow, 1918, p. 115.

individual management.[6] This evolution of the organs of proletarian administration of enterprises from collegial to individual leadership was a shift away *from training* the proletariat in the art of running enterprises and *towards actually running* them.

Individual leadership did not eliminate the collective nature of the proletarian organisation of the economy: only the execution of the general directives of the collective became an individual action. While the leadership was still in the hands of the former capitalist administration, and, consequently, cadres of proletarian 'managers' did not yet exist, collective supervision over them was needed. But after the switch in administration itself (and of the individual leaders of the enterprises, apparently almost two thirds were workers)[7] the issue of collective or individual leadership became a technical issue, and, from this aspect, individual leadership of productive labour without doubt turns out to be more beneficial than collegial because it guarantees the necessary consistency and clarity of command.

Individual leaders of the enterprises were appointed (just like the collegiums) by the organs of proletarian state power (VSNKh) *in agreement* with the corresponding trade union organs. To these individual leadership positions were appointed either workers who had learned the art of management (red directors), or representatives of the former administration whom the workers trusted.

The development and completion of the new proletarian organisation of the national economy occurred during, and under the strong influence of, a catastrophic decline in productive forces, as a result of which the developmental trends of the new organisation of the economy often intersected with trends towards collapse in the national economy, creating a very colourful and contradictory picture.

The internal logic of the development of socialist centralism meant that the original territorial (*horizontal*) organisation of the national economy was replaced by organisation by economic branches (*vertical*). While it was still a matter of taking control of the national economy and as long as the central organs of the proletarian organisation of the national economy were not yet functioning, the local organs, which were organised territorially, came to the fore of course. It was impossible to organise supervision of the capitalists cent-

6 See V. Gershgorn, 'Struktura i sostav glavkov i tsentrov' in No. 4, *Narodnoe khoziaistvo*, 1921, p. 56; similar statistics can also be found *in Otchet VSNKh VIII S'ezdu Sovetov*.

7 According to statistics in *Otchet VSNKh VIII S'ezdu Sovetov*, pp. 14–15, workers made up 63.5% of the total members of enterprise leaderships; this was approximately the same ratio among individual leaderships, because 86% of all enterprise leaderships were individual.

rally, and there was nobody capable of doing that. When it became a matter of ensuring the functioning of the national economy, then this, under the prevailing conditions of market suppression, required a 'central administration-type' [*glavkistskii*], i.e. proletarian-monopolistic, organisation of the national economy according to the branches of the economy; this represented the culmination by the proletariat of the unifying, organising tendency of monopoly capitalism, a tendency which found expression, on the one hand, in the creation of cartels (syndicates and trusts) in control of individual branches of the national economy, and, on the other, in the creation of production trade unions. For the real components of the national economy as a whole, given the current state of productive forces, are precisely its economic branches.

But just as capitalism moved from individual monopolies to a unitary organisation of the national economy, first to finance-capitalist concerns and later to state-capitalist trusts, so too the proletarian-monopolistic (central administration) organisation tended to move towards a unitary proletarian organisation of the national economy, thereby taking the final step towards the transition to socialism.

In essence, the entire grandiose process of organising the national economy of Soviet Russia was a (still incomplete) effort to create a unitary organisation of the national economy of the Republic. Thus, for example, the majority of the organs of the Supreme Council of the National Economy were formed by merging various organs of the former ministries with former zemstvo, city, public organisations, and with former private capitalist enterprises and their associations. This tendency towards unification could be seen in the fact that the people's commissars (initially the commissars of transport and foreign trade and then also of agriculture) became members of the Presidium of the Supreme Council of the National Economy and, as members of this Presidium, they were on the Collegiums of the People's Commissariats (of agriculture and finance); they were also at the joint meetings of the Presidium of the Supreme Council of the National Economy, the Presidium of the All-Russian Central Council of Trade Unions, and the Collegium of the People's Commissariat of Food Supply, etc; furthermore, the posts of the Chair of the Supreme Council of the National Economy and of the Extraordinary Plenipotentiary for Food Supply of the Red Army under the Council for Defense were combined in one person, etc.

This tendency was also illustrated by the creation (especially towards the end of the Civil War period) of several organs of a generic nature.

One such organ was the highest authority in production politics, the Central Production-Technical Commission under the Presidium of the Supreme Council of the National Economy, whose task was to establish the production programmes of the various branches of industry and agriculture, and also to resolve issues about new production methods and tasks. Analogous production commissions to examine the production programmes of the central administrations also existed under several production departments of the Supreme Council of the National Economy.

For the unification of transport and to bring a planned approach to the utilisation of transport resources, a top body was created for transport policy, the Supreme Council on Transportation (VSP) under the Council of People's Commissars. Its members included representatives of the People's Commissariat of Communication Routes, the Supreme Council of the National Economy, the People's Commissariat of Food Supply, the People's Commissariat of Military Affairs, etc. The Supreme Council on Transportation established the volume of food supplies and of military supplies that had to be shipped in the course of a month, etc.

To determine the most important enterprises and to ensure the normal or increased food ration for the employees and workers in these enterprises, there was a special Commission for the Supply of Workers under the People's Commissariat of Food Supply, a commission made up of representatives from the All-Russian Central Council of Trade Unions, the People's Commissariat of Labour, the Supreme Council of the National Economy, and other institutions.

To establish fixed prices on all products and materials, a Committee on Fixed Prices was set up under the Supreme Council of the National Economy, a committee made up of representatives of the People's Commissariat of Food Supply, the People's Commissariat of Finance, etc.

Under the Supreme Council of the National Economy, there was also a Commission for the Utilisation of Material Resources (abbreviated as the Commission for Utilisation or KI) of the Soviet Republic, made up of representatives of the Supreme Council of the National Economy, the People's Commissariat of Food Supply, and the People's Commissariat of Foreign Trade. The task of this commitee was to establish how much of each product had to be distributed amongst the population, how much had to be used to incentivise requisitioners and workers, how much was required for technical needs, how much was destined for export, and how much had to be put into a reserve fund. This commission reviewed and confirmed the material estimates, established the order of supply, the number of different categories of the population, the supply norms for these categories (workers, peasants, etc), and the norms of in-kind bonuses for procurements, etc. The plans and norms were devised by special organs of this commission. But alongside it, other distribution organs, the People's Commissariat of Food Supply, the Central Administration for Fuel, and others, continued to function. The tendency towards eliminating the multiplicity of the organs of distribution was not fully realized, it remained a tendency.

There was no actual, unitary centre of organisation of the national economy even by the end of the Civil War period. To a certain extent, the Council of Labour and Defence, formed from the Council of Defense, was a (completely unsatisfactory) substitute for such a centre. Its character and name had changed, once the so-called 'economic front' had become a priority, overshadowing the military fronts. The Council of Labour and Defense included both the Chairman of the Supreme Council of the National Economy and the People's Commissars of Food Supply, and of Communication Routes, and others.

More important, perhaps, was the unification of the national economic organisations at the local level, which was achieved in the soviets of the labour armies, to which not only the members of the Revolutionary Military Council of the army belonged, but also plenipotentiaries of the Supreme Council of the National Economy and of the economic commissariats. Both the provincial Councils of the National Economy and the provincial organs of the economic commissariats remained subordinate to the plenipotentiaries of their centres, although their activity became less fragmented (a consequence of the lack of a general, all-Russian centre) and more interconnected, if only on a narrow local scale.

The clearest expression of this tendency towards socialization, so typical of the proletariat, was that, despite the federal structure of the Soviet state, its economic organisation was in principle a *unitary* organisation, common to the entire federation. The most consistent uniformity was achieved in transport, communications, finance, and large-scale industry.

The tendency towards a unitary proletarian organisation of the economy was further illustrated by the fact that the vertical organisation of the national economy by branch, that had replaced the horizontal (territorial) organization, began to transform further into a complex vertical (functional) organisation.[8]

---

8 With the earlier horizontal organisation, the main line of subordination ran as follows:

district administration — provincial council of national economy — district administration

|

Supreme Council of the National Economy

With the later simple vertical organisation, it looked like this:

But this tendency too, which sought to transform the Supreme Council of the National Economy into a truly economic centre, remained a tendency that was not sufficiently realised.[9]

The tendency towards socialist centralism ran up against opposing tendencies towards decentralisation, which were rooted in the progressive breakdown of the national economy as a result of the ever deepening decline in productive forces.

The imperialist war, this cruellest crisis of world capitalism, had already to a significant extent destroyed the economic connections both in the world economy and within the national economy. The Civil War aggravated these processes severely, and created the tendency to transform the country which had already been combined into a uniform whole by the preceding capitalist development, into a conglomerate (a cluster) of individual regions, i.e. the tendency to break it down into a series of more or less independently existing districts, into pre-capitalist provinces.

The centralising tendency of economic development, therefore, ran up against its opposing trend – the *collapse of economic connections*, which led not only to a decline in large-scale industry, but also to extraordinary difficulties in maintaining the connections of economic associations; these difficulties were all the greater, the larger the territory covered by these associations. With the rupture of these economic connections, local economic connections, and above all supply from local resources, naturally came to the fore.

As long as no general organisation of the national economy had yet taken shape, its organisation, as we have noted, was along *territorial* lines: local coun-

---

districtadministration   district administration
| |
central administration   central administration
\   /
Supreme Council of the National Economy

With the trend by the end towards a vertical (functional) connection emerged, then it looked like this:

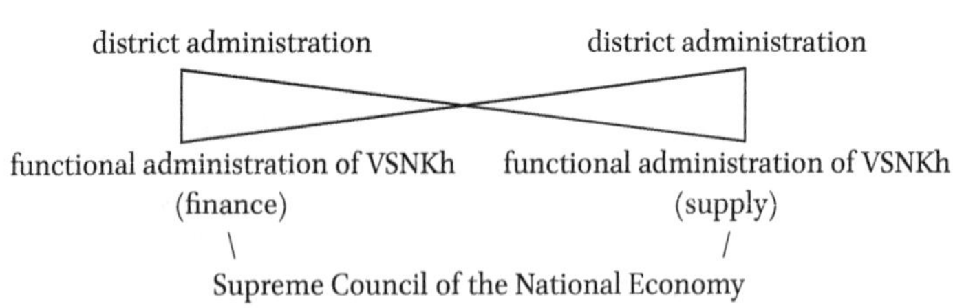

9 In the next part of our work, we will examine these trends in more detail.

cils of the national economy at thecounty, provincial and regional levels (1918). As a general organisation of the national economy of the Soviet Republic was created, this territorial organisation was replaced by organisation along production lines (the central administrations of 1919 and 1920). Regional and district councils of the national economy (and also the Supreme Councils of the National Economy of the individual Soviet Republics) were abolished, provincial councils were turned into administrative organs of small-scale industry, their field of activity narrowed, and they began to take on a purely local character (and in relation to those enterprises which were subordinated to the center – an auxiliary character) both in terms of supplying enterprises with production resources, and in terms of selling their products. But the continuing and worsening collapse of productive forces later saw a reappearance of the territorial principle, although in weakened form; on the one hand, in the far regions of Soviet Russia (including in the individual republics), economic representatives of the center emerged (the so-called industrial bureaus[10] and economic councils), which became regional centres; on the other hand, the circle of those enterprises which were subordinated to local organs began to widen (the division into categories).

The decentralising tendencies, having objectively consolidated the disintegration of the national economy into the component parts from which it had once originated (the provincial economies), reinforced the transformation of the national economy from an organism whose organs were its branches into a conglomerate (a cluster) of provincial economies. These tendencies were transforming Russia into a federation of economically (predominantly) independent districts which exchanged their surpluses with each other, i.e. they were provincializing Russia. These tendencies were nurtured by the actual collapse of the national economy and they reinforced that collapse.

At the same time, however, this decentralising trend was also a product of the extraordinary scale of the centralised proletarian natural economy, which, as we have seen, had absorbed a mass of small-scale and tiny enterprises, whose economic connections did not extend beyond the borders of small territories; and while we are speaking about these enterprises (and this is not only about them), this tendency strove to reduce the centralised economy to its normal scope, to restrict it to the large-scale economy. As a result of this struggle between these opposing tendencies, in 1920 all enterprises were divided into three categories, whereby the smallest enterprises (the third category) came

10 By the end of 1920, there were six: in Ukraine, in the South-East, in the Urals, in Siberia, in Kirghizia, and in Turkestan. See *Otchet VSNKh VIII S'ezdu Sovetov*,' VSNKh schema.

under the total control of the local councils of the national economy, while the medium-sized enterprises – the second category – were only administered by them.

The decentralising tendency was also constantly reinforced and greatly enhanced by the intolerable bureaucratism of the central economic organs, something that they all had in common with every other institution. One of the features of this bureaucratism was also a mind-numbingly pedantic observation of the rights accorded to every organ and an astounding inability to achieve a separation of duties in merged spheres; this caused all merged enterprises to break down unnecessarily into their constituent parts, and auxiliary enterprises to separate from main enterprises (e.g. the tanker fleet from the petroleum industry, the supply lines from the industrial enterprises, etc).

In precisely the same way, the tendency towards the unification of the entire national economy in the hands of the Supreme Council of the National Economy ran up against opposing tendencies rooted in this same decline in productive forces.

The decline in productive forces proceeded, as we have seen, unevenly. The large-scale economy (big industry, transport) was destroyed much more rapidly than the small-scale economy (small industry, agriculture). Under the extreme strain of the direct military costs of the Civil War, this led, as was shown above, to economic parasitism by the city and to the extraction of the resources, which were needed to fight the Civil War, from the peasantry by extra-economic force (in the final analysis, though, the peasantry preferred this force to that of the landowner-capitalist reaction).

But an inevitable consequence of this shift in the distribution of productive forces was that the further it went, the more *the economic base of the Soviet state (and city) shifted from large-scale industry to small-scale peasant agriculture*. It is enough to look at the following two columns to see this:[11]

	Gross production of large-scale industry as a % of 1917	**Requisitioning as a % of 1917**
1918	45	147
1919	34	290
1920	23	500

11 See *Stat. ezhegodnik* for 1918–1920, vol. I, p. 2, and *Sbornik stat. svedenii po SSSR*, p. 424.

The *decline* in large-scale industry, then, was more than *three quarters* and the increase in procurements *five-fold*, i.e. a more than twenty-fold change in the ratio between them.

This phenomenon was, on the one hand, a sign of the intensifying political hegemony of the proletariat, whose state power turned out to be able – in such conditions and on such a scale – to force the peasantry to help bear the costs of the Civil War (which was also a war for land), and, on the other hand, a sign of the growing significance and the growing hegemony of the petty bourgeois peasant economy.

This shift was inevitably reflected in the declining significance of the Supreme Council of the National Economy and the increasing significance of the People's Commissariat of Food Supply. In the organisational system of the Soviet national economy, the *replacement* of the hegemony of the Supreme Council of the National Economy with the hegemony of the People's Commissariat of Food Supply was simply a reflection of the fact that large-scale industry was declining while the importance of the small-peasant economy to the Soviet state and to the city was growing.

The extraordinary role of the Supreme Council of the National Economy in the system of economic authorities was really more of an idea from 1919 on; in reality, it increasingly became one authority among many, a People's Commissariat of Industry, primarily because another economic authority, independent of it, the People's Commissariat of Food Supply, grew steadily, becoming in practice the main axis of the entire economic organisation of Soviet Russia.

By 1919, the process of *dismantling* the Supreme Council of the National Economy had already begun. In 1920, the following economic branches were transferred from its leadership to that of the People's Commissariat of Food Supply: the fish, refrigeration, and dairy industries, and the procurement of industrial raw materials produced in agriculture; the merchant navy was moved to the People's Commissariat of Communication Routes. This process also continued after the Civil War was over.

The exceptional decline in large-scale industry and the large-scale economy in general and the rising importance of the petty bourgeois peasant economy to the Soviet state and to the city was also reflected in the changing mutual relations with the peasantry and its various groups.

The decline in productive forces, and the spread of the Civil War and of the rising costs associated with it, saw the proletarian state, as we have seen, bring increasing pressure to bear on its petty bourgeois economic base, whose importance grew more and more. This increasing pressure led to more strain on the mutual relations between the proletariat and the peasantry; it strengthened the counter-pressure from the peasantry, for in social relations a law applies that is analogous to Newton's third law of equal and opposite reaction.

This growing strain and the counter-pressure from the petty-bourgeois peasantry could be seen not only in its vacillations between revolution and counter-revolution, in the peasant uprisings led by kulaks and a bloc of the vestiges of the bourgeoisie and landowners; it could also be seen in the tendency, under the influence of this pressure, for the natural economic relations between the proletariat and the peasantry to revert back to commodity relations.

We will go into this phenomenon in more detail in the next part of this book, and we will note only the following now.

Under natural economic relations, everything produced is placed at the disposal of the organs of distribution. For the peasant economy, which to a significant degree was an economy for personal consumption, this would mean that the organs of distribution would have to give a large part of this production (and in most cases almost the entire production) back to the very same peasants. Therefore, in relation to the peasant economy, the transition to natural economic relations meant that the norms of peasant consumption of self-produced products were set, and all the remaining production of the peasant economy ('surpluses') had to be delivered to the state organs (the organs of the People's Commissariat of Food Supply), initially at fixed prices, but then free of charge, and in any event without any payment in kind, and only for the right to be included in the general state distribution plan for industrial products. This was the state of affairs in 1918–1919.

But the proletarian state was unable to maintain this situation. Above all, it turned out to be completely impossible, as we have seen, to make a true accounting of the production of the peasant economy, and, consequently, of its surpluses. This inability compelled the proletarian state to move to acquire the surpluses through requisitioning.[12] Instead of determining what the peasant had left over, they began to determine what the peasant should surrender.

---

12 In the collection, *Prodovol'stvennaia politika*, Moscow, 1920 in the article by Kaganovich, 'Uchet izlishkov ili razverstka,' p. 181, we read: 'It is possible to set norms for what is needed for the personal subsistence of the peasant, and, to take from him the surplus above these norms'. *This was the method used in the campaign of 1918–1919*.

But, in order to calculate the surpluses, it is necessary to determine the actual stockpiles at the disposal of the peasant economy. It is, however, almost impossible to do this when the harvest is already completed and threshing has been partially carried out, given the unbelievable ingenuity of the peasantry in partially hiding food stockpiles.

Considering the unsuccessful experience of 1918–1919, Narkomprod decided in summer 1919 to conduct a general accounting at the moment of completion of the harvest, when it would seem to be impossible to hide the grain.

And on the other hand, the simple supply of the peasantry as part of the fulfillment of state distribution plans was replaced by the *state collective exchange of products*, whereby the stockpile of products intended for the supply of the peasantry of a given region was distributed only in proportion to the fulfillment of the requisitioning, i.e. *in proportion to* the amount of agricultural products surrendered by the peasantry.[13]

Instead of surrendering the surpluses, i.e. an *undetermined* amount, and instead of supplying on the basis of the plan, i.e. also an *undetermined* amount, whereby these two amounts were in no way dependent on (linked with) each other, we began to move to requisitioning, i.e. providing a *determined* amount, while supply from a special product exchange stockpile was proportional to completion of the requisitioning. Supply now was a *determined* amount, which was moreover in a fixed relationship with the first *determined* amount. This signified a *tendency to return to product exchange relations between city and village*, between industry and agriculture. It signified a hidden change in the system of economic relations itself, a fundamental retreat in the face of the demands of the petty bourgeois peasant economy. This was a harbinger of the future return to product exchange relations with the peasantry.[14]

The failure of this attempt as well caused Narkomprod *to abandon this way of calculating surpluses in favour of mandatory apportionment*, which in the beginning was perhaps very rough and only gradually put in place, but which produced real success (author's italics throughout).

The following statement from this same author addresses the approximate nature of this method of requisitioning (p. 148): 'Requisitioning produced a quite mixed picture: requisitioning in various places yielded from 5 to 35 poods per desiatin'. One place, then, had to perhaps bear a *seven* times larger apportionment than another.

13 The germ of this idea can be found in the decree, 'On the Organisation of Product Exchange to Increase Grain Procurements' of 2 April 1918. § 3 of its instructions reads: 'Within the boundaries of each county, a product is distributed among rural district and district associations *in proportion to* the amount of grain and other food products surrendered by the population which has joined associations'.

And the decree 'On the Obligatory Product Exchange in Grain-producing Agricultural Localities' of 7 August 1918 declared: '§ 1. An *obligatory* order is established in the localities of the grain-producing provinces and counties that commodities from the processing industry be supplied *exclusively* in exchange for grain and other food products, and also for hemp, flax, leathers, etc. § 2 that commodities…be supplied only on presentation of…accounting receipts for the delivery of a *corresponding* amount of grain, forage cereals, and other food products to the delivery points'. (see *Sistematicheskii sbornik dekretov i rasporiazhenii pravitel'stva po prodovol'stvennomu delu*, book I, pp. 149 and 151) (author's italics throughout).

14 In 'Tezisy po voprosu o reorganizatsii Komproda' (see *Ekonomicheskaia zhizn'*, issue dated 27 March 1920), I wrote about the transition 'from the *obligatory surrender of all surpluses*…through a requisitioning method, *which does not determine how much the village*

But this was just a tendency. On the one hand, the number of agricultural products under monopoly was constantly expanding, and so commodity relations between the city and the countryside were being further suppressed; the goal of this expansion was to incorporate all agricultural products.[15] On the other hand, the aforementioned fundamental change in the nature of mutual relations between city and countryside was just the first step towards the return to product exchange relations between city and countryside.

The proportionality that was established between the surrender of agricultural products and the distribution of industrial products *was in no way equivalent*, i.e. it did not correspond to market relations.

Nevertheless, it would be completely wrong to deny the importance of this connection (product exchange). Thus, in the article we have already cited above from the collection *Prodovol'stvennaia politika*, the author, summarising his own experience of procurements, writes: 'In itself, agitation (to carry out requisitioning, L.K.) without a properly organised and strictly executed product exchange would not have much significance.…*Product exchange was the basis of agitation*'.[16]

The cause of the important influence that the relatively small amounts of industrial products had on the success of requisitioning was because the decline in industry, which was more severe than the decline in agriculture and played a greater part in the provisioning of the army, had led to an extraordinary shortage of industrial products particularly in the countryside. 'This terrible need', writes the same author, 'which the peasantry experiences for all products, will negate any agitation, if it [need, not agitation. L.K.] is not eased to even a

---

retains for itself, but how much it surrenders; the sum of products given up by the village during a particular requisition was set against a particular sum of commodities received by it'.

15 In the official theses, 'Razverstka, kak metod gosudarstvennykh zagotovok,' we read: 'Point 6…under Soviet power, the monopoly must gradually encompass *all* products. Leaving one or another product or part of it in the hands of a producer over the needs of the economy pours lifeblood into the dying capitalist system, because it supports private trade – speculation'. 'Point 10…Procuring some products through requisitioning and other products through buying and selling leads to agriculture shifting its focus to the production of those products which are sold under conditions of private trade, and also to the fact that monopoly products reach the speculative market prematurely'. See *Prodovol'stvennaia politika*, Moscow, 1920, 'Tezisy doklada M.I. Frumkina,' pp. 257–258. In the same collection, we find the decrees on requisitioning the following agricultural products: cereal bread, grain fodder, oil-seeds, hay, straw, potatoes, vegetables and others unrationed products (cabbage, beets, carrots, onions, etc), eggs, butter, honey, poultry, slaughter cattle (large cattle, sheep, pigs), fruits, mushrooms, flax, hemp, and wool.

16 P. 256, article Kaganovich, 'Prodotriady i prodpolk'. See also p. 177 (author's italics).

very small degree'. The more sharply industry declined and the more violently the Civil War raged, the more severely was the need felt for industrial products, i.e. an imbalance existed between the supply of industrial products and the demand for them. Therefore, the more that industry declined *and the more that product exchange stockpiles contracted, the stronger became the purchasing power of each product unit.*[17]

This could be seen in the movement of 'free' (underground) market prices, even in the capitals. Thus, in pounds of rye flour, the exchange value of six of the most important industrial products was on average for all of Russia:[18]

1912	40.6
1 September 1920	81.6

i.e. the exchange value *more than doubled.*

These figures refer to provincial and some county towns. In the countryside, this increase was undoubtedly far higher.

That this increase became ever sharper during the Civil War period can be seen in the movement of the price, expressed in pounds of baked (rye) bread, for one arshin of chintz even in Moscow:[19]

in March 1919	1.3
in July 1919	1.7
in March 1920	1.5
in July 1920	1.9
in February 1921	2.2

17 'The direct and significant effect of payment in kind is explained by the fact that, despite the widespread suspicious attitude towards the state commodity stockpile, this stockpile, while *insignificant* in absolute terms (expressed in poods, arshins, etc) compared with the good old days, represents a colossal force in the *market*. The price of industrial products in the village market increased five, ten and many more times more than the prices of agricultural products. Even in starving Moscow, the prices for industrial products rose more than for agricultural products. The reason for this is that *the supply of industrial products contracted many times more than the supply of agricultural products. Here, given the unilateral reduction in the state commodity stockpile, its purchasing power does not fall*, and indeed it can increase, if the supply of agricultural products grows'. See L. Kritsman, 'Tezisy po voprosu o reorganizatsii Komproda,' in *Ekonomicheskaia zhizn'*, dated 27 March 1920.

18 See S. Strumilin, 'Problema vysokikh khlebnykh tsen,' no. 4, *Ekonomicheskoe obozrenie*, 1923, p. 8.

19 Calculated according to data in *Stat. ezhegodnik 1918–1920 g.g.*, pp. 115 and 118.

Thus, as we have said, the proportionality between the yields of agricultural products through procurement and the distribution of industrial products (the scale of which varied greatly in different localities for arbitrary reasons having to do with product delivery), was not equivalent. At the same time, proportionality was usually established only in relation to grain (and potatoes in some districts), and was not differentiated at all by the individual products of agriculture and industry; these products were to a certain extent opposites to each other en masse.[20]

Ultimately, this was a *collective* product exchange, i.e. an exchange of products between the state and the peasant community (or cooperative), and within this community the poor peasants, i.e. those who surrendered less or nothing at all, received more.

But this tendency towards a radical change in the very nature of the economic mutual relations between proletarian industry and petty bourgeois agriculture, fostered by the decline in productive forces and the growing importance of the peasant economy, found expression, together with the aforementioned division of the economy into a legal and an illegal sector, in the stubbornness and vitality of the petty bourgeois economy, which with relentless pressure slowly transformed the economic relations that had been forced on it by the proletarian revolution, and that had held it back.

But the growing importance of the petty bourgeois economy was also reflected in the nature of the proletarian state's attitudes towards the various class strata in the countryside. There was a tendency to erase the class nature of proletarian politics in the countryside – a tendency to replace support for the village poor with support for cultural, remediable 'industrious owners'. The proletarian exclusivity dictated by the demands of the class struggle ran up against resistance from a stratum of the countryside which was rendered powerful by its economic role. This tendency was most clearly expressed in the decree of 20 December 1918, which completely abolished the Committees of the Village Poor, the objects of particular hatred from the well-to-do strata in the countryside.

Given the inherent limitation of the petty bourgeois, the serviceable or well-to-do owner-peasant agreed to the political hegemony of the urban proletariat, affirmed in the Soviet constitution,[21] but he was resolutely opposed to the hege-

20 In the next part of this book, we will examine in more detail the trends towards further development of commodity relations with the peasant economy.

21 § 24 of the Soviet Constitution reads: 'The All-Russian Congress of Soviets is composed of representatives of urban soviets (one delegate for 25,000 voters), and of representatives of the provincial congresses of soviets (one delegate for 125,000 inhabitants),' i.e. over

mony of the poor peasants. As a result of this, already in 1919 the hegemony of the poor peasant began to be replaced by the hegemony of the middle peasant, and moreover by a tendency towards the hegemony of the serviceable owner. Of course, as the class struggle became sharper in the Civil War period, this tendency too remained a tendency.

But the decline in productive forces did not only lead to an increase in the importance of the petty bourgeois peasant (and handicraft) economy, it also *reinforced the petty bourgeois nature of the countryside*. This was evident from the decline in the commercial part-time activities of the peasantry, which for the overwhelming majority of the peasants consisted of selling their own labour power, i.e. an expression of the *proletarian* nature of the countryside. The percentage of households doing commercial part-time work in individual provinces fell by 25–50%. This contraction of commercial activity was directly linked to the decline in industry, to the decline in demand for labour power in industry, construction, forestry, etc. As a result of this contraction of part-time commercial activity, which most peasants performed as proletarians supplying their own labour power, the peasants concentrated more and more on agriculture, i.e. they increasingly became small owners (petty bourgeois) who were connected with society exclusively through the products of their own economy.

The decline in productive forces, however, did not only reinforce the petty bourgeois nature of the peasantry, it led at the same time *to a petty bourgeois degradation* of large-scale industry and of the large-scale economy in general.

There ceased to be any continuity of the production process in large enterprises, as it was interrupted again and again by fuel shortages, by raw material shortages, and then by transport stoppages, or by something else. Large-scale industry ceased to function as large-scale industry.

This withering of large-scale industry and the sharp and protracted decline in the standard of living of the proletariat led *to an increase in absences*, i.e. to the utilisation of worker time not for production but for other purposes, most frequently for domestic activities (trips to secure food), to an increase *in industrial moonlighting* [*sovmestitel'stvo*], i.e. working simultaneously at the factory or plant and outside of it in small workshops, to an increase in *work on the side*. This transformed large public enterprises into a multitude of small independent handicraft-type workshops (using materials in the plant to make objects for sale on the market, such as lighters, dishes, etc). This ultimately led to the

50,000 voters (according to the constitution, voters are those individuals not engaged in wage labour and older than 18 years; this age group includes approximately half of the village population). See *Sbornik dekretov 1917–1918 g.g.*, pp. 65 and 69 and *Sbornik stat. svedenii po SSSR*, pp. 16–17.

growth of the direct *theft* of materials and manufactured goods for the purpose of selling them (in addition to the theft of materials for side jobs). All of these phenomena tended to *distort* the very social archetype of the industrial proletarian, the worker in public production, declassing him, *making him more like the archetype of the petty bourgeois* independent *commodity producer*.

Similar, but even more visible processes occurred for the same reasons among employees as well: *moonlighting proliferated*, meaning that employees worked everywhere and nowhere, *and* so too did *bribe-taking*, which the severest measures were unable to root out: both of these sores of Soviet bureaucratism turned the state employee from an employee into an independent contractor of his own services, and the institution into a simple function of his independent activity, something like a gift of nature. That these tendencies among the intelligentsia, which was so hostile to the dictatorship of the proletariat, did not encounter such ideological resistance as among the proletariat, meant that these phenomena found much sharper expression here.

The extent of this process is shown by the ratio of the 'extralegal' (S. Strumilin's term) earnings of a worker to his total wage. This ratio on average in Russia comprised:[22]

in 1917 0%
in 1918 14%
in 1919 20%
in 1920 20.5%

In individual months in 1920, this percentage rose sharply, sometimes doubling. And in relation to the total urban population, a very revealing sign of this was that in 1920 in the RSFSR (not including Turkestan) the census numbered 12.3 million urban inhabitants, while reports by the food supply organs showed 21.9 million people being supplied by the state, i.e. *78% more*.[23]

22 Calculated according to data from S. Strumilin, *Zarabotnaia plata*, etc, p. 33. These figures represent a very rough, rather underestimated evaluation. They were obtained by comparing wages and expenditures of workers. Expenditures before the war exceeded wages by only 3–4%, in 1919 in ten cities it was already 50% higher, and in 1919–1920 in individual cities it was already up to 100% higher, indeed even more, rising to 191% in Khar'kov. Expenditures exceeded wages all the more, the lower the wages were. In May 1918, then, among Leningrad workers in the highest group expenditures exceeded wages by only 2%, but in the lowest groups by 294%, i.e. expenditures were almost four times higher than wages (in the middle groups, expenditures exceeded wages, from the highest to the lowest group, by 42%, 55%, 84%, 162%). See ibid., p. 31,32.

23 Ibid., p. 30. Leningrad had 1.46 million inhabitants in 1918 according to the census (in

This change in the very nature of large-scale production and of the proletariat, a result of the effect of the decline in productive forces and in the standard of living of the workers, inevitably influenced the mutual relations between the enterprise and the individual worker, between the proletariat as the owner of socialised production, and the proletarian as worker and consumer.

The original system of payment and supply of the worker without consideration of performance, a system that aspired to be universal and to be expanded to the so-called free professions (doctors, and others), was not sustainable in conditions of declining productive forces and workers' declining living standards. Under these conditions, the tendency to return to performance-based forms of payment (wages) reappeared. This tendency could be seen in the change in the relationship between the high wages of a skilled worker and the wage of a labourer. This correlation initially fell (in the period from August 1917 to June 1918 from 2.44 to 1.39, i.e. almost by half), but later rose (by September 1918 to 1.75, i.e. by a fifth). But this tendency came to nought because of the declining importance of the money wage, so that in reality the real relationship between the highest and lowest wages fell as follows:[24]

7 August 1917	2.32
1 November 1917	1.68
1 June 1918	1.19
1 September 1918	1.30
1 February 1919	1,17
1 September 1919	1.09
1920	1.04

Of far more importance was a different feature of this same tendency, so-called *performance-related supply* [*tselevoe snabzhenie*], whereby a certain correlation was stipulated between the worker's consumption and his productive effectiveness (productivity of labour), initially on a collective basis (for groups of workers), and later for individual workers. Performance-related supply was relatively widely distributed in 1920 as one of the applications of the principle of 'shock work [*udarnost'*]'.

June), and 1.95 million according to bread ration cards, i.e. 33% more. The petty bourgeois degradation of this city, a consequence of the decline in productive forces and of the standard of living of the population, made a precise calculation impossible here as well.

24 Ibid., pp. 34–35.

In addition, bonus systems were used more and more, whereby in-kind bonuses were most important. All of these initially very complex systems, as they were implemented, became more and more like simple piece-work payment.

However, on the whole this tendency too remained just a tendency: by 1920, variation in workers' wages was, as we have seen, only 4%, i.e. a completely insignificant figure. But this also created a tendency to return to commodity relations, supported and fostered by the decline in productive forces and in the living standards of the workers.

Despite the quite widespread opinion that the tendencies towards naturalisation and centralisation of the national economy, which appeared both in the state-capitalist economic system (above all in Germany) and in our proletarian natural economic system during the Civil War period, were the product of the war and the war-induced decline in the productive forces of society and the decline in the living standards of the broad masses, we were able to see that precisely the opposing tendencies towards decentralisation and towards restoration of commodity relations were fostered by the decline in the productive forces of society and in the decline in the living standards of the broad masses.

But this had nothing to do with any mystical properties of this decline – it created nothing, it only destroyed; and, most importantly, this destruction was not uniform. The large-scale economy, whose functioning (work) was linked to an extended network of economic connections, turned out to be more vulnerable to the effects of the omnipresent and all-pervading Civil War, which ruptured all of the more or less important economic connections. This is why the large-scale economy experienced a protracted crisis in productive relations, and why it suffered destruction on a far greater scale. But this unevenness of destruction also led to a growth in the relative significance of petty bourgeois economic forms and to a petty bourgeois degradation of the large-scale economy. These both produced tendencies towards the destruction of economic relations, which corresponded to the nature of large-scale industry and which were forced by it on the entire national economy, if (for the already mentioned reasons) in distorted form.

CHAPTER 13

The Results of the Civil War

1. The actual periods of development of the revolution. 2. The boom trends. 3. Victory at the lowest ebb. 4. The creation of the new society.

The intertwined effect of these opposing tendencies so complicated the entire course of development of the new economic and social order that the actual, individual periods of this development are very difficult to discern, and then only contingently, i.e. after weighing the characteristic features of a given period.

The first six months of existence of the Soviet republic, from October 1917 to May–June 1918, were a period of pre-economic construction, dominated decisively by the process of organising the political power of the newly victorious proletariat. The proletariat had struggled under very difficult conditions against domestic and foreign enemies, which did not permit any thoughts of consolidating the new system once and for all. In economic terms, this period is marked by the destruction of the organisation of finance capital (the nationalisation of the banks); by the establishment of the political dictatorship of the proletariat over the bourgeoisie in the production process as well, although without the complete removal of the latter from the enterprises, which occurred only spontaneously and chaotically (compulsory subjection of the capitalists to worker supervision under threat of confiscation of the enterprise in the event of insubordination by the owner); by the attempt to demobilise industry (after October 1917); by the agrarian revolution (the expulsion of the landowners from the countryside and the seizure of land by the peasants); by the worsening crises in food supply, transport, and industry; and, finally, by the violence of German imperialism, which imposed unprecedented peace conditions on a defenseless country, tantamount to an economic death sentence (depriving the localities of food supplies, raw materials, and fuel).

For almost a year – from May–June 1918 to January–February 1919 – the proletarian economic administration was being created, and the crisis in food supply relations was being tackled. The Soviet Republic found itself under terrible pressure from German imperialism, which was strangling it after the Brest Peace; at the same time, the onslaught of the imperialist Entente powers began (the mutiny of the Czechoslovaks, the occupation of Black Sea ports, etc), which intensified after the collapse of German imperialism. In economic terms, this period was characterised by the following: establishment of the

 | HTTPS://DOI.ORG/10.1163/9789004765313-017

command power of the proletariat in enterprises as well (the nationalisation of industry); the first steps on the road to organising industry (organising the central administrations, which corresponded, in terms of the organisation of production, to capitalist syndicates and trusts); a significant contraction of the free market (by replacing private trade with state distribution); introduction of the state procurement of the products of the peasant economy; class differentiation in the countryside (organisation of the Committees of the Village Poor) and the even redistribution of peasant lands through the partial expropriation of large peasants to the benefit of middle peasants; organisation of Soviet agricultural producers (above all sugar-beets); a renewed mobilisation of industry; further exacerbation of the food supply crisis and continuation of the transport and industrial crises, and also of the fuel crisis; depopulation of the cities and shortages of the labour force, especially the skilled labour force. This period saw the organization of the Red Army, which defeated the Czechoslovaks and the Don Cossacks. The greatest obstacle in the struggle against this destruction was, alongside the Civil War, the crisis in food supply relations, the process of creating a new proletarian organisation of the national economy, as a consequence of which the former organisation was no longer functioning, while the new one was not yet functioning normally.

The following year – from January–February 1919 to January–February 1920 – was a period of deep shortages in material resources (food supply, raw materials, fuel, metals). Although the districts, which supplied not only foodstuffs and raw materials but also fuel and metals, found themselves already cut off from central Russia by the start of summer 1918, the effects of this were felt somewhat later. The Soviet Republic found itself under concentrated attack from the imperialist Entente powers, which surrounded it with a blockade to seal it off hermetically and sought to organise an assault by its vassals from all sides. In economic terms, this period was marked by the following: the process of unification of the national economy of the Republic – the initial functioning of the central administrations created in the preceding period, and the creation, on the one hand, of partial associations (syndicates, trusts), and, on the other, of organs to put into effect a general economic plan in individual spheres of economic activity; the feverish struggle of the enterprises against the strangulation threatening their existence; the developing use of substitutes and all possible ruses; the successful concentration of efforts in the arms industry and the procurement of wood fuel; completion of the entire economic apparatus (food supply, fuel, transport, etc) and at the same time the growth of bureaucratism in this apparatus and in the entire state apparatus in general; a terrible exacerbation of the crises in industry, fuel supply, and transport, and a continuation of the crises in the food supply and labour force; a contraction of industrial agriculture and of animal husbandry. In this period, the new apparatus of industry already existed, but it was unable to function as a result of shortages in the materials it required for its operation.

Finally, January–February 1920 to February–March 1921 was, on the one hand, a period of exit from the Civil War and of final consolidation of the new proletarian state and society, and, on the other hand, of formal intensification of the methods of proletarian economic construction also in relation to petty bourgeois economic forms; this was also a period of mounting contradiction between these methods and the petty bourgeois economy.

The Red Army, which strengthened and grew during the two-year struggle, defeated all the enemies of the Soviet Republic: in the East – Kolchak; in the South-East – Dutov; in the South – Denikin; in the North-West – Iudenich; and in the North – the Entente forces. By the end of 1920, the last serious redoubt of the Russian counter-revolution had been eliminated, its final card was trumped: the Crimea, where Denikin's and Wrangel's successors had settled. The mobilised arms industry ensured that the army had adequate supplies of military equipment, the supply of the Red Army was organised and functioned quite differently than before. Transport began to run more regularly. Procurements of food supplies increased. Supply of the workers and cities improved. The blockade ring was breached, and the blockade itself was broken. Not only the border states (including also France's vassal state, White Poland, whose offensive was the final serious intervention by international capital) began concluding peace treaties with the proletarian Soviet Republic, but the capitalist Entente states too saw a need, under pressure from their labour organisations (and for a number of other reasons), to resume economic relations with Soviet Russia. The vacillations among the intermediate strata tended to subside (although this tendency was interlaced with other tendencies as well): peasants surrendered their agricultural products, employees began to work without any ulterior motives.

In economic terms, this period saw the start of the restoration of connections with the world economy, the start of the restoration of domestic economic connections due to the shift in military actions to the border regions; it saw the initial easing of the various supply crises due to the restoration of a unitary agricultural-industrial territory (and consequently also of the connections between the Soviet centre and Siberian grain, Baku oil, etc), and the further completion of the entire economic apparatus. But at the same time, this period also saw a continuing growth of bureaucratism in the entire state, including the economic, apparatus; an increase in the military deformation [*deformatsiia*] of the economy caused by the enormous growth of the Red Army; the continuing destruction of the entire technical framework of the national economy; it saw an intensification of the tendency of the proletarian organisation of the economy to go beyond the limits of the large-scale economy and to draw into it the entire small-scale economy (nationalisation of small-scale industry, sowing committees [*posevkomy*]); and it saw a growth in the processes of disintegration of the unitary proletarian-natural economy (the dismantling of the VSNKh etc). This culminated in the greatest economic crisis at the end of 1920 and start of 1921, and, at the end of this period, in the growing political crisis (peasant uprisings, Kronstadt) as well.

Despite these extraordinarily burdensome conditions, despite the internal disruption caused by the complex interactions of external and internal factors, which so influenced the development of the proletarian revolution, – the proletarian natural economy, which had been created by this revolution and which had not yet acquired its final form, nonetheless achieved some famous successes, above all in the arms industry and in the supply of the Red Army. In the article, 'The Construction of the Red Army in the Revolution', we read:[1] 'The victory of the Red Army in the Civil War was not only our military, but also our *economic* and administrative victory. *It was our victory on the economic front.* After all, by the end of 1920 we had increased the numerical strength of the army to 5½ million. This army had to be outfitted, fed, armed. This army had to be deployed along an enormous 8000-verst front; during military operations, it had to be thrown with all haste from one end of the country to the other. And during this tremendous struggle, *we never experienced the kinds of difficulties with food, equipment, and military supplies for the army as were suffered by the army under tsarism or during the Kerensky era [Kerenshchina]*'.

1 See the article by V. Antonov-Ovseenko in the collection *Za 5 let*, p. 167. It should be noted that the author was one of the leading officials of the Red Army and, so to speak, an eyewitness. Typical here is an extract from a speech he cites by L. Trotsky at the VII Congress of Soviets in December 1919: 'Supply issues presented enormous difficulties for us. Our Soviet apparatus in this sphere underwent the severest of tests and *passed* them. There was a period when our plants were not producing a single bullet, a single rifle, a single machine-gun, or a single artillery-piece, a period when the old apparatus had disintegrated and when we had not yet seriously started creating a new one.... The last production month had a ten- to fifteen-fold increase over the first month when we began work.... *Our apparatus proved itself capable of rebuilding the arms industry*.... There is no longer any danger that we would fail because of the shortage of bullets, rifles, machine-guns and artillery, a danger that threatened us 8–10 months ago. This very fact, I say as an aside, is evidence that an apparatus which is capable of repairing the arms industry *in several months*, will be capable of repairing industry in general'. (author's italics). [*7 – i Vserossiiskii s'ezd Sovetov rabochikh, krest'ianskikh, krasnoarmeiskikh i kazach'ikh deputatov: Stenograficheskii otchet* (Moscow: Gosudarstvennoe izdatel'stvo, 1920), p. 89].

In other spheres of industry, the extreme degree of destruction of economic connections and the decline in productive forces reduced all efforts for the most part to nought. But in individual cases in the Soviet central region, where there were no civil war fronts, in branches of the extraction industry which did not need, then, supplies of raw materials, some successes were achieved. One example of this was the extraction of peat and Moscow region coal which comprised (in millions of poods):[2]

	Peat	Coal
1918	58	–
1919	67	25.5
1920	92	35

Average labour productivity across all of industry in 1920, based on gross output, apparently rose (see p. 265). The number of days when plants were idle fell more than three-fold in 1920 compared with 1919 and were even significantly lower than in 1917 (see p. 267).

Some successes were also achieved in transport, where in 1920, with the same level of capital repairs, running repairs increased over 1919 by 30%, almost reaching prewar levels (see p. 254). Water transport in 1920 outstripped – and significantly so – that of 1919 and 1918 (see p. 234).

Significant successes were achieved in logging as well (in millions of cubic sazhens):[3]

	Logged	Shipped
1918–1919	(4.2)	(3.2)
1919–1920	9.4 (9.4)	6.9 (7.1)
1920–1921	9.3	8.4

2 See Antonov-Ovseenko, p. 52.

3 See *Stat. ezhegodnik 1918–1920 g.g.*, vol. II, pp. 282–283. The figures in brackets are from *Lesozagotivitel'naia politika v obshchei sisteme narodnogo khoziaistva*, p. 8.

Consequently, the logged quantity more than *doubled*, and shipments rose by 2–3 *times*. Only this success prevented the complete paralysis of transport and industry, as wood, for example, in 1919 provided 88 % of fuel consumption (see p. 113).

Finally, the undeniable successes in the procurement of agricultural products (see p. 252) were already for the most part successes of the administrative (taxation) apparatus. The result of all this was, among other things, a significant drop in mortality (for the capitals, see p. 260).

But these successes remained only partial successes which were lost in the general catastrophic decline in productive forces, a product of the extraordinary duration and intensification of the Civil War.

The experiment, which was being conducted by international capitalism to reanimate the corpse of Russian capitalism – an experiment that included not only *the creation of the White Russia* of Kolchak, Denikin, and Wrangel' but also *persistent sabotage*, counter-revolutionary plots and uprisings inside Soviet Russia – failed completely. But those three years of the death throes of capitalism were costly years for the Russia of the proletarian and the toiler.

Under these conditions, the victory of the revolution could achieved only at the cost of a catastrophic decline in the productive forces of society, only when they were at an *extremely low* level.

Only at the cost of the extreme strain on all its forces, at the cost of the significant destruction and the petty bourgeois degradation of its own large-scale economic base, and at the cost of its own partial declassing process could the revolution, the heroic proletariat of Russia, prevail.

Only at the cost of this self-destruction could capitalism be destroyed and the counter-revolutionary resistance of capital and the landowners be crushed.

The objective task of the Civil War era was for *the revolution to assert itself*: to destroy the political dominance of capital, to destroy the economic dominance of capital (the expropriation of large capital), to organise the proletarian (Soviet) state, to control an integrated (agricultural-industrial) territory, to organise the proletarian management of large-scale public production, and to restore ties to the world economy (break the blockade).

Here, the military task – *taking control of an integrated economic territory* – became a priority, for this was the necessary *precondition* for the resolution of the remaining tasks.

The long duration and intensification of the Civil War, a result of the interference of international capital, and the resultant concentration and deepening of the proletarian revolution, meant that the proletarian organisation of the national economy of Soviet Russia in the Civil War era overcame exploitation, as we have seen, not only in large-scale capitalist production, but outside of it as well; it not only overcame exploitation (through the organisation of a proletarian economic administration), it also overcame the market. But here the economic politics of the proletarian revolution had gone beyond (for the sake of expediency) concerns of direct economic expediency, they had gone beyond the limits set for them by the preceding capitalist development, because overcoming the market in this context turned into its simple *suppression*, into a means not of development but of destruction of the productive forces of the small-scale economy and of its connections with the large-scale economy. So this economic policy and its organisational expression, the organisation of the national economy associated with it, inevitably ran up against resistance from opposing forces, which could be partially suppressed for a time, but which could not be overcome. This was why *the organisational structure* of the national economy of Soviet Russia in the Civil War era remained *incomplete* and why economic phenomena persisted that stood in sharp contradiction with this organisational structure. At the same time, this organisational structure was clearly *transitional in nature*, for its development was interrupted before it was able to be fully completed.

But the revolution performed its fundamental task. It was not able to end, and did not end, the class struggle, for no revolution can destroy classes if they are rooted in economic forms that they have not yet outlived. But *for the first time in the history of mankind* it transformed the class struggle, which before had happened within the framework and as a function of the *capitalist* order, into a class struggle within the framework and as a function of the *proletarian* order.

The entire history of mankind knows no other achievement which can be ranked alongside this achievement in terms of its world historical significance.

The revolution has done what revolution in general does: it created a *new* social order. It did so in rough outline and unfinished form, but it is not at all the task of revolution to finish and polish the new order. That is up to evolution, which unfolds *as a function of the new* social order created by the revolution.

APPENDIX

Three Years of the New Economic Policy of the Proletariat of the USSR

The Russian Revolution was the first *proletarian* revolution and the first stage of the world revolution of the proletariat; herein lies its *world* significance.[1,2] But it was not only an anti-capitalist revolution of the proletariat, it was also an anti-feudal revolution of the peasantry, and herein lies its *national* significance, vital to the overwhelming majority of the population of Russia.

However, the particular tasks which the Russian proletariat had to solve *after* its victory, were determined not only by this *dual* nature of the Russian Revolution, but also by the specific features of the *combination* of these two revolutions: the anti-capitalist revolution (this would have been a purely socialist revolution, had it not combined with the anti-feudal revolution) and the anti-feudal revolution (this would have been a purely bourgeois revolution, had it not combined with the proletarian revolution).

The world proletarian revolution did not remain a purely anti-capitalist revolution either, it was accompanied by a simultaneous peasant (and in part also bourgeois capitalist) anti-feudal revolution. It has been inevitably bound up *with the liberation of colonial peoples*, which world capital artificially maintains at a pre-capitalist stage of development, by simultaneously disrupting their former natural social relations and transforming the countries populated by them into their own agrarian appendages, into colonies.

But the peculiar feature of the Russian Revolution was not just that the combination of anti-capitalist and anti-feudal revolutions happened not on a world scale but on a national scale (making the Russian Revolution the prototype of the world revolution), as a result of which it took on a fundamentally different form: in place of two parallel, territorially separated revolutions, the anti-capitalist in the metropoles and the anti-feudal in the colonies, one *complex* revolution took place in one and the same country.

---

1 This appendix is intended to provide an albeit rough outline of the period of the revolution following the Civil War era. It is a reprint with minor changes of a brochure written at the start of 1924; it is of course designed differently than the book, and for this reason it contains several inextensive repetitions that unfortunately cannot be removed.

2 [Lev Kritsman, 'Tri goda Novoi Ekonomicheskoi Politiki proletariata Sovetskogo Soiuza,' *Zvezda*, no. 3, 1924, pp. 108–134].

 | HTTPS://DOI.ORG/10.1163/9789004765313-018

The main feature of the Russian Revolution was that *the Russian peasant economy was an agrarian appendage not only of Russian capital, but also of international* (West European) *capital.*[3] This, on the one hand, enabled the proletariat to act as the liberator of the entire nation from the colonial exploitation (the annullment of loans) threatening it and significantly facilitated the first steps of the revolution; but, on the other hand, this to an extraordinary degree *overburdened* the proletarian, anti-capitalist revolution with the tasks of the anti-feudal revolution, and meant that the Russian proletariat had to solve the question of the proletariat's position vis-à-vis the peasantry not only for itself, but also for the West European proletariat.

In the interest of developing the revolution, because of its offensive against capital and to consolidate the results of this offensive, the Russian proletariat more than once had to put on hold the immediate interests of socialist construction, of the Russian proletarian revolution – *to retreat* before the peasant revolution, to deviate from the direct high road in search of detours.

The very birth of the Russian proletarian revolution – the October overthrow – was associated with just such a retreat (and became possible because of it).

In the days of the October overthrow, the Russian proletariat took up not a proletarian agrarian program, but a peasant one; in agriculture, there was not a proletarian, but a peasant, expropriation of the expropriators, a division not only of the lands of the feudal lords, but also of capitalist agriculture (even if these lands did not become the property of the peasant petty bourgeoisie, but was given over to its use).

But this very retreat of the proletariat brought about the merging *of both revolutions* – the proletarian and the peasant. It gave the former the support it lacked of the huge majority of the population and the huge majority of the army; it gave the latter the cohesion and leadership it lacked. It welded together the revolution of the unorganised masses of the peasantry and the revolution of the organised proletarian minority of the population into a victorious revolution of the organised masses.

The destruction of the estate [*soslovie*] of the noble landlords, and moreover of the estates and estate system in general, and the destruction of the foundations of this system – landlord land ownership – in short, the destruction of *feudal* relations; exiting the imperialist war and cancelling the old loans and old treaties, i.e. the destruction of the *colonial* dependency on foreign capital

3 Approximately 60% of the grain (its main product), and 40–50% of all agricultural products, which was exported beyond the Russian village, went abroad.

forged by the imperialist war; finally the destruction of the *national* oppression, which weighed upon all the nationalities, made up almost exclusively of peasants, with the exception of the Great Russian nationality – this was the substance of the anti-feudal, peasant revolution.

But the peasant revolution can only undertake its work once the resistance of the ruling class, which is concentrated in the state organisation, is truly broken, if its state organisation is destroyed.

The peasantry is not in a condition to do this *on its own*. The peasantry is not capable of organising its own integration. It is not capable of overcoming its fragmentation, which is a necessary consequence of the atomisation of the peasant economy. This is precisely why all independent actions of the peasantry in the course of the entire history of mankind have invariably ended in defeat.

And this is precisely why the merger of the proletarian and peasant revolution meant that the role of leader and organiser of the peasant, anti-feudal revolution, a role played in earlier great revolutions by the bourgeoisie, was assumed *for the first time in human history* by the proletariat, which became the very hegemon of our revolution.

But the complex nature of the revolution inevitably ensured the complex nature of the counter-revolution as well.

The role of the proletariat as the leader of the peasant, anti-feudal revolution and the role of the capitalist bourgeoisie as one of the forces of the counter-revolution, which was simultaneously capitalist and feudal (manorial), these were two sides of one and the same social process.

But this complex nature of the counter-revolution meant, in turn, that the class struggle of the proletariat against capital became a necessary element (a constituent part) of the anti-feudal revolution, and the suppression of the counter-revolutionary resistance of capital a necessary *condition of the victory* of the anti-feudal revolution.

The crushing of the counter-revolutionary resistance of capital, however, under the conditions of the Civil War, i.e. a period when the very nature of the system of society has not yet been decided, is impossible without the elimination of the market. For the market is capital's source of life, the source of its power, and thus of its counter-revolutionary power, and, starved of the air it needs to survive, namely its ownership of the means of production, capital cannot survive.

The victory of the peasant revolution, then, is not possible without the suppression of the market.

This is why the peasantry, in the final analysis, gave its agreement to the suppression of the market. But this agreement to the suppression of the market (to the suppression of trade) was nothing less than a refusal to complete the anti-feudal peasant revolution, which, after all, would mean that the peasantry, entangled in feudal relations, would become a free peasantry, namely free producers of commodities, freely disposing of everything they produced. And precisely because the agreement of the peasantry to the suppression of the market was a refusal to complete the peasant revolution, the peasantry gave its agreement only after great vacillations. And each of these vacillations set a sixth of the earth in motion (and indirectly even more), for they were echoed in the advances of the White Armies from the Black Sea, from farthest Siberia to the centre of Russia, sometimes almost to Moscow itself.

And, of course, this agreement was only a *temporary* agreement.

Insofar as the world revolution has not yet changed relations between the proletariat and the peasantry (its petty bourgeois masses) in Russia, and did not place alongside the Russian proletariat the proletariat of even one of the advanced capitalist countries, then the very victory of the Russian Revolution, which was a victory of the proletariat and the peasantry, inevitably led to the future *retreat* of the Russian proletarian revolution before the peasant revolution.

For the victory meant that the *military* organisational significance of the proletariat took a back seat in the struggle being conducted jointly with the peasantry against the restoration of the landlords and the intervention of world capital.

The victory, i.e. the cessation of open struggle against the new system, and de facto recognition of it by its class enemies, meant that the suppression of the market *ceased* to be a precondition of the victory of the revolution in general, and thus also of the peasant revolution.

The great mass of the peasantry only grudgingly supported the suppression of trade when it was confronted by the choice of either a return of the landlords and being turned into a colony, or agreeing to the ban on trade; it rose up decisively against the ban on trade as soon as the struggle against the landowner and foreign capital was over. In this way, the military, and thus primarily *political, victory* of the proletariat inevitably led, under these conditions, to its *economic retreat.*

The New *Economic* Policy – the restoration of *market* relations and the possibility of also restoring and developing *capital* on this basis, while keeping the large-scale economy and political control in the hands of the proletariat – was precisely this *retreat.* It threw into stark relief the fact that our revolution was a complex revolution, not just an anti-capitalist revolution of the proletariat, but also an anti-feudal revolution of the peasantry.

The retreat from the proletarian revolution consisted primarily of the *restoration of market relations*. This meant not only the transition from natural economic relations to commodity-monetary relations, but also recognition of the fundamental *social* activity of people, i.e. recognition of the economic activity of every individual as a *private* matter. Thus, the proletarian socialist structure had economic forms (commercial principles) forced upon it that were alien to it. The retreat from the proletarian revolution meant, moreover, *the rejection of the exceptional nature* of the proletarian revolution, an inevitable consequence of the restoration of market relations. It allowed not only for the possibility of accumulating wealth and restoring the power of money, but also for the *possibility of restoring capitalist exploitation*, even if *materially* (in practice) within quite narrow limits: the restoration of capitalist exploitation, whereby the *basic* means of (large-scale) production, which had been expropriated from capital, remained in the hands of the proletariat; the accumulation of wealth, whereby political power, and thus also the collection of *taxes*, remained in the hands of the working class.

Retreat for the proletarian revolution – the New Economic Policy – means *completion* for the anti-feudal, peasant revolution. It finally transforms the great mass of the peasantry into *free* commodity producers. In addition to land and to liberation from all the bonds of serfdom, from colonial dependency and national oppression, it gives the great mass of the peasantry free access *to the market*.

If the victory of the peasant revolution, being a condition of its completion, i.e. the participation of the peasant masses in the market, was impossible without the suppression of the market while the Civil War was going on, then blocking the petty commodity producer's access to the market *after* this, when the suppression of the market ceased being necessary for the peasant revolution itself, would have meant the following: it would have made it more difficult for the petty bourgeois mass of the peasantry to enjoy the fruits of revolution, it would have held back the development of the productive forces of the petty economy. As a result of this, it would have produced an inevitable conflict between the proletariat and the great mass of the peasantry, a break in the alliance between the proletarian and peasant revolutions, a Russia-wide Kronstadt.

Restoration of market relations *after the victory of the revolution*, however, did not mean at all that there was no longer a possibility of continuing the proletarian revolution. It did not mean a defeat, but rather a retreat from the proletarian revolution, its *limitation and a change in the means of realising it*.

By affording the peasant revolution the chance *to come to its conclusion* unimpeded, it thus eliminated conflicts and frictions between the peasant revolution and the proletarian revolution. With the proletariat's refusal to *completely and immediately* implement the proletarian revolution (i.e. in those forms most beneficial to the proletarian revolution), the necessary *self-limitation* of the proletarian revolution both in its scale and in the methods of its realisation, this retreat opened up to the proletarian revolution the difficult, but under these circumstances the only possible, path for its continuation.

This inevitably meant, however, that the proletarian revolution would experience an extremely *difficult* path forward, as it forced unaccustomed methods (forms) of construction upon it, restricted its scope, and created the conditions for the simultaneous growth of the forces of its enemy, capital.

Since the announcement of the New Economic Policy – in earnest and for a long time, but not for ever[4] – three years have passed. Tensely and anxiously the Russian, the entire world, proletariat, has been seeking an answer to the fundamental question: what are the results of this retreat for the *proletarian* revolution? Is the newly created *proletarian* society developing, strengthening politically, and most importantly, economically *under these conditions of retreat* from the proletarian revolution? Or is the petty bourgeois, and this means bourgeois, flood washing away the solidified lava of the proletarian revolution?

The victory of the Russian Revolution in armed struggle against a world of enemies was bought at the cost of unheard-of sacrifices. The costs of the Civil War, which added to the costs of the imperialist war, led to such a decline in Russia's productive forces,[5] that it was impossible to revive them using the methods and thus also the power of the proletariat alone, and only of the Russian proletariat at that. To invoke Lenin's words here, this led to 'the collaboration of two classes: the workers and peasants, in which the 'Nepmen', i.e., the bourgeoisie, are now permitted to participate on certain terms'.[6] But this class collaboration is only within the framework of the class struggle. In Russia, the class struggle differs from that in other countries in that it happens *within the framework and on the basis of the Soviet system*, i.e. of the economic superiority (control of the *fundamental* means of production and exchange) and the political dictatorship *not of capital, but of the proletariat.*

4 [V.I. Lenin, 'Ninth All-Russia Congress of Soviets. December 23–28, 1921,' *Collected Works*, vol. 33 (Moscow, Progress Publishers, 1973), p. 160].

5 The scale of the decline in productive forces is best illustrated by two facts: in 1921–1922 in Russia, which used to supply half of the world's grain needs, had to import foreign grain, and not long before this the question was seriously raised of importing foreign coal to the Donbas.

6 [V.I. Lenin, 'How We Should Reorganise the Workers' and Peasants' Inspection. Recommendations to the Twelfth Party Congress,' *Collected Works*, vol. 33 (Moscow, Progress Publishers, 1973), p. 485].

The Soviet system is not yet a socialist system, but a societal system that *is transitioning* from capitalism to socialism. Classes still exist, including the class of capitalists (much diminished both in significance and power). Class exploitation still exists (sharply restricted in scope). Poverty, hunger, and unemployment still exist for some and shameless luxury for others. Prostitution, homelessness of children, old people, and invalids still exist, as does the need to stretch out a hand to the well-fed Nepman for alms. The peasant economy and the household economy still exist, and therefore so does the narrowness and limitedness of peasants and women. *But political power and control over the basic means of social production and exchange* (large-scale industry, transport, wholesale trade, and credit) are in the hands of the *proletariat,* which fought for *the conditions for socialist construction.*

Since the proletariat has not yet achieved socialism, i.e. a planned economy which puts an end to the commodity anarchy of economic life and to its costs and which guarantees the unobstructed development of the productive forces of society, then the basic question of the current period of our revolution is this: *is this transitional Soviet system creating the necessary conditions for the development of the productive forces of society,* of the productive forces of all of society and the productive forces of the large-scale economy that is in the hands of the proletariat?

The first question is the question whether the proletarian regime is a *progressive* regime; a second question is whether this progress is progress for *proletarian* society.

The proletariat, as the ruling class, is confronted, therefore, with three main tasks:

The first task is to raise the productive forces of the *entire* society, whereby under the current conditions the methods of the proletariat alone are not sufficient; this is why other methods are also permitted.

The second task is to develop specifically the productive forces of the large-scale economy, which the proletariat has taken over and maintained (*in this,* the New Economic Policy is no different from the old). Here, the proletariat must rely both on the internal forces of this large-scale proletarian economy, and on resources allocated from private capitalist and petty bourgeois enterprises via state taxes;[7] this task is simultaneously one of consolidating the new

---

7 The upturn in the large-scale economy, like the development of the Red Army, is a national necessity, for without it Russia will inevitably be transformed into a colony of international capital; here the interests of the proletariat and the petty bourgeoisie (above all the village petty bourgeoisie) coincide.

economic system of this large-scale economy, consolidating the power of the proletariat, and raising its living standard and cultural level.

The third task is to keep the class struggle within the framework of the Soviet system, in other words, to secure class collaboration on the basis of the Soviet system, which comrade Lenin[8] wrote about and which forms the basis of the alliance between the workers and peasants, both economic (their trade 'alliance') and political.

The supreme criterion of the degree of success in resolving these tasks, both here and everywhere, is *practice*. What are the facts?

Everyone understands that a time of struggle is not a time of economic upturn and not a time of an upturn in the workers' living standards – every worker knows this from his experience in every strike. Only in 1921 did the soviets' struggle for their existence cease; the financial year 1921–1922 was a year of unheard-of harvest failure and famine, the result of elemental disaster and destruction caused by the imperialist war, and by a Civil War which was so prolonged by the furious resistance of the exploiters. Only recently did the *first* year without war and failed harvest come to an end.

But a multifaceted upturn in the national economy of the Soviet Republic is now already beyond doubt.

The value of finished products of large- and medium-scale industry, which, with small exceptions, is in the hands of the proletariat, comprised (according to data of the TsSU in millions of gold roubles at prewar prices):

	In millions of roubles	As a percentage of 1920	Annual increase in percent
1920	518	100	–
1921	669	129	+29
1922	954	184	+43

Data for 1923 are not yet available. But in 1923, the industrial upturn continued. The gross value of all products of the mining and factory-plant industry comprised, according to Gosplan (in millions of gold roubles at prewar prices):

8 [For example, V.I. Lenin, 'Alliance Between the Workers and the Working and Exploited Peasants. A Letter to *Pravda*,' *Collected Works*, vol. 26 (Moscow, Progress Publishers, 1964), 333–335].

Financial year[9]	In millions of roubles	As a percentage of 1920–21	Annual increase in percent
1920–21	930	100	–
1921–22	1,355	146	+46
192–23	1,949	210	+44

In 1921, the activity of the New Economic Policy had not yet had an effect, but the cessation of war, and, in the second half of the year, the famine did have an effect. In 1922, the influence of the New Economic Policy was already being felt, as was the cessation of war and the reduction in the army, but the first six months saw the worst torments of the famine.

The financial year 1922–1923 was the first year in which our economy did not suffer any new blows from either war or hunger.

The general result of this has been an *upturn* in large-scale industry, indeed initially at a very sharp rate. Over the past two years, industrial production increased annually almost by *one-and-a-half* times, while before the war, in the years of the largest upturn, this increase was only 9% annually, i.e. about *five* times weaker.

The level attained is still very low – the gross production of large-scale and medium-scale industry comprised also in 1922–1923 only a little over a third (35%) of the prewar level. But the first step is the hardest. The upturn had only just begun.

This conclusion is completely corroborated by the figures for the main sectors of industry (VSNKh data):

	In millions of poods						
	1913	1918	1919	1920	1921	1922	1923
Coal production	1738.0	731.0	511.0	467.0	520.0	553.0	727.0
Petroleum production	554.8	245.0	273.0	243.0	246.0	290.0	325.0
Smelted iron	256.8	31.5	6.9	7.0	7.0	11.5	23.5
Open-hearth metal production	259.3	24.5	12.2	10.0	11.0	22.5	43.6
Cotton yarn production	16.0	–	1.0	0.8	0.9	3.6	4.7

9 The financial year runs from October 1 to October 1.

Throughout, the lowest value was reached in 1920, the final year of the war. In 1921 an upturn began, picking up steam in 1922. In 1923, this upturn continued.

This upturn in large-scale industry was an *intensive* upturn; at the same time labour productivity also rose.

According to data from VSNKh and TsSU, the gross product per worker in 1921–1922 (the financial year from 1 October to 1 October) doubled on average compared with 1920–1921.

In 1922–1923, the gross product per worker continued to grow and increased by almost a third (by 30%) according to Gosplan figures on the twelve most important sectors of industry in nine months of 1922–1923 compared with the same nine months of 1921–1922.

Here too, the prewar level of labour productivity was for the most part not reached. In fifteen closely examined textile factories, labour productivity in 1922 was already 60% of prewar productivity (this undoubtedly was roughly equivalent to the average), but for the hewers it was 96%, at the 'Krasnyi Treugolnik' factory it was 107%, and at the First Obraztsovaia Print Shop it was 145% of prewar productivity.

Most importantly, though, labour productivity grew. The 1921–1922 financial year was a year when large-scale industry as a whole worked at a loss (only a few individual sectors worked at a profit) and required subsidies from the state. But the rise in labour productivity and the lowering of production costs, as a result of the increased utilization of the plants, gradually turned one sector of large-scale industry after another from loss-making into profit-making entities for the state.

In 1922–1923, the state expended (according to VSNKh) 143 million commodity roubles on industry, and received about 115 million commodity roubles from taxation of industry;[10] but to this latter figure must still be added the deductions from the profits of industry for 1922–1923, which amounted in the current budget to about 24 million roubles[11] (in chervonets currency), but which in reality were probably a larger sum.

In this way, already in 1922–1923, industry *received from the state not many more resources*, perhaps no more at all, *than it itself gave to the state*, even though it expended large resources on expanding production.

10 According to Gosplan figures, 135 million commodity roubles, indexed to the first of the month. When the calculation is indexed to the 15th of the month, as VSNKh does, we get about 115 million commodity roubles.

11 The state budget includes data on the profits of industry in 1921–1922 and 1920–1923, but in reality industry in 1921–1922 turned a profit only in rare cases, and only on a small scale.

The general level of profits of industry in 1922–1923, which were spent predominantly on expanding production, was estimated – accurate figures do not yet exist – at 200–250 million roubles.

According to the preliminary budget of state industry for 1923–1924, 323 million roubles of pure income from industry was expected, of which 147 million roubles were from profits and 176 million roubles from taxes and excises. State expenditures were projected at 65 million roubles in subventions and 26 million roubles for maintenance and concentration. In addition, there were 4.5 million roubles in loans for terms longer than one year, a total therefore of approximately 105 million roubles.

What industry achieved or almost achieved already last year (parity between state expenditures on industry and income from industry) was almost achieved by the transport industry in the current 1923–1924 year, according to budget projections.

In 1922–1923, the income from the transport industry (according to Gosplan figures) was 310 million roubles, the expenditures (projected) were 428 million roubles, the state subsidy for the transport industry amounted to 118 million roubles. In 1922–1923, the state subsidy for the transport industry was projected in the amount only of about 40 million roubles.

In this way, *the state economy of the proletariat* (*taken as a whole*), i.e. state industry, transport, and the already profitable state trade and credit, was clearly becoming profitable and capable of expansion *at the expense of its own resources*.

The upturn in large-scale industry was accompanied by a growth and improvement of the position of the proletariat. The numerical size of the industrial proletariat according to figures from about 3,200 enterprises with three-quarters of all industrial workers (about 850,000 people) reached its minimum by 1 November 1921, and then the number began to rise: for one year from 1 January 1922 to 1 January 1923, the size of the industrial proletariat grew by almost 10% (and the value of products in 1922 in comparison with 1921 grew by 43%).

From 1 January to 1 October 1923, the size of the industrial proletariat (according to labour statistics) grew again by just over 10%.

For the entire (registered) factory-plant and mining industry (according to Gosplan figures), the size of the industrial proletariat comprised:

in 1921–22	1,243,000 people
in 1922–23	1,452,000 people
i.e. more than	209,000 people or 17%

The size of the industrial proletariat was far from reaching the prewar level, comprising in 1922–1923 only 56% of it, i.e. *a little over half*, but it was growing rapidly.

Evidence of this improvement in the situation of the proletariat was the growth of the real wage of the workers.

The average, annual wage of industrial workers comprised (according to Gosplan figures):

Financial year	In prewar roubles	Annual growth in percent
1920–21	100	–
1921–22	123	+23%
1922–23	153	+24%

Real wage grew, then, by *one-and-a-half* times in two years.

And the wage of industrial workers had still not yet reached the prewar level, comprising in October 1923, according to figures encompassing about 900,000 workers in enterprises with more than 250 people, (on average for all of Russia) 62% of the prewar level.[12]

In the capitals, the increase was more significant: thus, in the same month of October 1923, the average wage for all of Russia was 62% of the prewar wage, in Leningrad province 82%, and in Moscow 92%,[13] and for Moscow food industry workers it was even 113% of the prewar wage. However, for mine workers it was 38%, railway workers 46%, metalworkers 52%, and in all other sectors of industry it was over 70%.

12 The working class of many countries of central Europe can by no means boast that their real wage is much higher than the prewar level – quite the contrary.

Thus in March 1923, the real wage of skilled metalworkers as a percentage of the prewar wage comprised (according to the figures of the Statistical Bureau of Profintern): in England 75%, in Austria 63%, in Germany 57%, in Poland 43%, in the USSR in October 1923 52% (data from labour statistics).

In March–June 1923, the real wage of a Berlin labourer was 83% of the real wage of a Moscow labourer, and thus was lower not only in relative terms (in comparison with the prewar level) but also in absolute terms.

13 In January 1924, the wage of a Moscow worker *exceeded* the prewar level, comprising 102% of the prewar wage. But the average wage for all of Russia was still only 63% of the prewar level.

That the intensity of labour in Soviet Russia was no lower, but in fact higher, than before the revolution, is shown by an examination of the aforementioned more than 15 textile enterprises, in which the output per worker in 1922 was 60% of the output in 1912, and the (real) wage was about 50% of the wage in 1912.

Another calculation, undertaken by S. Strumilin, showed that for the first six months of 1923 the daily wage of an industrial worker increased by 5.5%, and labour productivity by 18%.

However low the level reached at a particular time, the fact of the multi-sided improvement of the situation of the proletariat and its material base, large-scale industry, is clear.

But just as certain is the upturn in the national economy as a whole. For small-scale industry, we have the following data on the value of its finished products (for 1920 according to census data, for 1921 and 1922 according to the evaluation of the TsSU in millions of roubles and at prewar prices):

	In millions of roubles	As a percentage of 1920	Annual growth in percent
1920	193	100	–
1921	260	135	+35
1922	413	214	+59

The equivalent figures for the leasing industry are as follows:

	In millions of roubles	As a percentage of 1920	Annual growth in percent
1921	66	–	–
1922	98	–	+48
1923	– no data available		

Small-scale industry, then, was continuing to grow, although it had not yet reached the prewar level (in 1922 it was about three fifths of prewar production).

But far more important is that the upturn was occurring also in the main sector of the small-scale economy – in agriculture. The first year of the *general* upturn in agriculture was this past year of 1923; before this, alongside the clear upturn in agriculture in the central and western part of the USSR, there was also a sharp fall in it in most other regions, under the influence of the extreme poverty, the failed harvest of 1921.

Total production of agriculture comprised (according to the calculations of Prof. N. Oganovskii) the following in prewar prices:

1922	3,995 million roubles
1923	4,540 million roubles

It therefore increased by almost 14%, i.e. *by one seventh in one year*, having reached three quarters of the prewar level of *all* of agriculture and 85–90% of the prewar level of *peasant* agriculture. And this was by no means the result of elemental causes: the harvest in 1923 was significantly worse than the previous year.

This upturn encompassed all sectors (although not to the same degree) and all agricultural regions of the USSR (with the exception of Kirgiziia).

Cultivation grew (according to the TsSU figures) for last year almost by *ten million desiatins*, amounting (according to the calculation of the TsSU) to about a 19% growth.

This includes an increase in sown areas (according to the calculation of the TsSU) that comprised:

for winter rye	21%
for spring wheat	44.5%
for oats	22.5%
for barley	73%
for potatoes	28%

(sown areas decreased only for millet and corn).

1923 was also a year of rebuilding for technical cultivations, i.e. the production of agricultural raw materials for industry.

Their sown areas (according to local data, corresponding to a summary in *Sots. khoziaistvo*) revealed for 1923 the following increases over 1922:

For potatoes, an increase from 2,351,000 to 3,016,000 desiatins, i.e. by 28% (whereby the sown area of potatoes was 11% larger than before the war, when it amounted to 2,718,000 desiatins).

For sugar beets, an increase from 162,000 to 200,000 desiatins, i.e. by 24%.

For sunflower, an increase from 1,470,000 to 1,556,000 desiatins, i.e. by 7% (whereby the sown area of sunflower was almost twice as large as before the war, when it amounted to 817,000 desiatins).

For flax, an increase from 800,000 to 976,000 desiatins, i.e. by 22%.

For hemp, an increase from 535,000 to 670,000 desiatins, i.e. by 25% (whereby the sown area of hemp was 15% larger than before the war, when it amounted to 584,000 desiatins).

For cotton, an increase from 55,000 to 200,000 desiatins, i.e. by 263% (almost four-fold).

For feed grasses, an increase from 540,000 to 731,000 desiatins, i.e. by 35%.

For shag,[14] an increase from 4,300 to 20,000 desiatins, i.e. by 365% (almost five-fold).

For tobacco[15] (in the Caucasus and in the Crimea), an increase from 1,800 to 15,500 desiatins, i.e. by 761% (almost nine-fold).

Livestock-raising (according to the data of Narkomzem of the RSFSR) also showed an increase in the number of livestock, although not as significant as the increase in sown areas in agriculture.

The increase in 1923 over 1922 was:

for horses	7% (including draught horses 5%)
for large cattle	9%
for sheep and goats	18%
for pigs	22%

Here, the increase in *young livestock* is especially rapid, promising an accelerated rebuilding of livestock-raising, which suffered greatly in the famine of 1921–1922 (in comparison with 1916, about two thirds of horses, about three quarters of large cattle, and about half of sheep, goats, and pigs remained).

The increase in young livestock in 1923 over 1922 was:

for horses	16%
for large cattle	25%

The secondary sectors of agriculture also expanded: the number of fowl rose in the central provinces in 1923 compared with 1922 from 30% to 130%.

The upturn in agriculture encompassed all provinces, apart from Kirgiziia. Thus, sown area (we are limiting ourselves here to agriculture) increased as follows:

14 VSNKh data.

15 VSNKh data.

in the grain-consuming region (where the increase in sown area began in 1921)	by 9%
in the grain surplus region	by 24%
in the South-East	by 30%
in Ukraine	by 17%
in Siberia	by 20%
in Kirgiziia it declined, but only	by 6%

This upturn was not, however, just a simple restoration of prewar conditions: in post-revolutionary agriculture, there was a definite shift in the direction of very rapidly increasing *intensive* cultivations, whose sown area in relation to total sown area comprised:

1913	10.5%
1922	11.8%
1923	12.0%

This multifaceted upturn in the entire national economy of the USSR, something which was achieved exclusively by means of *domestic* forces (without any reliance on foreign capital) – is an indisputable fact. Further evidence of it was the *growth in rail freight turnover*, which for 1922–1923 was a full *third* larger than for 1921–1922. This upturn extends both to large-scale industry, which is in the hands of the proletariat, and to petty capitalist and non-capitalist industry and to agriculture.

Here, the relative importance of large-scale industry, transport, and credit, which are in the hands of the proletariat, *has been growing*. In industry, the relative importance of large-scale industry did not see any kind of significant change either in comparison with leased industry (supplying about 5% of production[16]), or in comparison with all of small-scale industry. 65–70% of industrial production comes from large-scale industry, but the fundamental sectors of industry (the production of mineral fuels, metallurgy, etc) are almost exclusively in the hands of the proletarian state. Industry as a whole has grown significantly faster (by 2–3 times) than agriculture. This can be seen in the *growth of the cities*, which had lost a significant part of their population during the Civil War years. From 1920 to 1923, the population of Moscow grew by

16 In July 1923, of the total number of industrial workers, the following percentages were employed in private industry:

in all USSR	4.3%
in Leningrad	7.6%
in Moscow	13.6%

50%, of Leningrad by 45%, of cities of the Central Industrial Region by 20%; on average for all of Russia, the urban population (from data encompassing up to two thirds of the urban population) grew by 10%.

The characteristic relationship in the economy of our Soviet Union between the large-scale economy in the hands of the proletariat and the remaining part of the national economy can be seen *in the market,* and indeed in *domestic* trade.

More than three quarters of wholesale trade (according to the information from a census of urban trade carried out in 1923 by the TsSU) was *in the hands of the state,* and as a percentage of total wholesale turnover, we see the following:

state trade turnover	77%
cooperative trade turnover	8%
private trade turnover	15%

Here, the average turnover of a single state wholesale trade enterprise is almost five times greater than the average turnover of a single private wholesale trade enterprise (the cooperative turnover is almost the same as the private enterprise).

Only *half* of *wholesale-retail* trade was (according to the same data) in the hands of the state and of cooperatives. As a percentage of total wholesale-retail turnover, we see the following:

state trade turnover	39%
cooperative trade turnover	11%
private trade turnover	50%

The average turnover of a single state wholesale-retail trade enterprise was one and a half times larger than of a single private enterprise (and average turnover of a cooperative enterprise was one and a half times smaller than of a private enterprise).

Moscow accounted for almost half of the turnover of both wholesale and wholesale-retail urban trade.

Almost all of urban retail trade – *five sixths* – was in the hands of *private* traders (according to the same data).

As a percentage of total retail urban turnover, we see the following:

state trade turnover	7%
cooperative trade turnover	10%
private trade turnover	83%

Of this 83%, 52% is accounted for by the somewhat more robust trade of permanent institutions and 31% by market trade (the latter is undoubtedly not fully accounted for).

The average turnover of a single state enterprise, and also of a cooperative retail enterprise, was almost four times that of a private enterprise. Moscow accounted for one fifth of urban retail trade.

There are, unfortunately, no general statistics on rural trade. The taxed turnovers from rural trade, calculated by equalising collections (in the second quarter of 1923 according to Narkomfin data) were seven times smaller than the taxed turnovers of urban trade using the same method. In reality, however, the significance of rural trade is probably much greater.

Nevertheless, the above data on the correlation of various forms of urban trade are also characteristic, by all appearances, of total urban and rural trade as a whole.

Rural wholesale trade is insignificant and comprises (according to the same Nakomfin data) barely a *thirtieth* of urban wholesale trade. The same is also true of rural wholesale-retail trade, which is less than a *twenty fifth* of urban wholesale-retail trade. Since wholesale and wholesale-retail rural trade scarcely eluded statistical accounting in significant amounts, then these data indicate that urban wholesale and wholesale-retail trade accounts for almost all wholesale and wholesale-retail trade.

Retail rural trade, according to Narkomfin data, accounts for more than nine tenths of all (as calculated by Narkomfin) rural trade, and in reality even more than this, for retail trade is undoubtedly accounted for very incompletely. Of its total turnover, cooperative trade turnover (according to Tsentrosoiuz) accounts for 15–20%, i.e. about the same share accounted for in retail urban trade by state and cooperative trade combined; the remainder – 80–85% – is accounted for by private trade (as much as 90% by other estimates).

Thus, large-scale wholesale trade, which has the possibility to affect all of trade as a whole, is almost entirely in the hands of the state; half of medium wholesale-retail trade (the larger-scale trade) is in the hands of the state and the cooperatives, and half (the smaller-scale trade) is in the hands of private traders, i.e. trade capital; retail trade, predominantly small-scale, is almost entirely in the hands of private traders.

Changes in the correlation between state and cooperative trade on the one hand, and private trade on the other, can be ascertained with a certain degree of accuracy (in the absence of direct data on total trade) from information on the sales of those state enterprises which are subordinated to VSNKh and the Moscow SNKh.

About *two thirds* of the sales of state enterprises were accounted for by sales to state organs (i.e. by trade between state organs). The share of private individuals, judging from these data in 1922–1923, *did not grow*. Thus, in the course of 1922–1923 private individuals accounted for the following percentages of total sales (for the months from October 1922 to September 1923): 31, 20, 12, 17, 8, 12, 12, 10, 15, 14, 14, 10.

Foreign trade was completely in the hands of the state (the foreign trade monopoly). In 1922–1923, the till then constantly passive trade balance became an active trade balance. Exports surpassed imports by 23 million roubles. At the same time, by the end of 1923 the *welfare* imports [*blagotvoritel'nyi vvoz*] (Pomgol shipments), a result of the terrible famine from 1921–1923, almost disappeared. In 1921–1922, *welfare* imports were almost triple exports, in 1922–1923 they were a little more than a third of exports, and in the final quarter of 1923 they were *less than 0.5 % of exports*, i.e. they had almost vanished.

By volume, however, foreign trade comprised in 1922–1923 only one *sixth* of its volume in 1913.

The export of grain began on a significant scale only in 1923, for the most part in the final months of that year.

Credit, in reality, was also completely in the hands of the state.

The Soviet rouble in the course of these three years also depreciated even more quickly than before[17] (it depreciated especially quickly during the famine and at the start of the current year), but the significance of issuing (printing) paper money as a means of covering the state deficit declined thanks to the growth in income from taxes, and, more recently, from domestic loans as well.

In 1922–1923, the deficit comprised about 39 % of all expenditures, projected for the current year to be 20 %, and thus almost *half*.

The contemporary state of Soviet finances is already characterised by the fact that monetary reform might be placed on the agenda of priority tasks and adopted.

If we can add to all this that the Union of Soviet Republics is the only country in the entire world to establish – on the basis of the recognition of the market – an 'alliance of two classes – the workers and the peasants' satisfactory to both sides, that complete, unbreakable internal order reigns, ensuring the normal course of economic construction, then we can conclude that the Soviet

17 It is worth noting that the Soviet rouble is by no means the currency that depreciated the most. The German mark outstripped it long since; currently, the officially recognized depreciation of the Soviet rouble is 1:50 billion, while the German mark is 1:1 trillion, i.e. twenty times greater. From time to time, the rate of depreciation of the Polish mark also outstripped that of the Soviet rouble.

system is not only capable of surviving, but has also created the necessary conditions for the development of the productive forces of the whole of society. Alongside the upturn in productive forces of the whole of society, there has also been a quantitative and qualititative upturn in large-scale industry, which is in the hands of the proletariat, and a growth and upturn in the proletariat itself.

In short, *the proletarian regime showed itself to be a progressive regime, and the new society created by the proletariat is also being built under the difficult conditions of retreat from the proletarian revolution*, in which a new offensive is being prepared (and in part has already been prepared).

The very first peaceful year has revealed the gigantic, internal forces of the proletarian revolution.

And it is precisely this fact that unsettles world capital. Compared with earlier, the free Russian proletarians have achieved the same standard of living as the proletarians, the wage slaves of world capital in its new colony, in Germany, and if not today, then tomorrow, they will be relatively better off materially. What can be more dangerous, though, than free proletarians, living without capitalists, without an enterprise owner who 'gives' them work, and who are no worse off in relative terms than the wage slaves of capital?

The growth of internal power increases the external danger to the world's first proletarian republic. But the proletarian republic, in its struggle with the external capitalist threat, relies not only upon its own forces, but to a certain extent also upon the forces of the still enslaved world proletariat, and this compels capital to act with caution and even forces it, as recently happened in England, to officially recognise the Soviet state of the proletariat.[18]

The international situation of the USSR has grown stronger, even as the danger of a new attack by international capital on the Union of Soviet Republics has also grown, an attack on this unbearable thorn in the side of the capitalist globe.

But with the upturn in the Soviet society, which was developed by the proletariat, and with the upturn in the proletariat itself, not only external, but also internal, peril grows. For the New Economic Policy gives those economic forms that are not in the hands of the proletariat, including capitalist forms, the chance to survive and to develop.

To the extent that the New Economic Policy has been put into effect, *the rule of market spontaneity* has grown.

---

18 Under the pressure of England's recognition, a number of our bourgeois states have also recognized the USSR.

During the transition to the New Economic Policy, elemental market forces were restricted both in scale and form. The proletariat sought to restrict free trade within the framework of *local* trade turnover, and product exchange within the framework of *moneyless* product exchange, in accordance with which an *in-kind* food supply tax was the basis of the taxation system.

The retreat, however, was not limited to this. The proletariat quickly had to *remove* all limits on the market that affected both the scale and form of market activity. The freedom of local trade turnover, having thrown off territorial restrictions, turned into the freedom of trade turnover in all Russia. Moneyless product exchange broke through the forms restricting it, and was replaced by complex commodity-monetary and credit relations, just as the in-kind taxation system was replaced by a monetary taxation system.

There was the impression that the New Economic Policy gave birth to the market. In reality, however, it was not the New Economic Policy that gave birth to the market, but rather the market, forced underground during the Civil War era, that gave birth to and advanced the New Economic Policy of the proletariat. It cleared the way for the full completion of the anti-feudal revolution.

Given the colossal scale of the shifts, caused by war and revolution in the national economy of Russia, the growing dominance of market spontaneity found expression in the extraordinarily wide-reaching fluctuations in market conditions.

Their starting point was a sharp disruption in the relationship between industry and agriculture that existed before the war. At the start of the New Economic Policy, industrial production, for instance, was one *sixth* of the prewar level, while agricultural production was almost *three quarters* of the prewar level, i.e. in relative terms, the decline in industry was about five times larger than the decline in agriculture. Of course, at the same time agriculture became, to a far greater degree than it had been before the war, a producer for its own consumption, and this factor moderated somewhat the disruption that had occurred in the relationship between industry and agriculture. On the other hand, however, Russian agriculture before the war was the agrarian basis not only for Russian but also for European industry, and the rupture in relations with the world economy deprived it of foreign sales markets.

The result of all this was that a relative surplus of agricultural products began to appear, just as the war was coming to an end and the multimillion-man army was beginning to be reduced. In 1921, despite the partial failed harvest, the prices for industrial products (compared with prewar prices) were higher than for agricultural products.

The extraordinary failed harvest and famine of 1922 sharply changed the state of affairs, but only for *seven* months (from January to July 1922).

From August 1922, prices for industrial products once again began to exceed prices for agricultural products, and moreover, even more strongly.[19]

If in April 1922 industrial products were one and a half times cheaper than agricultural products (compared with the prewar period), in April 1923 they were already almost two times more expensive, and by October 1923 more than *three times more expensive*, than agricultural products.

This was the result of a harvest, which (according to TsSU calculations) in 1922 brought in 40% more grain than in 1921 (2.8 billion poods compared with 2 billion). Russia, which *imported* grain in 1922, once again became a land of cheap grain, and began exporting it. By setting high prices for industrial products and low prices for agricultural prices, the market spurred the development of industry, which had been more strongly squeezed than agriculture. But the colossal scale of the price shifts (within a year and a half, the ratio of the prices of industrial products to those of agricultural products had increased a little less than *five-fold*) was an expression of the complete dominance of the elemental forces of the market.

The crisis that developed in autumn 1923 was the start of a new spontaneous shift in the *opposite* direction (a fall in the prices of industrial products and a rise in the prices of agricultural products), as a result of which for *six* months the difference between industrial prices and agricultural prices almost *vanished* (in October of the previous year, this difference was 220%, by mid-March it was only a little more than 30%).

Price shifts of this kind – the difference between industrial prices and agricultural prices increased five-fold in the course of *a year and a half*, and then by *two and a half times* in the course of *six months* – were undoubtedly gigantic price shifts, huge waves tossed up by the elemental forces of the market.

They led to sales crises, alternately in industry and in agriculture, they held back the upturn in productive forces (which would have happened even more quickly without them), and they were a really serious economic burden. For almost a year, the 'scissors' problem has occupied the attention of the entire Soviet public as its core economic and social problem.

19 A graphic illustration of this price differential – the increase in the prices for industrial products and the simultaneous decline in the prices for agricultural products – has the appearance of open scissors, which was demonstrated by comrade Trotsky at a congress of our party; consequently, this price differential thus received the well-known name of 'scissors'. [Trotsky used the term 'scissors [*nozhnitsy*]' in his report on industry to the 12th Congress of the party in April 1923, see *Dvenadtsatyi s'ezd RKP* (*bol'shevikov*). *17–25 aprelia 1923 g*. (Moscow: Izdanie RIO VTsIK, 1923), p. 232.]

These price shifts, expressed as sharp fluctuations in the market situation, i.e. the rule of elemental market forces, make it a priority to place certain limits on these elemental forces, to introduce the state *regulation of trade* (drawing not only upon the political, but also on the economic, power of the Soviet state, thereby utilising large-scale industry, transport, credit, and wholesale domestic and foreign trade), i.e. to introduce measures for a real transition to a planned economy, to subordinate the market rather than to be subordinated to it.

The autumn crisis of 1923 gave a boost to a series of measures designed to regulate state trade (stipulating *fixed* prices that are obligatory for state economic organs, etc), measures which left the market (and partly the monetary) forms of economic interactions in place, but fundamentally changed their substance.[20] The monetary reform now under way has brought state intervention in *private* trade as well.

Real successes in matter of the state regulation of trade, drawing on the political and economic power of the Soviet state, allowed for a significant acceleration of the upsurge in the productive forces of the USSR.

Subordination of the market is possible, however, only as a result of the economic victory of the state economy over the private capital that was striving to manage the market in its own interests. But victory requires struggle. Furthermore, the initial period of the New Economic Policy from spring 1921 to autumn 1923–a period of developing elemental market forces, which expanded into ever newer spaces – is characterised not by struggle against a new bourgeoisie, but by collaboration with it, a consequence of the conditions of the transition of the proletariat to the New Economic Policy.

At the moment when, after six years of imperialist and civil war, the proletariat, victorious in the latter war, had the opportunity to take up the task of economic construction, the national economy of Russia was characterised by the following: an extreme decline in the productive forces of the country, a diversion of colossal national economic resources to the needs of the military apparatus, and an extraordinarily deep rupture in economic relations between

20 The specific character of the Soviet economic system became clear during the autumn crisis of 1923, which was weathered without any serious contraction in production, thanks, on the one hand, to the general *deferral of payments* (which to a significant extent served as mutual cover), and, on the other hand, to the upsurge in wages and the additional expansion of the market connected with it, in addition to the expansion of the market that was caused by lower prices. The moratorium on payments, i.e. rejecting the private economic principle, made it possible to wait for the results of this expansion of the market.

urban industry and agriculture. Russia experienced a most terrible *crisis of exhaustion.* Restoring the productive forces of the country and raising the living standards of the popular masses – after the end of the Civil War and once military costs had been sharply cut – relied on a need to overcome the rupture of economic relations between the city with its industry and the countryside with its agriculture. The problem of the economic *alliance* [*smychka*] *of town and countryside* became the *central* problem of the day.

But the necessary *tempo* of this restoration of economic relations between town and countryside could not be achieved by the forces of the economic organisations of the proletariat alone, either in their old form or in their new (commercial) forms. Nor could it be achieved, of course, by the forces of the economically fragmented great mass of the peasantry.

This is why it was necessary to permit and, even, it can be said, to cultivate to a certain extent private, i.e. capitalist, trade, as one of the forms of economic connection between town and countryside, without which the needed tempo of restoration of this connection could not be achieved.

Capital turned out to have something of a virtual monopoly on the restoration of the missing (destroyed) economic connections, something of a virtual *monopoly* in the sphere of *circulation.*[21]

So the period from the start of the New Economic Policy to autumn 1923 is marked by the *coexistence* side by side of capitalist trade on the one hand and state (and cooperative) trade on the other.

One condition of permitting the activity of trade capital was its recognition of the Soviet system, i.e. its activity was on the basis of and within the framework of this system.

That capital accepted these conditions was the result of the proletariat's *victory*; that the proletariat accepted this collaboration with trade capital, however, was the sharpest expression of the proletariat's *retreat.*

Trade capital took full advantage of the opportunities made available to it. Not only in the sense of developing its trading activity, i.e. essentially by restoring the economic connections between the town and village, but also by making use of state economic organs, above all utilising and deploying their resources, which became one of the basic forms of primitive capitalist accumulation.

This utilisation took many different paths, more often hidden paths than obvious ones. Thus, a study of the credit practices of the banks by the RKI

21 As we saw, in spring 1923 five-sixths of retail trade in the cities (and probably more in the countryside) was in the hands of private traders.

revealed that *direct* bank credit extended by banks to private firms was small, but indirect credit by accounting for bills of exchange of state economic organs played a larger role.

So, private individuals received the following:

Direct credits (as percentage of total)		**Indirect credits via accounting for bills of exchange of state organs (as percentage of total)**		
credits:		accounted-for bills of exchange		
In State Bank	0.3% (1922–23)	0.6% in January, 0.7% in February 1924		
In Industrial Bank.	7.4% (1922–23)	Bills of exchange for textile industry		Bills of exchange for state trade organs
		in Dec. 1923	18.1%	42%
		in Jan. 1924	12.2%	
		in Feb. 1924	8.7%	63.4%
In Moscow State Bank on 1 November 1923		Textile industry	33.9%	
Credit re bills of exchange	2.3%	Trade organs	14.3%	
Term loans	10%	Silicate industry	16.1%	
		Match syndicate	41.2%	
		Rubber trust	33.5%	

Consequently, a not insignificant part of the credits extended to state economic organs in fact fell into the hands of private individuals.

An RKI study of stock exchange transactions showed that private individuals received more cash for their products when selling them to state economic organs, than state organs received when selling to private individuals; and that, by contrast, private individuals received more credit when buying from state organs, than state organs received when buying from private individuals.

To these and any other legal transactions must also be added the direct paying off (bribing) of employees of state economic organs, as a result of which these organs, as a series of legal proceedings has shown, suffered millions in losses.

In other words, capital tries (and partly succeeds) to turn the state economic organs into an (illegal) tool of capitalist exploitation.

Collaboration with trade capital led to a simultaneous growth in the power both of the proletarian state economy and of trade capital. The New Economic Policy was not only, as it is often unilaterally described, *a period of primitive socialist accumulation*, but also *a period of primitive capitalist accumulation*, which was no less predatory than other periods of this kind. In one year, 1922–1923, trade capital pocketed many *hundreds* of millions of gold roubles from the meagre production of the impoverished land of the workers and peasants.

As a result, in 1923 trade capital kept hold of half of all wholesale-retail trade and almost all retail trade, i.e. sitting *at the nexus of* city and countryside, it was able to speculate on the aforementioned fluctuations in the market situation, increasing their scale.

The autumn crisis of 1923 was not only a turn away from retreat before the elemental forces of the market and a move towards attempts to regulate it, but also a turn away from any collaboration with trade capital to fight against it.

The first consequence of the crisis was that industry and trade *clashed with each other*.

If prior to this (in the period of rising prices for industrial products) trade drew most of its benefits from price increases, then industry could also sell its products at increased prices, although not as high as the traders' prices. But with the onset of the crisis, sales could be achieved only under conditions of lowered prices, and break-even sales were only possible for industry if fees and profits, the bulk of overhead costs, were *cut*.

A further consequence of the crisis was that the former space that allowed for the simultaneous development of *all* aspects of trade, both state (and cooperative) and capitalist trade, disappeared.

Within the narrow framework, which the crisis had created for sales, state (and cooperative) trade inevitably had to come into direct conflict with trade capital.

Collaboration with trade capital was replaced by a struggle against it. Trade capital became the enemy, and displacing it became the basic task of the struggle.

The crisis of autumn 1923 launched, then, the *second* period of the New Economic Policy, the shift *from retreat* to careful and methodical *attack*, to restricting the elemental nature of the market and combatting the trade capital riding its crest.

The shift to the attack on trade capital put the question of cooperatives onto the agenda. It is the task of cooperatives everywhere to fight against capital. In capitalist society, however, this fight does not affect the *foundations* of capitalism – large-scale industry and credit – it is therefore *a struggle within the framework* of the capitalist order, and cooperative ideology is a petty bourgeois dream of discreetly overcoming capitalism without a revolution that upsets petty bourgeois comforts. In Soviet Russia, where industrial and bank capital have already been *fully* expropriated, the cooperatives' struggle against capital, by rooting out its remnants (trade capital), becomes a real fight to destroy it, it takes on a *revolutionary* character. Under the influence of the crisis, Soviet cooperatives began to reorganise, transforming from trade organisations into organisations for fighting against trade capital.

The transition from collaboration with trade capital to fighting against could only weaken the Soviet patriotism of trade capital, which not only had to come to terms with the fact that the halcyon days of predatory primitive accumulation were over, but also had to defend the very possibility of its future development.

A change in economic relations inevitably brings a change in the realm of political relations as well. However, domestic (native) capital (while predominantly trade capital and thus mostly retail trade) cannot in itself become dangerous so soon. The fundamental internal danger is the presence of enormous masses of peasants who have been impoverished by the imperialist war and later by the Civil War,[22] and whose ranks were swelled by agricultural labourers [*batraki*] who received land, and by urban workers who fled during the Civil War from the starving cities to the countryside. All of these masses have land, but not the means to work it. Therefore, at the same time as the number of workers employed in industry grew, so too did the number of unemployed as a result of in-migration from the countryside, a product of the improving living standards of the industrial proletariat. The total number of unemployed on 1 December 1922 was 540,000 according to the VTsSPS. Currently (at the start of 1924) their number has exceeded one million.

Data from 78 provincial towns show that the number of unemployed rose in just over a year (from 1 November 1922 to 1 December 1923) from 319,000 to 767,000, i.e. more than double. The number of unemployed labourers rose from 61,000 to 195,000, i.e. more than triple. The number of unemployed industrial workers rose from 69,000 to 186,000, i.e. almost triple, although the number of employed industrial workers for the same period rose by more than 10 %. Both the number of employed and the number of unemployed industrial workers each rose by more than 100,000 people.

With the growth in industry and towns, the in-migration to the towns of part of the impoverished peasantry, and the freeing-up of their poorly utilised land, this internal danger, which could otherwise arise if the emboldened bourgeoisie tried to exploit their discontent, will recede. But precisely because such a danger exists, one of the most important tasks of the party is to agitate among the impoverished peasants, to bring them over to the side of the proletariat and to support the fastest possible reconstruction of industry. For improvement in the situation of the impoverished peasants also depends on this upturn

22 The poor peasants [*bedniaki*] alone, freed from all taxation, made up by autumn 1924 a quarter of all households. In 1922–1923, they accounted for only a seventh of the land and only a fifteenth of agricultural production (judging from the food tax).

in industry – the possibility of utilising their labour power in industry, and in forestry and construction work.

This task requires that poor peasants be liberated from the influence of trade capital and its agents in the countryside, the kulaks, and that kulaks not be allowed into peasant organisations (especially cooperative organisations), which in the hands of trade capital can become a tool for organising the peasantry around capital and under its leadership. One way of rallying the entire peasantry around the peasant bourgeoisie is the *slogan* of replacing the urge for land with the urge *for the market* as a slogan for *all of the peasantry*. In reality, this slogan for developing market relations among the poor peasants can bring them nothing, for their interest in the market for agricultural products is not as sellers but as buyers. As sellers, they bring a different product to the market, their labour power. This slogan is, on the contrary, merely a tool for deceiving them and for mobilising them under the banner of the peasant bourgeoisie.

Another internal danger emerges because, with the upturn in the country, the demand grows for an organisational intelligentsia (in the economic and political organs of the Soviet state), as does the level of demands placed upon it. The low cultural level and the relatively numerically small Russian proletariat threaten to cause a disparity between the need of the Soviet state and society for an intelligentsia which is proletarian in its class origins, and how to sustain and replenish it. If the workers, who took up these posts during the Civil War,[23] were to be pushed out by a bourgeois intelligentsia, and if, in particular, replenishment (training) of the intelligentsia were to be in its hands, creating (or rather preserving) knowledge of its privileges, then the bourgeoisie would also get the officer corps it needs. This is why raising the cultural level of the proletariat and taking over the replenishment apparatus of the organisational intelligentsia (the schools) is also one of the most important tasks of the party.

Breaking *the monopoly on education* is as much of an urgent task in the fight as the task of breaking the monopoly in the realm of circulation (of trade). This is why it is necessary, above all, to take over higher education.

Higher education has expanded significantly under Soviet power. The total number of students in them in 1914 was more than 65,000 (according to data provided by 55 of a total of 64 higher educational establishments). By 1921 (at the beginning of the New Economic Policy), the number was already over 197,000. On 1 October 1923, it was about 132,000, i.e. still *double* the total in 1914.

23 Currently in the party about 100,000 workers are not at the workbench, i.e. not working in factories and plants but rather in Soviet (economic, administrative, military, etc), trade union, and party organs. These 100,000 workers form the skeleton of the proletarian state.

Of this latter number, over 19,000, i.e. a seventh, were workers and the children of workers.[24] *19,000 workers in institutions of higher education!* Of the recent admissions in autumn 1923, already a quarter (25%, and in the capital cities 30%) of those accepted into institutions of higher education were workers and the children of workers. Furthermore, about 36,000 individuals, including over 22,000 workers (62.5%), studied at workers' faculties (*rabochie fakul'tety*) (preparing them for university).

Thus, in total, about *42,000* workers[25] received or prepared in the near future to receive higher education. This is more than half of all university students in 1914. Already by the autumn of next year, 1925, universities will have graduated *three thousand* proletarians.

The third internal danger is directly linked to the fact that the monopoly on education of the old bourgeois intelligentsia and the representatives of the former ruling classes has not yet been broken. This danger is a separation of the state Soviet apparatus from the masses of the working class and peasantry, to the extent that the connections between the representatives of bourgeois intelligentsia employed in state Soviet apparatus and the former ruling classes, connections which were destroyed by the violent whirlwind of revolution, have been restored.

The main cause of the current *Soviet bureaucratism* is a disconnect between the tasks (social functions) of the new state apparatus, including the economic apparatus, and its personnel makeup; it is the resultant disconnect between the power of the still numerically and low-skilled new proletarian intelligentsia, active in this apparatus, and the tasks that confront it; and it is the inadequate connection between this proletarian intelligentsia (and this means the state apparatus as well) and the masses of the working class and peasantry.

Mass training of a new proletarian (and peasant) intelligentsia allows for the actual renewal of the state Soviet apparatus in the near future. And the necessary alliance between this new intelligentsia (and this also means the state apparatus) and the mass of the working class is facilitated by the proletarianisation of our party currently under way: the inclusion into the party, in addition to the 50,000 workers engaged in production and the 100,000 working in state, trade union, and party bodies, of another 150,000 workers engaged in production, at the same time that the 200,000-strong non-proletarian, peas-

24 Over 36,000 students (about 28%) were peasants and the children of peasants. The remainder were mostly Soviet clerical employees and their children (about 32%). 14,000 students (about 11%) were members of the party and the Komsomol. All figures refer not to the USSR, but only to the RSFSR.

25 And about 45,000 peasants.

ant and intelligentsia, portion of the party is contracting. Thanks to this, our party includes in its ranks up to one *eighth* of the current number of industrial workers.

This task to fight against bureaucratism is bound up with a closely connected older task – *the continuation of economic construction,* in which the selection and training of suitable people for appropriate positions is one of the most important moments (requiring a number of years for completion), alongside the painstaking work of organisationally restructuring and adapting the various state organs to each other and to the market, i.e. to the mass of private households.

The New Economic Policy of the proletariat began as a policy of *retreat,* but not as a hasty retreat, rather as a retreat in order to *gather forces* (and inevitably this retreat gave the enemy the chance to gather their forces as well).

This gathering of forces allowed us in autumn 1923 to stem any further retreat and to begin the transition to a careful methodical attack on the elemental nature of the market and on trade capital.

This caution was justified because the basic tasks of the revolution in Russia have been resolved and the Russian proletariat is facing class-revolutionary tasks not within Russia, but outside of it – on the world stage.

Within Russia, the task is *to make use of the conditions, created by the revolution, for the construction of socialism,* to overcome the elemental nature of the market, to fight against the remnants of capitalism, to prepare also for a change in the personnel makeup of the state (economic, military, administrative, etc) apparatus, to improve the work of this apparatus, and so on.

This is the way to prepare for the impending, great, world-historically significant battles between the proletariat and capital, and also to make way for the transition to a socialist economy and a great technological revolution.

The three-year experience of this country of 130 million has shown that this path is the path to ultimate victory for the proletariat.

Glossary

All-Russian Central Council of Trade Unions [*Vserossiiskii Tsentral'nyi Sovet Professional'nykh Soiuzov* or VTsSPS] was elected by the All-Russian Conference of Trade Unions that was established in June 1917. Trade unions were caught in a dilemma due to their betimes interrupted legal status in Russia since the 1905 revolution. Should they be independent legal trade unions on the model of the mass Western socialist trade unions dedicated to incremental gains in workers' lives or should they embrace their often semi-legal status and dedicate themselves to a proletarian overthrow? With rising Bolshevik influence in the latter half of 1917, and especially once the Bolshevik dictatorship of the proletariat had become a reality, this dilemma became an existential one for the role of trade unions in the Soviet state. As trade unions in the course of the Civil War lost their influence in industry to government bodies, various factions inside the CPSU argued for degrees of more or less subordination, but the die was cast. In the course of the 1920s, they became a subordinate, strictly hierarchically organised arm of the Communist Party of the Soviet Union (CPSU). For a while under the New Economic Policy, trade unions were afforded some latitude as a bulwark against harmful bureaucratism in the state apparatus, although they were stripped of any of the class overtones of the prerevolutionary trade union battles. Culturally, trade unions were to fulfill a role, like the Red Army, as Lenin's 'School of Communism'. See also *Central Union of Consumer Societies; Food Detachments; Tsiperovich.*

All-Russian Committee for Relief of the Starving [*Vserossiiskii komitet pomoshchi golodaiushchim* or Pomgol] was set up in 1921 to support the starving during the 1921 famine in Russia. It was an umbrella term for two organisations: the All-Union Public Committee for the Relief of the Starving [*Vserossiiskii obshestvennyi komitet pomoshchi golodaiushchim*] set up by Patriarch Tikhon, the Patriarch of Moscow and All Russia; and the Central Commission of the Relief for the Starving [*Tsentral'naia komissiia pomoshchi golodaiushchim*] under VTsIK, and headed by Mikhail Kalinin, chair of VTsIK. See also *Prokopovich.*

All-Russian Extraordinary Commission for Combatting Counter-Revolution, Speculation, and Corruption in Office [*Vserossiiskaia Chrezvychainaia Komissiia po bor'be s kontr-revoliutsii, spekuliatsiei i prestupleniiami po dolzhnosti*, Cheka, or VChK] was created on December 20 (7), 1917 under Feliks Dzherzhinsky. Originally set up as an investigative body, the Cheka quickly acquired the power to arrest, imprison, interrogate with torture, and summarily execute often ill-defined enemies, including counterrevolutionaries, enemy agents, speculators, insurgents, and so on. Its influence, particularly under the conditions of the Civil War, extended into all areas of Soviet life, including the economy, transport, the military, and political organisations. With the change in political and economic emphasis initially ushered in by the New Economic Policy, the Cheka's methods became incompatible with the new era of economic, social, and political relaxation that marked these first years of the 1920s. Disbanded by decree on February 6, 1922, it was superseded immediately by the State Political Administration [*Gosudarstvennoe politicheskoe upravlenie*, or GPU] under the People's Commissariat of Internal Affairs [*Narodnyi komissariat vnutrennykh del*, or NKVD] of the RSFSR. With the formation of the USSR in 1922, it was expanded into the Unified State Political Administration [*Ob'edinennoe gosudarstvennoe politicheskoe upravlenie*, or OGPU]. Always dictatorial by design, the OGPU was tasked by the 1924 constitution with continuing the struggle against political and economic counterrevolution, espionage, and banditry, although not with the abandon of the earlier Cheka.

Antaeus was the son of the gods Poseidon and Gaea, one of the Gigantes in Greek mythology. He drew strength from the earth (Gaea) whenever he was in direct contact with her.

Arshin See *Units of Weights and Measures.*

Bagging (*meshechnichestvo*, variously, bagging, bag-trading, sack-trading, shuttle-trading, or profiteering). Baggers (*meshechniki*, variously, sack-traders, or bag-traders) conducted small-scale goods-trading, often grain and other foodstuffs, but also low-grade tobacco [*makhorka*], salt, and even currency. Initially a response to wartime shortages in 1916, baggers subsequently sought to circumvent the Provisional Government's grain monopoly on the railways, shuttling from place to place with bags or sacks [*meshki*] of grain often stolen from trains. During the Civil War, baggers continued their activities in the increasingly shortage-riven economy, as the new Soviet government sought to control food and goods supply by eliminating private trade and introducing a system of food allocation through ration cards. At times the target of campaigns by the government to stem their illegal but often indispensable activities, baggers were often denounced as speculators, although their activities had many motives from personal profit to self-survival. This was no truer than in the brutal famine of 1921, when they became an explicit target of the Cheka's attentions. This informal or illegal distribution of necessary products has been a common feature of Soviet life. See *New Economic Policy; Sukharevka.*

Batrak **(farmhand or agricultural labourer)** See *Sociopolitical classifications.*

Bedniak **(poor peasant)** See *Sociopolitical classifications.*

Bourgeois specialists (*spetsy*) See *Sociopolitical classifications.*

Brest Peace referred to the Brest-Litovsk Treaty signed on March 3, 1918 between Soviet Russia and the Central Powers. It was a cornerstone of the Bolshevik slogan of 'Peace, Bread, and Land' designed to win over a fractious and divided population that had experienced the tribulations and privations of world war. It alienated the Allied Powers which had wanted to keep Russia in the war. Despite efforts to maneuver through an impossible situation, most notably their rather quixotic demand of 'peace without annexations and indemnities', the Bolsheviks were ultimately forced to cede the Polish, Baltic, and part of the White Russian provinces, among other areas, to the Central Powers, and to recognise German-occupied Ukraine and the independence of Finland. Severe hardships were threatened by other treaty provisions, including payment of a prohibitive compensation in gold roubles for losses caused to Germany during the war, but the treaty was set aside by the armistice of November 11, 1918, and abrogated under the Treaty of Versailles. Among the economists debating whither Russia economically in the early years of the Soviet Republic, the Brest Peace was an object-lesson of the worst instincts of predatory and powerful capitalism. Kritsman regarded it as the clearest sign that German imperialism wanted to destroy a militarily helpless Soviet Russia, and that it would stop at nothing to defend world capitalism by strangling the new Communist state in the womb.

Bukharin, Nikolai Ivanovich (1888–1938) was a leading Marxist theorist of revolutionary pedigree, having been a Bolshevik since 1906. From 1907, he was a student in the Economics Department of the Faculty of Law of Moscow University, when he also agitated amongst the trade unions. He suffered periods of detainment by the Okhrana for his revolutionary activities and was sentenced to internal exile. In 1912, he fled abroad to Western Europe, where he came to know Lenin. He spent a peripatetic five years moving around Europe, engaged in often illegal *émigré* activities on behalf of the Russian revolutionary movement, and deepening his study of Marxist theory. He returned to Russia in May 1917, but only after periods of arrest in Japan and by local authorities in Cheliabinsk. He participated in the armed insurrection in Moscow in October 1917. He was a Central Committee member from 1917–34, and a full member of the Politburo from 1924–29. From December 1917 to February 1918 he was editor of the newspaper *Pravda*; from 1919–29, a member of the Executive Committee of the Comintern; and from 1924, an editor of the journal *Bol'shevik*. Bukharin found himself in opposition to Lenin at certain junctures, notably over the Peace of Brest-Litovsk. Bukharin's most famous publication, perhaps, was his 1920 *Economics of the Transitional Period* [*Ekonomika perekhodnogo perioda*], a turn away from his early embrace of the policies of 'war communism' and their assault on capitalist economic fundamentals, and a turn towards the New Economic Policy. Despite Bukharin's reputation as the darling of the party, this volume was quickly criticized by Lenin as insufficiently Marxist in its conceptions. Bukharin was too important an economic authority in the early 1920s to be safe to ignore, and Kritsman acknowledged this in his foreword. He did so somewhat backhandedly however, comparing his own concrete analysis of the socialist revolution to Bukharin's abstract analysis. Bukharin's future was not secure. In the intraparty struggles of the mid-1920s, he sided with Stalin, Zinoviev and Kamenev against Trotsky. From 1929 he was prominent in the Supreme Council of the National Economy [*Vysshii Sovet Narodnogo Khoziaistvo*, or VSNKh] of the USSR. With his slogan of 'Enrichissez-vous!', Bukharin's moderate path to peasant prosperity, as a prerequisite of future industrialisation in Soviet Russia, soon placed him at odds with Stalin's drive for forced, mass industrialisation and collectivisation. He was expelled from the Politburo, and from his posts in *Pravda* and in the Comintern, in 1929. In early 1937 he was expelled from the Central Committee and the party. He was arrested in February 1937, and tried in a show trial (the Trial of the Twenty-One) in March of the following year. He was shot on 15 March 1938. See also *Preobrazhenskii.*

Central Administrations [*glavnye upravleniia* or glavki] were administrative units in a ministry or other central institution in the early Soviet economic system. They were responsible to the Supreme Council of the National Economy for devising and enacting plans of activity in various sectors of the economy (e.g. Glavneft', Glavles, Tsentrotekstil', and so on). Vertically organised, they were often cumbersome bodies in charge of hundreds or thousands of plants. Jurisdictional disputes often arose between the central administrations and the regional councils of the national economy [*sovnarkhozy*]s. Kritsman discusses the system of central administrations at length. See also *Councils of the National Economy; Supreme Council of the National Economy.*

Central Statistical Administration [*Tsentral'noe Statisticheskoe Upravlenie* or TsSU] was set up by Sovnarkom in 1918 as the TsSU RSFSR, becoming the TsSU SSSR in 1923. It was the main statistical agency of the Soviet state, responsible for gathering and publishing a regular statistical accounting of all branches of the economy. It was the professional home for many of the economists, demographers, and statisticians featured in Kritsman's work on the state of the early Soviet economy.

Central Union of Consumer Societies [*Tsentral'nyi soiuz potrebitel'skikh obshchestv* or Tsentrosoiuz] was the body to which all consumer cooperative associations were forcibly subordinated in 1918. The cooperative system was organised territorially under Tsentrosoiuz, from basic cooperatives to regional unions [*raisoiuz*] to provincial unions [*gubsoiuz*]. As long as the NEP was in force, Tsentrosoiuz was able to reassert the older principles of cooperative activity, including joint-stock arrangements, admission fees, and elective managements, and to move away from the surplus grain seizures of 'war communism' to food taxes that permitted peasants to retain surplus crops for exchange through cooperatives. See also *All-Russian Central Council of Trade Unions.*

Cheka See *All-Russian Extraordinary Commission for Combatting Counter-Revolution, Profiteering, and Corruption.*

Commission for the Utilisation of Material Resources [*Komissiia po ispol'zovaniiu material'nykh resursov*, or Komissiia Ispol'zovaniia, or KI] was set up in 1918 and, once its apparatus was in place, assumed the functions of the Central Committee for Production in mid-1920. Kritsman was chair from 1920–21. Under the VSNKh, the Commission compiled lists of available products for distribution, determined how they were to be allocated, and assessed the demand for and supply of these products. As it dawned on VSNKh leaders that Sovnarkom would never cede the functions of its economic commissariats to VSNKh, the planned allocation of resources implicit in the commission's charge was undermined somewhat. Allocation decisions were also subject to military needs during the Civil War. Still, the Commission made impressive gains in drawing up plans of utilisation for multiple products, notably essential foodstuffs.

Committees of Poor Peasants [*Komitety derevenskoi bednoty* or kombedy; in Ukraine, *Komitety nezamozhnikh selian* or *komnezamozhi*] were set up in 1918 as organs of Soviet power in the countryside to help implement the policies of 'war communism'. Under conditions of critical food shortages, they were charged with distributing grain, assisting local food-supply, and redistributing 'hidden surpluses' from 'kulaks' to poorer strata of the peasantry. As such, they were also intended as instruments of socialist 'levelling' policies, an effort to combat the influence of the traditional peasant commune. The original intent was to exclude certain classes of peasants from membership in the kombedy, although persistent local autonomy and self-interest did not always ensure this. By late 1918, ca. 130,000 local committees existed across European Russia. *Komnezamozhi* were set up in Ukraine in 1919 after Soviet power had been restored there. Regional factors often meant that these committees could be helpful or decidedly unhelpful to Bolshevik grain procurement policies during the Civil War years. Indeed, kombedy became unpopular among local peasants when grain requisitioning was at its most violent, sparking disturbances, even uprisings, by peasants across European Russia in the course of 1918. By early 1919, many kombedy had been abolished, their functions assumed by newly elected local soviets, which some of their members joined. Here too, though, Bolshevik power was exercised less through local soviets than through armed grain-requisitioning detachments under 'war communism'.

Cossacks belonged to centuries-old military communities in Ukraine and Southern Russia, which had historically been deployed by successive tsars at critical moments and had gained certain privileges in return for that military service. In June 1918 the Soviet government leveled the Cossack communities with the rest of the communities in these regions. Cossacks saw action on both sides of the fighting during the Civil War, some for the Reds, others for the Whites.

Council of Labour and Defense [*Sovet Truda i Oborony*, STO] was the successor in December 1920 to the Council of Workers' and Peasants' Defense [*Sovet rabochei i krest'ianskoi oborony*] that had been set up two years earlier under Lenin's chairmanship. STO's main responsibility was the coordinated guidance of military economic matters in the new Soviet Russia. The chair of Sovnarkom was appointed chair of

STO, its members were the people's commissars, the head of the Worker and Peasant Inspection [Rabkrin], and the chairman of the All-Russian Central Council of Trade Unions [VTsSPS].

Councils of the National Economy [*Sovet Narodnogo khoziaistva*, sovnarkhozy] were subordinate to the VSNKh and were responsible for administering the economy at the local level in cooperation with local soviets and workers' councils. By mid-1918, there were 7 regional, 38 provincial, and 69 district councils. They sometimes found themselves in conflict jurisdictionally with the central administrations (glavki) that were spawned by VSNKh to control specific branches of the economy, such as textiles, oil, timber, and so on. See also *Supreme Council of the National Economy*.

Council of People's Commissars [*Sovet Narodnykh Komissarov* or Sovnarkom] was formed on 27 October 1917 by a decree adopted at the Second All-Russian Congress of Soviets, as the government of the new Soviet state. Trotsky counselled that these titles were less 'bourgeois' than minister and cabinet. It became the Council of Ministers [*Sovet ministrov*] in 1946. The first Sovnarkom was chaired by Lenin, and included leading Bolsheviks of the time, including Trotsky, Stalin, Lunacharskii, Vladimir Antonov-Ovseenko, Rykov, among others. A significant number of this original group were executed in the purges of the 1930s.

Czechoslovak Legion was made up of Czech and Slovak soldiers who volunteered to fight in the First World War on the Entente side in the hope of winning later Allied support for the independence of their ancestral homes in the Austro-Hungarian Empire. Buoyed by the support of Czech and Slovak political *émigrés*, their numbers grew to 100,000. After three years' war service in support of the tsarist army, the legionnaires experienced a rapid and radical change in the constellation of political forces around them after the October Revolution. Mistrusted by the Bolsheviks, the Legion was permitted to be evacuated across Siberia (so as not to be recruited by the White forces) and ultimately to France for continued fighting on the Entente side. With the German occupation of Western territories of Soviet Russia after the Brest Peace, evacuation proved slow, stretching the legionnaires along the railway from Penza to Vladivostok. In May 1918, the soldiers came into conflict with Hungarian POWs being evacuated westwards, and Trotsky, Commissar for Military and Naval Affairs, ordered that the Legion be disarmed. The legionnaires refused and rose up against the Bolsheviks. After a series of impressive successes in Siberia against the Red Army, the Legion moved westwards, finding common cause with anti-Bolshevik White governments on the way. As the Red Army continued to grow in organisation and effectiveness, the Legion eventually succumbed, abandoning Kolchak to his fate, and signing an armistice for safe passage to Vladivostok in early 1920, whence they were eventually evacuated to Europe. See also: *Brest Peace; Denikin*; *Dutov*; *Iudenich*; *Krasnov*; *Wrangel'*.

Denikin, Anton Ivanovich (1872–1947) was a prominent Russian military leader with battle credentials garnered as a general in the tsarist imperial army during the First World War, as Chief of Staff to Kornilov (whose coup attempt he supported), as Commander of the Southwestern Front after the February Revolution, and as Commander-in-Chief of the armed forces of South Russia during the Civil War. After some initial successes against the Red Army, his forces suffered defeat at Orel in late 1919, after which they were in near constant retreat. For a brief while, he formally – but unenthusiastically – succeeded the defeated General Kolchak as Supreme Ruler [*Verkhovnyy pravitel'*]. Denikin left Crimea for Istanbul and later London. In the emigration, he led a peripatetic existence but kept up a consistent critique of Bolshevik Russia. He survived various abduction attempts by the Soviets and died of natural causes in 1947 in the USA. See also: *Czechoslovak Legion*; *Dutov*; *Iudenich*; *Krasnov*; *Wrangel'*.

Desiatina See *Units of Weights and Measures.*

Don Cossacks See *Cossacks*; *Krasnov*.

Dutov, Aleksandr Il'ich (1879–1921) was ataman of the Orenburg Cossacks who joined the White movement. He was assistant commander of the Cossack regiment during The First World War. After the February Revolution, he became deputy chair of the Provisional Council of the Union of Cossack Forces [*Vremennyi sovet soiuza kazach'ikh voisk*], and then chair of the Second All-Russian Cossack Congress [*Obshchekazach'ii s'ezd*] in June 1917. By September, he was leader of the Orenburg Cossack Army. After the October Revolution, Dutov led a revolt against the Red Army in Orenburg, which by mid-1918 with the aid of the Czechoslovak Legion, had become a full-fledged counter-revolutionary uprising against Soviet power in the Urals. His inability to persuade other White generals to join forces with him undercut his uprising, and he was defeated by the Red Army. In 1920, he led his army out of Russia to China. In February 1921, he fell victim there to a Cheka assassin. See also *Czechoslovak Legion*; *Denikin*; *Iudenich*; *Krasnov*; *Wrangel'*.

Estate [*soslovie*]. See *Sociopolitical classifications.*

Fal'kner, Semen Anisimovich (1890–1938) was a Russian economist with expertise in monetary policy and economic history. His ideas on a near-limitless devaluation of money (*emissionoe khoziaistvo*) made him attractive to various economic schools at this time, not least Kritsman's group. Educated in Taganrog and in Germany prior to the revolution, he became a professor at Moscow University from 1917. Unaffiliated with any political party, he nonetheless was permitted to apply his expertise to the first steps of the Soviet state. He worked as a consultant to VSNKh from 1918, as one of the organisers of the Institute of Economic Studies [*Institut ekonomicheskikh issledovanii*] under Narkomfin from 1919, as a professor in the Department of Theoretical Economics in the Faculty of the Social Sciences from 1921 to 1925, and as a frequent consultant to state bodies in matters of planning, finance, and foreign trade from 1925. As head of the editorial and publication department of VSNKh, he had significant influence over what could, and presumably could not, be published on economic matters during this period, and was responsible for ushering into print not only original studies by leading Soviet economists but also Russian translations of leading works by international economists. His ultimate fate as a non-Marxist economist in an increasingly orthodox Marxist economic world in the course of the 1920s mirrored that of many of his colleagues. He was stripped of his editorial positions in 1930. A year later, the Communist journal *Bol'shevik*, in an article by E. Kol'man, levelled accusations of 'idealist and mechanistic theories, their own scholarly falsifications of the theory of pricing, production, money, agriculture' at him and other prominent economists (Bazarov, Sukhanov, Groman, Rubin, Iurovskii, Finn-Enotaevskii, Kondrat'ev, Chaianov) as part of the Prompartii trial. The accusations against them were a vivid sign of the changing times, a warning that the very words they had used in less politically claustrophobic times would now be used to hang them. Fal'kner was arrested 30 December 1934 accused of anti-Soviet activity and was sentenced to three years in exile the following year. Re-arrested in November 1937, he was sentenced to death, and shot in February 1938.

Food Detachments [*prodovol'stvennye otriady* or prodotriady] were procurement squads sent into villages to seize supplies from peasants who refused to send food to the cities. Such detachments had been sent by the Bolsheviks into grain-producing regions already in November 1917 to allay the food crisis, but their activities became more intense as the Civil War cut off the Bolsheviks from these regions. They were set up in large numbers starting in May 1918. They consisted of two groups: the *food requisition army* [*Prodovol'stvenno-rekvizitsionnaia armiia* or prodarmiia] under Nakromprod of the RSFSR, formed from mobilised troops and volunteers from factory committees; and armed food detachments under the Military Food Bureau [*Voennoe prodovol'stvennoe biuro* or Voenprodbiuro] that was part of the All-Russian Central Council of Trade Unions. During the years of the Civil War, food detachments under these two bodies numbered close to 100,000. The detachments and the army were disbanded with the establishment of the New Economic Policy in 1921. See also *People's Commissariat of Food Supply of the RSFSR.*

Food requisition army See *Food Detachments.*

Glavki See *Central Administrations.*

Glavleskom See *Main Forestry Committee.*

Gosplan See *State Committee for Planning.*

Glavpolitprosvet See *Main Political-Enlightenment Committee of the Republic.*

Gubsovnarkhoz See *Provincial Council of the National Economy.*

Industrial Bureaus [*Promyshlennoe biuro* or Prombiuro] were the authorised representatives of the Supreme Council of the National Economy [VSNKh] in the republics and large regions of the USSR. The first was established in Ukraine at the start of

1920, and subsequently in the Urals, in Siberia, and in the South-East of the RSFSR [*Prombiuro Ural'skoe*, *Prombiuro Sibirskoe*, and *Prombiuro Iugo-Vostoka RSFSR*]. The industrial bureaus were intended to wield broad authority in questions pertaining to local economic life on behalf of the centre, and to bring together the local sovnarkhozy, regional administrations, and so on. They existed until 1928.

Iudenich, Nikolai Nikolaevich (1862–1933) was a White officer who had emerged from the Russo-Japanese War as an infantry general and served as chief-of-staff of the tsarist army in 1913. He was in charge of all Russian forces in the Caucasus at various times during the First World War. After the October Revolution, he commanded the North-Western Army in the Baltic area, one of the smaller White armies which fought against the Bolsheviks. In October 1919, he penetrated Soviet territory and led an abortive offensive against Petrograd, as part of a grand strategy in support of a campaign against Moscow by another White general, Anton Denikin. After his defeat, Iudenich was arrested in January 1920 as he tried to flee to Western Europe. Diplomatic pressure from Britain and France secured his release, and he retreated to Estonia. He died in exile in France. See also: *Czechoslovak Legion*; *Denikin*; *Dutov*; *Krasnov*; *Wrangel'*.

Kafengauz, Lev Borisovich (1885–1940) was trained as an economist and statistician with long prerevolutionary credentials in the Russian revolutionary movement. He was best known for his published work on the problems of the creation and distribution of national income in industry. An activist since 1904, he was a Bolshevik propagandist in 1905–06 until coming under police scrutiny. He graduated from the Economics Department of the Faculty of Law at Moscow University in 1910, later becoming a professor there, but lost his position after taking part in strike activities against the state. He worked as a statistician from 1911 at the Moscow Commercial Institute, and on the newspaper *Russkie vedomosti* until 1917. He diverged from Lenin's Bolsheviks in the course of 1917, joining the Moscow organisation of the Mensheviks after February, and taking a critical public stance on Lenin's April Theses. He supported a collaborative relationship between workers and entrepreneurs on the basis of mutual concessions. In the summer, he was an elector to the Moscow Duma, and prior to October Deputy Minister of Trade and Industry. He regarded the economic travails of the Civil War years as partly a product of Bolshevik force, and in mid-1918 was critical of Sovnarkom's money and food supply policy. He opposed the nationalisation of large-scale industry. He left the increasingly beleaguered Mensheviks in 1919 to work at VSNKh. At a time when split loyalties were still briefly possible, he worked with Kadet-allied economists on an economic program for the rebuilding of Russia in the event of a collapse of Soviet power. Although arrested in 1920 on suspicion of belonging to the Kadet National Centre, he was freed for lack of evidence. He continued to work in VSNKh, in the Department of Statistics, gathering and publishing statistical data on the industry of the USSR until 1928. He was arrested in August 1930, accused of anti-Soviet activity, and exiled to Ufa until December 1932. From 1933–37, he continued to work in higher educational establishments in Moscow, notably the Institute of Steel, and at Moscow State University. He was deputy editor of the Technical Encyclopedia (*Tekhnicheskaia entsiklopediia*). In 1937–40, he was a member of the Institute of Economics of the Academy of Sciences of the USSR [*Institut ekonomiki AN SSSR*].

Kerensky, Aleksandr Fedorovich (1881–1970), a lawyer, was head of the Provisional Government from June to October 1917. He was a member of the Socialist Revolutionary Party in 1905 and joined the State Duma representing the Labour Group [*trudoviki*] in 1912. A prominent leader in the February Revolution in 1917, he was deputy chairman of the Petrograd Soviet and a member of the Provisional Committee of the State Duma. He served as Minister of Justice in the first Provisional Government, and as Minister of War from early May. He became Commander-in-Chief after the abortive Kornilov Affair. He escaped from the Winter Palace during the October insurrection, fleeing abroad. In the émigré centres of Europe, he published widely, and edited the newspaper *Golos Rossii* [*Voice of Russia*], and the journals *Dni* [*Days*] and *Novaia Rossiia* [*New Russia*]. After moving to the United States prior to World War Two, he concentrated his attention on his *émigré* activities, teaching, researching, and speaking publicly on Russian history. Bolsheviks coined the term *Kerenshchina* [Kerensky era] to refer to his time in office. It was later applied dismissively to any perceived petty bourgeois government that did not have the interests of the workers at heart. See also *Kondrat'ev*.

Khriashcheva, Anna Ivanovna (1868–1934) was a statistician who spent a year studying at the Department of Statistics at Berlin University in 1904–05. Her practical expertise derived from years of experience in zemstvo statistical bureaus in various provinces of the Tsarist empire, conducting statistical and census work with local populations, and accruing knowledge of rural and urban economies in the north and south of the empire. Involved in revolutionary circles since the 1890s, she was imprisoned for eighteen months for distributing illegal literature. As a textile worker in 1896, she was imprisoned again for eight months for agitprop activity amongst workers. Exile to Ufa province followed, where she met her future husband, P.I. Popov, also in political exile, the beginning of a long and fruitful professional collaboration. From 1909–17, she established herself as a leading statistician in the zemstvo movement, developing methods of registering, classifying, and consolidating the data being gathered on all aspects of local, rural life. In 1917, first the Provisional Government and then the Bolshevik government each recruited her to help compile statistics on the lands that had only recently come under their control, and about which they knew little. This knowledge became key to the very survival not only of the Soviet state but also of large swathes of the population as the vicious privations of the Civil War took hold. She became head of the Department of Agricultural

Censuses, and a member of the Collegium of the Central Statistical Office (TsSU) in early 1918. She used the 1917 agricultural census to collate data on 52 provinces and oblasts of Russia. Further annual censuses were conducted in the difficult conditions of the Civil War, in order to count the rural population, log their economic activities, sown areas, etc. Her work continued up to the 1926 census which had to answer basic questions of the now consolidating Soviet state: the state of agriculture in the USSR, the class composition of peasant households, and so forth. Her regular publications were fundamental sources for specialists on the peasant economy in particular, including Kritsman, with whom she shared an interest in evidence of developing social and class differentiation within the peasantry. From 1918 to 1926 she headed the Department of Agricultural Censuses under the Central Statistical Administration. From 1924 to 1926 and again from the end of 1927 to 1929 she headed the Department of the Dynamics of Agriculture in the TsSU SSSR. Her work was sidelined as forced collectivisation took over as a major economic priority in the USSR. Her zemstvo past became a liability, although her early revolutionary credentials, professionalism, and sense of service to the power of social transformation earned her the respect of her colleagues. She died in 1934. See also *Popov*.

Kolchak, Aleksandr Vasil'evich (1873–1920) was a former Arctic explorer and tsarist admiral who participated in the war with Japan in 1904 and took command of the Black Sea Fleet in the First World War. After the February Revolution, he was exiled to Great Britain and the US for counter-revolutionary activity. After the October Revolution, he returned to Russia via Omsk, and joined the Ufa Directory. He staged a coup and set up a dictatorship in Siberia, the Urals, and the Far East (*Kolchakovshchina*), assuming total control as 'Supreme Ruler of All Russia' in November 1918. In late 1919, he fled the Red Army into exile to Irkutsk. He was subsequently captured by the Bolsheviks there and executed in February 1920.

Kondrat'ev, Nikolai Dmitrievich (1892–1938), an economist, was one of the theoreticians and proponents of the New Economic Policy. He became famous for his theory on business cycles ('Kondrat'ev cycles'), namely that decades-long cycles of boom and depression characterised Western capitalist economies. In his teens, he joined the Socialist Revolutionary Party and was arrested and imprisoned for participating in textile strikes. An early tutee in economics classes at the University of St. Petersburg, he eventually graduated in 1915 from the Faculty of Law there. He studied for a professorship in the School of Political Economy and Statistics. He led an active academic life, publishing his first monograph in 1915 on a local zemstvo economy in Kostroma province, in keeping with his Socialist Revolutionary outlook. A year later, he was the head of the Agricultural Statististical-Economic Department [*Otdel sel'skokhoziaistvennoi ekonomiki i statistiki*] of the Zemskii Union of Petrograd [*Zemskii Soiuz Petrograda*]. After February 1917, his PSR work brought him into Prime Minister Kerensky's orbit as an SR activist and advisor on peasant matters. In the dying days of the Kerensky government, he was appointed Deputy Minister of Food Supply. After the October Revolution, he threw himself into academic research in the service of the new state, first as a teacher, and then from 1920–1928 as founder and director of the Market Institute [*Kon'iunkturnyi Institut*] under the People's Commissariat of Finances in Moscow He built this institute into one of the largest research institutes on issues related to trade, prices, and the market. He was arrested in 1922, marked for expulsion from Soviet Russia, but was saved by the intervention of the Deputy People's Commissar of Agriculture, N. Osinskii, who argued that this would interrupt his important statistical and economic work for the Soviet state. He undertook detailed comparative studies of goods and prices in Western European economies, and by 1923 he was working on a five-year plan of Soviet agricultural development. He published regularly on the boom-depression-recovery cycles of the world economy throughout the 1920s. In 1927, he openly expressed his doubts about a lack of balance in the five-year plan for the Soviet economy, predicting deep food shortages. Such views brought sharp criticism from leading Bolsheviks. The term 'Kondrat'evism [*Kondrat'evshchina*]', along with 'Chaianovism [*Chaianovshchina*]' relating to the leading agrarian economist, Aleksandr Chaianov, were coined to caricature their activities as a 'kulak-SR assault' on Soviet Russia (a harbinger of the later broader 'kulakism [*kulakovshchina*]'). This was no empty academic criticism, and in 1928 Kondrat'ev was removed from all his positions, and with other leading economists, including Teodorovich, Groman, and Sadyrin, was swept up in a wave of repression. Arrested in 1930, he was sentenced to an eight-year prison sentence. He was shot in 1938. See also *Oganovskii*; *Teodorovich*.

Krasnov, Piotr Nikolaevich (1869–1947) was a Russian military leader and ataman of the Don Republic with fighting credentials as leader of Cossack forces in the tsarist Imperial Army during the First World War and against the Bolsheviks after the October Revolution and during the Civil War. Immediately after the October Revolution, he had, at Kerensky's behest, led several hundred Cossacks to Petrograd in an attempt to reverse the Bolshevik victory. He was defeated, briefly imprisoned, and released, moving to the Don region to rally his forces. He did not enjoy smooth relations with other White generals, notably Denikin, and in early 1919 he fled to Europe after losing an election as Don ataman. In the emigration, he led a peripatetic existence fighting the Soviet government from abroad, and his fervent anti-Communism led him to collaborate with Nazi Germany during the Second World War. At the end of the war, he was repatriated by the British to Russia, where he was tried for participation in the Civil War and Operation Barbarossa. He was hanged in 1947. See also: *Czechoslovak Legion*; *Denikin*; *Dutov*; *Iudenich*; *Wrangel'*.

Kritsman, Lev Natanovich (1890–1938) was an economist and statistician who graduated from the Department of Chemistry of the University of Zurich. He published numerous scholarly works on the organisation and administration of the Soviet national economy, including the functioning of the economy during the Civil War, the reconstruction of agriculture after the war, problems encountered in the centralised planning initiative, and evidence of increasing socio-economic differentiation within the peasantry. His detailed examination of the effects of war and revolution on the social conditions of the countryside took up much of his energy in the latter half of the 1920s and beyond. He came of sound revolutionary credentials, becoming active in Russian Social Democracy as a teen, initially as a Menshevik. He was arrested several times, moving into foreign exile first in Vienna and then in Zurich, where he studied at both cities' universities. He earned a doctorate from Zurich, whereupon he returned to Russia in 1917, joining the RKP(b) a year later. From 1918, even though he was a member of the Left Communist faction, he was recruited to work in VSNKh, helping to draw up the initial nationalisation measures that would form the basis of what became known as 'war communism'. As the Civil War drew down, he took up a series of leading positions in the economic organs of the new Soviet state. He was chair of the Commission for the Utilisation of Material Resources in 1920–1921, and occupied various positions throughout the 1920s, including presidium member of Gosplan, director of the Agrarian Institute [*Agrarnyi institut*] of the Communist Academy, director of the Institute of Economics of RANION [*Institut ekonomiki Rossiiskoi Assotsiatsii nauchno-issledovatel'skikh institutov obshchestvennykh nauk*], deputy head of the Central Statistics Office, and deputy chair of the Commission for the Study of the Agrarian Revolution in Russia [*Komissiia po izucheniiu agrarnoi revoliutsii v Rossii*]. At various times, he served on the editorial boards of several newspapers and journals, including *Pravda*, *Na agrarnom fronte*, and *Problemy ekonomiki*. Kritsman's defense of the economic policies introduced during the Civil War years, his dislike of the NEP even as a strategic retreat, and his consistent support throughout the 1920s for strong and integrated economic planning as the only path forward for a socialist economy, brought him into conflict at various times with Lenin and other leading Bolsheviks. Moreover, he and his group of like-minded economists and statisticians conducted a protracted feud with the influential economist Alexander Chaianov and his band of scholars, whom he accused of underestimating both the capitalist substance of the peasant family economy and the rising processes of social differentiation within the countryside. Subject to public political criticism at least twice during the 1930s, Kritsman withdrew – or was withdrawn – from his various official positions, although publicly this was for reasons of ill health. Information on his final few years is scarce, and there are conflicting sources on whether he was shot in the repressions of 1937 or died of disease in 1938. See also *Commission for Utilisation of Material Resources*; *Gosplan*.

Kronstadt Uprising refers to a revolt against the Bolsheviks in March 1921 by some of the most radicalized sailors of 1917. After three years of war and economic misery, and in solidarity with striking workers in Petrograd and Moscow, the Kronstadt sailors made radical demands for an end to Bolshevik rule and a return to what they saw as the true ideals and goals of the October Revolution. Their revolt was brutally crushed. Opponents saw it as a stinging indictment of Bolshevik policies. To Kritsman, it was a direct product of the severe social dislocations and economic crises of the 1920–1921 period and a constant reminder that future Kronstadts were possible. See also *New Economic Policy*.

Krzhizhanovskii, Gleb Maksimilianovich (1872–1959) was a Soviet academician and scientist, who became chair of the State Committee for Planning [Gosplan] and director of the State Commission for the Electrification of Russia [*Gosudarstvennaia komissiia po elektrifikatsii Rossii* or GOELRO]. He studied at the St. Petersburg State Institute of Technology in the early 1990s, and became active in Social Democratic politics, for which he was arrested, imprisoned, and then sent into Siberian exile. He sought vainly to unite the party factions after the 1903 split in the RSDRP. After the failed 1905 Revolution, he focused on his engineering career, particularly on a new power station near Moscow and a possible hydroelectric plant in Saratov. After the February Revolution, he served in the Moscow Soviet and was responsible for fuel issues. From 1920, as head of GOELRO, he was key in theorising and planning the spread of electrification to industry and the entire country, a key interest of Lenin, who saw it as one of Communism's most tangible potential assets. He was involved in key big projects of the Soviet regime, including the Volga-Don and Dneprostroi projects. He was also involved in drawing up the First Five Year Plan for rapid industrialisation. From 1929–1939, he was Vice-President of the Academy of Sciences of the USSR [*Akademiia Nauk SSSR*], where he promoted the development of the technical sciences. In this capacity, he also oversaw the expulsion from its ranks of 'bourgeois specialists' to remove any potential harm they threatened to the socialist project. He explicitly termed this threat a veritable campaign against the USSR in his *Anti-Soviet Sabotage Exposed* published in 1929. At the end of the 1930s, letters revealed personal criticisms of Stalin, and he was stripped of his leadership positions, although not purged. He died in Moscow in 1959.

Kulak (wealthy peasant) See *Sociopolitical classifications*.

Land Planning Office [Zemplan] was part of efforts by Sovnarkom in the first years of the Soviet state to create a complete system of planning organs for all the major branches of the economy. These efforts included an Industrial Planning Commission [*Promyshlennaia planovaia komissiia* or Promplan], a Fuel Planning Commission [Central Commission for Fuel Planning [*Tsentral'naia komissiia toplivnogo plana*] under the Main Fuel Committee [*Glavnyi toplivyi komitet* or Glavtop], and a commission to draw up a plan of the agricultural and forest economy that later became known as the Land Planning Office [*Zemel'nyi plan* or Zemplan]. Other commissions were established to draw up plans for raw materials and for transport.

Larin, Iurii (Lur'e, Mikhail Aleksandrovich) (1882–1932) was a Marxist economist with expertise in the national economy of Germany, who helped shape the Soviet program of nationalisation of industry, workers' supervision of production, and the monopoly of foreign trade. He had strong activist credentials in Russian Social Democracy in the Crimea since 1902, and was responsible for founding the Crimean Union of the RSDRP [*Krymskii soiuz RSDRP*]. Arrested and sentenced to Siberian exile, he escaped in 1904 to the emigration, joining the Mensheviks in Geneva following the split in the RSDRP. He continued his revolutionary activism on his return to Russia in 1905 as head of the Kiev organisation of the RSDRP. In 1907, he began two years of activity in the Union of Mechanics of the Oil Industry [*Soiuz mekhanikov neftianoi promyshlennosti*] in the Caucasus. After a second period of emigration from 1914–17, he returned after the February Revolution of 1917 to become head of one of the groups of the Menshevik Internationalists. He switched parties to the Bolsheviks in August 1917, and participated in the October Revolution as a member of the Executive Committee of the Petrograd Soviet. A major force in Soviet economic policy, he was a founding member of VSNkh, joining its Presidium, and helped set up Gosplan and design the management structure for nationalised industries. During the years of the Civil War, Larin's original ideas on opening trade relations with the West, developing the coal industry in the Kuznetsk Basin, and irrigating Turkestan for cotton-growing were deemed impractical at the time. Distrusted by Lenin as a result, he was sidelined from state economic affairs and posted to the Soviet embassy in London in 1922. On his return in 1923, he became a sharp critic of Trotsky, a strong advocate of the NEP, but was later also a proponent of disenfranchising kulaks, raising taxes on the peasantry, and squeezing more labour productivity from industry. His latter years prior to his death were devoted to his advocacy against antisemitism in the USSR, and he published widely on this topic, earning him sharp criticism from his party. He died in 1932 of natural causes and was buried in the Kremlin Wall. His family did not escape repression. His widow Lena Larina was arrested and exiled to the gulag during the purges. His adopted daughter Anna Larina was married to Nikolai Bukharin, and she spent some 20 years in the gulag after Bukharin was purged.

Litoshenko, Lev Nikolaevich (1886–1943) was an economist and statistician who studied peasant land-use and the village economy prior to 1917, and peasant households, national economic budgeting, and the Russian national income after 1917. He graduated in 1909 from the Economics Department of Moscow University's Law School and was appointed as an assistant at the School of Political Economy of the Moscow Commercial Institute [*Moskovskii kommercheskii institut*]. He spent 1912 to 1914 on assignment abroad, returning to teach at Shaniavskii University in Moscow. During the First World War, he worked in the Statistical-Economics Department of the Union of Towns [*Soiuz gorodov*]. He worked with the Provisional Government after the February Revolution as an elected Kadet member of the Moscow City Duma. After October, he provided expert economic counsel to the new Soviet government, variously at the Central Statistical Administration, the People's Commissariat of Finance, and the People's Commissariat of Agriculture, while continuing to teach as a professor of economics at Moscow State University. From 1923 to 1927, he spent three periods of study in the USA. He worked with Popov in 1923 and 1924 drawing up budgetary balances among the branches of the new Soviet economy. Litoshenko believed that a strong wager on developing a class of independent farmers was the best way to increase agricultural productivity, although he recognised that Russia's traditions of the commune and Bolshevism's socialist policies were impediments to this. Indeed, he was critical of the disastrous effects of earlier forced requisitioning policies on the agrarian economy, particularly the destruction of an emerging class of prosperous peasants in the prewar period, and its replacement by a universally impoverished peasantry. He was guardedly optimistic about the shift to the NEP as the best path to the economic restitution of the peasantry, although he did not think it went far enough. In 1930, he was arrested for such views along with Kondrat'ev, Chaianov, among others, and sentenced to three years in prison and subsequent internal exile. He was permitted to return to work and teach in Moscow in 1932 but was rearrested in 1938. He was sentenced to hard labour and died in 1943 in the Kolyma gulag. See also *Khriashcheva*; *Popov*.

Main Forestry Committee [*Glavnyi komitet lesnoi promyshlennosti* or Glavleskom] was created in December 1918 by the Soviet government to manage the forestry industry, particularly the procurement of wood for fuel.

Main Political-Enlightenment Committee of the Republic [*Glavnyi politiko-prosvetitel'nyi komitet Respubliki or Glavpolitprosvet*] was created in 1920 under the People's Commissariat of Enlightenment of the RSFSR with the aim of guiding Communist propaganda activity. It was tasked with eliminating illiteracy, setting up workers' universities, libraries and peasant reading huts. The committee was chaired by N.K. Krupskaia. See also *People's Commissariat of Enlightenment of the RSFSR*.

Merezhkovskii, Dmitrii Sergeevich (1866–1941) was a Russian novelist and Silver Age poet, one of the founders of the Symbolist movement. His often mercurial political and philosophical positions put him at odds with all manner of people and regimes throughout his life. After the October Revolution, which he saw as an unmitigated disaster for Russia, he went into political exile in Europe for the rest of his life, dying of natural causes in Paris in 1941. His life-long hatred of Communism took him towards Europe's dictators in the 1930s, always regarding fascist (and especially Nazi) expansionism as less of a threat to the world than Communist expansionism. In his work, Kritsman referenced Merezhkovskii's novel *The Forthcoming Ham* [*Griadushchii kham*, 1905], in order to illustrate the attitude of the old Russian intelligentsia to the labouring masses, whom Merezhkovskii criticised as the 'coming boors'. Merezhkovskii later regarded the October Revolution as the embodiment of that prophecy, Russia now being in the grip of the 'Beast-Nation [*Narod-Zver*]'.

Meschanin, pl. meshchane (urban dweller) referred in the 19th century to a member of the lower groups of townspeople, including tradesmen and craftsmen. These urban dwellers were ultimately constituted as a legal estate [*soslovie*], allowing for each city to set up a society [*meshchanskoe obshchestvo*], headed by an elected elder [*starosta*], and an executive board [*meshchanskaia uprava*] to run its affairs. See also *Sociopolitical classifications*; *Soslovie*.

Meshcherskii, Aleksei Pavlovich (1867–1938) was a wealthy Russian banker and industrialist, active in the management of large machine-building enterprises. He was one of the organisers of the 'Kolomna–Sormovo' trust in 1913, and a member of the Council of the Petersburg International Commercial Bank. After October 1917, while his ultimate hope was for a non-Bolshevik government, he was involved in negotiations with Soviet leaders to create mergers of state and capitalist trusts. Lenin rejected his proposals, and VSNKh broke off negotiations with Meshcherskii in April 1918, deciding instead to nationalise plants and factories. He was arrested and imprisoned in Butyrki prison, but released in late 1918 after protracted negotiations, whereupon he fled illegally to Finland, and settled in Paris. He is buried in the *émigré* cemetery at Ste-Geneviève-des-Bois on the outskirts of Paris.

Meshechnichestvo. See *Bagging*.

Narkomfin See *People's Commissariat of Finance*.

Narkomprod See *People's Commissariat of Food Supply*.

Narkompros See *People's Commissariat of Enlightenment of the RSFSR*.

Narkomput' See *People's Commissariat of Communication Routes*.

Narkomtorg See *People's Commissariat of Trade*.

Narkomtrud See *People's Commissariat of Labour*.

Narkomvneshtorg See *People's Commissariat of Foreign Trade*.

Narkomvoendel See *People's Commissariat of Military Affair*.

Narkomzem See *People's Commissariat of Agriculture*.

Narodniki See *Populists*.

Natural economy is essentially a money-less economy, in which goods and resources are exchanged through direct bartering or are allocated by law or custom. In a natural economy, a majority of goods are produced domestically for direct consumption by the producers. It was often posited by Marxist thinkers of the time as in opposition to the capitalist form of economy. Indeed, some saw capitalism's earlier emergence as dependent on the destruction of the natural economy with its focus on exchange rather than on profit. Kritsman drew explicit comparison between the capitalist natural economy of Tsarist Russia that had allowed for a more complete utilisation of productive forces for the ends of war and the proletarian natural economy that was an attempt to take the first steps in the transition to socialism. He conceded that by 1921 the proletarian natural economy was already giving way to the return of the commodity economy with the launching of the NEP. See *New Economic Policy.*

New Economic Policy [*Novaia Ekonomicheskaia Politika* or NEP] was proclaimed by Lenin in March 1921 after a spate of popular unrest over the continuation of the harsh policies of the Civil War era, notably forced grain requisitioning. Near-insurrections in the Tambov region were accompanied by unrest in the cities and by a revolt of sailors in Kronstadt in February and March of that year. The NEP was a step back from the earlier economic policies, allowing the peasantry a degree of freedom of use of the land and its produce, and also permitting a certain degree of private enterprise in the economy. This allowed for the rise of 'baggers [*meshochniki*]', individuals who had engaged in private trade during the Civil War, and who in the NEP facilitated, in a semi-legal status, the new private goods market. These NEP-men were often vilified as speculators and black-marketeers by the Soviet authorities. The goal of the NEP was economic recovery and thus political survival for the Bolsheviks. The NEP was not uncontroversial and was rejected by many staunch Communists as a betrayal of the goals they had championed for so long. Indeed, Kritsman's defense here of the prior economic policies with all their faults, grew out of his dislike of the NEP as essentially a wrong political and ideological direction for Soviet Russia. See also *Bagging*; *Kronstadt Uprising.*

Oganovskii, Nikolai Petrovich (1874–1938) was an economist and statistician, who worked on agrarian issues. His published works supported the argument that Tsarist Russia, and later Soviet Russia, should wager on the internal vitality of the middle-sized peasant economy as a path to economic prosperity. He graduated from the Historical-Philological Faculty of Saint-Petersburg University in 1897. He gained several years' experience in the Military Statistics Committee of the Urals Regional Administration [*Voiskii statisticheskii komitet Ural'skogo oblastnogo pravleniia*], then, like many of his profession, in the local zemstvo movement. A Populist by sympathy, he worked until the October 1917 Revolution in a variety of publicistic and organisational roles where he felt he could best promote the evolutionary adaptation of the traditional peasant commune to the fast-changing economic and political conditions of the times. In the First World War, he served as head of the Statistics Office of the All-Russian Union of Zemstvos [*Statisticheskoe biuo Vserossiiskogo zemskogo soiuza*], but he also at times found common cause with the Popular Socialists, trudoviks, Left Kadets, and Socialist Revolutionaries in their advocacy for peasant and land reform. He opposed the Bolshevik Revolution, and until late 1918 advocated for agrarian reforms within oppositional centres in the Volga region and Ufa but left that to work in the cooperative movement. From 1918 to 1920, he headed the Economics Department of the Siberian Central Union [*Ekonomicheskii otdel Sibtsentrosoiuza*]. From late 1921, he returned to Moscow to work in the People's

Commissariat of Agriculture [Narkomzem], and for three years headed its Statistics Department. In mid-1922 he published an article critical of a single tax in kind on agricultural products, earning the ire not only of his colleagues in organisations like Narkomprod, but also of Lenin himself who recommended his removal from his post as editor of his journal *Agricultural Life* [*Sel'skokhoziaistvennaia zhizn'*]. In his own work, Kritsman singled out Oganovskii for significant inaccuracies in his statistics. Oganovskii was arrested in October, but instead of being sent abroad as the GPU ordered, he was released for work in Narkomzem, and took part in preparing the 'general plan' of Narkomzem for 1921–1922. Although he continued to work on planning, he opposed excessive rates of industrialisation as harmful to agriculture. He was arrested in 1931, sentenced to prison, and subsequently to internal exile in Bashkiriia. He continued living there after his release in 1935 and died three years later. See also: *Kondrat'ev*; *Teodorovich.*

Osinskii, Nikolai pseud. of Valerian Valerianovich Obolenskii (1887–1938) was an economist and statistician who published on agrarian and economic issues in the new Soviet state. He completed three years in the Faculty of Law at Moscow University in 1905 and became involved in revolutionary politics during the 1905 Revolution, joining the RSDRP(b) in 1907. In 1911, he was exiled first to Tver' and then to Khar'kov. He continued his revolutionary activities through 1917 and was a member of the Khar'kov Military Revolutionary Committee in October 1917. Soon after October, he was appointed head of the Russian State Bank, and then chairman of Vesenkha until March 1918. In Spring 1918, he co-authored the platform of the 'Left Communists'. Osinskii supported some of the harshest Bolshevik policies, such as Red Terror. As the Civil War drew to a close, however, he supported gradualist, supportive policies, such as the Bolshevik Sowing Committees [*posevkomy*], and became a strong advocate of the NEP. He also supported increased internal party democracy in the face of tightening restrictions, joining the Democratic Centralist intraparty group in the process, and later flirting with the Trotskyist oppositionists. From 1921–23, he was Deputy to the People's Commissar of Narkomzem, and deputy chair of VSNKh. He spent the following two years as a Soviet plenipotentiary in Sweden, returning in 1925 to serve three years in Gosplan in charge of its Central Statistics Administration (TsSU). He was deputy chair of VSNKh from 1929. He was arrested in 1937, while director of the Institute of the History of Science and Technology of the Academy of Sciences of the USSR [*Institut istorii nauki i tekhniki* AN SSSR] in Moscow, accused along with 45 others in the Moscow Center trial of former members of the Central Committee of the VKP(b). He was shot in 1938. See also *Sowing Committee.*

Paris Commune of 1871 briefly ruled Paris from 18 March to 28 May 1871. It resulted from a working class uprising in Paris after France's defeat in the Franco-Prussian War. Although the short-lived city rule was soon crushed by government forces, it became famous for the radical socialist reforms it espoused. Unlike the complicated and cautionary lessons it could draw from the Great French Revolution of 1789 onwards, the new Soviet government saw the Paris Commune as a more useable and self-serving revolutionary example from the past. In this view, the Commune failed because it had lacked a strong revolutionary party to guide it.

Party of Socialist Revolutionaries [*Partiia sotsialistov-revoliutsionerov*, PSR, SRs] grew out of the unification of several populist groups of the late 19th century. The party advocated terrorism in its fight against tsarism, assassinating several high government officials in the first five years of the twentieth century. The first congress of the PSR took place in Finland from December 1905 to January 1906, and adopted the party programme drafted by Viktor Chernov, its chief theorist. The programme called for a federated, democratic republic on the basis of popular franchise as the road to socialism, and the PSR tried to attract not only peasants, but also urban workers. The party soon split over ideological differences. A right wing, the later Popular Socialists [*Narodnye sotsialisty*], wanted to forgo terrorist acts in favour of legal activities. A left wing, the SR Maximalists, wanted to nationalize the land and industry and create a Toilers' Republic [*Respublika trudiashchikhsia*]. In the First World War, the PSR split into Defensists and Internationalists depending on their stance vis-à-vis support for the war. In 1917 they enjoyed significant influence in the Soviets, and cooperated in the Provisional Government, particularly in the person of Alexander Kerensky, Minister and Justice and later Prime Minister. While most SRs agitated against the Bolsheviks after October, the left wing of the party, the Left SRs, formed at the Fourth Party Congress in November–December 1917, cooperated with the Bolsheviks until the Peace of Brest-Litovsk, which they opposed as a betrayal of the revolution. The Right SRs were expelled from the soviets in June 1918, the Left SRs were expelled in July. The PSR organisations were suppressed by the Bolsheviks, and several leaders of the party were put on trial in Moscow in 1922. In the *émigré* centres of Paris, Berlin, and Prague, other leaders kept up their critique of Soviet Russia through publicistic activities. See also *Kerensky*; *Kondrat'ev*; *Populists*.

People's Commissariat of Agriculture [*Narodnyi komissariat zemledeliia* or Narkomzem] was established in 1917 on the day after the October Revolution and was charged with carrying out the agricultural and land policy of the new regime, notably the Decree on Land, and was responsible for the activities of local soviets and rural land committees. Narkomzem was dominated by Left SRs in the first six months after October, until they were forced out by the Bolsheviks. It included the Department of Soviet State Farms [*Otdel sovetskikh khoziaistv* or Glavsovkhoz]. It later included a Committee for the Organisation of Sown Area [*Komitet po organizatsii posevnoi ploshchadi* or Orgasev] responsible for the cultivation of vacated land. Nakomzem was also responsible for the procurement of perishable products and grain feed destined for the People's Commissariat of Food Supply [Narkomprod]. In practice, its areas of responsibility in procuring agricultural products and raw materials often overlapped and conflicted with those of other organs of VSNKh.

People's Commissariat of Communication Routes [*Narodnyi komissariat putei soobshcheniia* or Narkomput] was elected in 1918 by the All-Russian Executive Committee of Railway Workers [*Vserossiiskii ispolnitel'nyi komitet zheleznodorozhnikov* or Vikzhedor]. It functioned initially as the administrative arm of the railways. From 1920, it began to draw into its sphere of responsibility all forms of transport, including water transport, horse-drawn transport, as well as warehouse facilities, and so on.

People's Commissariat of Enlightenment of the RSFSR [*Narodnyi komissariat prosveshcheniia RSFSR*, Narkompros] was created on the day after the October Revolution. It was responsible for public education and enlightenment, and was tasked with introducing universal compulsory free education, training new pedagogical cadres, ensuring the separation of church and state in schools, organizing a state apparatus of enlightenment in the centre and in the localities, bringing the old scientific and creative intelligentsia over to the side of Soviet power. Its first head was Anatolii Lunacharsky. It had sections devoted to the eradication of illiteracy, to the supervision (and censorship) of literature, theatre repertoires, and of the still-new medium of film. It became the Ministry of Enlightenment [*Ministerstvo prosveshcheniia*] in 1946. See also *Main Political-Enlightenment Committee of the Republic*.

People's Commissariat of Finance [*Narodnyi komissariat finansov* or Narkomfin] was established the day after the October Revolution in 1917. From 1917–23, it was responsible for determining state income and expenditure, supervising the financial budgets of the people's commissariats, central administrations, and local soviets, introducing tax policy, conducting currency operations for the Republic, the production of banknotes, and so on.

People's Commissariat of Food Supply [*Narodnyi komissariat prodovol'stviia* or Narkomprod], set up in 1917, was responsible for procuring and distributing foodstuffs throughout the Civil War years and beyond. It was one of the central organs in the early years, when its responsibilities and activities were not always clearly delineated from those of VSNKh. The NEP encroached on its sphere of activities, and in 1924 it was replaced by the People's Commissariat of Domestic Trade [Narkomvnutorg] and later by the People's Commissariat of Trade [Narkomtorg]. See also *Food requisition army*.

People's Commissariat of Foreign Trade [*Narodnyi komissariat vneshnei torgovli* or Narkomvneshtorg] was established by Sovnarkom decree in 1920. It was initially the monopoly seller of Russian goods and products on the foreign market. During the years of the NEP, some large state enterprises and cooperatives were permitted to engage in some foreign-trade activity while observing the state monopoly on foreign trade. In 1925, it was combined with the People's Commissariat of Domestic Trade [*Narodnyi komissariat vnutrennei torgovli* or Narkomvnutorg] into a single all-union People's Commissariat of Trade [*Narodnyi komissariat torgovli* or Narkomtorg], and once again assumed the exclusive right to conduct foreign trade operations.

People's Commissariat of Labour [*Narodnyi komissariat truda* or Narkomtrud] was one of the first economic commissariats to be set up. Its collegium was appointed by the All-Russian Central Council of Trade Unions [*Vserossiiskii tsentral'nyi komitet professional'nykh soiuzov* or VTsSPS]. It was responsible for instituting the principles of the socialist organisation of labour, including the 8-hour workday, social security of workers, equality of men and women, and so on. Narkomtrud was largely responsible for the accounting of and dissemination of labour, ceding its labour protection and wage functions at this time to the trade unions. A Main Committee on Universal Compulsory Labour [*Glavnyi komitet po vseobshchei trudovoi povinnosti* or Glavkomtrud] was created in 1920 for the labour mobilisation of the population, particularly of the peasantry. Other organisations had responsibility for labour mobilisation at the same time, not least the NKVD.

People's Commissariat of Military Affairs of the RSFSR [*Narodnyi komissariat po voennym delam* RSFSR or Narkomvoendel] was the leadership organ of the army operating from 23 November 1917 to 12 November 1923. In the wake of the October Revolution, it was charged with democratizing and demobilizing the former tsarist army, of purging the army of perceived counter-revolutionary elements, and of organizing the Red Army with the incorporation of military specialists to provide some military continuity and consistency as the Civil War ramped up. See also *Food requisition army*.

People's Commissariat of Trade [*Narodnyi komissariat torgovli* or Narkomtorg] was formed in November 1925 by combining the People's Commissariat of Foreign Trade of the USSR with the People's Commissariat of Domestic Trade of the USSR. It was led by Aleksandr Tsiurupa until early 1926, when Lev Kamenev briefly took over until falling out of official favour. Anastas Mikoian took over the post in August. In 1930, Narkomtorg was split into the People's Commissariat of Foreign Trade of the USSR [*Narodnyi kommissarit vneshnei torgovli SSSR* or Narkomvneshtorg] and the People's Commissariat of Supply of the USSR [*Narodnyi kommissariat snabzheniia SSSR* or Narkomsnab].

People's Commissariat of Worker and Peasant Inspection [*Narodnyi komissariat raboche-krest'ianskoi inspektsii*, Rabkrin, or RKI] was created in 1920, and was headed by Stalin until 1922. It was something of a bellwether of the administrative and bureaucratic development of the new Soviet state. Initially responsible for reviewing and evaluating the work of state, local, and enterprise administrations, it was a response to the perceived disruptive effects of the bureaucratic turf-wars that had developed during the difficult years of the Civil War. By supervising the Soviet administration in toto, Rabkrin was intended as an antidote to the inefficiency and corruption that the new state believed it had inherited from the old Tsarist civil service when it had opted to import military and bourgeois specialists [*spetsy*] into the new order. It was charged with developing an explicitly Soviet civil service cut to the needs of this new regime. It soon became evident that Rabkrin was beset by many of the same bureaucratic pettinesses, red-tape, inefficiencies, and corruption of the old tsarist order. From 1922, efforts were made to regularise its work, and eliminate such issues. From 1924, it worked jointly with the Central Control Commission of the VKP(b) [*Tsentral'naia kontrol'naia komissiia VKP(b)*] as part of a broader move to combine the supervisory functions of state and party agencies, a direct response in part to Lenin's earlier published criticism of growing Soviet bureaucratism and the resultant peril of a potential split in the party. Rabkrin was reorganised in 1934 as the Commission of Soviet Control [*Komissiia sovetskoi kontrolia*] under the Sovnarkom of the USSR. See also *Sociopolitical classifications; Council of People's Commissars.*

Pood See *Units of Weights and Measures.*

Pomgol See *All-Russian Committee for Relief of the Starving.*

Poor Peasant (*Bedniak*) See *Sociopolitical classifications.*

Popov, Pavel Il'ich (1872–1950), a statistician, was responsible for drawing up (with L.N. Litoshenko) the budgetary balances for the branches of the new Soviet economy in the 1920s. His practical experience derived from years of work as a zemstvo statistician from 1898 to 1904 in Ufa, Samara, Smolensk, and Vologda. He went to Berlin in 1904 for two years of study at the Agronomics Academy. His revolutionary activities dated back to 1896, for which he was arrested and exiled to Ufa province, where he made important contacts with prominent revolutionaries (including Lenin and Tsiurupa). While there he met his future wife, Anna Khriashcheva, the beginning of a long and fruitful professional collaboration. On his return to Russia from his studies in Berlin, he spent the next decade working in the statistics departments of various regional zemstvos again. After October 1917, he became head of the statistics department of the People's Commissariat of Agriculture (Narkomzem), and for a short time in 1918 head of the department of statistics of VSNKh. From 1918 to 1926, he worked as a statistician in the Central Statistical Administration (TsSU) with the rank of People's Commissar. He did not join the Communist Party until 1924. Throughout the 1920s until his retirement in 1948, he continued working in various capacities in planning agencies of the Soviet state. See also *Khriashcheva; Litoshenko.*

Populists [*Narodniki*] were members of tsarist Russia's populist socialist movement [*Narodnichestvo*]. They disputed the Marxist contention that Russia had to pass through the capitalist stage of historical development on its path to socialism, wagering instead on the peasant commune as an embryonic form of communism. They advocated for the abolition of the autocracy, the introduction of agrarian reforms, and a socialist society based on the commune. Through agitational and publicistic activities, and later through terrorism, they sought to mobilise the peasantry against tsarism. From about 1860 to 1895, a succession of organisations articulated Populist ideals: Land and Freedom [*Zemlia i volia*], People's Vengeance [*Narodnaia rasprava*], Black Repartition [*Chernyi peredel*], People's Will [*Narodnaia volia*], among others. People's Will emerged in 1879 from a split in Land and Freedom and was responsible for the assassination of Tsar Alexander II in St. Petersburg on 1 March 1881. Government reprisals and a general decline in popularity undercut the movement, although other groups like the Party of Socialist Revolutionaries, Popular Socialists, and Trudoviks all espoused similar ideas as had the Populists. See also *Party of Socialist Revolutionaries*.

Preobrazhenskii, Evgenii Alekseevich (1886–1937), an economist, published widely on Soviet finance, food politics, the peasant commune, the NEP, and wrote popular primers on Soviet communism for the layman. His revolutionary pedigree was long, flirting with a number of revolutionary organisations before opting for the RSDRP in 1903, and later for the Bolsheviks. He conducted local revolutionary work up to the upheavals of 1917, experiencing several arrests along the way. After the October Revolution, he worked as leader of the local Urals Regional Committee of the party and joined the Left Communist faction of the party in 1918, where he became a close sometime ally of another economist and activist, Bukharin. In March 1921, when the Bolshevik regime seemed under threat from internal opposition and economic collapse, Preobrazhenskii opposed Lenin's conception of trade unions merely as conveyor belts rather than more autonomous bodies in the postwar economy. When the ban on organised factions was passed at the Tenth Party Congress in March 1921, his alleged factionalism cost him his Central Committee membership. Kritsman drew upon the economic studies he wrote in the course of the 1920s, and especially his (to Kritsman endearing) opposition to the NEP and his wager on rapid industrialisation and heavy industry for the future of Soviet Russia. Preobrazhenskii joined the board of the People's Commissariat of Finance in 1924. He often found himself in opposition to Lenin or Stalin among others, often on issues of freedom of dissent within the party, and on disagreements over strategies to deal with the often parlous economic situation in early Soviet Russia. These views brought him into Trotsky's orbit, a dangerous place to be by the mid-1920s. Preobrazhenskii promoted his policy of rapid industrialisation at a time when Communist Party doctrine, championed by Bukharin, envisaged the creation of a rich peasantry fully invested in the socialist cause *before* the full industrialisation of the country could begin. He was expelled from the party in late 1927. When Stalin changed course, however, and began to advocate for rapid industrialisation, Preobrazhenskii advised his fellow oppositionists in 1929 to fall in with the party line. He broke publicly with the now exiled Trotsky, and petitioned for permission to rejoin the party, which he did in 1930. He continued to conduct economic research in the early 1930s on light industry and state farms, but was arrested in 1933 as a member of a 'counter-revolutionary Trotskyist' group. He was sentenced to internal exile, expelled from the party, but then readmitted again all in short order. After publicly recanting his heresies in 1934, he was arrested in 1936, and again in 1937, this time to be sentenced and executed with indecent rapidity. See also *Bukharin*.

Prokopovich, Sergei Nikolaevich (1871–1955), a Russian economist and statistician, completed most of his higher education in Brussels and Bern. He conducted work on national incomes in the provinces of European Russia, focusing on peasant and labour politics. A sometime Populist in the late 19th century, he flirted with the moderate wing of Marxism, in particular Economism. This inclination kept him away from Lenin's radical Bolshevik policies of immediate revolution, instead focusing on the bourgeois stage of any revolution as an evolution towards socialist revolution. He briefly fell into the orbit of the Constitutional Democratic Party, but soon opted for no formal party affiliation. He became prominent in Russia's liberal movement in the early years of the 20th century. At times, he fell foul of the Okhrana for his political activities. During the First World War, he worked in the Moscow regional Military-Industrial Committee [*Voenno-promyshlennyi komitet*]. He welcomed the February Revolution and worked in various economic advisory capacities for the cooperative movement and the new Kerensky government. In various incarnations of the Provisional Government in 1917, he applied his expertise first as Minister for Trade and Industry, and then as Minister of Food Supply. Briefly arrested after the October Revolution, he opposed the new Bolshevik government and worked actively if in vain to restore the Provisional Government. He was permitted to continue his work during the Civil War years, albeit haltingly. In 1921, he was one of the organisers of the All-Russian Committee for Relief of the Starving. He was arrested in late 1921 accused of espionage for the contacts he had made with Western aid agencies, and he was exiled abroad. In emigration, initially in Berlin, he continued to publish on cooperative, agrarian, and economic issues. His particular interest in the reasons for the failure of the wartime economic policies and the transition to the NEP made his work of interest to Kritsman, as did his data analysis on the incomes of Russia's provinces in the first decades of the twentieth century. In the 1930s, he became interested in Soviet Russia's planning efforts and the First Five Year Plan. He died in Geneva in 1955. See also *All-Russian Committee for Relief of the Starving*.

Promysly was a term applied by agrarian statisticians to any outside income-producing work performed by members of a household (including crafts, trades, self-employment).

Posevkom See *Sowing Committee.*

Rabfak See *Workers' Faculty.*

Rabkrin See *People's Commissariat of Worker and Peasant Inspection.*

Razmychka See *Smychka.*

Revolutionary Military Council [*Revoliutsionnyi voennyi sovet* or Revvoensovet] was the supreme administrative and political leadership of the Red Army from 1918 to 1934. It was set up in 1918 by a decree centralising the strategic and military command of the new state. Its first chairman was Trotsky from 1918 until his removal from the post in January 1925 over his perceived political oppositionism. It was dissolved in 1934.

Sazhen See *Units of Weights and Measures.*

Scissors crisis became shorthand for an economic dilemma confronting the Soviet state in 1923. At the Twelfth Party Congress in 1923, Trotsky displayed a graph showing the growing gap between the prices of agricultural products and the prices of industrial products over the preceding year, as illustrated by the opening of the 'scissors' on the graph. This rising disparity between industrial and agricultural prices represented a crisis, in Trotsky's view, because it illustrated the pitfalls of uncontrolled market processes and threatened the recovering NEP economy that relied on strong peasant involvement. In his work, Kritsman explicitly invoked Trotsky's illustration as evidence that these fluctuating and elemental (anarchic) market forces were in dire need of regulation by the state by all political and economic means possible. See also *New Economic Policy.*

Second International was formed in 1889 in Paris to bring together socialist and labour parties in common cause against capitalism. It quickly chose an executive body, the International Socialist Bureau (ISB), located in Brussels. During the first part of the 20th century, it was consistently anti-militarist as the world descended into war. When its individual member parties in Europe chose to back their national states at the outbreak of war with Germany, the ensuing fragmentation within the International rendered it impotent, and it dissolved in 1916. Its various constituent parts went on to found similar organisations in its wake, most notably the Communist International. See also *Two-And-A-Half International.*

Seredniak **(middle peasant)** See *Sociopolitical classifications*

Smychka (alliance) referred to the Soviet state's declaration of the need for the interests of the workers and peasants, of the town and the countryside, to come together during the NEP period in an alliance or merger focused on the resolution of economic and social tasks facing the state. It was intended to reverse what had happened during the years of so-called 'war communism', namely the *razmychka* (separation) that had occurred between the city and the countryside. This had been the result of the rupture of economic relations between the two spheres of the national economy, a result of the collapse of large-scale industrial and agricultural production by 1920. The *smychka* envisaged ways of allowing the broad population to adapt to both the planning and market elements of the economics of the transition period in the 1920's. It grew to signify not only an economic alliance but also a cultural alliance between the workers and the peasants. Ignorance of conditions in the countryside always meant that the alliance would be an uneven one, and as the countryside failed to produce the hoped-for economic gains within this arrangement, the *smychka* gradually subsided in favour of the more direct and brutal methods of forced collectivisation of agriculture. In his work, Kritsman dismissed the *smychka* as a highly dubious and impractical idea, given the current state of the economic organisations of the proletariat and the state of the economically fragmented peasant masses See also *Committee of the Village Poor; New Economic Policy; Sociopolitical classifications.*

Sociopolitical classifications. Classifying and categorising the populations of tsarist Russia and Soviet Russia has involved as much political as social or economic delineation. They were often used by both regimes not so much as descriptors of occupation or even relative economic status as implicit (sometimes explicit) ascriptors of potential or perceived good or ill intent. This was especially evident in the tsarist and soviet classifications of the bulk of the population, the peasantry. *Batrak*, pl. *batraki* (farmhand or agricultural labourer) was a seasonal agricultural worker who owned no land and was hired by other peasants for specific farming tasks. *Bedniak*, pl. *bedniaki* (poor peasant) occupied or owned a little land but scraped out a subsistence living. In the intensifying class warfare particularly after 1917, the Bolsheviks regarded the *batraki* and *bedniaki* as the only peasants who could reliably meet the ideological purity test as non-exploiters of others' labour. *Seredniak*, pl. *seredniaki* (middle peasant) was poorly defined in terms of land or livestock ownership, and thus deemed in the Bolshevik view to be of questionable loyalty, still capable of exploitation of others, and of political vacillations within the fluctuating conditions of the Civil War and after. *Kulak*, pl. *kulaki* (wealthy peasant) denoted peasants who owned an (indeterminate) measure of land and employed hired labour. The term was the target of some government mistrust during the tsarist period, but during the Bolshevik period, it served as a blanket accusation by the Bolsheviks levelled against anyone deemed to be engaging in black marketeering (hoarding or withholding grain, and so on). Kritsman recognised the limits encountered by the state in applying some of these labels to the various class strata in the countryside, and even a tendency to erase the class aspect of proletarian politics there. He noted efforts (Osinskii was instrumental here) to coin less classist terms for the emergent petty bourgeoisie in the village by the end of the Civil War, such as the 'industrious owner' [*staratel'nyi khoziain*] that accompanied the setting up of the Bolshevik Sowing Committees in 1920, after the abolition of the intentionally divisive Committees of the Village Poor. As the 1920s progressed, the term became synonymous with class enemies, from whom *batraki*, *bedniaki*, and increasingly *serednіaki* required liberation. Into the 1930s, Stalin's dekulakisation policies (seizures of farms and peasant deportations to the gulag) were the culmination of this self-serving politicisation of the term *kulak*. Kritsman's research, particularly his later examination of processes of differentiation within the peasantry, traded on this politicisation of social discourse, especially the caricaturing of kulaks as rich peasants, black-marketeers, exploiters, and worse, counterrevolutionaries. *Spetsy* (bourgeois specialists) were skilled individuals employed in the tsarist economy who were brought into the post-revolutionary economy for their specific skills. In urgent need of specialists in all fields, the Soviet state in the interim brought in *spetsy* to help train this new generation of Communist specialists on the job. This term too carried an ideological taint, increasingly so as the 1920s wore on. Kritsman clearly regarded them as a short-term necessity, at least until a Red technical intelligentsia could be trained up. In his work, he often expressed his mistrust of what he saw as their intrinsically anti-Soviet motives, and thus of their potentially harmful influence on the Soviet economy in its formative stages. He felt the same about the role being played by military specialists [*voennye spetsy*] in the army as well. See also *Meshchanin*; *New Economic Policy; Osinskii; Sowing Committee.*

***Soslovie*, pl. *sosloviia* (estate)** Roughly equivalent to the traditional estate systems of Europe, Russia's *soslovie* system had come by the mid-19th century to designate hereditary groups of the population, including the nobility, clergy, townspeople, and peasantry, although these groups subsumed multiple sub-groups of the population within them as well. The estates were the antithesis in Soviet thought to the classes, and especially the proletarian stratum of the working class that would ultimately emerge from the frictions within the population, driving the process of revolution See also *Meshchanin*; *Sociopolitical classifications.*

Sovnarkom See *Council of People's Commissars.*

Sowing Committee [*posevnoi komitet* or *posevkom*] referred to a system of bodies set up in December 1920 by the Eighth Congress of Soviets. Strongly advanced by Osinskii, at that time on the board of the People's Commissariat of Food Supply [Narkomprod], it was an effort to find a way out of the agricultural crisis facing Soviet Russia at the end of the Civil War. It aimed to provide seed to peasant households in order to expand sown acreage and improve the productivity of the land. It acknowledged that the grain requisitioning policies of the early years, though necessary, had harmed the peasantry. While regarded as an emergency measure, the sowing committees were not seen as conflicting with the NEP and continued through its first year. See *Osinskii.*

Spetsy (bourgeois specialists) See *Sociopolitical classifications.*

State Committee for Planning [*Gosudarstvennyi komitet po planirovaniiu* or Gosplan] was set up in 1921 and was responsible for devising a series of plans that would govern all aspects of the Soviet national economy. After the economic ruin of the Civil War years, the NEP was intended as a breathing space for the economy's recovery, although the idea of a centrally planned, socialist economy, free from the anarchy of the market, was promoted alongside it. Gosplan was set up as an advisory arm of the Council of Labour and Defense (STO), that counted among its ranks many economic experts, including Kritsman, all tasked with carrying out economic investigations and making advisory recommendations up the administrative chain of command. Notwithstanding significant constraints on its autonomy through much of the 1920s, Gosplan as a body was a strong advocate for the introduction of some form of central planning into the Soviet economy as a major policy priority. Its star rose as central planning became an integral component of Stalin's policy of rapid forced industrialisation and collectivisation. See also *New Economic Policy*; *Council of Labour and Defense*.

Stinnes, Hugo (1870–1924) was a German industrialist and politician. He inherited his wealth from his father's coal mining businesses, and expanded into international shipping, and later steel. His business interests profited significantly from the First World War. Vehemently anti-Bolshevik, he became increasingly drawn into extreme right-wing German politics after the war, and began to purchase major German newspapers, which he moved to the right. For Kritsman, he represented the archetypal predatory capitalist oligarch.

Strumilin, Stanislav Gustavovich (1877–1974), an economist and statistician, was involved in devising a planned national economy for the Soviet state. He published notably on the economics of labour, including measures of labour productivity. He was an early political activist, involved in revolutionary activity in the late 19th century, joining the RSDRP in 1899, and siding with the Mensheviks after the 1903 split in the party. He graduated from the Petrograd Polytechnical Institute in 1914, and after the October Revolution he became a Professor of Economics at Moscow State University, and a series of other institutions of higher education. He headed statistics departments in various bodies, including the Petrograd Regional Commissariat of Labour and the All-Union Council of Trade Unions. He spent much of his active career from 1921 to 1937 in leadership positions at the State Committee for Planning and was a member of the Academy of Sciences of the USSR. He was active in international economics well into his eighties and died in 1974. See also *Gosplan*.

Subbotniks (lit. Saturdays) were days of volunteer unpaid physical labour, a kind of civil labour conscription for the Communist cause, such as street-cleaning, removing building rubble, repairs, etc. The first was instituted by the Bolsheviks in early 1919. They became a regular feature of the Soviet era.

Sukharevka was the colloquial name for a famous large market-bazaar in Sukharev Square in Moscow, sometimes briefly closed down, but more often tolerated by the

Bolshevik authorities. For Kritsman, it was clear evidence of the difficulty of eradicating elements of the capitalist commodity economy that persisted in the Soviet national and local economy throughout the Civil War years and into the NEP period See also *Bagging*; *New Economic Policy*.

Supreme Council of the National Economy [*Vysshii Sovet Narodnogo Khoziaistva*, Vesenkha, VSNKh] was set up in December 1917. It was tasked with regulating all economic life in Soviet Russia, as well as reconciling and uniting the activities of all central and local regulating agencies in all branches of the economy. Responsible for the policy of nationalisation, it enjoyed broad rights to confiscate, requisition, sequester, and create syndicates wherever it deemed it necessary. It was headed by a Presidium of 10–12 members, chosen at a congress of the Councils of the National Economy [*sovnarkhozy*], with the participation of representatives of the largest enterprises, trade unions, central administrations (*glavki*) of individual branches of industry and provinces of the *sovnarkhozy*. At the head of each production department was a collegium of 5–7 members appointed by the Presidium of VSNKh in agreement with the central committee of the respective branch trade union. It was a quasi-economic cabinet of the Council of People's Commissars, with members representing the commissariats, workers' councils, and so on. See also *Central Administrations; Council of People's Commissars*; *Councils of the National Economy*.

Taylorism referred to the theory of scientific work management developed by American engineer Frederick Winslow Taylor in 1911. It argued that labour productivity could be improved only by implementing scientific management techniques and optimised work methods. In this system, managers and workers should have clearly delineated fields of operation. Managers should be guided in their tasks by scientific principles, and should assign workers to a task according to the workers' aptitude for that particular task. Workers' performance and efficiency should be monitored. Kritsman regarded this system as nothing more than a cynical ploy of developed capitalism to squeeze more labour out of the worker. See also *New Economic Policy*.

Teodorovich, Ivan Adol'fovich (1875–1937) occupied leading positions in the economic apparatus of the new Soviet state immediately after the October Revolution. Unlike many of the economists and statisticians he dealt with in the economic debates in Soviet Russia's early years, and while he authored works on the agrarian question and the history of Russia's populist and revolutionary movements, his pedigree was largely revolutionary in nature, if not without its controversial aspects. Of gentry heritage, he graduated from the Faculty of Natural Sciences of Moscow University in 1896, where he became involved in the student protest movement. From the end of the nineteenth century up to October 1917, he experienced periods of arrest, internal exile, and foreign emigration for his labour-organizing activities in a variety of organisations of the RSDRP. He sided with the Bolsheviks in the party split in 1903. On his return from a period of exile after February 1917, he served in the Petrograd City Duma, and was a Central Committee member of the RSDRP(b) as it planned for insurrection. From August, he worked in the Petrograd State Duma on food supply matters. After the October Revolution, he was briefly the first People's Commissar of Food Supply, although a month later he quit the party and government (continuing to serve in the latter until December), because he believed that political power should be shared in a coalition government with other socialist parties and groupings. During the years of Civil War, he saw first-hand the effects of the harsh economic policies, while participating in the partisan movement against Kolchak's regime in Siberia. From 1920–1928, he was on the board of the People's Commissariat of Agriculture, and its Deputy People's Commissar from 1922. From 1925, he directed the International Agrarian Institute, and was General Secretary of the Peasant International from 1928. He disagreed with Kritsman over whether the party should pursue the economic policies of the civil war period or embrace the New Economic Policy, writing firmly in favour of the latter as the best opportunity for developing a strong socialist peasantry as a basis for future industrialisation. While in the People's Commissariat of Agriculture, he supervised the work of the economist Kondrat'ev. In 1928–29, he found himself charged with 'rightist-opportunist errors' for his earlier views, and in late 1930 was caught up in accusations against Kondrat'ev and others. Teodorovich was stripped of his official positions, and wrote a letter to *Pravda* publicly expressing contrition for his earlier faulty understanding of the NEP. From 1929–1935, he was a member of the Society of Former Political Prisoners and Exiles [*Obshchestvo byvshikh politkatorzhan i ssyl'noposelentsev*], an organisation set up for victims of tsarist oppression, and editor and publisher of its journal *Hard Labour and Exile* [*Katorga i ssylka*]. He was arrested in 1937 on charges of participation in an anti-Soviet terroristic organisation, and shot. See also *Kolchak*; *Kondrat'ev*; *Oganovskii*.

Thünen, Johann Heinrich (1783–1850) was a north German economist who published his famous multivolume treatise, *Der isolierte Staat in Beziehung auf Landwirtschaft und Nationalökonomie* (*The Isolated State in Relation to Agriculture and Political Economy*) in 1826, in which he developed his theory of marginal productivity in an agricultural land model.

Trotsky, Leon (Lev) Davidovich born Bronshtein (1879–1940), was a life-long Russian revolutionary activist. His activities in populist and Social Democratic circles in the late 1890s brought him arrest and exile to Siberia. He later moved into exile in London, where he collaborated with Lenin on the newspaper, *Iskra*. At the Second Congress of the RSDRP in 1903, he supported Lenin's position that led to the split in the party, although he became alienated by some of Lenin's actions and gravitated towards other prominent more moderate Social Democrats. In the 1905 Revolution, he played a prominent role as chair of the St. Petersburg Soviet of Workers' Deputies. For his efforts, he was again exiled to Siberia, but escaped abroad once again. His second period of exile took him to Vienna, where he engaged in various publicistic and journalistic endeavours, mostly devoted to finding a non-factional position to adopt vis-à-vis the fractured RSDRP. Trotsky returned to Russia in May 1917, becoming leader of the *Mezhraiontsy*. This group, and Trotsky, merged with the Bolsheviks in August 1917. Trotsky became very prominent in the Bolshevik leadership and in the preparations for armed insurrection, helping to set up the Military Revolutionary Committee. After October, Trotsky was the first People's Commissar of Foreign Affairs, in which capacity he played a major role in deliberations over the Brest Peace. His iconic status was really burnished during the Civil War, however, when, as People's Commissar of Military and Naval Affairs of the Soviet Union [*Narodnyi Kommissar voennym i morskim delam SSSR*] from 1918 to 1924, he set up the Red Army and secured victory in the Civil War. He advocated severe militarised policies to win the Civil War, and proposed preserving some of the harshest of those methods to secure economic reconstruction of this devastated and starving country. He briefly advocated forming labour armies of forcibly mobilised and militarised peasants to this end. His advocacy was undermined in the first half of the 1920s by his almost perpetual conflict with the RKP(b) leadership over ideological and organisational issues, culminating on the so-called 'literary discussion' of 1924, a polemic launched by the party against his interpretation of the significance of the October Revolution. He clashed with Stalin in 1926 to 1927, this time over the latter's policy of 'Socialism in One Country'. Isolated and vilified, Trotsky was expelled from the Politburo in 1926, the party and the Comintern in 1927, and then from the USSR in 1929. His peripatetic existence as a revolutionary of real stature in the international communist movement took him to Turkey, France, Norway, and ultimately Mexico. He was murdered there on 20 August 1940 by a Stalinist agent. See also *Food Detachments*.

Tsiperovich, Grigorii Vladimirovich (1871–1932), an economist, studied and wrote on syndicalism and trusts. He was an active participant in the revolutionary movement before 1917, for which he was arrested and spent ten years in Siberian exile. During the 1905 Revolution, he returned to active participation in the events in Khar'kov, where he again came to the attention of the Okhrana. He attended Petersburg University in 1907, and for the next few years was a Social Democratic activist among his fellow students and among trade unionists and workers in the city. He was again arrested, and, after a short term of imprisonment, emigrated. He became a Menshevik Internationalist, and after the February Revolution he worked in the Economics Department of the Petrograd Soviet. He soon joined the *Novaia zhizn'* Social Democratic group [*Novozhiznentsy*]. After the October Revolution, he agitated among the workers, joining the Bolsheviks in 1919 while head of the Petrograd

Council of Trade Unions [*Petrogradskii sovet profsoiuzov*]. He was a delegate to the Second Congress of the Comintern in 1920 as part of the Trade Union Commission. He also belonged to the Red International of Trade Unions [*Krasnyi Internatsional profsoiuzov* or Profintern]. Throughout the 1920s, he worked on the Leningrad Council of the National Economy [*Leningradskii sovnarkhoz*] and led the Leningrad Regional Planning Commission [*Oblastnaia planovaia komissiia*] for the latter half. Into the 1930s, he was prominent in the Leningrad Industrial Academy [*Leningradskaia promyshlennaia akademiia*], and the Institute of Technology and Technological Policy [*Institut tekhniki i tekhnicheskoi politiki*] of the Communist Academy. He died of natural causes in 1932. See *All-Russian Central Council of Trade Unions.*

TsSU See *Central Statistical Administration.*

Two-And-A-Half International (also the Vienna Union) was an international conference of socialists who met in Vienna in 1921 in an effort to create an alternative to both the remnants of the Second International that had collapsed in 1914 and the increasingly bolshevised Communist International (Comintern) that was founded in 1919. See also *Second International.*

Units of Weights and Measures *Pood* was a unit of weight used in much of the tsarist empire. It was equivalent to ca. 16 kg or 36 lbs. *Arshin* was a traditional unit of measurement equivalent to 28 inches or 71.1 cm. *Sazhen'* was equivalent to three arshins (7 feet or 2.13 metres). *Verst* [*versta*] was equivalent to 500 sazhens (0.663 miles or 1.067 km). *Desiatina* was equivalent to 2.7 acres or 10,926 square metres (the official Treasury designation) or 3.6 acres or 14,568 square metres (the proprietor's designation).

VChK See *All-Russian Extraordinary Commission for Combatting Counter-Revolution, Profiteering, and Corruption.*

Verst See *Units of Weights and Measures.*

Vishnevskii, Nikolai Mikhailovich (1891–1938), an economist, published works in the early 1920s on the organisation of food supply products, on agricultural statistics, and on the census of RKP members in 1922. In 1930, he led a group in the Economics-Statistical Sector of Gosplan SSSR [*Ekonomicheskii-statisticheskii sector Gosplana SSSR*]. He was arrested in 1930 accused of participation in a counter-revolutionary organisation and for exerting a harmful influence on economic policies. He was sent to the gulag, and then to internal exile. He was re-arrested in 1937 accused of fleeing his place of exile, and was shot in 1938.

Volost' referred to a rural municipality, an administrative authority encompassing several village communities.

***Vorwärts* (*Forward*)** was the central organ of the Socialist Workers' Party of Germany (SAPD) and began publishing in 1876. It printed major pieces by Friedrich Engels and other socialist theoreticians.

VSNKh See *Supreme Council of the National Economy.*

Workers' Faculty [*Rabochii fakul'tet*, or rabfak] was an educational institution specifically designed for workers in early Soviet Russia as a way of removing the traditional barriers to higher education and opening up the new Soviet institutions to ideologically trained working-class members. See also *Sociopolitical classifications (spetsy)*.

Wrangel', Petr Nikolaevich (1878–1928) was a former tsarist general and baron, who participated in the war with Japan in 1904 and served on the South-Western Front in the First World War. After the October Revolution, he led anti-Bolshevik forces during the Civil War, succeeding General Denikin as Commander-in-Chief of the White army in Southern Russia in 1920. After defeat by the Bolsheviks, he and his remaining forces were evacuated to Constantinople. In emigration, he engaged in military matters, notably his creation in 1924 of the Russian All-Military Union [*Russkii obshchevoinskii soiuz*, or ROVS], which united the bulk of the participants of the White Movement in the Emigration. In 1927 he moved to Brussels, dying of tuberculosis after a few months. See also: *Czechoslovak Legion*; *Denikin*; *Dutov*; *Iudenich*; *Krasnov*.

Zemstvo system was made up of organs of self-administration in rural areas. The system was set up by imperial statute in 1864 as part of the emancipation legislation. Zemstvos were set up in 34 provinces of European Russia. Each zemstvo was responsible for managing zemstvo property and funds, building and maintaining local roads, supplying food in emergency situations, insurance of property, developing local trade and industry, supporting public education and health, and other tasks. The district and provincial zemstvos each had regular assemblies which elected three-year term executive boards [*zemskaia uprava*] chaired by marshals of the nobility. The zemstvos lacked real executive power, and so they depended on the cooperation of local police and other tsarist officials over whom they had no control. They relied on the minimal taxes on real estate and businesses they were permitted to collect. Counter-reforms under Alexander III sought to increase the influence of the nobility in the zemstvos. Despite their limitations, the zemstvos drew in almost all classes of the population. They turned out to be real training grounds of practical experience in the realms of education, public health, and agricultural innovation for generations of teachers, doctors, agronomists, statisticians, and veterinarians. Many of the economists who figured so prominently in the economic and administrative policies of the first decade of the Soviet regime earned their laurels in the zemstvo movement.

Bibliography

Newspapers and Journals

Biulleten' VSNKh (Moscow)
Ekonomicheskaia zhizn'
Ekonomicheskoe obozrenie
Narodnoe khoziaistvo
Prodovol'stvie i revoliutsiia
Sotsialisticheskii vestnik
Statistika truda
Vestnik statistiki (Moscow)
Vorwärts (Berlin)
Zhilishchnoe tovarishchestvo: zhilishche i stroitel'stvo (Moscow, 1922–1929)

Books and Articles

Amosov, I. and A. Savich 1921, *Problema material'nogo ucheta v sotsialisticheskom khoziaistve*. Petrograd: Izd. otdel Petrogradskogo soveta narognogo khoziaistva.

Bogdanov, N. 1919, 'Organizatsiia sovetskikh khoziaistv', *Narodnoe khoziaistvo*, no. 6.

Bol'shakov, A 1924, *Sovetskaia derevnia (1917–1924 g.g.): ekonomika i byt*. Leningrad: 'Priboi'.

Bukharin, Nikolai 1920, *Ekonomika perekhodnogo perioda*. Moscow: Gos. Izd-vo.

1920 *Dva goda diktatury proletariata, 1917–1919*. Moscow: Otdel readaktsionno-izdatel'skii.

1922, *Ekonomicheskoe rassloenie krest'ianstva v 1917 i 1919 gg*. Moscow: Mospoligraf.

1922, *Eksportnye vozmozhnosti Rossii. Statistiko-ekonomicheskii ocherk*. Moscow: Izd. N.K.V.T.

1923, *Ezhegodnik Kominterna*. Petrograd-Moscow, Izd-vo Kommunisticheskogo internatsionala.

1924, Fal'kner, S. *Problemy teorii i praktiki emissionnogo khoziaistva*. Moscow, Ekonomicheskaia zhizn'.

1921, Gul', R. *Ledianoi pokhod: s Kornilovym*. Berlin: Izd-vo S. Efron.

1924, Khriashcheva, A. *Gruppy i klassy v krest'ianstve; k XIII s'ezdu RKP(b)*. Moscow: Tip. MKKh.

1922, Kogan, P.; and I. Shenkman, *Eksportnye vozmozhnosti Rossii. Statistiko-ekonomicheskii* ocherk. Moscow: Izd. N.K.V.T.

1922, Kondrat'ev, N.D. *Rynok khlebov i ego regulirovanie vo vremia voiny i revoliutsii*. Moscow: 'Nauka'.

1924, Kondrat'ev, N. and N. Oganovskii. *Perspektivy razvitiia sel'skogo khoziaistva SSSR*. Moscow: Novaia derevnia.

1924, *Kratkii otchet Gosplana, 1921–1923*. Moscow.

1921, *Krest'ianstvo v voine i revoliutsii; statistiko-ekonomicheskie ocherki*. Moscow: 14-ia tip. V.S.N.Kh.

Kritsman, L. 1928 'Ob ocherednoi zadache proletarskoi revolutsii', in *Narodnoe khoziaistvo*, no. 5.

Kritsman, L 1921, *Ob edinom khoziaistvennom plane*. Moscow: Gosizdat.

Kritsman, L and Iu. Larin 1920, *Ocherk khoziaistvennoi zhizni i organizatsiia narodnogo khoziaistva Sovetskoi Rossii, 1 noiabria 1917–1 iiulia 1920 g*. Moscow: Gos. izd.-vo.

Krzhizhanovskii, G. 1924, *Tovaroobmen i planovaia rabota*. Moscow.

Larin, Iu. 1923, *Itogi, puti, vyvody novoi ekonomicheskoi politiki*. Moscow: 'Moskovskii rabochii'.

Lenin, N. 1923, *Razvitie kapitalizma v Rossii*. Moscow: Gos. Izdat.

1921, *Lesozagotovitel'naia politika v obshchei sisteme narodnogo khoziaistva*. Moscow: Gos. izd.vo.

Litoshenko, L. 1923, *Krest'ianskii biudzhet v 1922–1923 g*. Moscow: Tsentral'noe statisticheskoe upravlenie.

1924, *Materialy po statistike truda rabotnikov transporta*. Moscow.

1923, *Na novykh putiakh. Itogi novoi ekonomicheskoi politiki 1921–1922 gg*. 4 vols. Moscow: Izd. Soveta truda i orobony.

1923, *Narodnoe khoziaistvo Rossii za 1921–1922 g.g. Statistiko-ekonomicheskii ezhegodnik*. Moscow: 'Ekonomicheskaia zhizn'.

1924, *Narodnoe khoziaistvo SSSR v tsifrakh*. Moscow: TsSU.

1921, *Obzor sostoianiia i raboty transporta k 1921 g*. (*Materialy k dokladu IX s'ezdu sovetov*). Moscow: Moscow: 11-ia tipo-litografiia M.S.N.Kh.

Oganovskii, N. 1922, *Statisticheskii ezhegodnik 1918–20 gg*. Moscow.

Oganovskii, N. 1923, *Ocherki po ekonomicheskoi geografii RSFSR*. Moscow.

Oganovskii, N. 1924, *Ocherki po ekonomicheskoi geografii S.S.S.R.: v sviazi s mirovym khoziaistvom, po noveishim statistcheskim materialam*. Moscow: 'Novaia derevnia'.

Osinskii, V. 1922, *Vosstanovlenie krest'ianskogo khoziaistva v Rossii i nashi zadachi*. Moscow: Izd. Narkomzema, 'Novaia derevnia'.

Osinskii, V. 1922, *Vosstanovlenie krest'ianskogo khoziaistva v Rossii i nashi zadachi*. Moscow: Izd. Narkomzema, 'Novaia derevnia'.

1920, *Otchet VSNKh VIII s'ezdu sovetov*. Moscow.

1922, *Piat' let vlasti Sovetov*. Moscow: Izd. VtsIK.

Pletnev, D.D. 1922, *Sypnoi tif*. Moscow.

Popov, P. 1921, *Proizvodstvo khleba v R.S.F.S.R. i federiruiushchikhsia s neiu respublikakh*. Moscow: Gos. izdat.

Preobrazhenskii, E. 1921, *Finansy v epokhu diktatury proletariata*. Moscow: Narodnyi komissariat finansov.

1920, *Prodvol'stvennaia politika*. Moscow: Gos. izd-vo.

Prokopovich, S.N. 1918, *Opyt ischisleniia narodnago dokhoda 50 gub. evropeiiskoii Rossīi v 1900–1913 g.g.* Moscow: Sovet Vserossiiskikh kooperativnykh s'ezdov.

1921, *Russkaia promyshlennost' v...godu*. Moscow: Redaktsionno-izdatel'skii otdel.

1920, *Sbornik dekretov 1917–1918 g.* Moscow.

1918, *Sbornik dekretov i postanovlenii po narodnomu khoziaistvu*. Moscow: Sklad izd., 1918–, 4 volumes.

1924, *Sbornik statisticheskikh svedenii po SSSR*. Moscow: TsSU.

1919–20, *Sistematicheskii sbornik dekretov i rasporiazhenii pravitel'stv po prodovol'stvennomu delu*. Nizhni-Nogorod-Moscow, 4 vols.

1918, *Statisticheskii ezhegodnik na ... god*, Moscow: 1918.

Strumilin, S. 1923, *Zarabotnaia plata i proizvoditel'nost' truda v Russkoi promyshlennosti v 1913–1922 g.g.* Moscow: Voprosy truda.

1923, *Syr'evye problemy tekstil'noi promyshlennosti*. Moscow.

1918, *Trudy 1-go Vserossiiskogo S'ezda Sovetov Narodnogo Khoziaistva*. Moscow.

1921, *Trudy sel'sko-khoiziaistvennoi sektsii Instituta Ekonomicheskikh Issledovanii*. Petrograd: n.p.

1924, *Trudy zemplana*. Moscow: Novaia derevnia.

Tsiperovich, G. 1919, *Sindikaty i tresty v Rossii*. Moscow: Izd. Vserossiiskago soveta professional'nykh soiuzov.

Vishnevskii, N. 1920, *Printsipy i metody organizovannogo raspredeleniia produktov prodovol'stviia i predmetov pervoi neobkhodimosti*. Moscow, 10-ia Gos. tip.

Vishnevskii, N. 1922, *Statistika i sel'sko-khoziaistvennaia deistvitel'nost'*. Moscow.

1923, *Vserossiiskaia perepis' chlenov RKP 1922 g.* 4th ed. Moscow.

1922, *Za 5 let*. Moscow: Krasnaia nov'.

Index

www.ingramcontent.com/pod-product-compliance
Lightning Source LLC
Chambersburg PA
CBHW071334230926
51849CB00002B/398
* 9 7 8 9 0 0 4 7 6 5 3 0 6 *